WARRANT: THE CURRENT DEBATE

WARRANT: THE CURRENT DEBATE

Alvin Plantinga

New York   Oxford
OXFORD UNIVERSITY PRESS
1993

Oxford University Press

Oxford   New York   Toronto
Delhi   Bombay   Calcutta   Madras   Karachi
Kuala Lumpur   Singapore   Hong Kong   Tokyo
Nairobi   Dar es Salaam   Cape Town
Melbourne   Auckland   Madrid

and associated companies in
Berlin   Ibadan

Copyright © 1993 by Alvin Plantinga

Published by Oxford University Press, Inc.
200 Madison Avenue, New York, New York 10016

Oxford is a registered trademark of Oxford University Press

Library of Congress Cataloging-in-Publication Data
Plantinga, Alvin.
Warrant : the current debate / Alvin Plantinga.
p.   cm.   Includes index.
ISBN 0-19-507861-6; ISBN 0-19-507862-4 (pbk.)
1. Knowledge, Theory of.   2. Belief and doubt.   I. Title.
BD161.P58   1993   121'.6—dc20   92-13183

2 4 6 8 9 7 5 3

Printed in the United States of America
on acid-free paper

Preface

The theory of knowledge is currently flourishing, perhaps as never before. There are some, of course, who loudly proclaim the death of epistemology. This seems to me less premature than confused: what they observe is the breakdown of *classical foundationalism,* which is only one epistemological program among several, even if a historically important one. Confounding species with genus, they shrilly announce the demise of the latter. It is as if someone, noting the demise of Eastern European communism, should proclaim the death of political systems and government generally.

There is some excuse for this confusion. Classical foundationalism has been dominant in Western epistemology ever since the Enlightenment; more broadly and more exactly, it is really classical *deontologism*—the view that epistemic responsibility and fulfillment of epistemic obligation and duty are of crucial epistemic importance—together with its consequent internalism that has been thus dominant. Although classical foundationalism has fallen into ruins in the last half of the present century, the same most emphatically cannot be said for classical deontologism and internalism.

Nevertheless, one of the most exciting developments in twentieth-century theory of knowledge is the rejection of deontology and the sudden appearance of various forms of externalism. More precisely, this development is less the appearance than the *reappearance* of externalism in epistemology. Externalism goes a long way back, to Thomas Reid, to Thomas Aquinas—back, in fact, all the way to Aristotle. Indeed, we may venture to say that (apart, perhaps, from Augustine and some of the skeptics of the later Platonic Academy) internalists in epistemology are *rarae aves* in Western thought prior to Descartes. It is really externalism, in one form or another, that has been the dominant tradition; internalism is a recent interloper. We may therefore see present-day externalists as calling us back to our first epistemological love, after a brief and ill-starred fling with the seductive siren of internalism. In this book and its sequels, I hope to heed that call.

My topic, therefore, is the theory of knowledge. In the theory of knowledge, naturally enough, we try to come to some understanding of knowledge. But where and how shall we start? First, there is nearly universal agreement that knowledge requires truth; a person knows that all men are mortal only if it is *true* that all men are mortal. Of course we sometimes use the term 'knows' as if it were within ironic quotes, as when we say that a good Marxist knows that the idea of objective truth is no more than a piece of bourgeois sentimentality. Sociologists of knowledge sometimes seem to take this ironic use of the term as its basic use, so that '*S* knows *P*', as they use it, means little more than that *S* believes *P*, or is strongly convinced of *P*, or perhaps is committed to *P*, or is such that the scientists of his culture circle announce *P*. But let us set such aberrant notions aside, for the moment, and agree that knowledge requires truth. Second, it is widely (though not universally*) agreed that knowledge, whatever precisely it is, also involves belief; a person knows that all men are mortal only if, among other things, she *believes* that all men are mortal (where here the term 'believes' is to be taken in the classical sense of 'thinking with assent'; it does not imply lack of certainty or *mere* belief).

There is wide agreement that knowledge requires true belief; but as far back as Plato's *Theaetetus*, there is also recognition that it requires more. I may believe that I will win a Nobel Prize next year; by some mad chance my belief may be true; it hardly follows that I know the truth in question. What more is required? What is this elusive further quality or quantity which, or enough of which, stands between knowledge and mere true belief? What is it that, added to true belief, yields knowledge; what is it that *epistemizes* true belief? (We cannot properly assume that it is a *simple* property or quantity; perhaps it is more like a vector resultant of other properties or quantities.) This quality or quantity, however, whatever exactly it may turn out to be, is the subject of this book and the sequels, *Warrant and Proper Function* and *Warranted Christian Belief*. Contemporary epistemologists seldom focus attention on the *nature* of this element (although they often ask under what conditions a given belief has it); and when they do, they display deplorable diversity. Some claim that what turns true belief into knowledge is a matter of epistemic dutifulness, others that it goes by coherence, and still others that it is conferred by reliability. I shall argue that none of these claims is correct, and (in *Warrant and Proper Function*) suggest a more satisfactory alternative.

Epistemology is extremely difficult, in many ways more difficult than, say, the metaphysics of modality. The latter requires a fair amount of logical acumen; but it is reasonably easy to see what the basic concepts are and how they are related. Not so for epistemology. *Warrant, justification, evidence, epistemic normativity, probability, rationality*—these are all extremely difficult notions. Indeed, each of those terms is really associated with a whole class of difficult and analogically related notions, where a big part of the difficulty is discerning how the members of each class are related to each other and to the members of the other classes. Coming to clarity on them and their relatives and discerning the relations among them is strenuous and demanding; yet it is the only way to progress in epistemology. What is needed is hermeneutics, understanding, interpretation. Here the way to progress is not to turn directly to the issue itself, proceeding in lofty abstraction from what others have said and thought on the

---

*For a discussion of dissenters, see Robert Shope, *The Analysis of Knowing* (Princeton: Princeton University Press, 1983), pp. 171–92.

matter. There is an impressive tradition on these topics, going back to the beginnings of modern philosophy and indeed to the beginnings of philosophy itself. Furthermore, epistemology is at present in lively ferment; there are many penetrating and imaginative contemporary contributions to this and neighboring issues; it would be at best churlish to ignore them. Still further, it is unsatisfactory to consider only, say, coherentism *überhaupt;* for while we may thus come to understand coherentism taken neat (the Platonic Form of coherentism, we might say), any flesh-and-blood coherentist will have her own additions and subtractions, her own modifications, which may result in a position stronger (or weaker) than coherentism as such, and in any case may make a real contribution to our understanding of the issues. My ultimate aim is to come to a satisfying and accurate account of warrant; but to do so we must first pay close attention to what our contemporaries suggest (concurring where possible, opposing where necessary).

I begin with *internalism,* the tradition dominant since the Enlightenment. First, there is the carefully crafted foundationalist internalism of Roderick Chisholm (chapters 2 and 3). To understand Chisholm and other internalists properly, however, we shall have to make a preliminary *excursus* (chapter 1) into the classical internalism of Descartes, Locke, and others; here we note the roots of internalism in *epistemic deontology,* the view that epistemic duty and obligation are of crucial epistemic importance. After Chisholmian internalism I turn to coherentism. For classificatory purposes, I take it as a form of internalism; and in the next three chapters I consider coherentism *überhaupt* (chapter 4), the coherentist views of Laurence BonJour (chapter 5) and contemporary Bayesian versions of coherentism (chapters 6 and 7). Third (chapter 8) there is the more attenuated internalism of John Pollock; I see Pollock's view as in transition from internalism to externalism.

After arguing that internalism, classical or otherwise, holds no real promise for a correct account of warrant, I turn to externalism. Given the recent history of epistemology, externalism seems new, innovative, perhaps even radical; on a longer view, however, internalism is a departure from the main tradition in Western epistemology, which, as I noted, has been externalist. The dominant form of contemporary externalism is *reliabilism;* I consider (chapter 9) the reliabilist views of William Alston, Fred Dretske, and Alvin Goldman. Reliabilism has its charms; but it omits a crucial component of warrant (or so, at any rate, I shall argue): that of *proper function or absence of dysfunction.* The idea of our cognitive faculties' functioning properly in the production and sustenance of belief is absolutely crucial to our conception of warrant; this idea is intimately connected with the idea of a *design plan,* a sort of blueprint specifying how properly functioning organs, powers, and faculties work. The last chapter offers a preview of coming attractions: a brief and preliminary account of that elusive notion *warrant,* an account that seems at once subtler, more accurate, and more satisfying than any of the theories in the field.

In the second volume, *Warrant and Proper Function,* I shall outline this theory in more detail. The first two chapters will be a general development of the theory, involving in particular an examination of the notion of proper function and its colleagues: purpose, damage, design plan, malfunction, and the like. Then in the next eight chapters I shall explore general features of our cognitive design plan, explaining how my account of warrant applies in each of the main areas of our epistemic establishment: knowledge of myself, knowledge by way of memory, knowledge of other persons, knowledge by way of testimony, perception, *a priori* knowledge and belief, induction, and probability. Then comes a chapter on a more general or structural feature of our epistemic establishment: the question whether warrant has a foundationalist structure. Finally, in the last two chapters of *Warrant and Proper Function* I argue that naturalism in epistemology flourishes best within the context of supernaturalism in theology or metaphysics: the prospects for a naturalistic epistemology are intimately intertwined with a theistic view of the world. I therefore conclude that naturalistic epistemology is indeed viable; it offers the best chance for success; but only if set in the context of a broadly theistic view of the nature of human beings.

It would be nice to have a name for this theory. 'Proper Functionalism' comes to mind; it has the advantage of a certain pleasing ambiguity, as well as the advantage that a view whose name contains 'Functionalism' gets (at present) an automatic leg up. 'Proper Functionalism', however, does not come trippingly off the tongue and I am inclined to prefer 'The Theory of Proper Function' a name suggested by William Hasker. Whatever we call it, the theory in question is, broadly speaking, an example of epistemology 'naturalized'. This account of warrant is in some ways similar to that of Thomas Reid; at any rate it is in the spirit of Reid's work (as perhaps also in the spirit of Aquinas and Aristotle). Of course, I am not entering the lists in order to provide a good or satisfactory interpretation or account of Reid's thought.

The projected (but so far unwritten) third volume of this series, *Warranted Christian Belief*, will be an application of the theory developed in *Warrant and Proper Function* to Christian and theistic belief. Although these three volumes form a sort of series, they are designed to be self-contained and can be read separately.

The three volumes together develop the ideas underlying my Gifford Lectures in Aberdeen in 1987 and my Wilde Lectures in Oxford in 1988. I am grateful to both sets of electors for the honor of the invitations, and for giving me an opportunity to work out these ideas. Given the debt my views owe to Thomas Reid, it was gratifying and interesting to be able to lecture on them at Aberdeen, only a few miles from his birthplace, and the scene of his early work. I should also like to thank Professors Robin Cameron and James Torrance and the other members of the philosophy and theology departments at the University of Aberdeen, for their wonderful hospitality during the months my wife and I visited there. I must express similar gratitude to Professor Richard Swinburne for similar hospitality during our stay in Oxford.

These ideas also played a prominent part in Payton Lectures at Fuller Theological Seminary in 1987, Norton Lectures at Southern Baptist Seminary in 1988, lectures at the 1986 Wheaton Philosophy Conference, and lectures at the 1986 NEH Summer Institute for Philosophy of Religion in Bellingham, Washington; I am extremely grateful to all of these audiences (but perhaps particularly the participants in the NEH Summer Institute) for criticism and stimulation, from which I benefited greatly. I am also grateful to the National Endowment for the Humanities for a Fellowship for 1987 and to the University of Notre Dame for sabbatical leave for the same year.

In writing these books I have received a great deal of help from many people; I am grateful to them all for penetrating criticism, stimulating discussion, and wise counsel; without their help these books would have been much the poorer. Indeed, the number of people from whom I have received help is embarrassingly large (with so much help from so many people, why aren't these books better than they are?) I must make special mention of Felicia Ackerman, William Alston, Robert Audi, Laurence BonJour, Roderick Chisholm, Robin Collins, Marian David, Michael DePaul, Fred Dretske, Aron Edidin, Richard Feldman, Richard Foley, John Foster, Carl Ginet, Lee Hardy, William Hasker, Kenneth Konyndyk, Patrick Maher, George Mavrodes, Caleb Miller, Richard Otte, Michael Partridge, John Pollock, Philip Quinn, William Ramsey, Del Ratzsch, Bruce Russell, James Sennett, Thomas Senor, Robert Shope, Caroline Simon, Ernest Sosa, Leopold Stubenberg, Richard Swinburne, Fred Suppe, Bas van Fraassen, Edward Wierenga, Nicholas Wolterstorff, Stephen Wykstra, and Dean Zimmerman. Some of these—BonJour, Collins, Dretske, Russell, Senor, Suppe, van Fraassen, and Zimmerman, for example, but especially Alston—went so far as to give me extensive and detailed written comments on various portions of the manuscripts; to them I am particularly grateful. Others—the members of the Notre Dame Monday Colloquium Group and the Calvin College Tuesday Colloquium group—discussed and criticized parts of these books over periods of many months; to them also I am especially grateful. I have learned more than I can say from discussion with all of these people and their comments on various parts of the manuscripts. No doubt many will see that their criticisms aren't properly met and their insights not properly incorporated (or worse, not properly acknowledged); to them I can only apologize.

Large parts of chapter 1 appeared in *Philosophy and Phenomenological Research;* I am grateful to the editors for permission to republish them here. Parts of chapter 2 appeared in *Philosophical Analysis: A Defense by Example,* edited by David Austin (Dordrecht and Boston: Kluwer Academic Publishers, 1988).

Finally, I must express special gratitude to Martha Detlefsen, who did her formidable best (against nearly insurmountable odds) to keep both me and these books properly organized.

Notre Dame, Indiana   A. P.
April 1992

Contents

WARRANT: THE CURRENT DEBATE

1

Justification, Internalism, and Deontology

My topic is warrant: that, whatever precisely it is, which together with truth makes the difference between knowledge and mere true belief. More specifically, my topic is contemporary views of warrant. I shall begin by looking briefly at the twentieth-century received tradition with respect to warrant; but first, how shall we initially pin down, or locate, or characterize this property or quantity I propose to discuss? It is that which distinguishes knowledge from mere true belief, of course; but note also that there is obviously something *normative* or *evaluative* about warrant. To attribute warrant to a belief is to *appraise* that belief, and to appraise it favorably; and we use such terms as 'warranted', 'justification', 'justified', and the like as "terms of epistemic appraisal."[1] To say that a belief is *warranted* or *justified* for a person is to evaluate it or him (or both) *positively;* his holding that belief in his circumstances is *right*, or *proper*, or *acceptable*, or *approvable*, or *up to standard*. We evaluate a person's beliefs (more exactly, her *believings*) as warranted, or justified, or rational, or reasonable, contrasting them with beliefs that are unwarranted, unjustified, irrational, unreasonable. The evidentialist objector to theistic belief,[2] for example, claims that a theist who believes in God without evidence or argument is so far forth unwarranted and unjustified in that belief; he offers a negative appraisal of the belief or its holder. (Perhaps he claims that in believing in God in that way she is flouting some duty, or (more charitably) is suffering from a sort of cognitive dysfunction, or (still more modestly) that the module of our cognitive establishment that issues in theistic belief is not aimed at truth but at something else.)[3]

In the same way we may appraise the belief that all contemporary flora and fauna arose by way of random genetic mutation and natural selection from primitive forms of life, which in turn arose via similarly ateleological processes

[1]Roderick Chisholm's phrase: see *Theory of Knowledge,* 2d ed. (Englewood Cliffs, N.J.: Prentice-Hall, 1977), p. 5.

[2]See my "Reason and Belief in God," in *Faith and Rationality: Reason and Belief in God,* ed. A. Plantinga and N. Wolterstorff (Notre Dame: University of Notre Dame Press, 1983), pp. 24ff.; and see my *Warrant and Proper Function* (New York: Oxford University Press, 1993), chap. 1, end of sec. 1 and beginning of sec. 2.

[3]See "Reason and Belief in God," pp. 27ff.

3

from inorganic material. And of course the less spectacular beliefs of everyday life are also subject to such evaluation and appraisal. We appraise a person's *beliefs,* but also her skepticisms or (to use another Chisholmian term) her withholdings, her refrainings from belief. An unduly credulous person may believe what she ought not; an unduly skeptical (or cynical) person may fail to believe what she ought. Further, we may hold a belief more or less strongly, more or less firmly; we appraise not only the belief itself, but also the *degree* to which it is accepted. If I believe that Homer was born before 800 B.C. and believe this with as much fervor as that New York City is larger than Cleveland, then (given what are in fact my epistemic circumstances) my degree of confidence in the former proposition is excessive and unwarranted.

Finally, warrant comes in degrees. Some of my beliefs have more by way of that quantity for me than others. Thus my belief that I live in Indiana has more by way of warrant, for me, than my belief that Shakespeare wrote the plays commonly attributed to him; my belief that $2 + 1 = 3$ has more warrant than my belief that the Axiom of Choice is equivalent to the Hausdorff Maximal Principle. (This is not to say, of course, that I am not equally rational and equally justified in accepting these beliefs to the degrees to which I do in fact accept them; for I believe the latter member of each pair less firmly than the former.) But then we can distinguish *degrees* of positive epistemic status, at least for a given person.[4] Initially, then, and to a first approximation, warrant is a normative, possibly complex quantity that comes in degrees, enough of which is what distinguishes knowledge from mere true belief.

Second, a problem that is less trivial than it initially seems: what shall we *call* this quantity? I propose to call it 'warrant'; but those of us brought up in that benighted pre-Gettier era learned at our mother's knee that knowledge is *justified true belief;* and even in this enlightened post-Gettier age we still think of justification and knowledge as intimately related. So why not call this property 'justification'? Because it would be both misleading and unfair. 'Justification' suggests duty, obligation, requirement; it is redolent of permission and rights; it brings to mind exoneration, not being properly subject to blame—it connotes, in a word (or two) the whole deontological stable. And the problem is that one of the main contending theories or pictures here (one with impressive historical credentials going back at least to Descartes and Locke) explicitly explains the quantity in question at least partly in terms of fulfilling one's epistemic duties, satisfying one's epistemic obligations, conforming to one's epistemic requirements. To use the term 'justification', then, as a *name* for that quantity would be to give this theory and its relatives a confusing and unwarranted (if merely verbal) initial edge over their rivals. So 'justification' is not the

---

[4]Take either of these pairs and call them 'A' and 'B' respectively. There is the degree of warrant had by those beliefs that have no more of that quantity (for me) than B, the degree displayed by those that have more than B but less than A, and the degree enjoyed by those that have as much or more than A. Of course in fact the classification will be much more fine-grained than this: there will be beliefs with less warrant than B, beliefs with more than A, and beliefs that fall between A and B in warrant but differ from each other.

right choice. In earlier work[5] I borrowed Roderick Chisholm's more neutral term "positive epistemic status" as my official name for the quantity in question. That locution, however, is too long; so I shall use the term 'warrant' in its place. Of course, 'warrant' has deontological associations of its own (even if they are not quite so insistent); perhaps (as Ernest Sosa suggested in conversation) 'epistemic aptness' is a better term. On balance, however, I prefer 'warrant'—but we must be careful not to be misled by its residual deontological insinuations.

I. Internalism

The main story of twentieth-century epistemology is the story of three connected notions: justification, internalism, and deontology. I propose to begin my study of contemporary views of warrant by examining some *internalist* theories of warrant; but what *is* this 'internalism'? What does it mean to call someone an internalist? The term is in considerable disarray. Different people use it differently; it expresses distinct ideas loosely related by analogies and family resemblance. How can we gain an understanding of internalism? What is the central notion here, the notion in terms of which we can see how the rest of those loosely related ideas hang together? What is the source of the attraction of internalism, and what makes it plausible? And how is it connected with the fundamental question of the nature of warrant?

The basic internalist idea, of course, is that what determines whether a belief is warranted for a person are factors or states in some sense internal to that person; warrant conferring properties are in some way internal to the subject or cognizer. But in *what* way? The pH level of my blood is a condition internal to me, as is the size of my heart; but clearly these are not internal in the relevant way. So what is the relevant way? The first thing to see, I think, is that this notion of internality is fundamentally *epistemic*. Warrant and the properties that confer it are internal in that they are states or conditions of which the cognizer is or can be *aware;* they are states of which he has or can easily have knowledge; they are states or properties to which he has cognitive or epistemic access. But not just any old epistemic access will do; I have epistemic access to the distance from the earth to the moon and to the depth of the Pacific Ocean (I own an encyclopedia), but that is not access of the relevant sort. What is required is some kind of *special* access. Perhaps (as Chisholm suggests) S can determine by *reflection alone* whether a belief has warrant for him; or perhaps he can determine with *certainty* whether a belief has the property that grounds and confers justification; or perhaps there is a certain kind of mistake—a mistake about warrant or the properties that confer it—that he cannot nonculpably make. So the relevant sense of 'internal' is strongly epistemic; the

[5]For example, "Positive Epistemic Status and Proper Function," in *Philosophical Perspectives, 2, Epistemology, 1988*, ed. James Tomberlin (Atascadero, Calif.: Ridgeview, 1988).

internalist holds that a person has some kind of special epistemic access to warrant and the properties that ground it.

The externalist, by contrast, holds that warrant need not depend upon factors relevantly internal to the cognizer; warrant depends or supervenes upon properties to some of which the cognizer may have no special access, or even no epistemic access at all. Take a paradigm externalist view: that of the early Alvin Goldman, for example, who holds "to a first approximation" that a belief has warrant if and to the degree that it is produced by a reliable belief-producing mechanism.[6] What makes this view externalist? Why isn't it internalist? After all, my belief-producing mechanisms, unlike my house or my car, are surely internal to me. What makes the claim externalist, I suggest, is that the properties that on this view confer warrant are not such that I need have any special kind of epistemic access to them. On externalist views, warrant-making properties are such properties (of a belief) as *being produced by a reliable belief-producing mechanism,* or *standing in a causal chain appropriately involving the subject of belief,* or *standing in probabilistic relation R to certain other relevant propositions;* and none of these properties is one to which we have the relevant kind of special access.

The basic thrust of internalism in epistemology, therefore, is that the properties that confer warrant upon a belief are properties to which the believer has some sort of special epistemic access. But why think a thing like that? What is the source of internalism, and why is it attractive? To see why, we must turn to a different but connected idea: that of epistemic *justification.*

II. Justification

It would be colossal understatement to say that Anglo-American epistemology of this century has made much of the notion of epistemic justification. First, of course, there is the widely celebrated "justified true belief" (JTB) account or analysis of knowledge, an analysis we imbibed with our mothers' milk. According to the inherited lore of the epistemological tribe, the JTB account enjoyed the status of epistemological orthodoxy until 1963, when it was shattered by Edmund Gettier with his three-page paper "Is Justified True Belief Knowledge?"[7] After 1963 the justified true belief account of knowledge was seen to be defective and lost its exalted status; but even those convinced by Gettier that justification (along with truth) is not *sufficient* for knowledge still mostly think it *necessary* and *nearly* sufficient for knowledge: the basic shape or contour of the concept of knowledge is given by justified true belief, even if a quasi-technical fillip or addendum ("the fourth condition") is needed to appease Gettier. Of course there is an interesting historical irony here: it isn't easy to find many really explicit statements of a JTB analysis of knowledge prior to Gettier. It is almost as if a distinguished critic created a tradition in the very act

    [6]"What Is Justified Belief," in *Justification and Knowledge: New Studies in Epistemology,* ed. George Pappas (Dordrecht: D. Reidel, 1979), p. 10.
    [7]*Analysis* 23 (1963), pp. 121–23.

of destroying it.[8] Still, there are *some* fairly clear statements of a JTB analysis of knowledge prior to Gettier. Thus, according to C. I. Lewis, "Knowledge is belief which not only is true but also is justified in its believing attitude."[9] A. J. Ayer, furthermore, speaks of knowledge as "the right to be sure";[10] for reasons that will be clearer a bit further along, I believe this is a statement of a JTB account of knowledge. And even if there are few explicit published statements, there is an extensive and impressive oral tradition.

So one element in the received epistemological tradition in the twentieth century is that justification is necessary and (with truth) nearly sufficient (sufficient up to Gettier problems) for knowledge. But what exactly *is* justification? Here we are offered a wide and indeed confusing assortment of alternatives. Consider the following: In the third edition of *Theory of Knowledge* (1989) Roderick Chisholm speaks of the question 'what is knowledge?' and suggests that

> The traditional or classic answer—and the one proposed in Plato's dialogue, the *Theaetetus*—is that knowledge is *justified* true belief. (p. 90—see also the quotation from *The Foundations of Knowing* in n. 8)

According to Roderick Firth,

> To decide whether Watson knows that the coachman did it we must decide whether or not Watson is justified in believing that the coachman did it. Thus if Watson believes that the coachman did it, we must decide whether his conclusion is based rationally on the evidence.[11]

Laurence BonJour[12] holds that the traditional JTB account of knowledge is "at least approximately correct" (pp. 3–4); he continues:

---

[8]Thus, for example, in Roderick Chisholm's *Perceiving: A Philosophical Study* (Ithaca: Cornell University Press, 1957) there is an analysis of knowledge, but one that makes no explicit reference to justification:
"S knows that h is true" means (i) S accepts h; (ii) S has adequate evidence for h and (iii) h is true. (p. 16)
In the first edition of *Theory of Knowledge,* published in 1966, which was after Gettier but before it was widely recognized that Gettier had done in the JTB analysis, Chisholm again offers an analysis of knowledge, and again one in which justification plays no explicit role:
S knows at t that h is true, provided (1) S believes h at t; (2) h is true; and (3) h is evident at t for S. (p. 23)
(In a footnote, Chisholm refers to Gettier's paper, acknowledges Gettier's point, and proposes a repair; this was one of the first rivulets in what was to become a mighty rushing river of responses to Gettier.) In *The Foundations of Knowing* (Minneapolis: University of Minnesota Press, 1982), however, Chisholm speaks of "the traditional definition of knowledge": "Now we are in a position to define the type of justification presupposed by the traditional definition of knowledge. . . . " And after defining it he goes on to say, "And so we retain the traditional definition of knowledge:
S knows that p = Df p; S believes that p; and S is justified in believing that p." (p. 47)
[9]*An Analysis of Knowledge and Valuation* (La Salle, Ill: Open Court, 1946), p. 9.
[10]*The Problem of Knowledge* (London: Macmillan, 1956), p. 28.
[11]"Are Epistemic Concepts Reducible to Ethical Concepts?" in *Values and Morals,* ed. A. Goldman and J. Kim (Dordrecht: D. Reidel, 1978), p. 219.
[12]*The Structure of Empirical Knowledge* (Cambridge: Harvard University Press, 1985).

We cannot, in most cases at least, bring it about directly that our beliefs are true, but we can presumably bring it about directly (though perhaps only in the long run) that they are epistemically justified. (p. 8)

It follows that one's cognitive endeavors are epistemically justified only if and to the extent that they are aimed at this goal, which means very roughly that one accepts all and only those beliefs which one has good reason to think are true. To accept a belief in the absence of such a reason . . . is to neglect the pursuit of truth; such acceptance is, one might say, *epistemically irresponsible*. My contention here is that the idea of avoiding such irresponsibility, of being epistemically responsible in one's believings, is the core of the notion of epistemic justification. (p. 8)

If a given putative knower is himself to be epistemically responsible in accepting beliefs in virtue of their meeting the standards of a given epistemological account, then it seems to follow that an appropriate metajustification for those principles must, in principle at least, be available *to him*. (p. 10)

Hilary Kornblith joins BonJour in linking justification with epistemically responsible action:

Justified belief is belief which is the product of epistemically responsible action; epistemically responsible action is action guided by a desire to have true beliefs. The epistemically responsible agent will thus desire to have true beliefs and thus desire to have his beliefs produced by reliable processes.[13]

Earl Conee and Richard Feldman claim that:

Doxastic attitude D toward proposition p is epistemically justified for S at t if and only if having D toward p fits the evidence S has at t.

Conee adds that:

A person has a justified belief only if the person has reflective access to evidence that the belief is true. . . . Such examples make it reasonable to conclude that there is epistemic justification for a belief only where the person has cognitive access to evidence that supports the truth of the belief. Justifying evidence must be internally available.[14]

William P. Alston considers and rejects an account of justification in terms of responsibility or duty fulfillment and proposes instead that:

S is J_{eg} ['$_e$' for 'evaluative' and '$_g$' for 'grounds'] justified in believing that p *iff* S's believing that p, as S did, was a good thing from the epistemic point of view, in that S's belief that p was based on adequate grounds and S lacked sufficient overriding reasons to the contrary.[15]

---

[13]"Justified Belief and Epistemically Responsible Action," *Philosophical Review* (January 1983), p. 48.

[14]Conee and Feldman, "Evidentialism," *Philosophical Studies* (1985), p 15 (There is an examination of Conee and Feldman's evidentialism in my *Warrant and Proper Function,* chap. 9); and Conee, "The Basic Nature of Epistemic Justification," *Monist* (July 1988), p. 398.

[15]"Concepts of Epistemic Justification," *Monist* (January 1985), p. 71. Chapter 9 (pp. 184ff.) contains a consideration of Alston's view of justification.

"Adequate grounds," furthermore, "are those sufficiently indicative of the truth of *p*."[16] Alston also reports that he finds "widely shared and strong intuitions in favor of some kind of accessibility requirement for justification."[17]

According to Ernest Sosa:

> What does matter for justification is how the subject performs with respect to factors internal to him, . . . it does not matter for justification if external factors are abnormal and unfavorable so that despite his impeccable performance S does not know.[18]

> The evil demon problem for reliabilism is not Descartes' problem of course, but it is a relative. What if twins of ours in another possible world were given mental lives just like ours down to the most minute detail of experience or thought, etc., though they were also totally in error about the nature of their surroundings, and their perceptual and inferential processes of belief acquisition accomplished very little except to sink them more and more deeply and systematically into error? Shall we say that we are justified in our beliefs while our twins are not? They are quite wrong in their beliefs, of course, but it seems somehow very implausible to suppose that they are *unjustified* [his emphasis].[19]

In "Justification and Truth," Stewart Cohen holds that the demon hypothesis entails that "our experience is just as it would be if our cognitive processes were reliable" and hence that we would be justified in believing as we do in fact, when our cognitive processes *are* reliable. So reliability, he argues, cannot be a necessary condition of justification. He also seems to join BonJour in thinking of justification as a matter of epistemic responsibility. Keith Lehrer joins Cohen in elaborating this view:

> Imagine that, unknown to us, our cognitive processes, those involved in perception, memory and inference, are rendered unreliable by the actions of a powerful demon or malevolent scientist. It would follow on reliabilist views that under such conditions the beliefs generated by those processes would not be justified. This result is unacceptable. The truth of the demon hypothesis also entails that our experiences and our reasonings are just what they would be if our cognitive processes were reliable, and therefore, that we would be just as well justified in believing what we do if the demon hypothesis were true as if it were false. Contrary to reliabilism, we aver that under the conditions of the demon hypothesis our beliefs would be justified in an epistemic sense. Justification is a normative concept. It is an evaluation of how well one has pursued one's epistemic goals. Consequently, if we have reason to believe that perception, for example, is a reliable process, then the mere fact that it turns out not to be reliable, because of some improbable contingency, does not obliterate our justification for perceptual belief. This is especially clear when we have good reason to believe that the contingency, which, in fact, makes our cognitive processes unreliable, does not obtain.[20]

[16]"An Internalist Externalism," *Synthese* 74, no. 3 (March 1988), p. 269.
[17]Ibid., p. 272.
[18]"Knowledge and Intellectual Virtue," *Monist* 68 (1985), p. 241.
[19]"Beyond Skepticism, to the Best of Our Knowledge," *Mind,* 97, no. 386 (April 1988), p. 164.
[20]Cohen, "Justification and Truth," *Philosophical Studies* 46 (1984), pp. 281, 282, 284; and Lehrer, "Justification, Truth and Coherence," *Synthese* 55 (1983), pp. 192–93.

The early Alvin Goldman, on the other hand, takes a very different view:

> The justificational status of a belief is a function of the reliability of the process
> or processes that cause it, where (as a first approximation) reliability consists
> in the tendency of a process to produce beliefs that are true rather than false.[21]

And according to the later Goldman of *Epistemology and Cognition:*[22]

> (P1*) A cognizer's belief in p at time t is justified if and only if it is the final
> member of a finite sequence of doxastic states of the cognizer such that some
> (single) right J-rule system licenses the transition of each member of the se-
> quence from some earlier state(s) [where] . . . (ARI) A J-rule system R is right
> if and only if R permits certain (basic) psychological processes, and the instan-
> tiation of these processes would result in a truth ratio of belief that meets some
> specified high threshold (greater than .5) (pp. 83, 106).

Now: how shall we understand this blooming, buzzing confusion with
respect to justification? There seem to be at least four central ideas in these
quotations. First, of course, there is the pervasive connection between justification and warrant or knowledge. Second (BonJour, Cohen, Kornblith, the first
Alstonian notion), justification is a matter of *epistemic responsibility;* a belief is
justified if the person holding it is not guilty of epistemic irresponsibility in
forming or maintaining it.[23] Third (Alston, Conee, Lehrer and Cohen, Cohen,
Sosa, Lehrer), we have the suggestion that there is an *internalist* component to
justification (Goldman seems to demur): the believer must have cognitive access to something important lurking in the neighborhood—whether or not he
is justified, for example, or to the *grounds* of his justification (that by virtue of
which he is justified [Alston]), or to the connection between those grounds and
the justified belief. Of course this must be some kind of *special* access; perhaps
S can determine by reflection alone, for example, whether he is justified (Alston, Conee, Lehrer and Cohen, BonJour, Chisholm). Fourth, there is to be
found in many of the quotations the idea that justification is a matter of *having
evidence,* or at least depends upon evidence (Alston, Firth, Conee, Conee and
Feldman, Chisholm).

  Finally, there is another and broader (if vaguer) notion of justification also
evident in some of the quotations (Lehrer and Cohen, Cohen, Sosa): one that is
hard to put at all precisely but seems to be a generalization of the notion of
justification taken deontologically. This is the idea that everything is going
properly from the perspective of the knowing subject, or insofar as the knowing
subject himself is concerned, *as* knowing subject. What is involved in the
"perspective of the knowing subject," or "the knowing subject as the knowing
subject"? This isn't entirely easy to say. Part of what is involved, however, is
that the way in which the subject's experience is connected with the world is
excluded. Perhaps he is a brain in a vat, or perhaps his experience is induced by
a Cartesian demon and is wholly misleading; nevertheless he is justified if

---

[21]"What Is Justified Belief," p. 10.

[22]Cambridge: Harvard University Press, 1986.

[23]As we shall see in the next chapter, this is also a central theme in Chisholm's account of
warrant.

everything goes right from there on, so to speak—if, in particular, he reasons aright and forms the appropriate beliefs given the course of his experience. Call this *broad justification*. There will be different ways of filling in what it is for things to go right from there on. It could be a matter of forming beliefs responsibly (Cohen), or in such a way as to properly pursue one's epistemic goals (Lehrer and Cohen); it could be a matter of a sort of intrinsic fittingness relating experience and belief (see chapter 3); and it could also be a matter of faculties downstream of experience (reasoning and belief formation, say) *functioning properly*, being subject to no dysfunction.

So we have several different suggestions as to what justification is: being formed responsibly, being reliably produced, being such that the believer has adequate evidence, being formed on the basis of an internally accessible and truth conducive ground, being an evaluation of how well the believer has pursued her epistemic goals, and so on. There is also the connection with knowledge, with internalism, and with evidence. How shall we understand this welter of views as to the nature of justification? And how does it happen that justification is associated, in this way, with evidence? And what is the source of the internalist requirement, and how does it fit in? And why is justification associated, in this way, with knowledge?

III. Classical Deontologism

Here what we need is history and hermeneutics: archaeology, as Foucault says (although, *pace* Foucault, there is no reason to think we will uncover a hidden political agenda). We must go back to the fountainheads of Western theory of knowledge, those twin towers of Western epistemology, Descartes and Locke. For *some* topics—the nature of proper names, perhaps, or the question of serious actualism (that is, the question whether objects can have properties in possible worlds in which they do not exist)—a grasp of the history of the topic is not obviously essential to a grasp of the topic. Not so for internalism and epistemic justification: to understand the contemporary situation of those notions we must look carefully at their history, in particular at some of the ideas of Descartes and, perhaps even more important, Locke. Commonly (and correctly) thought of as the fountainheads of the tradition of classical foundationalism, Descartes and Locke are equally and perhaps even more significantly the fountainheads of the tradition of classical internalism.[24] Contemporary discussion has paid scant attention to the source and origin of the internalist tradition. This has led to confusion, and failure to see the main issues with real

[24]Historians may point out that the internalist tradition goes much further back, at least as far back as the later Platonic Academy, and perhaps back to the Stoics and to Plato himself. I don't propose to dispute the point; but the internalist tradition is very much in eclipse in medieval philosophy, and certainly the important proximate sources of the contemporary version of that tradition are Descartes and Locke.

I am indebted in what I say about Locke to Nicholas Wolterstorff's forthcoming book *When Tradition Fractures*.

clarity, or even (more modestly) the degree of clarity we can attain. Here the ahistoricism of contemporary analytic philosophy has served us ill. To get a proper understanding of justification and internalism, to understand the basic internalist insight, we must trace that tradition back to its source in Descartes and (more crucially) Locke. I have neither the space nor the competence for a really proper historical investigation here; what follows, I fear, is little more than a gesture in that direction. It is an important direction, however, and it is there we must look in order to understand contemporary internalism.

The first thing to see is that for Descartes and Locke the notion of *duty* or *obligation* plays a central role in the whole doxastic enterprise. Rodericks Firth[25] and Chisholm[26] (and other contemporaries) point out that there is a strong normative component in such basic epistemological concepts as justification and warrant; Chisholm (as we shall see) goes on to claim that this normative component is really *deontological,*[27] having to do with (moral) duties, obligations, requirements. In the contemporary context it required a real insight to see clearly the normative character of these epistemic concepts. For Descartes and Locke, however, deontological notions enter in a way that is explicit *in excelsis.* Their thought—that duty and warrant are closely related—is not, of course, inevitable; you might think that we have little or no control over our believings, so that we have few significant duties in connection with them. Or you might think that while indeed we have considerable control over what we believe, the deontological notions of obligation, duty, and permission do not apply; the most we can say, you think, is that some beliefs (or some habits of belief formation and retention, or some epistemic strategies) are more valuable in themselves or more useful to us than others, but no belief or way or strategy of forming and holding beliefs is such that it is obligatory either to accept it or to reject it.

For Descartes and Locke, however, deontological notions enter crucially. Following Augustine (*De Libero Arbitrio*) Descartes gives his classical account of the origin of error:

> But if I abstain from giving my judgment on any thing when I do not perceive it with sufficient clearness and distinctness, it is plain that I act rightly. . . . But if I determine to deny or affirm, I no longer make use as I should of my free will, and if I affirm what is not true, it is evident that I deceive myself; even though I judge according to truth, this comes about only by chance, and I do not escape the blame of misusing my freedom; for the light of nature teaches us that the knowledge of the understanding should always precede the determina-

[25]See, for example, his "Are Epistemic Concepts Reducible to Ethical Concepts?" pp. 215ff.
[26]See, for example, *Perceiving,* part I; *Theory of Knowledge* (Englewood Cliffs, N.J. : Prentice-Hall, 1st ed., 1966; 2d ed., 1977; 3d ed., 1989), pp. 11ff. in 1st ed. and pp. 12ff. in the 2d; and *The Foundations of Knowing* (Minneapolis: University of Minnesota Press, 1982), pp. 7ff.
[27]From the Greek *déon* (that which is obligatory). There is no direct connection here with the metaethical position according to which the basic ethical notion is that of duty; I use the term just to point to the fact that the variety of normativity under consideration is that exemplified by *duty* and *obligation* (even if, *pace* Ross and Prichard, that is not the primary ethical notion).

tion of the will. It is in the misuse of the free will that the privation which constitutes the characteristic nature of error is met with.[28]

According to Descartes, error is due to a misuse of free will, a misuse for which one is guilty and blameworthy ("and I do not escape the blame of misusing my freedom"). There is a *duty* or *obligation* not to affirm a proposition unless we perceive it with sufficient clarity and distinctness; that there is such a duty is something we are taught by "the light of nature."[29] According to Descartes, *being justified* is being within our rights, flouting no epistemic duties, doing no more than what is permitted. We are justified when we regulate or order our beliefs in such a way as to conform to the duty not to affirm a proposition unless we perceive it with sufficient clarity and distinctness.

In his *Essay Concerning Human Understanding,* Locke is, if anything, even more explicit about this deontological component of the epistemic:

> Faith is nothing but a firm assent of the mind: which if it be regulated, as is our duty, cannot be afforded to anything, but upon good reason; and so cannot be opposite to it. He that believes, without having any reason for believing, may be in love with his own fancies; but neither seeks truth as he ought, nor pays the obedience due his maker, who would have him use those discerning faculties he has given him, to keep him out of mistake and error. He that does not this to the best of his power, however he sometimes lights on truth, is in the right but by chance; and I know not whether the luckiness of the accident will excuse the irregularity of his proceeding. This at least is certain, that he must be accountable for whatever mistakes he runs into: whereas he that makes use of the light and faculties God has given him, and seeks sincerely to discover truth, by those helps and abilities he has, may have this satisfaction in doing his duty as a rational creature, that though he should miss truth, he will not miss the reward of it. For he governs his assent right, and places it as he should, who in any case or matter whatsoever, believes or disbelieves, according as reason directs him. He that does otherwise, transgresses against his own light, and misuses those faculties, which were given him.[30]

Here again there is the clear affirmation that we have an epistemic or doxastic duty: a duty, for example, not to afford a firm assent of the mind "to anything, but upon good reason." To act in accord with these duties or obligations is to be within one's rights; it is to do only what is permissible; it is to be

---

[28]Meditation 4 in *Philosophical Works of Descartes,* ed. Haldane and Ross (Cambridge: Cambridge University Press, 1911; reprint, New York: Dover, 1955), vol. 1, p. 176.

[29]In "What is Cartesian Doubt?" (presently unpublished), Nicholas Wolterstorff argues that on the best understanding of Descartes, he didn't really mean to insist that there is a duty or obligation to affirm a proposition only if it is clearly and distinctly perceived. What he meant instead is that a proposition constitutes *scientia* for us only if it meets that condition. Wolterstorff's interpretation of Descartes makes sense of much of what Descartes says; in the long run he may be right. Still, Descartes certainly *seems* to say, here, that I am obliged to refrain from believing a proposition that is not clear and distinct (for me); this is how he has commonly been understood; and it is this common understanding that is relevant to the formation of the twentieth-century received tradition with respect to justification.

[30]*An Essay Concerning Human Understanding,* ed. A. C. Fraser (New York: Dover, 1959), IV, xvii, 24, pp. 413–14; hereafter referred to as *Essay.*

subject to no blame or disapprobation; it is to have flouted no duties; it is to be deontologically approvable; it is, in a word, to be *justified*. Indeed the whole notion of epistemic justification has its origin and home in this deontological territory of duty and permission, and it is only by way of analogical extension that the term 'epistemic justification' is applied in other ways. Originally and at bottom, epistemic justification *is* deontological justification: deontological justification with respect to the regulation of belief.

Now perhaps Descartes accepts a justified true belief account of knowledge; for he thinks that one is justified only in accepting just those propositions that are clear and distinct; and those propositions are just the ones he thinks we know. Locke, however, clearly does not; for him, knowledge and belief are two quite different states, and duty or obligation applies only to the latter. Your duty, he says, is to regulate your beliefs in such a way that you believe a proposition only if you have good reasons for it; those reasons would be propositions that are certain for you, and of which, accordingly, you have knowledge. But knowledge itself does not involve fulfillment of duty, epistemic or otherwise; indeed, here the dual concepts of obligation and permission do not really apply. Knowledge, he says, is a matter of noticing connections among ideas, and is only of what is certain. But if a proposition is certain for me, he holds, then there is no question of regulating my belief with respect to it. The reason is that I have no control with respect to such propositions, so that whether I believe is not up to me. Speaking of self-evident propositions, he says "all such affirmations, and negations, are made without any possibility of doubt, uncertainty or hesitation, and must necessarily be assented to, as soon as understood" (*Essay*, IV, vii, 4, p. 269). While Locke speaks here of just one of the several kinds of items of which we can have certainty, he clearly thinks the same thing about the others.

So Locke does not equate warrant—that quantity enough of which is sufficient, with truth, for knowledge—with epistemic justification, or, as we could call it to remind ourselves of the reference to duty and obligation, *deontological* epistemic justification. Nevertheless, deontological justification is of the very first importance for him as it is for Descartes. His central thought is that being justified in holding a belief is having fulfilled one's epistemic duties in forming or continuing to hold that belief. He adds (in agreement with Descartes) that if I go contrary to my epistemic duty, I lose a most important epistemic quality; and both hold that if I do so, then, although I may happen to "light on the truth," it will be (no thanks to me) only by mere chance, by accident. (An important component of our idea of knowledge is that if a person just *happens* to "light on truth," if he believes what is true by chance or accident, then the belief in question may be as true as you please but does not constitute knowledge.)[31] This thought—the thought that being justified in holding a belief is having fulfilled one's epistemic duties in forming or continuing to hold that belief—is the *fons et origo* of the whole internalist tradition. It is this notion of

[31] In *Warrant and Proper Function*, chap. 2, I explain what underlies this thought and what the force of 'by accident' is here.

deontological justification that is the source of internalism: deontology implies internalism. Let me explain.

IV. Deontology and Internalism

First, on the Cartesian–Lockean deontological conception of justification, whether *S*'s beliefs are justified, obviously, is up to *S* and within her control. He who has justification, says Locke, "may have this satisfaction in doing his duty as a rational creature, that though he should miss truth, he will not miss the reward of it [that is, of being justified, having done his duty]." The classical internalist thinks we need give no hostages to fortune when it comes to justification; here our destiny is entirely in our own hands. The fates may conspire to deceive me; I could be wrong about whether there is an external world, or a past, or other persons; for all I can be really sure of, I may be a brain in a vat or the victim of a malevolent Cartesian demon who delights in deception; I may be wholly and hopelessly deceived. Even so, I can still do my epistemic duty; I can still do my best; I can be above reproach. Justification (unlike, say, a strong constitution) is not something that *happens* to a person; it is instead a result of her own efforts. Perhaps I can't take credit for my good digestion or my charming disposition; I can take credit for being justified. As the classical deontologist sees things, justification is not by faith but by works; and whether we are justified in our beliefs is up to us.

It is really this deontological feature of the classical conception of justification that leads to the internalist result; but to see just how, we must make a brief detour through a steep and thorny area of ethics. Most of us will agree that a person is guilty, properly blamed, properly subject to censure and moral disapproval, if and only if she fails to do her duty (where among her duties might be that of *refraining* from doing certain things). So

> (a)   you are properly blamed for failing to do something *A* if and only if it is your duty to do *A* (and you fail to do it).

Of course we also think that someone who has done no more than what she nonculpably thinks duty permits or requires, is not culpable or guilty in doing what she does, even if we think that what she has done is wrong. You are the governor and it is up to you to decide whether a certain prisoner is to suffer the death penalty. You reflect as carefully and impartially as you can and make your decision; perhaps you believe that it is your duty in the circumstances not to commute the death sentence and let the law take its course. Then I shall not properly hold you blameworthy or guilty for doing what you do, even if I think you made the wrong decision. You cannot be faulted for doing what you think is the right thing to do—provided, of course, that you came to that judgment in a nonculpable way. (If you formed the judgment out of vengefulness, or pride, or lordly contempt for those whom you take to be your inferiors, then things are very different.) So we also have

(b)   If a person nonculpably believes that doing A is morally required or permitted, then she is not guilty (not to be blamed) for doing A; and if she nonculpably believes that refraining from doing A is morally required or permitted, then she is not guilty (not to be blamed) for refraining from doing A.

It is plausible to add, still further, that if I believe that it is my duty, all things considered, to do A, then I am guilty, culpable, morally blameworthy if I do *not* do A.[32]

Sadly enough, however, these principles taken together appear to lead to trouble. For suppose I nonculpably think I am permitted to refrain from doing A. Then by (b) I am not guilty and not to be blamed for thus refraining; but then by (a) doing A is not my duty. So if I nonculpably think it is not my duty to do something A, then it is not my duty to do A; and if I nonculpably think it is not my duty to refrain from doing A, then it is not my duty to refrain from doing it. Furthermore (given the addition to (b)), we can argue similarly that if I think it is my duty to do A, then I am culpable if I do not do A, in which case it is my duty to do A. But isn't this consequence wrong? You and I might argue at considerable and heated length about what duty requires in a given set of circumstances. Perhaps I think you ought to commute that sentence; you think the right thing to do is to let it stand. You could not sensibly claim that since you do in fact believe that is your duty, and believe that nonculpably, you automatically win the argument. It isn't given in advance that I am always right about what my duty requires, so long as I am nonculpable in holding the opinion I hold. If that were so, why should I come to you, asking for advice as to what my duty really is, in a given situation? So (a) and (b) both seem correct; taken together, however, they seem to entail a proposition that is clearly false.

Here, as Aquinas says, we must make a distinction. An attractive way out of this quandary is offered by the distinction between *objective* and *subjective* duty or rightness. You are guilty or blameworthy if you fail to do your *subjective* duty, but not necessarily guilty for failing to do your *objective* duty. Guilt, being properly blamed, being properly subject to censure—these things go with violation of subjective duty. Perhaps my objective duties are constituted by virtue of their being, of the options open to me, the ones that contribute most to the greatest good; or perhaps they are constituted by God's commands; or perhaps they are the ones that bear a certain particular relation of fittingness to the circumstances. Then a person might well not know or be able to see that a given action was the right one, the dutiful one, in the circumstances. Perhaps I suffer from a certain sort of moral blindness; I simply cannot see that I have an obligation to care for my aging parents. Then I am not blameworthy for failing to care for them, unless my moral blindness itself somehow arises from dereliction of duty. Assume, just for purposes of argument, that the ground of the obligation not to steal is the divine command "Thou shalt not steal." I could

[32]As the apostle Paul points out, those who think eating meat is wrong are blameworthy if they eat it, even if in fact it is not (objectively) wrong: "But if anyone regards something as unclean, then for him it is unclean" (*Romans* 14:14).

hardly be blamed for stealing if I (nonculpably) didn't know that stealing is wrong or didn't know, of a given act of stealing I am performing, that it is wrong, or didn't know, of a given act of taking something, that it is indeed an act of stealing. You are guilty, or to blame, or properly subject to censure only if, as we say, you *knowingly* flout your duty. Ignorance may be no excuse in the law; but nonculpable ignorance is an excusing condition in morality. Indeed, it is sometimes also an excusing condition in the law; according to the M'Naghten Rule you aren't legally culpable if you cannot tell right from wrong.

Now how, exactly, does this help with respect to the above quandary? Well, the problem was that (a) and (b) seemed to entail that I couldn't make a nonculpable mistake about what my duty was; but that seemed wrong, since it is perfectly sensible for you to challenge my belief as to what duty requires, even if you don't for a moment believe that I arrived at that belief culpably. And the resolution is that while I can't make a nonculpable error about my *subjective* duty, the same does not hold for my *objective* duty; but what we dispute about, when we dispute about what my duty, in a given circumstance, is, is not my subjective but my objective duty. It is easy enough, in the right circumstances, to make a mistake about *that*.[33]

Given that no one is guilty for doing what she nonculpably believes is right, you might expect that we would ordinarily be receptive to the claim of ignorance as an excusing condition. The fact is, however, that in many circumstances we are extremely reluctant to accept such a claim. I take part in a racist lynching: you will not be impressed by my claim that, after careful reflection, I considered that the right thing to do. We are deeply suspicious of such claims. We are not ordinarily receptive to the claim, on the part of murderer or thief, that, after due consideration, she thought the course she took most appropriate, morally speaking, of those open to her.

The reason, I think, is that there are many moral beliefs we don't think a properly functioning human being can (in ordinary circumstances) nonculpably acquire. We do not think a well-formed, properly functioning human being could honestly arrive at the view that it does not matter how one treats his fellows, that if inflicting suffering on someone else affords me a certain mild pleasure, then there can be no serious objection to my so doing. We do not think a person could honestly come to the view that all that matters is his own welfare and pleasure, other persons being of value only insofar as they contribute to that end. It is not, of course, that we think it *logically* impossible (in the broad sense) that there be persons who honestly arrive at such views; it is rather that we think it simply would not, more exactly, could not happen, given ordinary circumstances and what is in fact the nature of human beings. A theist

---

[33]Can we explain subjective duty in terms of objective duty or vice versa? Or, if that is too much to hope for, can we at least state an interesting relation between the two? Perhaps: according to Alan Donagan (*The Theory of Morality* [Chicago: University of Chicago Press, 1977], chap. 2.3, pp. 52–57, and chap. 4, pp. 112ff.), my subjective duty is that which it would be objectively right to blame me for not doing. In the other direction, a proposition states an objective duty for me if and only if it is true, and is such that if I knew it, then it would state a subjective duty for me.

will be likely to view this as a matter of God's having created us in such a way that we can simply *see* that heinous actions are indeed heinous; nontheists will account for the same fact in some other way.

In either case, however, we are likely to think that if a cognitively nondefective person comes to believe that such actions are perfectly right and proper, it must be because of some fault in him. Perhaps at some time in the past he *decided* to accept these views, and the pressure of that commitment has brought it about that these beliefs are now second nature to him. A part of what is involved in our blaming people for holding corrupt beliefs, I think, is our supposing that a human being whose faculties are functioning properly, and who is blameless in forming and holding her beliefs, will *reject* these beliefs, just as we think a human being whose faculties are functioning properly will accept *modus ponens* as valid but fail to pay the same compliment to Affirming the Consequent. We think a properly functioning human being will find injustice—the sort depicted, for example, in the story the prophet Nathan told King David[34]—despicable and odious. Only a cognitively defective person could conscientiously come to think that the behavior of the rich man in that story is anything but morally abhorrent; any normal adult who gives the matter a moment's thought can see that injustice of that sort is wicked and reprehensible. (Indeed, we need not limit ourselves to adults: small children often exhibit a very well developed sense of justice and fairness.) In the face of this natural tendency or prompting, to accept such behavior as perfectly proper requires something like a special act of will—a special act of *ill* will. Such a person, we think, *knows better*, or at any rate *should have* known better; she chooses what in some sense she knows to be wrong. And if, on the other hand, we think a person really *does* lack this inclination to see these actions as morally wrong, then we think he is in some way defective, that some of his cognitive faculties are not functioning properly.

We therefore object, from a moral point of view, to certain kinds of actions that (in the short term anyway) are entirely conscientious; we hold that a person may be doing what is wrong or wicked or impermissible even if he thinks that way of acting is quite in accord with his obligations—even if, indeed, he thinks the action in question is part of his duty. Our objection here is that he *ought not* to think that action permissible or obligatory; and the fact that he *does* think so shows (if his cognitive faculties are functioning properly) that at some point he has culpably done something that has clouded his own moral vision. We think those whom we thus hold responsible really know better. They have rejected what is plain to anyone of goodwill. They have ignored or suppressed the promptings and leadings of nature—the natural tendency to find unjust behavior reprehensible, for example—and have instead chosen a different route, perhaps one that legitimates a desire for self-aggrandizement, one that gives free rein to that perverse and aboriginal sin, *pride*. So there is a link, here, between objective and subjective duty, a link we think provided by our nature. This link is constituted by the fact that—so, at

[34]*2 Samuel* 11–12.

any rate, we are inclined to think—a certain kind of mistake is not possible for a well-formed human being who is acting (and has acted) conscientiously.

So for a large and important class of cases we think objective and subjective duty coincide, and do so because of our cognitive constitution; there is a large class of cases in which a properly functioning human being can just see (all else being equal) that a certain course of action is wrong. Now it is this same thought—the thought that in a large class of cases objective and subjective duty coincide—that underlies classical internalism. This coincidence of objective and subjective duty is the driving force behind the classical internalism of Descartes and Locke. We can see this in more detail as follows.

A. The First Internalist Motif

According to Locke and Descartes, epistemic justification is *deontological* justification. And here they are clearly thinking of *subjective* duty or obligation; they are thinking of guilt and innocence, blame and blamelessness. If I do not have certainty but believe anyway, says Descartes, "I do not escape the blame of misusing my freedom." Locke, clearly enough, is also thinking of subjective duty ("This at least is certain, that he must be accountable for whatever mistakes he runs into"). But then the first internalist motif follows immediately:

M1. *Epistemic justification (that is, subjective epistemic justification, being such that I am not blameworthy) is entirely up to me and within my power.*

All that is required is that I do my subjective duty, act in such a way that I am blameless. All I have to do is my duty; and, given that ought implies can, I am guaranteed to be able to do that. So justification is entirely within my power; whether or not my beliefs are justified is up to me, within my control. My system of beliefs may be wildly skewed and laughably far from the truth; I may be a brain in a vat or a victim of a malicious Cartesian demon; but whether my beliefs have justification is still up to me.

B. The Second Internalist Motif

Descartes and Locke, I say, are speaking there of subjective duty. But of course they are also speaking of *objective* duty. Descartes claims that it is clear to us that we must not give assent to what is uncertain: "the light of nature," he says, "teaches us that the knowledge of the understanding should always precede the determination of the will." And Locke holds that it is my duty to regulate my belief in such a way that I believe only what I have good reasons for, that is, only what is epistemically probable with respect to my total evidence.[35] One

---

[35]That is, the body of beliefs that are certain for me. Both Locke and Descartes are classical internalists, but also, of course, classical foundationalists. Say that a proposition is *basic* for me if I accept it, but do not accept it on the evidential basis of other beliefs; $2 + 1 = 3$ would be an

who does otherwise, he says, "transgresses against his own light, and misuses those faculties, which were given him." Such a person, he says, "neither seeks truth as he ought, nor pays the obedience due his maker, who would have him use those discerning faculties he has given him, to keep him out of mistake and error." To regulate my belief in this way is my *objective* duty; what makes an act of believing permissible or right is its being appropriately supported by the believer's total evidence. But Locke also holds that this is my *subjective* duty; if I do not regulate my belief in this way I am blameworthy, guilty of dereliction of epistemic duty. (Merely *trying* to regulate it thus is not sufficient; I must *succeed* in so doing if I am not to be blameworthy.) Objective and subjective duty thus coincide. Similarly for Descartes: if you give assent to what is not certain then (*ceteris paribus*) you are blameworthy, have flouted subjective duty as well as objective duty. So the second internalist motif:

> M2.   For a large, important, and basic class of objective epistemic duties, objective and subjective duty coincide; what you objectively ought to do matches that which is such that if you don't do it, you are guilty and blameworthy.

And the link is provided by our nature: in a large and important class of cases, a properly functioning human being can simply see whether a given belief is or is not (objectively) justified for him. (In the same way, in the more general moral case, certain heinous acts, so we think, are such that a properly functioning human being cannot make a nonculpable mistake as to whether those acts are morally acceptable.)

The second internalist motif has three corollaries.

First: if it is your subjective duty to regulate your belief in this way, then you must be able to see or tell that regulating belief this way is indeed your duty. Locke and Descartes clearly hold that a dutiful, conscientious person whose cognitive faculties are functioning properly will not make a mistake as to what is the right method or practice for regulating belief. Descartes claims that it is clear to us that we must not give assent to what is uncertain: "the light of nature," he says, "teaches us that the knowledge of the understanding should always precede the determination of the will." And Locke says that the person who does not regulate his belief according to the evidence "*transgresses against his own light,* and misuses those faculties, which were given him*" (my emphasis). So the first corollary:

---

example. Say further that a belief is *properly basic* for me if it is basic for me and I am justified, violating no epistemic duties, in accepting it in the basic way. Then according to Locke and Descartes, the only propositions that are properly basic for me are ones that are certain; and these are the propositions that are self-evident to me, such as $2 + 1 = 3$, or immediately about my own mental life, such as *I am appeared to redly,* or (perhaps) *I believe that $7 + 5 = 12$.* (There is a good deal of unclarity about just which propositions are properly basic, according to Descartes and Locke; this is not the place to enter that discussion.) So propositions of these kinds are properly basic; any other proposition I believe is such that if I am justified in accepting it, I must believe it on the basis of propositions that are properly basic. For a fuller characterization of foundationalism and classical foundationalism, see chapter 4, and see my "Reason and Belief in God," pp. 47–59.

C1   *In a large and important set of cases, a properly functioning human being can simply see (cannot make a nonculpable mistake about) what objective epistemic duty requires.*

To grasp the second corollary, we must note first that (according to both Descartes and Locke) I do not determine *directly,* so to speak, what it is that I am obliged to believe and withhold. According to Locke, I determine whether a given belief is acceptable for me or justified for me by determining something else: whether it is supported by what is certain for me—whether, that is, it is probable with respect to what I know. Similarly for Descartes: I do not *directly* determine whether a proposition is acceptable or justified for me; I do it by determining whether or not it is *clear and distinct* for me. So I have a way of determining when a belief is justified for me; to use a medieval expression, I have a *ratio cognoscendi* for whether a belief is justified for me. As we have seen, Descartes and Locke think that a well-formed human being cannot (in those basic cases) make a conscientious error as to whether a given belief is justified for her; but then, in those cases, she will also be unable to make a conscientious mistake about whether a given belief has the property by which she *determines* whether that belief is justified for her. Locke and Descartes therefore believe that a well-formed, conscientious human being will (at least in that large and important basic class of cases) be able to tell whether a given belief has the property that forms the *ratio cognoscendi* for justification. So the second corollary:

C2   *In a large and important class of cases a properly functioning human being can simply see (cannot make a nonculpable mistake about) whether a proposition has the property by means of which she tells whether a proposition is justified for her.*

As we have just seen, Locke and Descartes hold that I have a means of telling whether a given proposition is justified for me; I do it by determining whether it is supported by my total evidence (Locke) or whether it is certain for me (Descartes). But note that what *confers* justification on a belief for me, the *ground* of its justification, is, as they see it, the very same property as *that by which I determine* whether it is justified for me. According to Locke, the *ratio essendi* (to invoke the other half of that medieval contrast) of justification is the property of being supported by the believer's total evidence, whereas according to Descartes it is the property of being certain for the believer. But then the ground of justification (the justification-making property) is identical with the property by which we determine whether a belief has justification: *ratio cognoscendi* coincides with *ratio essendi*.[36] (This is not, of course, inevitable; in

[36]I don't mean to suggest that Locke and Descartes were clear about the distinction between *ratio essendi* and *ratio cognoscendi;* like the distinction between modality *de re* and modality *de dicto,* and the distinction between the necessity of the consequent and the necessity of the consequence, this is a case of an important piece of philosophical lore known to every medieval graduate student but disastrously lost in the Renaissance rejection of all things scholastic.

the case of measles, velocity, blood pressure, weight, and serum cholesterol our *ratio cognoscendi* does not coincide with the *ratio essendi*.)

If so, however, then there is another kind of error a properly functioning dutiful human being cannot make; such a person is so constructed that (in that class of basic cases) she cannot conscientiously come to believe, of the justification-making property, that a given belief has it when in fact it does not. According to Locke, a properly functioning human being could not both be appropriately dutiful in forming her beliefs (in these cases), and also mistakenly believe, of some proposition, that it was supported by her total evidence; according to Descartes, such a person in such a case could not mistakenly come to think that a belief was certain for her when in fact it was not. We have a certain guaranteed access to the *ratio cognoscendi* of justification; but if *ratio cognoscendi* and *ratio essendi* coincide, then we also have guaranteed access to the latter. So the third corollary:

> C3   *In a large, important and basic class of epistemic cases a properly functioning human being can simply see (cannot make a nonculpable mistake about) whether a proposition has the property that confers justification upon it for her.*

Now the fact of the matter seems to be, *contra* Locke, that cases in which it is obvious what my total evidence supports are, after all, relatively few and far between. It is easy enough to make a nonculpable mistake about what my total evidence supports; it is often difficult indeed to tell whether a belief has (what Locke sees as) the *ratio cognoscendi* of justification. Perhaps Locke sometimes saw this; significantly enough, he sometimes retreats to the weaker view that what confers justification is the belief's being such that *upon reflection* I *think* it is supported by my evidence. Here it seems clear that I do have the requisite special access.

C. The Third Internalist Motif

There is still another and somewhat less well defined internalist motif here. According to Locke and Descartes, I have a sort of guaranteed access to whether a belief is justified for me and also to what makes it justified for me: I cannot (if I suffer from no cognitive deficiency) nonculpably but mistakenly believe that a belief is justified or has the justification-making property. This is the source of another internalist motif; for it is only certain of my states and properties to which it is at all plausible to think that I have that sort of access. Clearly you don't have this sort of access to the pH level of your blood, or the size of your liver, or whether your pancreas is now functioning properly. The sorts of things about which it is plausible to hold that you can't make a mistake, will be, for example, whether you believe that Albuquerque is in New Mexico, whether you are now being appeared to redly, whether you are trying to get to Boston on time, or whether you are trying to bring it about that, for every proposition you consider, you believe it if and only if it is true. So the justification-making property will have to attach to such states as my believing thus and so, my being appeared to in such and such a fashion, my aiming at a given state of affairs, my trying to do something or other, and the like. These states are the ones such that it is plausible to hold of them that I cannot make a nonculpable mistake as to whether I exhibit them. But they are also, in some recognizable, if hard to define sense, internal to me—internal to me as a knower or a cognizing being. Thinking of justification in the deontological way characteristic of classical internalism induces *epistemic* internalism: and that in turn induces internalism of this different but related sort. It is not easy to think of a name for internalism of this sort, but perhaps the name 'personal internalism' (calling attention to the way in which my beliefs, desires, experience, and aims are crucial to me as a person) is no worse than some others.

Of course it is not *necessary* that the things to which a person has this special access are internal in this sense; there could be a being who had guaranteed and indeed logically incorrigible access to properties that were not in this way internal to him. If the bulk of the theistic tradition is right, God is essentially omniscient: but then it is impossible (impossible in the broadly logical sense) that he err on any topic whatever, internal to him or not. Not so for us.

One final point. It is clear that Descartes and Locke each embrace a version of *doxastic voluntarism:* the view that we have at least some voluntary control over our beliefs. Of course both hold that I cannot withhold assent from what is genuinely self-evident; thus, according to Locke (as we saw), "all such affirmations, and negations, are made without any possibility of doubt, uncertainty, or hesitation, and must necessarily be assented to, as soon as understood" (*Essay* IV, vii, 4, p. 269); and Descartes would concur. But Descartes thought there were many propositions—propositions that are not initially self-evident for me—such that it is within my power to accept them and within my power to reject them; and it is my duty to accept them only if they are or become certain for me. (Of course, he recognized that it might take a certain discipline to be able to reject all beliefs that are less than certain; perhaps one must reflect on the fact that the senses often deceive us, or on the dream argument, or on the hypothesis that we might be in the doxastic control of a malicious demon. In fact Descartes suggests somewhere that it might be a good idea to reread the first couple of his *Meditations* when tempted to believe what is less than indubitable; in the same spirit Victorians encouraged youths tempted to idleness to read inspirational poetry extolling industry.)[37] Similarly for Locke: he held that it is up to me whether I deliberate, although once I have gone through this process and see that a given belief is strongly supported by what is certain for me, then it is no longer up to me whether I accept it. But many beliefs, he

---

[37]For example, Isaac Watts's "How Doth the Little Busy Bee." The first verse:

How doth the little busy bee
Improve each shining hour,
And gather honey all the day
From every opening flower!

This poem is the one that was parodied to devastating effect by Lewis Carroll's "The Crocodile" ("How doth the little crocodile improve his shining tail, . . . ").

thought, are such that prior to reflection I have a strong inclination to accept them, which inclination is resistible.[38] It is possible for me to accept them and possible for me to withhold them; and he held that the latter is what duty requires. It is my duty to withhold assent unless the candidate for belief is supported by what is certain for me. So should we add doxastic voluntarism as a fourth internalist motif?

I don't think so. First, note that in the typical case where a belief suggests itself—even a belief that is not certain—it is not the case that it is within my power to accept it and within my power to reject it. Driving down the road I am confronted with what appears to be an approaching automobile; it is or- dinarily not, in such a case, up to me whether I believe that there is an auto- mobile approaching. (And, *pace* Descartes, it doesn't help much to reread the first couple of his *Meditations*.) When I see a tree, or the sky, it is ordinarily not within my power to withhold such propositions as *there's a tree there* or *today the sky is blue*. You offer me a million dollars to believe that the population of the United States exceeds that of China; I can try my hardest, strain to the uttermost; it will be in vain. But does epistemic deontologism as such imply the denials of these facts? Not at all. Perhaps Descartes' and Locke's views do; and perhaps epistemic deontologism implies a doxastic voluntarism of *some* sort, a sort of weak doxastic voluntarism; but it does not as such imply that there are any beliefs at all such that merely by an act of will I can either acquire or lose or withhold them. One who construes justification deontologically need not be- lieve that it is ever my duty, in given circumstances, to believe or withhold a given proposition. Perhaps instead my duty is to follow Locke's advice and reflect on the question whether the belief in question is supported by my evidence; perhaps it is my duty to adopt or strive to adopt policies of a certain sort. It is within my power to adopt policies that influence and modify my propensities to believe; I can adopt such policies as paying careful attention to the evidence, avoiding wishful thinking, being aware of such sources of belief as jealousy, lust, contrariety, excessive optimism, loyalty, and the like. Perhaps it is my duty to cultivate the epistemic or doxastic virtue Ernest Sosa speaks of; and perhaps a belief of mine is justified in case it is epistemically virtuous, the sort of belief that an epistemically virtuous person would hold in that context. Of course, even this implies at least a certain degree of *indirect* control over my beliefs. Suppose I am at present epistemically vicious and it is my duty to achieve intellectual virtue. Then it is within my power to achieve this state; but the beliefs I would hold were I epistemically virtuous would presumably be different from the beliefs I would hold if I persisted in my epistemically vicious condition; so I have at any rate a certain indirect control over what I believe. But this control may be as indirect and tenuous as you please.

Internalism, therefore, is a congeries of ideas loosely connected and analogi- cally related. If we go back to the source of the internalist tradition, however, we can see that internalism arises out of deontology; a deontological concep- tion of warrant (or, as in Locke's case, of an aspect of warrant) leads directly to

---

[38]See Wolterstorff, *When Tradition Fractures*.

internalism. Seeing internalism as thus arising out of deontology permits us to see why it includes just the elements it does, and how those elements are related.

V. Back to the Present

Suppose we return to the twentieth century; we are now in a better position, I think, to understand the swirling diversity it presents with respect to justification. According to the twentieth-century received tradition, as we saw above, (1) justification is necessary and (along with truth) nearly sufficient for knowledge, (2) there is a strong connection between justification and evidence, and (3) justification involves internalism of two kinds (epistemic and personal internalism). Further, justification itself is taken as a matter of epistemic responsibility or aptness for epistemic duty fulfillment (Firth, Lehrer, Cohen, Kornblith, Chisholm), as an "evaluation" of how well you have fulfilled your epistemic goals (Lehrer and Cohen), as being believed or accepted on the basis of an adequate truth conducive ground (Alston), as being produced by a reliable belief-producing mechanism (Goldman), as being supported by or fitting the evidence (Conee, Conee and Feldman, Firth, many others), and as a matter of things going right with respect to the knowing subject *qua* subject. The project was to try to understand this diversity, and to see what underlies the close connection of justification with knowledge, the internalist requirement laid upon epistemic justification, and the stress upon evidence in connection with justification. I think it is now easier to understand this diversity.

By way of pursuing this project, note first that the basic Cartesian–Lockean idea of justification as fulfillment of epistemic duty or obligation is, of course, directly reflected in the work of all of those (for example, BonJour, Cohen, Kornblith, and, preeminently, Chisholm) who see justification as epistemic responsibility or aptness for epistemic duty fulfillment. This deontological conception of epistemic justification is the basic and fundamental notion of epistemic justification; other notions of epistemic justification arise from this one by way of analogical extension. Deontological justification is justification most properly so-called.[39] (In the next chapter I shall examine Chisholm's detailed attempt to explain warrant in terms of justification thus construed.)

Turn now to the second notion of the nature of justification: that it is or essentially involves having adequate evidence for the belief in question. We often say that a belief is justified when the believer has what we think of as sufficient *evidence* or *reason* for the belief, or (perhaps more exactly) that under those conditions the believer is justified in holding that belief. According to the 'evidentialism' of Conee and Feldman, you are justified in believing B just if you have sufficient evidence for it, or (as they put it) just if it fits your evidence. (Thus Conee: "Such examples make it reasonable to conclude that there is

---

[39]Thus William Alston: "I must confess that I do not find 'justified' an apt term for a favorable or desirable state or condition, when what makes it desirable is cut loose from considerations of obligation and blame." "Concepts of Epistemic Justification," *Monist* (January 1985), p. 86.

epistemic justification of a belief only where the person has cognitive access to evidence that supports the belief.")[40] Indeed, this equation of being justified with having evidence is so pervasive that the justified true belief analysis of knowledge has often been put as the idea that you know if and only if your belief is true and you have adequate evidence for it.[41] How does this association of justification with evidence come about? The answer is easy, given the central historical position of Descartes and, more particularly, Locke. To be justified is to be without blame, to be within your rights, to have done no more than what is permitted, to have violated no duty or obligation, to warrant no blame or censure. Now suppose you agree with Locke that among your duties is that of not giving "firm assent" to any proposition (any proposition that is not certain for you, that is, self-evident or appropriately about your own mental life) without having good reasons, that is, evidence for it. Then, naturally enough, you will think that no one is justified in accepting such a belief without evidence or reason. Indeed, you may eventually go so far as to use the term 'justified belief' just to *mean* 'belief for which one has good reasons'.

Two further points here. (a) Conee and Feldman do not make the deontological connection: they do not say that the *ratio essendi* of justification is duty fulfillment, with the chief duty being that of believing (or, more plausibly, trying to bring it about that you believe) only that which fits your evidence. But there are plenty of contemporaries and near contemporaries who do; W. K. Clifford (that "delicious *enfant terrible*," as William James calls him) trumpets that "it is wrong, always, everywhere, and for anyone to believe anything upon insufficient evidence";[42] his is only the most strident in a vast chorus of voices insisting that the or a primary intellectual duty is that of believing only on the basis of evidence. (A few others in the choir: Sigmund Freud,[43] Brand Blanshard,[44] H. H. Price,[45] Bertrand Russell,[46] and Michael Scriven.[47] And (b) there are two quite different possibilities for the evidentialist; she might be holding, on the one hand, that the very *nature* of justification is believing (or trying to bring it about that you believe) on the basis of evidence (that justification just *is* believing or trying to believe in that way) or she might hold, more plausibly, that the nature of justification is fulfillment of epistemic duty, the chief among those duties being that of believing or trying to believe only on the basis of evidence. (Since Conee and Feldman do not mention epistemic obligation, it seems likely that they are to be taken the first way.)

[40]*Monist* (July 1988), p. 398; and see my n. 14.

[41]For example, in Chisholm's *Perceiving* (p. 16). In the first edition of *Theory of Knowledge*, however, he rejects that definition (p. 20).

[42]"The Ethics of Belief," in *Lectures and Essays* (London: Macmillan, 1879), p. 183.

[43]*The Future of an Illusion* (New York: Norton, 1961), p. 32 (the first German edition was published in 1927).

[44]*Reason and Belief* (London: Allen & Unwin, 1974), pp. 400ff.

[45]*Belief* (London: Allen & Unwin, 1969), pp. 85ff.

[46]"Give to any hypothesis which is worth your while to consider just that degree of credence which the evidence warrants." *A History of Western Philosophy* (New York: Simon & Schuster, 1945), p. 816.

[47]*Primary Philosophy* (New York: McGraw-Hill, 1966), pp. 102ff.

Turn next to broad justification, the idea that things are going right from the perspective of the epistemic agent, or with respect to the epistemic subject as subject, or with respect to everything downstream of experience. This is an easy analogical extension of the deontological notion of justification. On that deontological notion, your experience might be wholly deceptive (you might be a brain in a vat, or the victim of a Cartesian demon); nevertheless, you are justified if you do your epistemic duty and form the beliefs your circumstances (and duties) require. Here the notion of things going right with respect to the epistemic subject as subject is just the notion of doing one's epistemic duty, being epistemically responsible. But it is an easy analogical step to the idea of things going aright with respect to other conditions relevantly internal to the knower and hence to the idea of everything's going right from the perspective of the epistemic subject or with respect to the epistemic subject as subject.

Lehrer and Cohen speak of epistemic justification as an evaluation of how well you have accomplished your epistemic goals. Here the idea is not that you have duties or obligations; it is rather that you have or may have epistemic goals: and you are justified to the degree that your epistemic behavior is a good way of attaining those goals. And here the word 'rationality' might be more appropriate than 'justification'. What is really at issue is *Zweckrationalität*, means–end rationality, appropriateness of your means to your goals. This notion is similar to Richard Foley's conception of epistemic rationality, powerfully expounded in *The Theory of Epistemic Rationality*.[48] Lehrer and Cohen's notion is not directly connected with the classical deontological conception of justification; however, it does have a sort of indirect connection. If you become doubtful that there *are any* specifically epistemic duties, or perhaps think there are some, but doubt that fulfilling them can play a large role in the formation and governance of belief, then this notion of means–ends rationality may seem an attractive substitute. Perhaps there is no such thing as epistemic duty; even so, however, there is such a thing as pursuing your epistemic goals well or badly, and it is not unnatural, given your doubts about the former, to think of justification in terms of the latter.

Finally, there is the conception of justification to be found in both the old and the new Goldman. According to the old Goldman (to a first approximation), a belief is justified if and only if it is produced by a reliable belief producing process or mechanism (see pp. 197–199). According to the new, a belief is justified if it is the last item in a cognitive process that is licensed by a right set of J rules; and a set of J rules is right in case it has a high truth ratio in nearby possible worlds.[49] Here I think there is little connection with the classical notion of justification as involving fulfillment of epistemic duty. True, in the later Goldman there is the notion of a *rule,* and of a process *permitted* by a rule. But rules of this sort have nothing to do with duty or obligation; there is nothing deontological about them. Goldman's use of the term, I think, is to be understood another way: suppose you use the term 'justification' as no more

[48]Cambridge: Harvard University Press, 1987.
[49]See p. 200. For a criticism of the old Goldman, see my "Positive Epistemic Status and Proper Function," 24–32. For a criticism of the new, see my chapter 9.

than a *name* for what is necessary for knowledge and (together with truth) sufficient for it up to Gettier problems; and suppose you also think, with Goldman, that fulfillment of epistemic duty, no matter how fervent and conscientious, is substantially irrelevant to knowledge. Then you might find yourself using the term in just the way he uses it. Here there is only a fairly distant analogical connection with the classical conception.[50]

So much for the main contemporary conceptions of justification; they can all be understood, I think, in terms of their relation to the classical deontological conception. But the same can be said for the contemporary connection between justification and internalism. According to Conee, "Justifying evidence must be internally available"; his idea is that the evidence in question cannot be evidence you could get from your world almanac, for example, but must rather be evidence you can come up with just by reflection. Alston "find[s] widely shared and strong intuitions in favor of some kind of accessibility requirement for justification." Here there is a reflection of the classical connection between deontological justification and epistemic internalism; it is the influence of classical deontologism that is responsible for those widely shared intuitions. Internalism in the personal sense is also widespread (just as we should expect, given the relation between internalism in the two senses). Thus Lehrer and Cohen argue that reliabilism must be wrong about justification: "The truth of the demon hypothesis (where my beliefs are mostly false) also entails that our experiences and our reasonings are just what they would be if our cognitive processes were reliable, and therefore, that we would be just as well justified in believing what we do if the demon hypothesis were true as if it were false" (see p. 9). Here the idea, clearly, is that only what is internal to me as a knower in the personal sense, in the way in which my beliefs and experiences are, is relevant to justification. This may be understood, I think, as a reflection of the connection between deontological justification and internalism.

Now classical deontological internalism has a certain deep integrity. The central notion is that we have epistemic duties or obligations; this induces internalism of both the epistemic and the nonepistemic sorts; and the central duty, Locke thinks, is to believe a proposition that is not certain only on the basis of evidence. Chisholm's carefully crafted internalism, as we shall see, exhibits all of these features, except that according to Chisholm the central epistemic duty is to try to achieve epistemic excellence. Other contemporary accounts, however, sometimes seize on one or another of the elements of the classical package, often in such a way that the integrity of the original package is lost, or at least no longer clearly visible. (I argue this point with respect to Alston in chapter 9 below.) For another example, consider Conee and Feldman, who see justification as a matter of having adequate evidence, and hold that this evidence must be internally available to the believer. This makes sense if combined, as in Locke, with the idea that justification is fundamentally a

---

[50]Another example of a distant analogical connection: the internalism of John Pollock's *Contemporary Theories of Knowledge* (Totowa, N.J.: Rowman and Littlefield, 1986). See my chapter 8, pp. 162ff.

deontological matter of duty fulfillment. They say nothing about the latter, however, which leaves the internalism unmotivated and the connection between it and evidentialism obscure.

Lehrer and Cohen, to take still another example, speak of justification as "an evaluation of how well you have pursued your epistemic goals." The internalism they display fits at best dubiously with this conception of justification. Suppose justification is an evaluation of how well you are pursuing your epistemic goals; it is then presumably an evaluation of the appropriateness of the means you use to the goals you choose. Suppose your doxastic goal is, for example, believing truth, or attaining salvation, or achieving fame and fortune: why would there be any necessity that you be able to tell, just by reflection, let's say, how well suited your means are for achieving those goals? And why think that only what pertains in a direct way to your experiences and beliefs is relevant to this question of how well those means fit those goals? What reason is there to think that an evaluation of how well you were pursuing your epistemic goals would have to measure something such that only your beliefs and your experiences would be relevant to it? The internalism of the classical conception lingers, but its root and foundation are no longer present.

By way of conclusion then: justification, internalism, and epistemic deontology are properly seen as a closely related triumvirate: internalism flows from deontology and is unmotivated without it, and justification is at bottom and originally a deontological notion. Given a proper understanding of these three, furthermore, we can gain some understanding of the kaleidoscopic variety of contemporary thought about justification and its connection with warrant. (As a bonus, we are also able to understand the connection between justification and evidence.) The most interesting question, of course, is whether the twentieth-century received tradition is correct here; can warrant (apart, perhaps, from a fillip to mollify Gettier) be explained in terms of justification? It is time to consider that question, and there is no better way to do so than by turning to the work of Roderick Chisholm, the subject of the next chapter.

2

Classical Chisholmian Internalism

Over the past thirty years or so, Roderick Chisholm has presented a series of ever more refined and penetrating accounts of the central notions of the theory of knowledge. Clearly we can do no better than to start by considering his seminal and exemplary work. Chisholm's central epistemological project, perhaps, has been the development of *epistemic principles:* noncontingent conditionals whose antecedents specify a relation between a person *S* and a proposition *A,* and whose consequents specify that *A* has a certain epistemic status for *S—certainty,* perhaps, or *acceptability,* or *being beyond reasonable doubt,* or *being known.* Chisholm's attention has been directed less explicitly to exploring the *nature* of warrant (or 'positive epistemic status', as he calls it) than to stating those epistemic principles; he has been less explicitly concerned with what warrant or positive epistemic status *is* than with the question under what conditions a belief has it. But of course he does propose a view as to what warrant is, and that is where I propose to focus our attention. What, according to Chisholm, *is* warrant or positive epistemic status? What is its nature?

The answer I propose to explore first is "classical Chisholmian internalism," the answer he gives in his books *Theory of Knowledge*[1] (first and second editions) and *The Foundations of Knowing*[2] (hereafter *TK* and *FK*). The principal thing to see here, I think, is that Chisholm's answer stands squarely in the tradition of classical internalism. He concurs with the fundamental deontological intuition of the latter; he sees warrant or positive epistemic status as essentially connected with *deontological epistemic justification,* the condition of having satisfied one's epistemic duties or obligations. Of course his view differs, in interesting respects, from that of Descartes and Locke. For example, they limit knowledge to what is certain; he does not. Further, he writes as if warrant just *is* justification, in the sense that what makes the belief that *P* a case of knowledge for *S* is just the fact that believing *P* is an especially good way for *S* to fulfill his epistemic duty. Descartes and Locke, however, do not see duty

---

[1]New York: Prentice-Hall; the first edition was published in 1966, a second in 1977, and a third in 1989.

[2]University of Minnesota Press, 1982. I call this view "*classical* Chisholmian internalism" because it is characteristic of Chisholm's epistemological thought from his early work through at least *Foundations of Knowing.* Some of his more recent work, as we shall see in the next chapter, displays a significantly different character. His *most* recent work, however, seems to be a return to classical Chisholmian internalism.

fulfillment as essentially involved in knowledge. As they see it, knowledge is only of propositions that are certain for *S*—propositions that are self-evident to him, for example. But (as they think) we have little or no voluntary control over whether we believe propositions that are certain for us; hence there is little scope for duty and its fulfillment with respect to believing these propositions. Still, Chisholm's basic suggestion is that warrant or positive epistemic status is to be understood in terms of fulfillment of epistemic duty; and that idea displays obvious continuity with the thought of Descartes and Locke, for whom questions of epistemic duty and obligation are of central concern.

I. The Central Idea

Chisholm begins his inquiry by introducing an undefined technical locution: "*p* is more reasonable than *q* for *S* at *t*"; here the values for *p* and *q* will be such states as *believing that all men are mortal* and *withholding the belief that all men are mortal*—that is believing neither it nor its denial.[3] When one believes or withholds something, then, Chisholm assumes, there is indeed something one believes or withholds. If I believe that Venus is about the same size as Earth, then there is something I believe, namely *Venus is about the same size as Earth*. I concur: suppose we call the things that can be thus believed and withheld *propositions,* ignoring, for the moment, the difficult questions as to what sorts of things propositions are (classes of possible worlds?[4] items from some unusually large and powerful language? brain inscriptions? divine thoughts?), whether there are "singular propositions," whether propositions have *constituents,* whether they sometimes have *persons* and other concreta as constituents, whether, if a proposition has constituents, it has them *essentially,* whether some propositions exist contingently, whether there is or could be a set or perhaps a proper class of all propositions, and so on. Given 'is more reasonable than' as an undefined term, Chisholm goes on to define a battery of "terms of epistemic appraisal" as he calls them: 'certain', 'beyond reasonable doubt', 'evident', 'acceptable', and so on. A proposition *A* is *beyond reasonable doubt* for a person, for example, if it is more reasonable for her to accept that proposition than to withhold it; and *A has some presumption in its favor for her at t* just if accepting it then is more reasonable than accepting its negation. The epistemological principles Chisholm presents are formulated by way of these terms of epistemic appraisal.

Now Chisholm introduces 'is more reasonable than' as an undefined locution; but of course he intends it to have a sense, and to have a sense close to the

---

[3] I ignore here the complication occasioned by the fact that in *Foundations of Knowing* Chisholm recasts his epistemological theory in terms of direct attribution of properties, thus abandoning the earlier formulations in terms of believing or accepting propositions. Everything I say about his views can be restated so as to accommodate this shift, though in some cases at the cost of considerable complication.

[4] As I see it, the fact is they couldn't possibly be sets of possible worlds, or sets of *any* sort; see my "Two Concepts of Modality," in *Philosophical Perspectives, 1, Metaphysics, 1987,* ed. James Tomberlin (Atascadero, Calif.: Ridgeview, 1987), p. 208.

sense it has in English. In *FK* he says that "Epistemic reasonability could be understood in terms of the general requirement to try to have the largest possible set of logically independent beliefs that is such that the true beliefs outnumber the false beliefs. The principles of epistemic preferability are the principles one should follow if one is to fulfill this requirement" (p. 7). In his earlier *TK* he is a bit more explicit about intellectual requirements and explains reasonability in terms of a somewhat different requirement:

> We may assume that every person is subject to a purely intellectual requirement: that of trying his best to bring it about that for any proposition *p* he considers, he accepts *p* if and only if *p* is true.

He adds that

> One might say that this is the person's responsibility or duty *qua* intellectual being. . . . One way, then, of re-expressing the locution '*p* is more reasonable than *q* for *S* at *t*' is to say this: '*S* is so situated at *t* that his intellectual requirement, his responsibility as an intellectual being, is better fulfilled by *p* than by *q*'. (p. 14)

I said Chisholm stands in the classical internalist tradition; here we see the first and deepest connection with that tradition. Reasonability, as Chisholm explains it, is a *normative* concept; more precisely it is *deontological:* it pertains to requirement, duty, or obligation. That deontological character need not be strictly *moral* or *ethical;* for perhaps an epistemic requirement is not a moral duty. Perhaps it is a *sui generis* form of obligation.[5] But even if epistemic obligation is *sui generis,* it shares important elements of structure with moral obligation: there is supervenience, defeasibility, the application of the *prima facie*/all-things-considered distinction, the characteristic relations among permission, obligation, and prohibition, and so on. And Chisholm's central claim here is that a certain requirement, or responsibility, or duty, or obligation lies at the basis of such epistemic notions as evidence, justification, positive epistemic status, and knowledge itself; for knowledge is defined in terms of reasonability together with truth[6] and belief.

So here Chisholm endorses a fundamental intuition of the classical internalist tradition: there are epistemic duties; and justification, being justified in one's beliefs, is the state of forming and holding beliefs in accord with those duties. Here Chisholm also endorses, at least by implication, the First Internalist Motif (see p. 19). On the view he presents, it is sufficient for my beliefs'

---

[5]As argued by Roderick Firth. See his "Chisholm and the Ethics of Belief," *Philosophical Review* 68 (1959), pp. 493ff. Chisholm, on the other hand, has steadfastly seen epistemic justification as a species of ethical justification. See his "Firth and the Ethics of Belief," *Philosophy and Phenomenological Research,* 51 (1991).

[6]It isn't that (on Chisholm's view) the truth of *p itself* is sufficient, together with a high enough degree of reasonability, for knowledge. In order to deal with Gettier problems, Chisholm introduces the notion of *defective evidence;* roughly speaking, a belief is defectively evident for me if the basic propositions (again, roughly speaking, propositions that are concerned with what is self-presenting for me) that make it evident for me also make evident for me at least one false proposition; he then adds (still roughly speaking) that *S* knows *p* only if *p* is nondefectively evident for *S*. For details, see *FK,* pp. 46–48.

having positive epistemic status for me—even the highest levels of that quantity—that I do my epistemic duty, fulfill my epistemic obligation. But then whether my beliefs have positive epistemic status for me is up to me, within my control. I need only do my duty, to achieve that condition, and whether I do my duty is up to me.

The suggestions made in *FK* and *TK* as to what our intellectual requirement is differ in a more than superficial way; neither, furthermore, is exactly right. If the second suggestion were correct, one's duty as a being capable of belief might be satisfied by trying not to consider any propositions at all, or trying to consider only propositions that are obviously true or obviously false; if the first were correct, I could satisfy my epistemic duty by trying to restrict my attention as much as I could to propositions of simple arithmetic, considering and believing as many propositions of the form $n + 1 > n$ as possible. Obviously something must be said about *other* epistemic values here: the importance of considering *important* propositions, of having beliefs on certain crucial topics, of avoiding unnecessary clutter and frivolous dilettantism, perhaps of having a coherent system of beliefs, and so on. The basic idea, however, is that our epistemic duty or requirement is to try to achieve and maintain a certain condition—call it 'epistemic excellence'—which may be hard to specify in detail, but consists fundamentally in standing in an appropriate relation to truth. This is a duty I have "*qua* intellectual being"—that is, just by virtue of being the sort of creature that is capable of grasping and believing (or withholding) propositions. We must pay a price for our exalted status as intellectual beings; with ability comes responsibility. And the idea, presumably, is that *all* intellectual beings have this responsibility: angels, devils, Alpha Centaurians, what have you—all are subject to this requirement or obligation. The obligation in question, furthermore, unlike, say, the obligation to repay the $10,000 you have unwisely borrowed from your children, is not one that can be discharged in a moment; it is a long-standing (indeed permanent) requirement to try to bring about and maintain a certain relatively complex and many-sided state of affairs. This state of affairs, whatever exactly it is, is such that trying to bring it about involves many actions over a considerable period of time.

The *FK* version is relatively unspecific, saying only that '_____ is more reasonable than . . . for S at *t*' can be understood in terms of "a general requirement attaching to intellectual beings"; the *TK* version is more specific, specifying that '_____ is more reasonable than . . . for S at *t* if and only if S is so situated at *t* that his intellectual requirement is better fulfilled by _____ than by . . . .' So suppose we consider the latter formulation. What stands out, here, is that Chisholm states the intellectual duty or obligation or requirement as one of *trying* to bring about a certain state of affairs. One's duty as an intellectual being is not that of bringing it about that one has a large set of beliefs, most of which are true; it is instead that of *trying* to bring about this state of affairs. My requirement is not to succeed in maintaining epistemic excellence; my requirement is only to *try* to do so. Presumably the reason is that it may not be within my power to succeed. Perhaps I don't know how to achieve epistemic excellence: or perhaps even though I do know how, I simply can't manage it. So my duty is simply to *try* to bring about this state of affairs. And of course here the First Motif is once more evident. Achieving justification, achieving a state in which my beliefs have positive epistemic status for me, is clearly within my control and up to me. All I have to do is try to achieve epistemic excellence; and of course whether or not I try to achieve that state is within my control and up to me.[7]

But *how* can I try to bring about such a state of affairs? In the general case, what one does to try to bring about some state of affairs is to take some action one thinks will bring about or contribute to the bringing about of that state of affairs. A university president, for example, has a duty to try to see to it that his university flourishes; he discharges this responsibility by taking actions that he thinks will contribute to its flourishing. Second, Chisholm's explanation of 'is more reasonable than' presupposes that my requirement to try to bring about a certain state of affairs can be better fulfilled by my doing one thing *A* than by my doing another thing *B*. How would that go? Well, clearly if I believe that *A* would tend to produce the state of affairs in question but do not think *B* would, then I can better fulfill that requirement by *A* than by *B*. But even if I think both *A* and *B* would contribute to producing that state of affairs, it could still be that I could better fulfill the requirement by *A* than by *B*. Perhaps I think *A* would contribute much *more* to the realization of the intended state of affairs; or perhaps I think it is much more *probable* that *A* would contribute to that realization than *B;* or perhaps I believe more *strongly* that *A* would than that *B* would.

Now how does this apply in the case in question, the case of my being obliged to try to achieve epistemic excellence? First, I must have some idea as to what to *do* to achieve it. I need not have a *correct* idea as to what to do, but if I haven't any idea at *all,* nor even any idea how to find out what to do, then I cannot even try to do so. I have no idea how to make a computer out of wood and string, nor do I know whether it can be done. If you order me to do it, I can't even try to comply. (I could idly tie a couple of two-by-fours together and claim I was trying, but I would not be speaking the truth.) Similarly in the present case; I cannot try to achieve epistemic excellence unless I have some beliefs as to how to bring about that state of affairs. Second, if I *do* have beliefs as to how such a project should go, then (all else being equal) I can best satisfy my obligation to try to bring about the state of affairs by acting on those beliefs. Suppose it is my duty to try to be in Boston at a certain time; then the way for me to fulfill this duty is to act on my beliefs as to what I can do to get there then. This is true even if some of these beliefs are false. Suppose I believe I can get there on time only by flying through Detroit; then the way for me to try to

[7]As we saw in chapter 1 (pp. 23ff) still another classical internalist claim is that we have a certain control, possibly only indirect, over our believings and withholdings. Clearly the classical Chisholm endorses this notion as well. Strictly speaking, of course, all that Chisholm's statements straightforwardly presuppose is that it be within my power to *try* to bring it about that I have a large set of beliefs in which true beliefs outnumber false beliefs. Perhaps I could try to bring about this state of affairs even if I had no control whatever over what I believe (and then again perhaps not). But in fact Chisholm seems clearly to believe that a person *does* have at least *some* degree of control over what he believes and withholds. It does not follow, of course, that all or even any of *S*'s believings must be within his *direct* control.

get there on time is to fly through Detroit—even if, as it turns out, I am wrong, and in fact can get to Boston on time only by flying through Chicago.

We must make one qualification here. It may be that I am in some way *blameworthy* or properly subject to reproach in holding this false belief; perhaps I should have known better. Perhaps I hold the belief in question only because of laziness, or carelessness, or inattention. Under *these* conditions, acting on my belief might not be the best way to satisfy my obligation. You reproach me for not trying to get to Boston on time; I reply (by way of attempted self-exculpation) that I tried my best to get there then, but failed simply because of a false belief about plane schedules; you point out that I didn't even bother to make inquiries and arrived at my belief by relying on vague memories or just guessing. Then I may still be scored for flouting my obligation to try my best to get to Boston on time; I did not fulfill that duty.

Take another example. I have an obligation to try to bring up my children properly; I am obliged to try to bring it about that they enter adulthood in spiritual, moral, mental, and physical health. I can't even *try* to do this if I have no ideas at all about what to do—no ideas, for example, about what sorts of training and discipline are likely to produce the desired result. And if I *do* have beliefs about how to achieve the end in question, then the best way for me to fulfill this obligation is to act on these beliefs. Suppose it turns out that my beliefs are false, and acting on them wholly counterproductive: that doesn't show that I didn't try my best and doesn't show that I didn't satisfy my obligation thus to try. Perhaps I believed on good authority that it is an excellent idea to put your small children on a low-fat diet in order to help prevent cholesterol buildup later in life. Suppose, as it happens, I was wrong; low-fat diets are dangerous for young children.[8] If, later on, my children fail to display normal growth patterns, I am not properly held responsible for failing to try to bring them up in such a way as to promote their health. I did the best I could but was misinformed; I was mistaken but not blameworthy. And clearly if I *do* believe that fatty food is unhealthy, then I am so situated that I can better fulfill my obligation to try to bring them up in a healthy manner by withholding it from them than by feeding them large quantities of it. The qualification, again, would apply where I hold this belief but do so carelessly, or with what Aquinas calls 'undue levity', or where I should have known better. In such cases, perhaps, I fail to try hard enough; in such cases I can be blamed for failing to fulfill that obligation. But if I (nonculpably) believe that the best way to achieve the goal in question is to take a certain line of action, then I have *prima facie* fulfilled my obligation to try to bring about this state of affairs by taking that line of action.

So my obligation is to try to achieve epistemic excellence, and the way to do so is to act on what I believe is the way to achieve that state. But then the Second Internalist Motif and its corollaries (see pp. 19–22) are also satisfied. The ground of warrant, that which confers warrant upon a proposition for me,

---

[8]"Particularly during the first two years of life, low-fat diets can interfere with normal growth." *Harvard Medical School Health Letter* (May 1989).

is the aptness for fulfilling epistemic duty of my accepting that proposition. But in the typical case the degree of that aptness will depend upon the degree to which the proposition in question seems to me to be true; and that is something to which I have a sort of guaranteed access. Thus C2 (see p. 21) is satisfied. But so is C3 (p. 22). For what is my *ratio cognoscendi* here; how do I tell whether a given proposition is such that accepting it will contribute substantially to the fulfillment of duty to try to achieve epistemic excellence? Well, one way would be by determining how much or how strongly it seems to me to be true. The more strongly the proposition in question seems to me to be true, the more apt accepting it is for fulfillment of my epistemic duty. *Ratio essendi* and *ratio cognoscendi*, therefore, coincide. And of course the third motif is also exemplified: for *trying to do something or other* is surely in an important and recognizable (if hard to define) sense internal.

II. Classical Chisholmian Internalism Rejected

I propose to argue two points with respect to the main contours of classical Chisholmian internalism. First, the epistemic principles Chisholm offers do not in fact fit with his official claim that warrant is a matter of fulfilling epistemic obligation; if warrant is what he officially says it is, then most of his epistemic principles are clearly false. This suggests a certain tension in Chisholm's thought between what he officially *says* warrant is, and how he actually thinks about it. Second, I shall argue that positive epistemic status *cannot* be thus explained. My claim is that the fulfillment of epistemic obligation or requirement is nowhere nearly sufficient for warrant; it is also (though perhaps a bit more dubiously) unnecessary for it. Taking 'justification' in its original and most natural sense, what I shall argue is that justification is wholly insufficient for warrant; it is also not necessary for it.

A. *P1*

Let us begin by considering two of the six "epistemic principles" Chisholm offers in *FK*. These principles, he says, are *necessarily* true if true at all (*FK*, p. 57); and they specify conditions under which a person and a proposition are so related that the latter has some degree of warrant—being certain, or acceptable, or evident, for example—for the former. According to the first of these principles,

> P1   If the property of being *F* is self-presenting, then, for every *x*, if *x* has the property of being *F* and if *x* considers his having that property, then it is certain for *x* that he is then *F*. (*FK*, p.12)

An instance of P1, says Chisholm would be:

> P1a   If the property of being sad is self-presenting, then, for every *x*, if *x* has the property of being sad and if *x* considers his having that property, then it is certain for *x* that he is then sad. (*FK*, p.12)

To say that *p* is *certain* for *S* is to say that it is beyond reasonable doubt for him (is such that accepting it is more reasonable for him than withholding it) and that furthermore there is no proposition *q* such that accepting *q* is more reasonable for him than accepting *p* (p. 8); so if *p* is certain for *S*, then it has the maximal degree of warrant for him. A proposition *p* is *self-presenting* for a person *S* if and only if necessarily, if *S* considers *p* and *p* is true, then *S* believes *p* (pp. 12–13); examples would be propositions of the sort *S is appeared to redly, S is sad,* and *S believes that Albuquerque is in New Mexico.* In the case in question, therefore (the case of the person who is sad), there is no proposition *q* such that *S* can better fulfill his epistemic requirement by accepting *q* than by accepting the proposition that he is sad. So if *S* is sad and considers whether he is, then the proposition that *S* is sad has, for *S*, the highest degree of positive epistemic status.

Now perhaps it is natural to attribute the impressive degree of warrant enjoyed by this proposition (and others like it) to the fact that it is indeed self-presenting. What is responsible for its exalted condition, you think, is just the fact that it is indeed self-presenting: the fact that it is necessarily such that if it is true and *S* considers it, then *S* does in fact believe it. It is impossible that this proposition be true and *S* consider it but fail to believe it. But here there is a problem. Suppose warrant or positive epistemic status is what Chisholm says it is: why should the fact that this proposition is self-presenting, in Chisholm's sense, confer maximal epistemic status upon it? Indeed, a proposition's being self-presenting seems to *preclude* its having such status. The suggestion is that if I feel sad, then believing that I feel sad is a good way of fulfilling my duty to try to achieve epistemic excellence; it is *so* good, in fact, that nothing else I could do would be a better way of fulfilling that duty.

But suppose I feel sad, at *t:* could it really be that believing that I feel sad is any way at all (let alone a maximally excellent way) of trying to fulfill my epistemic duty? In any case I can think of, if doing something *A* is a way in which I can try to bring about some state of affairs, *A* will be such that it is at least logically possible for me to consider it and carry it out, and also at least logically possible for me to consider it and fail to carry it out; there will be possible worlds in which I consider it and carry it out, but also worlds in which I consider it and do *not* carry it out. This is not so in the present case. For the proposition that I am sad is self-presenting; hence (according to Chisholm) it is not possible in the broadly logical sense that I should in fact be sad and consider whether I am, but refrain from believing that I am. But if that is how things stand, how could this proposition be such that at *t* I can better fulfill my epistemic duty—my duty to try to achieve epistemic excellence—by accepting it than by rejecting or withholding it? Perhaps you think I might be able to fulfill an epistemic duty (when I am sad) by, say, asking myself whether I am sad (I can consider whether to consider my phenomenal field and then either do it or not). You might add that if I do consider that question under those conditions, I will in fact believe that I am sad, so that my not believing that I am sad might show that I am not doing my epistemic duty. Perhaps so; but even if so, that does not show that I can satisfy any epistemic duty by believing that I am sad; what satisfies my duty, under *that* scenario, is my *considering* whether

I am sad. If the fact is I *am* sad and I consider this proposition, then whether or not I accept it is simply not up to me; but then accepting this proposition cannot be a way in which I can fulfill my obligation to the truth, or, indeed, *any* obligation to try to bring about some state of affairs. Suppose I've just fallen off a cliff: could I be subject to an obligation to try to bring something about, which is such that I can better fulfill it by falling *down* rather than, say, by falling up or remaining suspended in midair? Hardly.

Chisholm's fundamental idea seems to be that the rational creature, the being capable of beliefs, considers the various propositions that come to his attention at a time *t*, deciding which to accept and which to withhold. If he is epistemically dutiful, he will make these decisions in the service of an effort to fulfill his duty to the truth, his duty to try to achieve and maintain epistemic excellence; and a proposition will have positive epistemic status (warrant) for him, at *t*, to the degree to which he can fulfill this obligation by accepting it. But if the proposition in question is self-presenting, then if it is true and he considers it, he already believes it. He cannot consider it, and then decide whether to accept it; if it is true and comes to his attention, then it is not up to him whether he believes it.

So there is a deep difficulty with supposing that the sort of proposition I would express by saying 'I feel sad' or 'I am appeared to redly' achieves its high epistemic status by virtue of being self-presenting. As a matter of fact, if warrant is what Chisholm says it is, then its being self-presenting for me would *preclude* its having warrant for me; for propositions that are self-presenting, for me (as Descartes and Locke noted), are not such that whether I accept them is, in the appropriate way, under my control. And this suggests that, contrary to what Chisholm officially says, he does not really think of warrant as simply a matter of aptness for fulfilling epistemic duties. The sorts of propositions he thinks of as self-presenting do, no doubt, have impressive epistemic credentials; but the status they have is not that of being such that a person can best fulfill that epistemic requirement by accepting them. *That's* not the sort of epistemic status they have.

But now suppose Chisholm is wrong about the propositions he says are self-presenting—the sorts of propositions Chisholm thinks of as self-presenting—the ones typically expressed by such sentences as 'I feel sad' and 'I am appeared to redly'. Suppose these propositions do in fact enjoy the high degree of warrant or positive epistemic status he says they do, but suppose they are *not*, in fact, self-presenting in his sense. Suppose it is or could be within my power to consider such a proposition as *I am appeared to redly* (when in fact I am) and then either accept or reject it. Suppose (by dint of enormous concentration and effort) I could train myself *not* to accept this proposition when I am thus appeared to and consider whether I am thus appeared to. Perhaps I could undergo some sort of strenuous regimen, so that at its conclusion it is within my power deliberately to refrain from believing that I am appeared to redly, despite the fact that I am thus appeared to. Then beliefs of this sort would not be disqualified for warrant—at any rate not for the previous reason. But would it then be correct to say that these propositions had maximal warrant (taking the latter to be what Chisholm officially says it is)? I think not. If P1 is correct, then it is necessarily the case that anyone who considers a proposition that is both true and of the sort in question is someone for whom that proposition has maximal warrant. Under those conditions, she and that proposition are so related that there is no proposition *q* such that she can better fulfill her epistemic requirement by accepting *q* than by accepting *p*. But suppose these propositions are *not* self-presenting for *S;* then clearly they are not related this way. Due to a brain lesion or the machinations of a malevolent Cartesian demon, I might be deeply but nonculpably convinced, of the proposition[9] I express by the words 'I am appeared to redly', that it is never true. Then the way for me to try to achieve epistemic excellence would be to try to *reject* that proposition, even when in fact I am appeared to redly.

Alternatively, a clever but unscrupulous epistemologist might offer me a subtly fallacious argument, convincing me both that this proposition—call it 'P'—is false and that I ought not to accept it. His argument might go as follows:

(1)   P entails that there is at least one person.

(2)   Necessarily, if there are any persons, then they are composed of more than one but finitely many molecules.

(3)   For any person *S* and number *n,* if *S* is composed of *n* molecules, then it is possible that there be a person composed of *n* − 1 molecules.

(4)   Anyone who carefully and reflectively considers (1) − (3) and be- lieves them, and sees that (1) − (3) entail the denial of P, ought not to accept P.[10]

This argument may be mistaken, but that does not mean I couldn't be taken in by it. And if I *were* (through no fault of my own) taken in by it and convinced of its conclusion, then surely it would *not* be the case that I could fulfill my epistemic obligation—my obligation to try to achieve epistemic excellence— better by believing P than by withholding it, or believing its denial. As I argued (pp. 34–36), how I can best fulfill my obligation to try to bring about a certain state of affairs depends (among other things) upon what I believe as to how to bring about that state of affairs. If I believe that the best way to bring it about is to take a certain line of action, then (provided, anyway, that in acquiring *that* belief[11] I did not flout my duty to the truth) I can best satisfy that obligation by taking that line of action. I must do the best I can, according to my own lights. (Who else's?)

[9]Here I assume, for simplicity, that there are singular propositions and that such a proposition as the one I express by saying 'I am appeared to redly' can be true at one time and false at another.

[10]See Peter Unger, "Why There Are No Persons," in *Midwest Studies in Philosophy*, Vol. IV, *Studies in Metaphysics*, ed. Peter French, Theodore E. Uehling, Jr., and Howard Wettstein (Minneapolis: University of Minnesota Press, 1979), pp. 203–4.

[11]Of course I might have been perverse or frivolous or careless in acquiring some other belief involved in my acquiring *that* belief; to put the matter more exactly perhaps we may proceed as follows. Say that belief *b* is *an ancestor* of belief *a* for me if it is a belief I acted upon in acquiring *a* or a belief I acted upon in acquiring some ancestor of *a*. If *a* is the belief that the best way for me to bring about *S* is to take action *A*, and if I did not flout my duty to the truth in acquiring *a* or any ancestor of *a*, then I can fulfill my duty to try to bring about *S* by acting on *a*.

Accordingly, there are two relevant facts here. The first is that if a belief really *is* self-presenting, in Chisholm's sense, then whether I hold that belief on a given occasion is not up to me. But then I am not so situated with respect to that belief that either accepting or withholding it could be the best way for me to fulfill my duty to the truth—my duty to try to achieve epistemic excellence. And second, even if it *were* within my power to accept or withhold such a belief, it still would not follow that I can best satisfy this obligation by accepting it; I might believe that most such beliefs are false, or that my obligation to the truth, in these circumstances, requires that I refrain from accepting it. These two facts suggest that Chisholm himself isn't really thinking of certainty—that particular maximal form of warrant—as a matter of aptness for fulfilling my epistemic requirement. He isn't really thinking that a belief is certain for me if and only if I am so situated with respect to it that I can better fulfill my duty to the truth by accepting it than by accepting any other proposition. Finally, the beliefs Chisholm thinks of as self-presenting surely do have great warrant or positive epistemic status; but this status is not that of being (if true) overwhelmingly apt for the fulfillment of epistemic duty. In *Warrant and Proper Function* I shall try to say what sort of positive epistemic status or warrant they have, and why they have so much of it.

B. P5a

Now suppose we consider Chisholm's P5, which I shall divide into two principles, P5a and P5b (and shall also state it in terms of propositions rather than properties):

> P5a   For every x, if (i) x perceptually takes there to be something that is F, and if (ii) his perceiving an F is epistemically in the clear for x, then it is beyond reasonable doubt for x that he perceives something that is F.
>
> P5b   If conditions (i) and (ii) are fulfilled and furthermore x's perceiving something that is F is a member of a set of propositions which mutually support each other and each of which is beyond reasonable doubt for x, then it is evident for x that he perceives something that is F. (*FK*, p. 21)

I shall comment only on P5a. We have two locutions that require explanation: 'perceptually takes there to be something that is F' in the first couple of lines, and 'epistemically in the clear for x' in the third. Take the second first: a proposition is *epistemically in the clear for x* if and only if it is not disconfirmed by the conjunction of all those propositions that are such that it is more reasonable for S to accept them than to accept their negations (for details, see *FK*, pp. 18ff.). Second, 'perceptually takes there to be something that is F' is to be understood as follows: "The property of being F is a sensible property such that x is appeared to in such a way that he directly attributes to himself the property of being appeared to in that way by something that is F" (*FK*, p. 20). Sensible properties, says Chisholm, are such properties as "being red, round, yellow, putrid, rough (to the touch)" and the like. What this means, therefore, is that a person perceptually takes there to be something that is *F* if he is appeared to in a certain way *Z*, believes that there is something that appears to him in way *Z*, and believes that that thing has the property of being *F*. You look out of your window at your backyard; you are appeared to in the characteristic way that goes with perceiving a yellow playhouse. If, under those conditions, you take it that there is something that is appearing to you in that way, and that the thing appearing to you in that way is yellow, then you perceptually take there to be something that is yellow. Finally, recall that a proposition is beyond reasonable doubt for *x* just if believing that proposition is a pretty good way for *x* to fulfill his epistemic duty. (In the counterexample I offer here, therefore, I shall assume with Chisholm that a person has a considerable degree of control over what he believes.)

P5a, I believe, is defective in more than one dimension. First, I shall argue that (as in the previous case) if positive epistemic status is what Chisholm says it is, then P5a is not necessarily true: a person could satisfy the antecedent of P5a with respect to some proposition and nonetheless utterly fail to fulfill his epistemic obligation in believing that proposition, so that the proposition would not be beyond reasonable doubt for him. Suppose Paul, like the rest of us, is such that when he is appeared to redly (under normal conditions) he has an inclination to believe that he perceives something red. Paul, however, has read his Kant. He has a deep concern for the dignity and autonomy of free, rational creatures such as himself. It seems to him a bit undignified, possibly even faintly ridiculous, to be pushed around in this way by his passional or impulsive nature. He therefore solemnly decides to edit his cognitive nature, thus demonstrating his autonomy, his independence of natural tendencies, and his mastery over his lower nature. He undertakes a regimen to free himself from the tyranny of these impulses; by dint of long and arduous training, he develops the power to withhold the normal or ordinary belief in many perceptual situations. For example, when he is appeared to in that characteristic way one is appeared to upon perceiving a large, fully developed oak from 40 yards, he is able (at the cost of considerable effort) to withhold the belief that he is perceiving a large tree. (Sadly enough, he also develops an unfortunate tendency to patronize those more ordinary mortals who have not thus enhanced their rational autonomy.) Further, he trains himself to acquire unusual beliefs in ordinary perceptual situations. On occasions when he is aurally appeared to in the way one is appeared to upon hearing church bells, the belief *he* forms is that there is something that is appearing to him in that way, and that it is bright orange.

On a given occasion, therefore, he is appeared to in that church-bell way and, in accord with his training, forms the belief that the thing appearing to him in this way is orange. That he is thus perceiving a thing that is orange, we may suppose, is epistemically in the clear for him; it is neither confirmed nor disconfirmed by the conjunction of propositions beyond reasonable doubt for him. The antecedent of P5a is therefore fulfilled, for Paul. Yet surely it is not the case that he can then better fulfill his duty to the truth by accepting the proposition that he is perceiving something orange than by withholding that proposition. Forming beliefs in accord with this foolish and arrogant policy of his is no way to fulfill any duty at all. If positive epistemic status is fundamentally a matter of deontological justification, therefore, P5a is not necessarily true. Someone who instantiates its antecedent may still be failing to do his epistemic duty.

Perhaps you think this example unduly fanciful; if so, there are plenty that are less esoteric.[12] Suppose I form the belief *all horses are white* and form it in some epistemically culpable fashion. (Perhaps the Lone Ranger and Silver make a guest appearance in my hometown; I am very much impressed by their magnificent appearance and hastily generalize to the belief in question.) Later I hear a horse whinny and form the belief that I am being appeared to in that fashion by a thing that is white. Then I am not properly fulfilling my duty by forming the belief in question. Still, I satisfy the antecedent of P5a: I perceptually take there to be something that is white, and the proposition that I do so, we may suppose, is neither confirmed nor disconfirmed by the conjunction of propositions beyond reasonable doubt for me, so that it is epistemically in the clear for me.

Still further, it is clear, I think, that in the sorts of situations P5a is designed to apply to, positive epistemic status is not (or is not merely) a matter of deontological justification. Return to Paul of the paragraph before last and alter his situation a bit. As in the previous case, he is such that when he is appeared to in one sense modality, he forms beliefs appropriate to another; only this time it is due not to some project born of pride and foolishness, but instead to a brain lesion or perhaps a whimsical Cartesian demon. When Paul is aurally appeared to in the church-bell fashion, therefore, he finds himself with a powerful, nearly ineluctable tendency or impulse to believe that there is something that is appearing to him in that fashion, and that that thing is orange. He does not know about this quirk in his epistemic equipment, and his lack of awareness is in no way due to dereliction of epistemic duty. Indeed, Paul is unusually dutiful, unusually concerned about fulfilling his epistemic duties; fulfilling these duties is the main passion of his life. And let's add that those around him suffer from a similar epistemic deficiency. They have all been manipulated in this way by demons or Alpha Centaurian cognitive scientists; or they all suffer from similar lesions due to radioactive fallout from a missile test. Then, surely, Paul is doing his epistemic duty *in excelsis* in believing as he does; but the proposition in question has little by way of positive epistemic status for him. He is deontologically justified, and more; for in working as hard as he does to achieve epistemic excellence, he performs works of epistemic supererogation. Using the term not as a synonym for 'warrant', but in a neutral way, we may say that there is a kind of positive epistemic status his beliefs have: they were formed in accord with a serious and determined effort to live dutifully.

Nevertheless there is also a kind of positive epistemic status this belief lacks for him, a kind crucial for knowledge: it lacks warrant. For *that* sort of positive

---

[12]As was pointed out to me by Aron Edidin.

epistemic status, it is not sufficient that one satisfy one's duty and do one's epistemic best. Paul can be ever so conscientious about his epistemic duties, and still be such that his beliefs have very little warrant. And the reason, fundamentally, is that even though he is doing his epistemic duty to the uttermost, his epistemic faculties are defective; this deprives the belief in question of any substantial degree of that quantity.

III. Justification versus Warrant

Suppose we briefly review our conclusions thus far. The discussion of Chisholm's principles displays a certain pattern: in both cases we noted first that if positive epistemic status is what Chisholm officially says it is, then the principle in question is wholly unsatisfactory. This is not, in these cases, a matter of fine tuning; it is not as if by further chisholming we could find a satisfactory set of principles substantially like the ones in question. The difficulties go deeper than that. What the classical Chisholm officially says is that warrant is a matter of a proposition's being so related to a person that he can better fulfill his duty—that of trying to bring it about that he is in the right relation to the truth—by accepting the proposition in question than by, for example, withholding it. But if this is what warrant is, then in a wide variety of cases—cases of the sort I mentioned above—Chisholm's principles yield wholly wrong results. In many of these cases, the way for a person to try his best to achieve epistemic excellence will depend, naturally enough, upon what he (nonculpably) believes about the way to achieve epistemic excellence. In particular, if a person is strongly (and nonculpably) convinced of the truth of a proposition—if that proposition seems obviously true to him—then (barring defeating conditions) the way for him to try to achieve epistemic excellence is to accept it; and the more obvious it seems to him, the more status of *this* sort it has for him. But Chisholm's principles don't anywhere nearly yield this result.[13]

This suggests that, despite his official statements on the nature of warrant or positive epistemic status, Chisholm does not or does not consistently think of it as a matter of aptness for fulfillment of epistemic duty. He implicitly thinks of it as also involving something else. And here he is surely correct. Epistemic dutifulness or deontological justification is attractive from an internalist perspective; but reflection on Chisholm's principles reveals that it cannot possibly be anywhere nearly sufficient for warrant. No degree of dutifulness, no amount of living up to one's obligations and satisfying one's responsibilities—in a word, no degree of justification—can be sufficient for warrant.

[13]In "Chisholmian Internalism," in *Philosophical Analysis: A Defense by Example,* ed. David Austin (Dordrecht: D. Reidel, 1987), I argue the same points with respect to Chisholm's principles P2, P3, and P4 (and also with respect to his account of confirmation); I argue that in each case the principle would be false if warrant were what Chisholm officially says it is, and that in fact warrant is not, in the cases to which the principles are designed to apply, a matter of aptness for epistemic duty fulfillment. Reflection on the explicit definition of knowledge (*FK*, pp. 46–47) reveals the same thing, although I will not take the space to argue the point here.

A couple of final examples. (If you are already convinced, please skip the next couple of pages.) Suppose I develop a rare sort of brain lesion that causes me to believe that I will be the next president of the United States. I have no evidence for the proposition, never having won or even run for public office; my only political experience was an unsuccessful bid for the vice-presidency of my sophomore class in college. Nevertheless, due to my cognitive dysfunction, the belief that I will be the next president seems to me obviously true—as obvious as the most obvious truths of elementary arithmetic. Now: am I so situated that I can better fulfill my obligation to the truth by withholding than by accepting this proposition? Can I better fulfill my obligation to try to bring it about that I am in the right relation to the truth by withholding than by accepting it? Surely not. That I will be the next president seems to me to be utterly and obviously true; I have no awareness at all that my cognitive faculties are playing me false here. So if I try to achieve epistemic excellence, I will count this proposition among the ones I accept. The way for me to try to achieve epistemic excellence in these circumstances, I should think, is for me to act on what I (nonculpably) believe about how best to achieve this end. But this proposition seems obviously true to me; so, naturally enough, I believe that the way to achieve epistemic excellence here is to accept it. We may add, if we like, that I am exceptionally dutiful, deeply concerned with my epistemic duty; I am eager to bring it about that I am in the right relation to the truth, and am trying my level best to do so. Then, surely, I am doing my epistemic duty in accepting the proposition in question; nevertheless that proposition has little by way of warrant for me. Even if by some mad chance I will in fact be the next president, I do not know that I will be.

A last example: perhaps you think that what goes *in excelsis* with satisfying duty is *effort;* perhaps (in a Kantian vein) you think that genuinely dutiful action demands acting contrary to inclination. Very well then, suppose this time, Paul (due to lesion, demon or Alpha Centaurian) is utterly and nonculpably convinced that his nature is deeply misleading. Like the rest of us, he has an inclination, upon being appeared to redly, to believe that there is something red lurking in the neighborhood; unlike the rest of us, he believes that this natural inclination is misleading and that on those occasions there really isn't anything that is thus appearing to him. He undertakes a strenuous regimen to overcome this inclination; after intense and protracted effort he succeeds: upon being appeared to redly he is able to withhold the belief that something red is appearing to him, and finally to form, on those occasions, the belief that nothing red is appearing to him. His devotion to duty costs him dearly. The enormous effort he expends takes its toll upon his health; he is subject to ridicule and disapprobation on the part of his fellows, who view his project as at best Quixotic; his wife protests his unusual behavior and finally leaves him for someone less epistemically nonstandard. Determined to do what is right, however, Paul heroically persists in doing what he is nonculpably convinced is his duty. It is obvious, I take it, that even though Paul is unusually dutiful in accepting, on a given occasion, the belief that nothing red is appearing to him, that belief has little by way of warrant for him. Epistemic duty fulfillment, even epistemic works of supererogation—these aren't anywhere nearly sufficient for warrant.

But neither are they necessary for it.[14] Suppose there is the sort of epistemic duty Chisholm suggests: a duty to try to bring it about that I attain and maintain the condition of epistemic excellence; and suppose I know this, am dutiful, but also a bit confused. I come nonculpably to believe that our Alpha Centaurian conquerors, for reasons opaque to us, thoroughly dislike my thinking that I am perceiving something that is red; I also believe that they are monitoring my beliefs and, if I form the belief that I see something red, will bring it about that I have a set of beliefs most of which are absurdly false, thus depriving me of any chance for epistemic excellence. I thereby acquire an epistemic duty to try to withhold the beliefs I naturally form when I am appeared to redly: such beliefs as that I see a red ball, or a red fire engine, or whatever. Of course I have the same epistemic inclinations everyone else has: when I am appeared to redly, I am powerfully inclined to believe that I see something that is red. By dint of heroic and unstinting effort, however, I am able to train myself to withhold the belief (on such occasions) that I see something red; naturally it takes enormous effort and requires great willpower. On a given morning I go for a walk in London; I am appeared to redly several times (postboxes, traffic signals, redcoats practicing for a reenactment of the American Revolution); each time I successfully resist the belief that I see something red, but only at the cost of prodigious effort. I become exhausted, and resentful. Finally I am appeared to redly in a particularly insistent and out-and-out fashion by a large red London bus. "Epistemic duty be hanged," I mutter, and relax blissfully into the belief that I am now perceiving something red. Then this would be a belief that was unjustified for me; in accepting it I would be going contrary to epistemic duty; yet could it not constitute knowledge nonetheless?

The conclusion to be drawn, I think, is that justification properly so-called—deontological justification—is not so much as necessary for warrant. Justification is a fine thing, a valuable state of affairs—intrinsically as well as extrinsically; but it is neither necessary nor sufficient for warrant. Chisholm's powerful and powerfully developed versions of deontological internalism—classical Chisholmian internalism—must be rejected.[15]

In chapter 1, I argued that in the twentieth century received tradition in Anglo-American epistemology—a tradition going back at least to Locke—sees justification as essentially deontological but also as necessary and nearly sufficient (sufficient up to Gettier) for warrant. Although this is an attractive, in-

---

[14]Unless, of course, *there are* no epistemic duties to regulate and maintain beliefs in a certain way. If there are no such duties, then any belief is automatically and trivially justified.

[15]Let me say once more that what I mean to reject here is Chisholm's account of what positive epistemic status *is*. Much of his effort has gone into the project of stating and revising his epistemic principles; these principles seem to me to be close to truth, particularly if appropriately qualified with a clause specifying that S's faculties are functioning properly (see chaps. 1 and 2 of my *Warrant and Proper Function* [New York: Oxford University Press, 1993]) in producing and sustaining the belief in question. On the other hand, I do not concur with Chisholm that these principles will in general be noncontingent, that is, necessarily true if true at all.

deed, a seductive approach to an understanding of warrant, it is nevertheless at bottom deeply flawed. No amount of dutifulness, epistemic or otherwise, is sufficient for warrant. My doing my duty in accepting a proposition (or the proposition's being apt, even maximally apt, for epistemic duty fulfillment, for me) isn't anywhere nearly sufficient for that proposition to have warrant or positive epistemic status for me. Knowledge does indeed contain a normative element; but the normativity is not that of deontology. Perhaps this incoherence in the received tradition is the most important thing to see here: the tension between the idea that justification is a deontological matter, a matter of fulfilling duties, being permitted or within one's rights, conforming to one's intellectual obligations, on the one hand; and, on the other, the idea that justification is necessary and sufficient (perhaps with a codicil to propitiate Gettier) for warrant.[16] To put it another way, what we need to see clearly and first of all is the vast difference between justification and warrant. The lesson to be learned is that these two are not merely uneasy bedfellows; they are worlds apart. Classical deontologism is no better off than classical foundationalism. We have learned to acquiesce or rejoice in the demise of classical foundationalism; but the classical deontologism that lies at its root is no better off.

[16]There is a second incoherence in the received tradition (or perhaps a special case of the first). According to that tradition, justification in many areas requires *evidence;* if I am to be justified in accepting the view that the earth is round, for example, I must have evidence of some sort—testimonial evidence, if nothing else. Now on the one hand justification is supposed to be sufficient or nearly sufficient for warrant. But on the other, if a belief of mine is to have warrant for me by virtue of being accepted on the basis of some *ground,* then that ground must be appropriately related to the belief in question. And the problem for the received view is one that is by now familiar; I can be *deontologically* justified in believing A on the basis of B even if B is *not* appropriately related to A. I may be doing my level best; I may be performing works of magnificent epistemic supererogation; even so (by virtue of epistemic malfunction) I may believe A on the basis of a ground that is ludicrously inadequate. Perhaps (by virtue of demon, tumor, or Alpha Centaurian) I believe that Feike can swim on the basis of the 'ground' that nine out of ten Frisians cannot swim and Feike is a Frisian; and perhaps I am maximally dutiful in the entire situation and have been all my life. Clearly *warrant* requires that the ground in question really *be* evidence of one sort or another; but I can be *deontologically* justified, and *completely* justified, in believing on the basis of a ground that is in fact no evidence at all.

3

Post-Classical Chisholmian Internalism

We have been examining the conception of warrant I call 'classical Chisholmian internalism' : the conception developed in Chisholm's work up through *Theory of Knowledge* (*TK*) and *Foundations of Knowing* (*FK*). This conception is classically Chisholmian, but also classically internalist, in that it displays the motifs of the classical epistemic internalism of Descartes and Locke—an internalism that arises from deontology, from considerations of duty and obligation. Classical Chisholmian internalism displays a certain interesting development. Consider those epistemic principles to be found in *TK* and *FK:* noncontingent conditionals whose antecedents specify that S is in some condition or other and whose consequents specify that some belief of S's has some degree or other of warrant or positive epistemic status. Now in the first (1966) edition of *TK,* interestingly enough, these principles[1] were all so stated that their antecedents, if true, specify that S is in a *self-presenting* condition: he is being appeared to redly, or believes that Albuquerque is in New Mexico, or is trying to get to Boston.

These self-presenting conditions, Chisholm thinks, are the *ground* of the warrant enjoyed by a belief $B;$ they are what confers such warrant upon it; they are (if you like supervenience) that upon which warrant supervenes. But they also display another interesting peculiarity: it is also plausible to think that one cannot *mistakenly believe* that she is in such a condition. The mark of a self-presenting condition (*FK,* p. 10) is that necessarily, if a person is in the condition and considers whether she is, she believes that she is: hence it is impossible, when you are in such a condition, to consider whether you are and fail to believe that you are. It is equally plausible to suppose, however, that it is impossible, when you are *not* in the condition in question, to consider whether you are in it, and believe that you *are.* A self-presenting condition has this distinction: you cannot be *mistaken* in thoughtfully or reflectively attributing it (or its complement) to yourself. So self-presenting conditions are epistemically internalist conditions: conditions to which the agent has some special epistemic access. Indeed, they are internalist *in excelsis,* in that the agent enjoys a sort of infallibility with respect to them.

[1]Principles A–C, in *TK,* pp. 44–47.

Various difficulties[2] required that these principles be modified, and in the second edition of *TK* their antecedents no longer specify only self-presenting conditions.[3] According to *FK*, furthermore,

> Examination of our principles makes clear that, according to them, our knowledge is not a function *merely* of what is self-presenting. Principle P2 refers to what I have called "the uncontradicted"; this involves the logical relations that one attribution may bear to others. If these relations obtain, that they obtain will not be self-presenting. (p. 25)

The internalist requirement, however, though not satisfied as straightforwardly, is nonetheless still satisfied. Chisholm continues:

> But, I would say, one can always ascertain by reflection whether or not they obtain. Similar observations hold of "the epistemically unsuspect" (that which is "epistemically in the clear"), referred to in principles P3, P4 and P5. (pp. 25–26)

So principles P3, P4, and P5 are not such that their antecedents specify self-presenting conditions. Nevertheless, the conditions they do specify are still of a sort to which we have special access: their presence can be determined "by reflection alone." The last principle, however—Principle P6—differs from the other five in that whether its antecedent holds is not something S can determine by reflection alone. For this reason, significantly enough, Chisholm proposes to call P6 not an "epistemic" principle, but a "quasi-epistemic" principle.[4]

So there is a certain movement away from the strongest forms of epistemic internalism. In *FK* the conditions specified in the antecedents of the principles are no longer self-presenting. Nevertheless, those conditions are still such that we have special access to them. They may not be self-presenting for us—our access isn't as special as all *that*—but we can still always determine by reflection alone whether or not they hold. And the source of this epistemic internalism, as we have seen, is epistemic deontologism, the idea that warrant is essentially a matter of aptness for epistemic duty fulfillment.

I. Post-Classicalism Explained

But a significantly different understanding of warrant appears in some of Chisholm's more recent work. In "The Place of Epistemic Justification"[5] Chisholm takes the locution '*x* is more reasonable for *S* at *t* than *y*' as primitive,

[2]See, for example, Herbert Heidelberger, "Chisholm's Epistemic Principles," *Nous* 3 (1969), pp. 73–82.

[3]Consider, for example, principle B in the first edition of *Theory of Knowledge* (Englewood Cliffs, N.J.: Prentice-Hall, 1966) and its successor in the second edition (1977).

[4]"But the *de re* principle, P6, is an exception. For antecedent (i)—'if x perceives y to be F'—is not something that can be ascertained merely by reflection. The requisite sense of 'perceives', as we have defined it, involves a causal relation between the object of perception and the perceiver. And one cannot determine by reflection whether or not such a relation obtains. Hence I suggested that P6 might be called a 'quasi-epistemic principle'" (*FK*, p. 26).

[5]See his "The Coherence Theory of Knowledge," in *Philosophical Topics* 14, no. 1 (Spring 1986), p. 85.

partially explaining it by laying certain constraints upon it.[6] What is most striking, however, is that here Chisholm no longer explains reasonability (and hence warrant) in terms of a duty to try to achieve epistemic excellence. As a matter of fact he proceeds in precisely the opposite direction: "I have previously written, incautiously, that one's primary intellectual duties are to acquire truth and to avoid error. What I should have said is that one's primary intellectual duties are to believe reasonably and to avoid believing unreasonably."[7] This is a considerable step away from the views we have been considering. Previously, warrant was explained by way of the satisfaction of epistemic or intellectual duties; reasonability (and hence warrant) was to be understood in terms of the fulfillment (or aptness for fulfillment) of the general duty or obligation to try to achieve epistemic excellence. Here, on the contrary, warrant is to be explained in terms of believing reasonably, and one's intellectual or epistemic duties are to believe reasonably and avoid believing unreasonably. But then of course we cannot also understand a belief's being reasonable (and hence having warrant) for *S* as a matter of its aptness for the fulfillment of *S*'s epistemic duty.

When we turn to Chisholm's "Self-Profile,"[8] we find a deeper development of the same notions. There is, first, reiteration of the claim that epistemic concepts are *normative* concepts; but once again, there is a move away from the idea that they are *deontological* concepts. More significant, however, there is here the Brentanoesque suggestion that these normative epistemic concepts pertain not to duty and permission but instead to *intrinsic value*. "What I will say presupposes Aristotle's insight according to which knowing is, as such, intrinsically good." On classical Chisholmian internalism, warrant is a deontological property; on the the post-classical view, however, it is an *axiological* property; it pertains to value and goodness rather than to duty.

To understand the post-classical Chisholm we need the notion of a *purely psychological property*. Although he gives a chain of definitions culminating in a definition of this notion,[9] what he says about it more informally (together

---

[6]For example, the intended sense of the locution is such that "It provides us with the material by means of which we can answer the question of the Theaetetus: 'What does one add to the concept of *true belief* to get the concept *knowledge?*'"; and (continuing the internalist theme) "The relevant sense of *reasonable belief* is one which is such that a believer can ascertain by himself at any time which of his beliefs are reasonable for him at that time" (ibid., p. 86).

[7]Ibid., pp. 90–91. (So far as I know, what Chisholm had previously written is that one's duty is, not actually to *achieve* intellectual excellence, but to *try* to achieve it.)

[8]In *Roderick M. Chisholm*, ed. Radu Bogdan (Dordrecht: D. Reidel, 1986), pp. 52ff.

[9]Say that a property *involves* another property if it is necessary that whoever conceives of the first also conceives of the second (so that, for example, the property *being unmarried* involves the property *being married*); a property *implies* another if necessarily, the second is exemplified if the first is (so that the property *being a brother* implies the property *being a parent*); and a property *includes* another if necessarily, whatever exemplifies the first also exemplifies the second (so that the property of being a brother includes the property of being male) (ibid., pp. 31–32). Say further that a *restricted* property is a property such that (1) only individual things can have it; (2) any individual that can have it, can have it or fail to have it at any time at which it exists; and (3) it is possible that there are many individuals that have it and many individuals that do not have it (p. 36). Thus the property *being green* will be restricted; the property of being thirteen years old will not. Further, say that a *purely qualitative* property is one such that "(i) it is possibly such that only *one*

with a couple of examples) may suffice: purely psychological properties, he says, are "those properties to which we have privileged access. Every such property is necessarily such that, if a person has it and if he attributes it to himself, then his attribution is evident in the strongest sense of the term."[10] Examples, I take it, would be *being appeared to redly, judging that 7 + 5 = 12, trying to achieve epistemic excellence, hoping that you will be able to repay the money you unwisely borrowed from your children,* and the like. Chisholm then explains that a person's "*evidence-base*" at a time is "the conjunction of all the purely psychological properties that that person has at that time"; he replaces "*A* is more reasonable for *S* than *B*" by "*A* is epistemically preferable to *B* for *S*" and continues:

> Generally speaking, we may say that, if taking a doxastic attitude *A* is epistemically preferable for a person *S* to taking a doxastic attitude *B*, then *S*'s evidence-base is such that having that evidence-base and taking *A* is intrinsically preferable to having that evidence-base and taking *B*.

He goes on to say that we can systematically reduce our epistemic concepts to those of the theory of intrinsic value, an example of such a reduction being

> (ED8) Believing *p* is epistemically preferable for *S* to believing *q* = def. Those of *S*'s purely psychological properties which do not include believing *p* and believing *q* are necessarily such that having those properties and believing *p* is intrinsically preferable to having those properties and believing *q*.[11]

thing has it; and (ii) it is a restricted property that includes every restricted property it implies or involves" (p. 37). Chisholm gives judging, endeavoring, being pleased, wishing, wanting, hoping, and feeling as examples. And finally, say that a property is *purely psychological* if it is a property that is such that every restricted property it implies, involves a property that is purely qualitative.

[10]Ibid., p. 37. This is not an official analysis or definition; if it were, the official account of reasonability would be circular. It is instead simply a means to enable the reader to identify the class of properties he proposes to discuss.

[11]Ibid., pp. 37, 53. In quoting (ED8) I have corrected a misprint by replacing the term 'epistemically preferable' which occurs in line 4 of the definition as printed in Chisholm's text, by the term 'intrinsically preferable', which is what he obviously intends.

Richard Foley points out a technical problem here. Consider self-presenting properties, such as *being sad*. According to Chisholm, you can't have such a property, consider whether you have it, and fail to believe that you have it. Further, the proposition that I have a self-presenting property (when I do), Chisholm thinks, is certain for me; it has the highest degree of reasonability. Now why does it have such an exalted status? According to (ED8), it is for the following reason. Take the set *S* of my purely psychological properties at the time in question, and delete from the set any property that includes believing that I am sad: having the properties in the resulting set *S** and believing that I am sad has very much more intrinsic value than exemplifying the properties in that set and believing some other proposition. But what properties will be in *S**? To get *S** we must delete the property *believing that I am sad* and any property that includes it—for example, the conjunctive property *being sad and considering whether I am sad*. We don't eliminate either *being sad,* however, or *considering whether I am sad,* since neither of these includes *believing that I am sad* (even though their conjunction does). *S**, therefore, will be such that necessarily, anyone who exemplifies the properties in it believes that he is sad. But then what is so valuable about exemplifying the properties in *S** and believing that you are sad? Why is that a more valuable state of affairs than exemplifying those properties and believing some other proposition—for example, that all men are mortal? After all, it isn't even possible to exemplify the properties in *S** and *fail* to believe that you are sad.

Clearly this suggestion fits with that of "The Place of Epistemic Justification," according to which our epistemic duty is to believe reasonably. The state of affairs consisting in my believing reasonably is an intrinsically good state of affairs; furthermore, it is my epistemic duty to pursue it, to try to realize or actualize it. But then of course *believing reasonably* is not itself to be understood by way of the fulfillment of epistemic duty. Consider a case in which someone S reasonably holds some belief B: on classical Chisholmian internalism, what makes B reasonable for S is that by accepting it S can fulfill her epistemic duty to try to achieve epistemic excellence. On the post-classical, axiological view, however, what makes B reasonable for S is just that S displays a certain evidence-base E, where B and E are so related that the state of affairs consisting in someone's having E and holding B is an intrinsically good state of affairs. This post-classical conception is clearly internalist, in that warrant or positive epistemic status is explained in terms of purely psychological properties to which the epistemic agent has privileged access. The internalism, however, does not arise from deontology; for it is not the case that warrant is to be understood in terms of such concepts as aptness for the fulfillment of epistemic duty.

According to the classical, deontological Chisholm,[12] what confers warrant is a matter of doing one's epistemic duty, acting in an epistemically responsible manner, doing that which is such that neglecting it is blameworthy. According to the post-classical axiological Chisholm, on the other hand, what confers warrant is there being the right relationship between evidence-base and belief, a relationship such that when they stand in it, then the resulting whole displays a certain intrinsic value. The sort of intrinsic value involved, as we shall see in more detail, is not specified. Depending on the sort involved, we can see several different contemporary views as versions of post-classical Chisholmian internalism: coherentism, for example, in both its classical (see the next two chapters) and Bayesian (see chapters 6 and 7) manifestations, as well as the evidentialism noted in chapter 1 and the different versions of evidentialism to be noted in chapter 9 of *Warrant and Proper Function*.

II. Problems with Post-Classical Chisholmian Internalism

I propose to make four critical observations about this view. First, it is relatively uninformative; it tells us little about what warrant or positive epistemic status *is*. Second, this new view, while it holds on to the epistemic internalism of classical Chisholmian internalism, loses the principal philosophical motivation for internalism in moving away from deontology. Third, it is not the case (contrary to the post-classical Chisholm) that for a given belief B, there is a set S of evidence-bases such that *necessarily*, B has warrant for me if and only if it

---

[12]As for the classical Locke, at least so long as we leave out of account those propositions that are certain for us (says Locke) by virtue of being self-evident or appropriately about our own mental states.

occurs in connection with a member of that set S. And consequently, fourth, it is a mistake to suppose that the warrant a belief enjoys for S can be understood as a function solely of the psychological properties S exemplifies.

A. Axiological Inspecificity

On the axiological view we don't really *have* an answer to the question *what is warrant?* We did on the classical view: there warrant was the relation in which a proposition stands to a person S when S can fulfill his epistemic duty by accepting it, the degree of warrant depending upon the degree to which S's accepting it is apt for the fulfillment of that duty. On the post-classical view, however, we are told only that warrant is or supervenes upon the occurrence of certain belief/evidence-base pairs—pairs $<E, B>$, such that a certain intrinsic value attaches to any state of affairs consisting in someone's having E and holding B.

But of course there are a thousand kinds of states of affairs that are intrinsically valuable: love, for example, but also happiness, kindness, peace, justice, truthfulness, faithfulness, loyalty, pleasure, courage, beauty, trustworthiness, moral dutifulness. There are also many epistemic intrinsic goods, such as believing the truth, speaking the truth, doing your epistemic duty and forming beliefs responsibly, holding coherent beliefs, holding beliefs for which you have sufficient evidence, believing what on sufficient reflection you *would* believe, being such that your beliefs are produced by reliable belief producing mechanisms, being such that your cognitive faculties are subject to no dysfunction, and many more. The post-classical view is thus much less specific than the classical one. On the classical view (as on the post-classical) warrant consists in an intrinsically valuable state of affairs, but the *kind* of intrinsic value is specified: it is that of the fulfillment of epistemic duty. On the post-classical view, a belief's having warrant is also a matter of its being an element in an intrinsically valuable state of affairs; but about the type of intrinsic value in question we are told only that it is *not* that of the fulfillment of duty. I look out the window and see a tiger lily; that is, I exemplify a certain set E of purely psychological properties (I am appeared to in a certain characteristic tiger-lily-like way and exemplify the rest of some set of purely psychological properties that go with seeing a tiger lily); I form the belief that I see a tiger lily. Now what is it that confers warrant upon this belief, under those conditions? Why does this belief have more warrant than, for example, the belief that I see a tiger? The axiological answer: the first situation has more intrinsic value than the second. But what kind of intrinsic value *is it* that is at issue? All we have by way of answer: it is not the the kind of intrinsic value exhibited by cases of duty fulfillment. But isn't this unduly uninformative? About all we seem to be able to say here is that the type of intrinsic value involved in warrant is the type of value displayed by a state of affairs consisting in someone's exemplifying a belief/evidence-base pair $<E, B>$ which is such that when a person holds B while displaying E, then B has warrant for her.

Or perhaps the problem is not just that the answer is uninformative, but that it is unintuitive, implausible. It is certainly true that when I exemplify the properties in E, it is better that I believe that I see a tiger lily than a tiger. But *why* is it better? Well, of course the second belief is false and the first one true. More poignantly, if I form the second belief under those circumstances, I am at best in deep psychological trouble and at worst insane; forming that belief under those circumstances is a sign of a deeply disordered psyche. But these reasons for preferring the one situation to the other are not the relevant ones, according to the axiological view. What *is* relevant, according to that view, is simply that the state of affairs consisting in someone's exemplifying the set of properties in E and holding the first belief is intrinsically more valuable than someone's displaying those properties and holding the second. If there is such a difference in intrinsic value, it is not easy to detect.

B. Internalism Unmotivated

Second, I'd like to emphasize how very different this post-classical perspective is from classical Chisholmian internalism; and the heart and soul of this difference, as I see it, directly concerns the central notions of internalism. The axiological conception loses the connection with internalism and hence loses the philosophical motivation for it. As we saw in chapter 1, deontology implies internalism; but if we move away from deontology, if we suppose that what confers justification is not my being above reproach or acting responsibly, in accord with my duty, but rather a certain appropriateness of belief to evidence-base, then we lose that reason for accepting the internalist motifs. On the classical view, B has warrant for me to the degree that I can fulfill my epistemic duty—my duty to try to achieve epistemic excellence—by accepting it. This will be a duty, of course, only for "intellectual beings," as Chisholm puts it— beings capable of grasping concepts and holding beliefs. Even then, however, it will be a (subjective) duty only for well-formed, nondefective intellectual beings. There may be those who by virtue of cognitive malfunction and through no fault of their own simply cannot see that it is their duty to under- take this project; such persons are not to be blamed for failing to undertake it. There may also be those who (perhaps like some French philosophers) believe it is their duty to try to spread as much darkness and confusion as possible; if such a person forms this belief nonculpably (by virtue of cognitive malfunction, perhaps, rather than a prideful effort *pour épater le bourgeois*) then she too is not to be blamed for failing to pursue the road of duty. But well-formed cognitively healthy persons will not, in the typical case, be able mistakenly but nonculpably to believe that epistemic duty requires a course of action incom- patible with the pursuit of epistemic excellence.

Further, the *ground* of warrant, that which confers warrant upon a belief for me, is the aptness of my accepting that proposition for fulfilling my epistemic duty. Here again, if there is to be coincidence of objective and subjective duty, if we are guilty and worthy of blame for failing to do what is our objective duty, then (in the cases in question) well-formed human beings must not be able to believe falsely but nonculpably that a given candidate for belief is such that I can fulfill my epistemic duty by accepting it. But of course this is easily satisfied on the classical view. In the typical case the degree of that aptness will depend upon the degree to which the proposition in question seems to me to be true; and that is indeed something to which I ordinarily have special access.

These pressures toward internalism disappear when we turn to the post-classical Chisholm. Suppose we turn our backs on deontology; suppose we believe that what confers justification upon a belief *B*, for me, is not my having acted in accord with my duty (in forming and maintaining it) but rather some relation that holds between *B* and the set of purely psychological properties I exhibit. If duty is not involved, why suppose that to be justified I must have any sort of access at all, special or otherwise, either to the fact (if it is a fact) that this relation constitutes or confers warrant, or to the fact that a given belief bears that relation to the totality of my purely psychological properties? Suppose warrant is a relation between the totality of my purely psychological properties and my beliefs (a relation such that it is intrinsically good that it be ex-emplified); why think that I would have to have any sort of special access to this relation? This relation between evidence-base and belief might be such that we cannot ordinarily tell whether our beliefs and evidence-bases stand in it. It might be a relation such that it is easy enough for us to believe that it obtains when it does not. It might be a relation such that a person's evidence-base and beliefs can stand in it, even if that person can't so much as grasp or form a conception of it. It might be a kind of fittingness such that some kinds of creatures are able to detect its presence but others cannot, even though they are capable of belief. It might be a kind of fittingness that only an expert can detect; or it might be one such that we can detect it only by virtue of a certain stroke of epistemic luck—the sort of luck denied those unfortunates who are brains in a vat or deceived by Cartesian demons.

In "The Place of Epistemic Justification," as we saw, Chisholm partially explains the locution '*x* is more reasonable for *S* at *t* than *y*' by laying certain constraints upon it; one of these constraints is that "The relevant sense of reasonable belief is one which is such that a believer can ascertain by himself at any time which of his beliefs are reasonable for him at that time" (p. 86). But the question is: why say this? Why lay this down as an initial constraint on locating the notion to be explained? For the earlier classical view, there was a clear answer: the deontological connection. But for the later post-classical view this connection vanishes; and with it goes the reason for the epistemic internal-ist dimension of the view. The internalism lingers, like the smile of a Cheshire cat, after its raison d'être has disappeared.

C. No Set of Evidence-Bases Necessarily Connected with Warrant

According to Chisholm's later view, warrant, for one of my beliefs for a given belief *B*, consists in a certain relationship that holds between *B* and my purely psychological properties. More exactly, there are some evidence-bases such that if *B* occurs in conjunction with *those* evidence-bases, then it has warrant; but other evidence-bases such that if it occurs in connection with *them,* then it does not have warrant. As we have seen, this is so far compatible with a wide variety of views as to what sort of intrinsic value warrant involves, and hence with a wide variety of views as to what warrant *is.* It is compatible with *coherentism,* for example, according to which what counts for warrant is the appropriate relation among my beliefs, the rest of my purely psychological properties being irrelevant.[13] It is also compatible with *evidentialism,* the view that what counts is the evidential relation between *B* and the relevant purely psychological properties. In *Warrant and Proper Function,* I argue that *B* has warrant for you only if it is produced by your cognitive faculties functioning properly, the degree of warrant it displays depending upon the degree to which you are inclined to accept it: the intrinsic value of which Chisholm speaks could also be the value attaching to the relation between *B* and your evidence-base when both are produced by properly functioning epistemic faculties.

But Chisholm takes a further step here, and a fateful one at that: he claims that for a given belief *B,* there is a set *S* of evidence-bases such that, *necessarily,* *B* has warrant for me if and only if it occurs in connection with a member of that set *S.* What is distinctive is the idea that for any belief *B* there is a certain set of evidence-bases *S* such that *B*'s occurring in connection with a member of *S* is both necessary and sufficient, in the broadly logical sense, for *B*'s having warrant. Take a given belief *B* you now hold: the one thing relevant to the question whether *B* has warrant for you is the question what purely psychological properties you now display; there will be a set of purely psychological properties such that having some member of that set as your evidence-base will be both necessary and sufficient (in the broadly logical sense) for *B*'s having warrant for you.

I think this is mistaken. Before trying to explain why, however, we must state the view a bit more exactly. Begin by recalling Chisholm's reduction of epistemic concepts to the concept of intrinsic value:

> (ED8) Believing *p* is epistemically preferable for *S* to believing *q* = def. Those of *S*'s purely psychological properties which do not include believing *p* and believing *q* are necessarily such that having those properties and believing *p* is intrinsically preferable to having those properties and believing *q*.

Now consider what is involved in (ED8). Say that a *maximal set S of purely psychological properties* is a set of psychological properties such that (1) it is possible for a cognizer to have every property in *S,* and (2) it is not possible for a cognizer to have every property in any superset of *S;* and say that a *maximal psychological property P* is the property of having every property in some maximal set of purely psychological properties. Further (where *B* is a belief) say that a *maximal set diminished with respect to B* is the result of deleting from a maximal set every property that includes believing *B;* and say that a *maximal psychological property diminished with respect to B* is the property, for some maximal set of psychological properties diminished with respect to *B,* of having every property in that set. Of course there will be pairs <*B, P*>

[13]See chapter 4, pp. 78ff.

whose second member is a maximal psychological property diminished with respect to B and whose first member is B; call these *epistemic pairs*. According to Chisholm, some epistemic pairs display more by way of intrinsic value than others. There will be true (indeed, necessarily true) propositions of the form $<Bi, Px>$ *has more intrinsic value than* $<Bj, Py>$; and if you exemplify $<Bi, Px>$ and I exemplify $<Bj, Py>$, then Bi will have more warrant for me than Bj does for you. There will be an ordering (perhaps only partial) of epistemic pairs in terms of intrinsic value; this ordering will induce another ordering in terms of level or *degree* of intrinsic value (the details of the ordering can be adjusted to suit). So for each epistemic pair, there will be a degree or level of intrinsic value; and if I exemplify a given pair $<Bx, Pi>$, then Bx will have for me the degree of warrant appropriately related to the degree of intrinsic value displayed by $<Bx, Pi>$. More precisely (if more pedantically) for any belief B and degree of warrant d, there is a set C of epistemic pairs (each of whose first members is B) such that, necessarily, for any person S and time t, B has d for S at t if and only if S then exemplifies some member of C. Alternatively, for any belief B and degree of warrant d, there is a set C^* of evidence-bases such that, necessarily, for any person S and time t, B has d for S at t if and only if some member of C^* is S's evidence-base at t.[14] Less precisely but more intelligibly, the degree of warrant now enjoyed by one of my beliefs depends only upon which purely psychological properties I now exemplify.

This is the claim I mean to dispute; I shall argue that, for a given belief of mine and a given degree of warrant, there is no set of evidence-bases such that, necessarily, the belief displays that degree of warrant if and only if my evidence-base is a member of that set. I don't mean to dispute the claim that some belief/evidence-base pairs display more intrinsic value than other such pairs; that is as may be. But even if this claim is true, *that* value is not what constitutes warrant. I shall argue that many of the epistemic pairs $<B, P>$ I exemplify are such that (1) B has a great deal of warrant (perhaps a degree sufficient for knowledge), and (2) there are other conditions in which I could exemplify the same pair but B have little warrant for me. I shall also argue that there are many epistemic pairs $<B, P>$ I exemplify such that (1) B has little or no warrant for me, and (2) there are other conditions in which I could exemplify the same pair but B have a great deal of warrant for me. But if I am right in these arguments, then it is false that for any belief B there is a set of evidence-bases such that, necessarily, B has warrant if and only if it is accompanied by one of those evidence-bases. It is false that all that counts, in determining the degree of warrant a belief of mine has, is the evidence-base I then display.

So on to the arguments. First, note that our cognitive equipment could have been quite different from what it is. Clearly, we (or, to beg no questions, a species similar to us) could have been so constructed that quite different phenomenal properties would have been associated with a given belief when it constitutes an item of high epistemic status for us. We could have had a sensory apparatus of a very different sort: for example, we could have been endowed

---

[14]Here I am indebted for a correction to Toomas Karmo.

with the sort of sense by which a pit viper can determine the distance and direction of a mouse by detecting its body heat; we could have had the kind of directional awareness that enables birds to navigate vast distances without so much as a glance at a map; we could have had an awareness of the force and direction of the earth's magnetic field that according to some is bestowed upon sharks; we could have had the sort of acoustically based sensory equipment that enables a bat to thread its way with great precision and at high speed through a nasty set of obstacles in a completely dark cave. And of course quite different phenomenology could go with such different senses, including psychological properties no human being has ever exemplified. So the set of pairs $<B, P>$ in the hierarchy will include pairs whose first members include phenomenal properties no human being has ever enjoyed. Similarly, there may be or could be cognizers who grasp a much broader range of propositions than we do, so that they grasp and believe and reject propositions completely beyond our ken; hence the pairs in the hierarchy will also include some whose second member is a proposition no human being has ever grasped. Of course this is no problem, so far, for Chisholm; it is only that the field of epistemic pairs, for a given degree of warrant, is broader than we might have initially thought.

Next, note that we *learn* what beliefs to form under given phenomenal conditions, what beliefs to form for a given (complex) way of being appeared to. We learn how to judge distance, for example; and we learn that, despite appearances, railroad tracks do not really converge in the distance and that people and automobiles are not actually smaller when viewed from the top of a tall tower. What we learn depends upon circumstances and upon *contingent* circumstances; our circumstances could have been such that we should have learned something quite different. A large oak tree viewed at fifty yards under standard conditions displays a certain phenomenal appearance, as does a mountain goat on a dark crag viewed at 350 yards under good lighting conditions. Furthermore, if I am practiced at viewing mountain goats, I can take a good look at one 350 yards or so away and thereby know both that it is a mountain goat and that indeed it is about 350 yards away. This takes a certain amount of practice or learning; a mere tyro might *guess* that what he sees is a goat at 350 yards, but the seasoned old mountain woman *knows*. It isn't *necessary*, however, that the phenomenal properties that in fact go with seeing a mountain goat at 350 yards should confer warrant on the belief that it is 350 yards distant. If different atmospheric or lighting conditions were the norm, or if our sensory apparatus had been differently constructed, *that* way of appearing—the way that *in fact* goes with seeing a mountain goat at 350 yards—might well have gone with the belief that it was 100 yards off. What confers positive epistemic status upon the belief in question under the phenomenal circumstances in question is not just those phenomenal circumstances; what you have learned is also relevant.

But then for Chisholm's view to be correct, what you have thus learned will have to be represented or included, somehow, in the purely psychological properties you display at a given time. Perhaps you will have, at any such time, a very large set of beliefs of the sort: *when it looks like **that**, it is a mountain goat* *at 250 yards; when it looks like* **that***, it is a mountain goat at 300 yards, when it looks like* **that****, it is a mountain goat at 500 yards,* and so on; or perhaps what you have learned will be represented by a sort of feeling of appropriateness, or fit, between its looking like *that** and the judgment that it is a mountain goat 300 yards away, or perhaps in still other ways. Assume, for the sake of simplicity, that what you have learned is represented by beliefs of this sort. Now from a post-classical Chisholmian perspective, what is it about your evidence-base that confers warrant upon your belief that you see a mountain goat at 300 yards? Such facts, of course, as that it looks like *that**, and that you believe that when it looks like *that** it is a mountain goat at 300 yards. But what about that latter belief, the belief that when it looks like *that** it is a mountain goat at 300 yards? What is it that confers warrant upon *it*? It is hard to see how it could be some relation between that belief and the rest of the purely psychological properties I display at the time in question. Even if a mere tyro had the same belief, it would not have the same degree of warrant. It looks as if what counts for warrant, on this axiological view, must be more than a relation between the belief in question and the purely psychological properties you exhibit at the time in question; the course of your *past experience* is also relevant.

But now to the heart of the matter. I propose to argue that the degree of warrant one of your beliefs *B* has does not depend merely upon the purely psychological properties you display; in different circumstances, the same epistemic pair $<B, P>$ can be associated with vastly different degrees of warrant. Consider first so-called *a priori* beliefs—such beliefs as $2 + 1 = 3, 31 - 6 = 25$, **Complex Constructive Dilemma** *is a valid argument form, sets are neither true nor false,* and *if all men are mortal and Socrates is a man, then Socrates is mortal.* Each of these is a proposition I believe, and each, I believe, has a great deal of warrant for me. Now according to post-classical Chisholmianism, what confers warrant upon these beliefs for me is their being associated with the right evidence-bases. But what could it be, about my purely psychological properties, that thus confers warrant upon them? The Chisholmian answer, I suppose, is that it is the phenomenal properties to which we refer when we say that we can simply *see* that the proposition in question is true (and perhaps what we simply see is not just that it *is* true, but that it *must* be true). Perhaps (and then again perhaps not) this is a matter of the clarity and distinctness of which Descartes spoke. Locke spoke in the same connection of an "evident luster"; a self-evident proposition, he says, "displays a kind of clarity and brightness to the attentive mind." Perhaps Descartes and Locke don't have the matter precisely right; perhaps the phenomenology involved is not exactly clarity or brightness or luster.[15] Still, something *like* what they say must be true from the post-classical perspective. If what confers warrant on a simple self-evident belief *B* for me is the intrinsic value of its conjunction with certain other purely psychological properties, then presumably those other purely psychological properties will be the phenomenal properties I exemplify when I contemplate or attentively consider *B*.

[15]See chapter 6 of my *Warrant and Proper Function* (New York: Oxford University Press, 1993), pp. 105–106.

But of course we, or creatures similar to us, could have been constructed quite differently. Consider, for example, the first 25 primes. Most of us cannot simply see, with respect to each of them, that it is indeed prime; we need to calculate, some of us in fact requiring pencil and paper. But of course we could have been constructed in such a way that we *could* simply see, with respect to any member of this set, that it is prime; perhaps in fact there are angels or Alpha Centaurians who can do exactly that. Such creatures would have the same sort of knowledge of these propositions as most of us have of the simplest propositions of elementary arithmetic. So consider an epistemic pair $<B, P>$ where B is the belief, say, that 67 is a prime, where P is a purely psychological property reduced with respect to B, and where $<B, P>$ is such that I could know B if P were my evidence-base; there are accordingly possible circumstances in which I exemplify $<B, P>$ and know B—circumstances in which B has a very high degree of warrant for me. I want to argue that there are other possible circumstances in which I exemplify $<B, P>$ and am such that B has very little warrant for me—but if so, then, clearly enough, for B there is no set of evidence-bases such that *necessarily*, B has warrant for me if and only if it is accompanied by some member of that set.

So suppose I am captured by a group of unscrupulous but extremely knowledgeable Alpha Centaurian superscientists intent upon a cognitive experiment (or suppose that I am a victim of a Cartesian demon who delights in deception). In the course of conducting their experiment, the scientists (or demon) modify my cognitive faculties. Consider the propositions of the form *n is prime* where *n* is a natural number between 23 and 200 (inclusive); my captors bring it about that I believe every third proposition of this form and disbelieve the rest. Thus I believe that neither 23 nor 24 is prime, but do believe that 25 is. Further, for each of those propositions I believe—*25 is prime, 28 is prime, . . . 67 is prime, . . . 199 is prime*—they so modify my faculties that when I consider it, I undergo the very sort of phenomenology that in fact goes with simply seeing that, say, 5 is prime. In the case of each of these propositions it seems to me that I can simply see that it is true in just the way I can simply see that $2 + 1 = 3$ is true. Similarly for the ones I believe to be false; each of them is such that when I consider it I undergo the phenomenology that goes with seeing, for example, that $31 + 32 = 277$ is false. I therefore think I can simply see that 67 is prime, just as I can simply see that $2 + 1 = 3$ and just as I think I can simply see that 5 is prime. When I consider *67 is prime,* it has for me precisely the phenomenology that goes with simply seeing that a simple arithmetical proposition is true. But of course my faculties have been modified so that they no longer function properly; in particular, most of the propositions of the form *n is prime* that I think I can simply see to be true are false, and most of the ones I think I can simply see to be false are true. It is, so to speak, only by accident that I have the right phenomenology with respect to *67 is prime;* my captors could just as well have given me the phenomenology that goes with seeing that a proposition of the form *n is prime* is *false.*

It is clear, I think, that under these conditions *67 is prime* has very little by way of warrant or positive epistemic status for me. Although it is true and necessarily true, I surely do not know that it is. So if I were in this condition of epistemic malfunction—brought about by a malicious Cartesian demon, inquisitive Alpha Centaurians, or perhaps a rare brain lesion—then I could display the phenomenology that goes with just seeing that 67 is prime, but nonetheless be such that that proposition has little or no positive epistemic status for me. But then consider that epistemic pair $<B, P>$ where B is the belief that 67 is prime and P is a purely psychological property reduced with respect to B and where the pair is such that I could know B if P were my evidence-base. Clearly I could exemplify that pair but be such that B has very little by way of warrant for me. But of course I could also exemplify that pair and be such that B has a great deal of warrant for me. So the degree of warrant a belief has for me does not depend merely upon the purely psychological properties I exemplify at the time in question. It also depends upon whether or not my faculties are functioning properly in producing that belief in me then. And if that is so, there is no set of evidence-bases such that, necessarily, the belief in question has warrant if and only if it is associated with a member of the set.

Let me be clear about the logic of the situation. According to the post-classical Chisholm, the *only* thing that can confer warrant or positive epistemic status upon a belief B for me is my exemplifying an appropriate evidence-base. For any belief B and each degree of warrant d, there is a set E of evidence-bases—that is, maximal purely psychological properties reduced with respect to B—such that necessarily, for any person S, B has d for S if and only if S exemplifies a member of E. What we have seen so far is that the evidence-bases that typically accompany high warrant for us are not *sufficient* for such warrant; in other conditions (pathological conditions) a person might exemplify the evidence-base but have very little by way of warrant for B. It is worth noting (though not inconsistent with what Chisholm says)[16] that we can also proceed in the opposite direction: having one of the evidence-bases that for us accompany high warrant for a belief B is also not *necessary* for B's having high warrant. We can see this as follows. For us, the phenomenology that accompanies seeing, for example, that $7 + 5 = 12$, is (on post-classical Chisholmianism) a matter of its seeming obvious or clearly true not only that the proposition in question is *true* but that it *must* be true, couldn't be otherwise. But presumably this is not necessary; there could be creatures who see that $7 + 5 = 12$ is true but do not see that it couldn't be false; perhaps, indeed, they lack the conception of necessary truth. Surely God could make creatures whose phenomenology, with respect to truths of this sort, differed from ours in just this way; and perhaps he could compensate them, for their failure to perceive the necessity of these propositions, by conferring upon them the ability to see directly (without inference or calculation) the truth of many more arithmetical propositions than we can.

[16]Chisholm's claim is that for any belief B, there is a set E of evidence-bases such that necessarily, B has warrant for S if and only if S displays a member of E. But, of course, for a given belief B, E might include evidence-bases we human beings never exemplify; perhaps they involve modes of experience foreign to us.

What we have here is a whole class of beliefs such that the degree of warrant they have for *S* does not depend merely upon *S*'s exemplifying the right purely psychological properties; we must also ask whether *S*'s faculties are functioning properly. But of course the same holds with respect to beliefs of other sorts. Consider memory beliefs: on Chisholm's view what confers warrant upon a given memory belief—that this morning I had an orange for breakfast, for example—is the sort of phenomenology I undergo when I consider the question what I had for breakfast. When I ask myself this question, that belief suddenly appears, simply occurs to me, pops into my mind, we might say, along with a sort of past-tinged phenomenology that is hard to describe but familiar to all. But of course a Cartesian demon or Alpha Centaurian cognitive scientist could modify my memory faculties. Say that my *memory field* is the set of propositions that constitute what I at present seem to remember, together with the negations of those propositions.

Now imagine that a Cartesian demon, acting out of sheer malicious whimsy, alters my faculties by redistributing over my memory field the phenomenology that in fact goes with propositions I do indeed remember. The distribution is completely random and is such that no more than a quarter of the propositions I seem to remember are true. Then what I seem to remember, even if true, will have very little by way of warrant or positive epistemic status for me, although of course I will be deontologically *justified* in accepting it. Such beliefs will certainly not constitute knowledge. The reason is that even if, as it happens, it is a true belief that is accompanied by the phenomenology in question, it is just by epistemic accident that this phenomenology goes with that belief; the demon could just as well have conferred that phenomenology upon a false belief. So these beliefs will have very little warrant for me—even though under *other* circumstances, when I exemplify the same epistemic pairs, the true beliefs in question *do* constitute knowledge. What we see once more is that exemplifying one of the evidence-bases that in fact accompany a belief *B*'s being of high warrant for me is not sufficient for that high degree of warrant; more is required, and the more has to do with the proper function of cognitive equipment.

The same point can be made with respect to perceptual beliefs. Consider the evidence-bases that in fact accompany perceptual beliefs for which I have a high degree of warrant: I think we can see that having one of those evidence-bases is not sufficient, in the broadly logical sense, for those beliefs having that degree of warrant. Suppose, once more, I am being arbitrarily manipulated by an Alpha Centaurian or Cartesian demon or am subject to some other pathology-inducing condition, and consider the phenomenology, the purely psychological properties, that in fact go with perceiving a large oak tree at 40 yards: suppose the Alpha Centaurians give me those properties at random intervals, with no correlation at all with my being in the presence of oak trees. Naturally enough, on those occasions I believe that I perceive an oak. These beliefs, however, will surely have little by way of warrant for me, despite the fact that they are accompanied by evidence-bases that in other, more happy circumstances accompany that belief's having a high degree of warrant for me. In this case as in the others I will of course be deontologically justified in accepting the beliefs I do accept, and I will also undergo the right phenomenology; but due to the pathology those beliefs will have very little by way of warrant for me— much less than such beliefs have for someone whose faculties are functioning properly.

Now in the conditions envisaged, my belief that I perceive an oak is false; on those occasions I do not perceive a tree at all. But we can easily modify the example to get a similar one where the belief in question is true. Suppose I see a quick furry blur bound across the space between a couple of trees in my back yard: I may form the belief *a squirrel just ran from* **that** tree to **that** tree. Clearly, once more, the Cartesian demon could arrange for me to have that sort of experience on a completely random basis; if it should happen to occur just after a squirrel did run from *that* tree to *that* tree, then, though the belief is true, it has next to no warrant. Surely it does not constitute knowledge, as it might if my faculties were functioning properly.

I have been arguing that, *pace* the post-classical Chisholm, it is false that for any belief B I might have, there is a set of evidence-bases E such that, necessarily, B has warrant for me if and only if it is a member of E. I argued this by finding beliefs B for which there are no such Es; the argument proceeded by way of finding a B and an evidence-base E such that in *normal* conditions one who holds B and has E as evidence-base is such that B has warrant for her, but in *other* conditions, conditions of cognitive malfunction, a person might hold B, have E as her evidence-base, and be such that B has no warrant for her. Another way to argue the same point is to find a belief B and evidence-base E such that, (1) as we are in fact constituted, one who holds B and has E is such that B has no warrant for her, but also (2) in other conditions a person who held B and had E could be such that B did have warrant for her.

So consider the unfortunate Paul of the last chapter (p. 42), who formed beliefs of the wrong modality: when appeared to in the church-bell fashion, he formed the belief that something was appearing to him in that fashion, and that it was orange. Now as things presently stand, it is clear, I think, that beliefs of these sorts do not have warrant. Paul's pathologically induced belief has no warrant, and even if it happened, on a given occasion, to be true, it would not constitute anything like knowledge. But of course things could have gone differently. Suppose God (or evolution, or both) had designed human beings in quite a different fashion—or, to avoid avoidable questions about what is involved in being a human being, suppose God had created a species capable of knowledge whose members were a lot like human beings but differed in certain crucial respects. Just as we are by nature such that when appeared to by something that is red, we form the belief that we are appeared to in that way by something that is red, so these creatures are by nature such that when appeared to in the church-bell fashion, they form the belief that they are appeared to that way by something that is orange. Imagine further that although these beings are often appeared to in that orange fashion, they inhabit a planet on which they seldom (if ever) visually perceive that an object is orange; atmospheric conditions make that for the most part impossible. (It is only once a year or so that one actually sees something that is orange and sees that it is orange.) Add that as a matter of fact nearly everything on this planet that makes the church-bell sound in question *is* orange. Now imagine that there is a certain common but rarely visible orange bird that makes the church-bell sound. When the inhabitants of this planet catch a glimpse of this bird (without seeing its color) and hear it make that sound, they form the belief that there is something appearing to them in the church-bell fashion and that it is orange. Why wouldn't this belief have a high degree of warrant for them—indeed, why couldn't it constitute knowledge? And this even though in Paul's case *his* similar belief and evidence-base are such that the latter confers no warrant upon the former?

D. *Psychological Properties Insufficient for Warrant*

I argued in the preceding section that the post-classical Chisholm is mistaken in arguing that for any belief B I might have, there is a set E of evidence-bases such that, necessarily, B has warrant for me if and only if it is a member of E. But of course this shows that warrant is not a function simply of what epistemic pairs I exemplify. Given that I hold a belief B, it is not the case that whether B has warrant for me depends solely on the purely psychological properties I display; purely psychological properties are not the only thing relevant. But then we should expect that Chisholm's post-classical account of knowledge will be mistaken. And I think it is easy to see that it is.

According to the post-classical Chisholm, the basic component of the concept of warrant is *evidence*. Take a case where you know something B—that $7 + 5 = 12$, for example, or that you had an orange for breakfast. In any such case you will have an appropriate evidence-base E, which will make B evident for you; the evidence *itself* is really a degree of intrinsic value, the degree that the combination of such evidence-bases as E with such beliefs as B displays. Evidence is the basic component of warrant, for the post-classical Chisholm, but it isn't the whole shooting match; Gettier situations may bring it about that a belief is evident for you but does not constitute knowledge for you. Chisholm proposes a codicil to deal with Gettier problems. When a belief is evident for you, we may say that your evidence-base makes it evident for you. Now an evidence-base can sometimes make a *false* proposition evident for you (thus Smith might give me overwhelming inductive evidence that he owns a Ford when the fact is he's just amusing himself at my expense and owns no car at all). But then, says Chisholm, your belief B constitutes *knowledge* for you if and only if your evidence-base makes B evident for you, and furthermore your evidence-base makes no false proposition evident for you.[17]

It is easy to see, I think, that this account is insufficient; we need only reflect on the examples I have given. Take the example (p. 59) where, for every third proposition of the form *n is prime* (*n* between 23 and 200), my Alpha Centaurian captors playfully give me the phenomenology that goes with simply seeing that a number is prime. I consider the proposition *67 is prime;* on the post-classical Chisholm's account of knowledge, this proposition is then evi-

---

[17]For details, see *Roderick M. Chisholm*, pp. 40ff.

dent for me (since it is accompanied by the right purely psychological properties). It is also true, and my evidence-base need make no false proposition evident for me; but then on the above account it constitutes knowledge for me. But surely it doesn't. Or take the case (p. 62) where the demon every now and then and at random gives me the phenomenology that normally goes with the belief *a squirrel just ran from* **that** *tree to* **that** *tree*. If he gives me that phenomenology just after a squirrel did in fact run from *that* tree to *that* tree, the belief will be true and evident, and the evidence-base need make no false proposition evident. But then, once more, that belief constitutes knowledge; and surely it does not.

Justification most properly so called, as we saw in chapter 1, is a matter of deontology; it crucially involves duty, permission, obligation, and the like. As we saw in chapter 2, justification so construed is wholly insufficient for warrant, and also unnecessary for it. What we have seen in this chapter is that justification taken the post-classical Chisholmian way—as a sort of intrinsic value that necessarily attaches to certain belief/evidence-base pairs—is also nowhere nearly sufficient for warrant. So we have two quite different Chisholmian accounts of justification, and neither is anywhere nearly sufficient for warrant. Justification construed either of these two ways is a specification of that vaguer and more capacious notion of justification I called 'broad justification' according to which a proposition is justified for you if you believe it and everything 'downstream of experience' is 'going properly'. What we have so far seen, then, is that neither of these two Chisholmian versions of broad justification is nearly sufficient for warrant.

We shall return to broad justification and to other versions of it; but we can already see in a preliminary way that no such version is at all likely to be correct. That is because they all neglect the important contribution of the *epistemic environment* to warrant. With deontological justification (justification most properly so called), all that counts is whether I do my epistemic duty; the vagaries of my cognitive environment are not relevant. On Chisholm's post-classical conception, all that counts for the justification of a belief is the right set of purely psychological properties; again, my cognitive environment is irrelevant. But neither sort, as we have seen, is sufficient for warrant; and the insufficiency has to do with the neglect of the cognitive environment. Suppose I am transported instantly and without my knowledge to a distant planet where the cognitive environment is very different (elephants, for example, are invisible, but give off a sort of radiation that causes human beings to be appeared to as if a trumpet is sounding nearby), so that while I do acquire a few true beliefs, it is just by happy cognitive accident. Suppose further that everything downstream of experience is going properly; do I really have knowledge of the few true beliefs I accidentally acquire? We shall have to look into this matter further; but initially one thinks not.

Our present concern, however, has been with the version of broad justificationism developed by the post-classical Chisholm. What we have seen is that what determines the warrant a belief has for me on a given occasion is not simply the evidence-base, the purely psychological properties I exemplify then.

Considerations of proper function and pathology are also relevant. The later Chisholm's views as to what constitutes warrant or positive epistemic status, like those of the earlier Chisholm, are not the true story. The epistemic principles he proposes, particularly if accompanied by a codicil to the effect that *S*'s cognitive faculties are working properly, may be correct or nearly so; but the account of the nature of warrant is fundamentally flawed. In *Warrant and Proper Function* I shall try to develop a better answer.

Chisholm's varieties of internalism, therefore, are not adequate. But there are other varieties of internalism. In particular, there is *coherentism*. Coherentism, as I said earlier, is perhaps best thought of as a sort of special case of post-classical Chisholmianism; strictly speaking, therefore, we already have the materials for seeing that it is inadequate. That is no substitute, however, for detailed consideration of it, and it is to this that we turn in the next chapter.

4

Coherentism

As we saw in the previous couple of chapters, Chisholmian internalism has impressive historical credentials. Coherentism, the subject of this chapter, has a lineage only slightly less impressive; both as a theory of truth and as a theory of justification it enjoyed enormous vogue during the second half of the nineteenth and first quarter of the twentieth centuries. Like music, coherentism had its three great B's: Francis Bradley, Bernard Bosanquet, and later (as one born out of due time) Brand Blanshard. During the next fifty years or so (with the rejection of absolute idealism and everything connected with it) coherentism fell on evil times. Now, however, it is flourishing once again and has such doughty advocates as Keith Lehrer[1] and Laurence BonJour,[2] who adopt coherentism as an account of warrant or justification, and Nicholas Rescher,[3] who adopts it as an account both of warrant and of truth. Furthermore it has spawned a whole new variety or subspecies: probabilistic or *Bayesian* coherentism. In this chapter I shall ignore my own *caveat* (Preface, p. vii) and consider coherentism *überhaupt;* I shall argue that it does not afford the resources for a satisfying account of warrant or positive epistemic status. In chapter 5, I shall take a specific example, arguing the same conclusion with respect to the variety of coherentism admirably presented by BonJour in *The Structure of Empirical Knowledge*.[4] Then in chapters 6 and 7 I shall turn to probabilistic or Bayesian coherentism, thought of first as an account of warrant and second as an account of rationality.

   Our first problem, naturally enough, is to characterize coherentism. This problem is not wholly trivial: there is considerable confusion as to what coherentism is and no generally accepted account of the relevant coherence relations. It is worth noting initially, however, that coherentism is nicely thought of as a variety of the post-classical Chisholmian internalism of the preceding chapter. So thought of, the sort of intrinsic value appealed to is,

[1]For example, *Knowledge* (Oxford: Oxford University Press, 1974), and "The Coherence Theory of Knowledge," *Philosophical Topics* 14, no. 1 (Spring 1986).
[2]*The Structure of Empirical Knowledge* (Cambridge: Harvard University Press, 1985).
[3]*The Coherence Theory of Truth* (Oxford: Oxford University Press, 1973).
[4]In "Coherentism and the Evidentialist Objection to Theistic Belief," in *Rationality, Religious Belief, and Moral Commitment*, ed. Robert Audi and William Wainwright (Ithaca: Cornell University Press, 1986), pp. 129–33, I consider and criticize the brand of coherentism to be found in Lehrer's *Knowledge* (Oxford: Oxford University Press, 1974).

naturally enough, coherence (however exactly the latter is to be thought of); and since coherence is a relation just among *beliefs*, the only relevant "purely psychological properties" would be beliefs.

Part of the motivation for coherentism, I think, has been similar to Locke's motivation for deontological internalism. Conceding that it might not be within our power to bring it about that all our beliefs are true, Locke claimed that, even so, we can at least make sure that we do our epistemic duty in forming our beliefs. Similarly, part of the attraction of coherentism is the thought that even if there is no guarantee that we will or can reach the truth, it is at least within our power to bring it about that our beliefs are coherent. Perhaps that is the best we can do, but perhaps that is also enough for mere mortals. Of course it isn't as easy as one might think to achieve coherence (as we shall see in the next chapter); in fact it isn't even easy to achieve logical consistency, and no amount of effort will guarantee it. A coherentist who recognizes this difficulty (and thus loses that motivation for coherentism) can nonetheless retreat to the Chisholmian, Brentanoesque stance: coherence is an intrinsically valuable state of affairs, and it is coherence that confers warrant, whether or not it is within our power to attain it.

The best way to understand coherentism, I think, is by contrasting it with foundationalism, whose structure is at least initially clearer. Foundationalism comes in many varieties, but perhaps the most famous and important brand of foundationalism goes back to Descartes and Locke. As we saw in chapter 1, Descartes and Locke were the fountainheads of the *deontological* tradition with respect to warrant and hence also the fountainheads of the *internalist* tradition with respect to it. Descartes and Locke are therefore the sources of classical deontologism and classical internalism; but they are also the sources of classical *foundationalism*. We shall get to classical foundationalism later (pp. 84–86); but let us begin here by thinking about foundationalism more broadly. Suppose we start with a partial account of foundationalism, focusing on those features that relevantly distinguish it from coherentism. And since the foundationalist sometimes accuses the coherentist of endorsing *circular reasoning*, we shall pay special attention to the foundationalist's rejection of such reasoning.

I. Ordinary Foundationalism

We form, discard, maintain, and modify beliefs. And a salient characteristic of our way of doing these things is that we sometimes do them on the basis of *evidence*. Taking the term 'evidence' in perhaps its most familiar sense (at any rate most familiar to *philosophers*), the evidence on the basis of which I form a given belief will be *some other proposition or propositions* I believe; in the preceding chapter I called such evidence 'propositional' evidence. There is, for example, the evidence for relativity theory, or for the proposition that the gospel of John was composed late in the first century A.D., or for the claim that life began on earth more than three billion years ago via the mechanisms suggested by A. G. Cairns-Smith.[5] Of course this is just one use of the term: clearly there are other, analogically related uses, and in chapter 10 of *Warrant and Proper Function* I shall explore some of them.

Foundationalism—a family of views that has had an extraordinarily illustrious career in Western thought—takes its fundamental inspiration from the first kind of evidence, from propositional evidence. It starts from the apparent cleavage between those beliefs you accept on the evidential basis of other beliefs, and those you accept in the *basic* way—accept, but not on the evidential basis of other beliefs. One attributes to Aristotle the property of being the fountainhead of foundationalism (subject, as Quine says in another connection, to contradiction by scholars, such being the penalty for attributions to Aristotle). Aristotle and some of his medieval followers are classical foundationalists—*ancient* classical foundationalists, as I shall call them, to distinguish them from such modern classical foundationalists as, for example, Descartes, Malebranche, Locke, Leibniz, Berkeley, Hume, and a thousand lesser lights. Modern classical foundationalism, obviously enough, has been the dominant tradition in epistemology, in the West, since the seventeenth century.

The foundationalist, therefore—call him a *generic* foundationalist, since we are here concerned with what is common to all foundationalists—starts from the distinction between beliefs we accept in the basic way and those we accept on the evidential basis of other beliefs. Thus I believe $23 \times 48 = 1,104$ on the evidential basis of such propositions as $3 \times 8 = 24, 3 \times 4 = 12, 12 + 2 = 14$, and the like. His idea is that every belief is either basic or accepted on the basis of other beliefs (and given the definition of basicality I just gave, here he will encounter no disagreement); he adds that in a correct or healthy human system of beliefs, there *are* basic beliefs, and every nonbasic belief will be accepted on the basis of other beliefs that offer evidential support for it, in such a way that every belief is supported, finally, by basic beliefs, beliefs in the foundations. These beliefs, of course, are not accepted on the basis of others; the basis relation is finite and terminates in the foundations.

An immediate and important consequence of this fundamental idea is the rejection of *circular* reasoning: that is, the foundationalist finds fault with a system of beliefs in which a belief A_0 is accepted on the evidential basis of a belief A_1, which is accepted on the basis of A_2, which is accepted on the basis of $A_3, \ldots$, which is based on A_n, which is based on A_0.[6] Thus suppose I believe

(1)   Life originated in tide pools during an n-year stretch some m years ago

on the basis of my beliefs that

(2)   Conditions C then obtained

and

---

[5]See Robert Shapiro, *Origins* (New York: Summit Books, 1986), pp. 190ff.

[6]Here we have the simplest kind of circular reasoning; the kind where each belief A_i is based on just one belief A_j, from which it gets all its warrant. What I shall say is easily generalized.

(3) The probability that life would arise on earth during an *n*-year stretch when condition *C* obtained is high.

Suppose I believe (3) on the evidential basis of my belief that

(4) The probability that life would arise in a single tide pool during a 100-year stretch under condition *C* is $1/p$;

and suppose finally that I believe (4) on the basis of my belief that life did indeed arise in tide pools during an *n*-year stretch, which would be monumentally improbable on any assignment significantly less than $1/p$ to the probability that life would arise, under condition *C*, in a single tide pool during a 100-year stretch. That is, suppose I believe (4) on the basis, among other things, of (1). Then, says the foundationalist, my system of beliefs is defective by virtue of containing a circle in the basis relation.

Now it is often said that the central difference between foundationalism and coherentism lies just here: the coherentist does *not* object to circular reasoning, "provided the circle is big enough."[7] Indeed, so the suggestion goes, the coherentist goes further; he *revels* in circular reasoning, for it is precisely in such circular chains that he sees warrant as arising. He must therefore suppose, if this characterization is correct, that the basis relation in a noetic structure does not simply *transfer* warrant: it somehow *generates* it, at least if the chain involved is sufficiently long. On this view (so the story goes) *every* belief is accepted on the basis of other beliefs; none holds the privileged position of being basic or foundational; and apart from coherence considerations, none is more warranted than any other. Suppose we begin by looking into this alleged opposition. Can it really be that the coherentist does not reject circular reasoning, instead recommending it as the path of true philosophy? And why does the foundationalist reject circular reasoning? Why do *we* reject it? And how shall we characterize foundationalism?

A. Basis and Support

The ordinary foundationalist begins by observing that we accept some beliefs on the evidential basis of other beliefs. Thus I may learn from you that Paul was either at the party or at the bar, and from the bartender that he wasn't at the bar; I then form the belief that Paul was at the party on the basis of these other two beliefs. Of course it isn't entirely easy to say precisely what it is to believe *B* on the evidential basis of *A*. I don't believe *B* on the basis of *A* just because *A* is the or a *cause* of my believing *B*;[8] but no doubt the relation in question involves a causal element of *some* sort. Further, believing *B* on the basis of *A* does not

---

[7] "So Edward Caird used to tell us—'There is no harm in arguing in a circle if the circle is large enough.'" William Temple, *Studies in the Spirit and Truth of Christianity* (London: Macmillan, 1914), p. 43.

[8] Suddenly seeing Sylvia, I form the belief that I see her; as a result I become rattled and drop my cup of tea, scalding my leg. I then form the belief that my leg hurts; but though the former belief is a (part) cause of the latter, it is not the case that I accept the latter on the evidential basis of the former.

require that I explicitly infer B from A, although that would certainly be a significant special case of the relation. On the other hand, it does require that I *believe* both A and B, and that, at any rate, I have in the past believed both A and B *occurrently*, not just dispositionally. Perhaps the best the foundationalist can do here (in addition to correcting misapprehensions) is to give examples and hope for the best.

Now if I believe a proposition A but do not believe it on the evidential basis of other beliefs I hold, then A is basic for me. (It does not follow, of course, that A is certain, incorrigible, indubitable, unrevisable, maximally warranted, or believed more firmly than any belief that is not basic for me; many criticisms of foundationalism miss the mark just because they treat basicality as if it did entail one or more of those items.) Certain beliefs about my own immediate experience—the sort of belief I might express by such sentences as 'I am feeling tired' or 'It seems to me that I see something red' or even (in a Chisholmian vein) 'I am being appeared to greenly'—are typically basic for me. It would be at best difficult for me to believe the proposition that I seem to see something red on the evidential basis of *other* propositions; such beliefs are ordinarily basic for me. Similarly, many beliefs that we accept *a priori* are also typically basic for us. I believe the corresponding conditional of *modus ponens* (as well as various instances of it) and a host of other obvious truths of mathematics and logic in this basic way; the same goes, I daresay, for you.

B. Proper Basicality

According to the modern classical foundationalist, beliefs of the previous two sorts are not only *basic* for us; they are also *properly* basic for us. Roughly speaking, a belief is properly basic for me if it is basic for me, and also meets some other condition C, differing choices for C leading to different varieties of foundationalism. We might say, for example, that a belief is properly basic for me in case it is basic and has a certain degree of warrant for me. How much warrant? Here again there are options. We could hold that a belief is properly basic for me only if it has so much warrant that it is *certain* for me (has the maximal degree of warrant for me); or we might say that it is properly basic for me if it has enough warrant so that I *know* it (or have some special type of knowledge of it). Alternatively, we could say that it is properly basic for me if I am *not irrational* in accepting it, am *justified* in accepting it, am *within my epistemic rights* in accepting it.[9] Thus the evidential objector to theistic belief[10] holds that one is not justified, not within her epistemic rights, in accepting belief in God without evidence (without proofs or arguments); and (so he says) hence belief in God is not properly basic in this sense. Aquinas, on the other hand, would hold that a person could certainly be within her epistemic rights in believing in God in the basic way, but belief in God taken in the basic way

[9]Of course in the deontological justified-true-belief tradition this is to say that it has a certain degree of warrant for me.

[10]See my "Reason and Belief in God," in *Faith and Rationality: Reason and Belief in God*, ed. A. Plantinga and N. Wolterstorff (Notre Dame: University of Notre Dame Press, 1983), pp. 17ff.

cannot constitute *knowledge* (that is, *scientia*) that there is such a person as God. Such modern classical foundationalists as John Locke (on still a third hand) proposes that a belief—any belief—is properly basic for me only if it is either self-evident or appropriately about my own immediate experience.

Of course many other sorts of belief are often taken as basic, and with respect to these the modern classical foundationalist will not be indulgent. Suppose I seem to see a tree: I have that characteristic sort of experience that goes with seeing a tree. I may then form the belief that I see a tree, or that there is a tree there (more realistically, something like *that tree must be more than one hundred feet tall!*). In the typical case, that belief will be basic for me; I will not ordinarily accept the proposition that I see a tree on the evidential basis of other beliefs I hold.[11] In particular, I will not ordinarily accept this proposition on the basis of the *belief* that I have that special seeming-to-see-a-tree or being-appeared-to-treely sort of experience, for I will not ordinarily believe this latter proposition at all. (I will not, ordinarily, be paying any attention to my experience; I will be concentrating on the tree.) And here the modern classical foundationalist will disapprove. She need not deny, of course, that we do *in fact* accept such perceptual beliefs in the basic way, but in her view such beliefs are not *properly* basic; for the modern classical foundationalist holds that only self-evident beliefs and (appropriate) beliefs about my own mental states are properly basic. Hence, she thinks, a perceptual belief is unwarranted if it is not accepted on the evidential basis of propositions that are either self-evident or appropriately about my own immediate experience.

Similarly, consider a memory belief—that you had breakfast this morning, for example. Once more, you do not believe this proposition on the basis of some belief about your experience—for example, the proposition that you *seem to remember* that you had breakfast this morning. Here again the modern classical foundationalist may concede that *in fact* we often do accept memory beliefs in the basic way; he will deplore this tendency on our parts, however, for in his view—his official view, at any rate—memory beliefs are not properly basic.

According to the foundationalist view some of my beliefs are basic for me: the rest, naturally enough, are nonbasic for me, held on the evidential basis of other beliefs I hold. If things are going properly, however, I will not (of course) believe a given proposition on the basis of just *any* proposition; I will instead believe A on the basis of B only if B *evidentially supports* A. Foundationalists of varying stripes, naturally enough, have made different suggestions as to the further characteristics of this relation. Descartes seemed to think that the only support worth its salt is deductive support. Locke added inductive evidence. (The facts that Feike is a seventeen-year-old Frisian and 19 out of 20 seventeen-

---

[11]It is of course consistent with this that there should be beliefs $B_1, \ldots, B_n$ such that I cannot hold the one in question without holding the B_i; perhaps I couldn't form some of the concepts involved without holding some other beliefs. But it wouldn't follow that I accepted the belief in question on the evidential basis of the B_i. (Perhaps I couldn't have the concept *14* without believing that $14 > 1$; then I couldn't believe $12 + 2 = 14$ without believing that $14 > 1$; it wouldn't follow that I believe the former on the evidential basis of the latter.)

year-old Frisians can swim evidentially support the proposition that Feike can swim.) Peirce added *abductive* evidence: the sort of evidence provided (for example) for special relativity by the null result of the Michelson-Morley experiment, muon decay phenomena, the Hafele-Keating experiment involving jet transport of cesium clocks, and so on.

Say that *S's noetic structure* is the set of propositions he believes, together with certain epistemic relations that hold among him and them. An account of *S's* noetic structure will specify, for example, which of his beliefs are basic and which nonbasic. It will also include something like an index of degree of belief, specifying, for each proposition he believes, how firmly he believes it. (We could add, if we like, that it specifies for each proposition to which he affords some degree of confidence, the degree of confidence he affords it.) Further, it will include, for any belief *B* that is a member of it, an account of which beliefs (and which sets of beliefs) *support B*, and the degree and kind of support they provide for it. It will also include an *epistemic history* of each belief, specifying the conditions under which the belief was formed and has been sustained, and a *deontological history*, which specifies for each belief whether it was formed and has been sustained in accord with epistemic duty. Finally, it will include a *coherence index* of the structure, which measures both the coherence of the structure as a whole and, for each of its members, its coherence with the rest of the structure. Still other properties of a noetic structure are relevant and important in some contexts, but I shall ignore them for now.

1. Six Foundationalist Theses

Now foundationalism is a *normative* thesis about noetic structures; more exactly, it is a connected group of such theses. It is a group of theses about how a system of beliefs *ought* to be structured, about the properties of a correct, or acceptable, or rightly structured system of beliefs. The normativity in question could be *deontological:* one who conforms to his intellectual duties, on this suggestion, will be such that his noetic structure satisfies the theses.[12] The normativity could be *axiological:* the state of affairs consisting in the existence of a noetic structure that satisfies the theses in question is intrinsically valuable.[13] The normativity could be *aretaic:* there are (intrinsically or extrinsically) valuable noetic or intellectual states; there are also the corresponding intellectual virtues, the habits of acting that produce or promote or enhance those valuable states of affairs; and the noetic structure of a person with the appropriate intellectual virtues will satisfy the theses in question.[14] The normativity in question could be understood in terms of what an *idealized* human being would be like, as in some of the Bayesian literature (see the next couple of chapters). Finally, the normativity could be 'functional' as we might call it: the sort involved when we say of a diseased heart or knee or immune system that it isn't functioning properly, isn't working the way it ought to work; and the

---

[12] As in classical Chisholmian internalism.

[13] As in post-classical Chisholmian internalism.

[14] As is suggested by some of Ernest Sosa's work.

claim would be that a properly functioning noetic structure (the noetic structure of a person whose epistemic faculties were functioning properly) would satisfy the theses in question. Foundationalism as such is neutral among these options, although—as I argue in *Warrant and Proper Function*—the last is most apposite if it is *warrant* that is at issue.

So foundationalism is a connected group of normative theses about noetic structures. Our present concern is with only some of these theses: those relevant to the alleged dispute between foundationalists and coherentists. And a noetic structure is what it should be, says the former, only if the beliefs it contains are either properly basic or believed on the basis of propositions that support them. Just to have a term, say that a noetic structure that is what it ought to be is *proper*. Then, according to the foundationalist,

(I) A proper noetic structure will have a foundation: a set of beliefs not accepted on the basis of other beliefs.

Next, the foundationalist accepts some theses about the relation of evidential support (call it the *supports* relation) and the believed-on-the-basis-of relation (the *basis relation*, for short):

(II) The supports relation is irreflexive.

Although of course every proposition *entails* itself, no proposition provides *evidential support* for itself, that is, no proposition is such that a properly functioning human being could believe it on the evidential basis of itself. From this perspective, the term 'self-evident' is something of a misnomer. A self-evident proposition is not one for which the evidential support is provided, oddly enough, by *itself;* it is rather a proposition that is evident in itself and thus requires no evidential support.

(III) The basis relation is irreflexive in a proper noetic structure.

It may be doubted that anyone is so benighted as to believe a proposition *A* on the evidential basis of *A;* but even if it could be done, it clearly should not be done.

The basis relation (in a proper noetic structure) and the supports relation coincide on irreflexivity; they diverge on asymmetry. For:

(IV) The supports relation is not asymmetrical

and

(V) The basis relation is asymmetrical in a proper noetic structure.

The supports relation, clearly enough, is not asymmetrical. Special relativity provides evidential support for muon decay phenomena, and muon decay phenomena also provide evidential support for relativity theory. A person could sensibly accept relativity theory on the evidential basis of muon decay phenomena, but it is also true that a person could sensibly accept muon decay on the basis of relativity. For one who is convinced of the Axiom of Choice, that axiom could serve as her evidence for the Hausdorff Maximal Principle; for the former entails the latter. But someone else already convinced of the latter could properly use it as his evidence for the former; for the latter entails the former. A person might find it obvious that there are no nonexistent objects and use this truth (as I see it) as her evidence for his view that proper names in fiction ('Captain Marvel', 'Hester Prynne') that do not name existent objects do not name any objects at all. On the other hand, someone who held that such names name nothing could properly take that fact as part of his evidence for the claim that there are no nonexistent objects.

But even if the supports relation is not asymmetrical, the basis relation, in a proper noetic structure, *is* asymmetrical. If my belief that A is accepted on the evidential basis of my belief that B, then my belief that B must not be based on my belief that A. More exactly, suppose N is a proper noetic structure. Then if the belief that A (in N) is based upon $B_1 \ldots B_n$, none of the B_i will be based upon A. If my belief that life arose in antediluvian tide pools is based on, among others, my belief that the probability that life would arise in a given tide pool in a hundred-year period (under the conditions that then obtained) is $1/n$, then (if my noetic structure is proper) my belief that that probability is $1/n$ will not be based on the proposition that life arose in this way, and there were n tide pool/100-year pairs available. If my evidence for special relativity is, say, the muon decay phenomena and the Hafele-Keating experiment, then it will not also be the case that my evidence for muon decay is special relativity.

So the basis relation, in a proper noetic structure, is asymmetrical. More generally,

(VI)   The basis relation, in a proper noetic structure, is noncircular.

In a proper noetic structure it will not be the case that a belief A_0 is accepted on the evidential basis of a belief A_1, which is accepted on the basis of A_2, which is accepted on the basis of $A_3, \ldots$, which is based on A_n, which is accepted on the basis of A_0.

2. Against Circularity

Now *why*, exactly, does the foundationalist object to circular reasoning? What exactly is objectionable about it? The answer is not trivially obvious. Of course, if the basis relation (in a proper noetic structure) were *transitive*, then we could see why circular reasoning would be objectionable. For suppose this relation were transitive: then if there were a circular path in my noetic structure, there would be some proposition A that I believe on the evidential basis of A itself; and this, according to the foundationalist, is either impossible or at any rate not a way to achieve warrant. The fact is, however, that the basis relation need not be transitive in a proper noetic structure; I can quite properly believe *A* on the basis of *B* and *B* on the basis of *C* without believing *A* on the basis of *C*. Perhaps things are different for a suitably *ideal* reasoner; for perhaps a person who is *aware* of believing *A* on the basis of *B* and *B* on the basis of *C* (and who has intellectual powers of an appropriate order) will also believe *A* on the basis of *C*. But there is no reason to think transitivity thus required for us ordinary mortals. So this isn't the answer.

But now recall (by way of making progress toward the answer) that warrant comes in degrees; some of my beliefs, obviously, have more warrant than others. (The belief that it *looks from here* as if that peak is triangular will have a higher degree of warrant, for me, than the proposition that it really *is* triangular.)

According to the typical foundationalist, a proposition can have or acquire warrant in at least two ways. On the one hand, it can be properly basic, can achieve warrant just by being accepted in the right circumstances; on the other, it can acquire warrant by virtue of *warrant transfer,* by virtue of being believed on the basis of some other proposition that already has warrant.[15] The *degree* of warrant enjoyed by a nonbasic belief will depend on at least two factors: the degree of warrant enjoyed by the propositions on the basis of which it is believed, and the strength of the supports relation holding between it and them. In the extreme case, a proposition *B* believed on the basis of a proposition *A* may have as much warrant as *A* itself—perhaps where *A* obviously and self-evidently entails *B*. (If you tell me that you are thirty-five years old, my belief that you are over thirty, even if based only on my belief that you are thirty-five, may enjoy as much warrant, for me, as does the belief that you are thirty-five.) In other cases the warranted proposition may display much less warrant than the warrant-conferring proposition; but in *no* case will the warrantee enjoy *greater* warrant than the warrantor. If my warrant for a proposition *A* arises from my believing it on the basis of another proposition *B*, then my warrant for *A* cannot exceed my warrant for *B*.

Here two caveats are necessary. First, a proposition believed on the basis of another may have a higher degree of warrant than that other by virtue of deriving some of its warrant from other sources. Suppose I have a relatively dim or vague memory of having seen Paul at the New Year's Eve party two months ago; you tell me that you distinctly remember seeing Eleanor at the party, and I know that Eleanor seldom attends parties without Paul. Then my belief that Paul was at the party is based partly on my beliefs that you saw Eleanor there and that she seldom attends parties without Paul; for my warrant for believing the proposition in question is greater than it would have been had I had only my memory to go on. It therefore receives part of its warrant from being believed on the basis of the propositions that Eleanor was there and that she never goes to parties without Paul. Nevertheless, it may have a higher degree of warrant, for me, than is enjoyed by either of those propositions; for it also

15This is so according to the *typical* foundationalist; there is of course the special case of foundationalism (perhaps scarcely deserving the name) according to which all beliefs are properly basic and there is no warrant transfer; on this version everything is foundations and there is no superstructure.

receives some warrant, for me, from my memory of having seen Paul there, dim and vague as that memory may be. The foundationalist need not hold, therefore, that if A is believed on the basis of B, then the warrant of A cannot exceed that of B; he holds instead that, if A's warrant is derived *entirely* from its being believed on the basis of B, then its warrant cannot exceed B's.

Second, things are a bit more complicated when we turn to the case where my warrant for a proposition A arises from my believing it on the basis of *several* propositions—$B_1, \ldots, B_n$, say. The foundationalist will not hold that my warrant for A cannot exceed my warrant for the *conjunction* of the B_i. Of course for *some* propositions believed on the basis of others—conjunctions of those others, for example—this would be no more than the sober truth; but for others—disjunctions of the B_i, for example—it is plainly false. Nor will he want to hold that A's warrant cannot exceed the warrant of the least warranted of the B_i: my warrant for a disjunction $B_1 \ v \ B_2$ may derive entirely from its being believed on the basis of B_1 and B_2, but its warrant may nonetheless exceed theirs.[16] About all the foundationalist can say generally here is that if the warrant of a proposition A derives entirely from its being believed on the basis of the B_is, then A's warrant will be a function of the warrant of the B_is, together with the degree to which they support A; and in no case can A have more warrant than that of the disjunction of the B_is.

In sum, when a belief B enjoys an increase or access of warrant by being believed on the basis of other propositions, we have *warrant transfer* from a belief that already has it to another. And here we meet a seventh foundationalist thesis, one crucial to the whole foundationalist picture:

(VII)   Warrant does not increase just by virtue of warrant transfer.

We are now in a position to see more clearly why circular reasoning is objectionable from a foundationalist point of view. For the sake of simplicity, suppose we confine our attention to the special case where A_0 is believed solely on the basis of A_1, A_1 solely on the basis of $A_2, \ldots, A_{n-1}$ on the basis of A_n, and A_n on the basis of A_0; and let us add that none of the A_i receives any warrant from any source other than its being believed on the basis of A_{i-1}. (The application to the more general case is easy enough to make.) Say that B is *directly warranted* by A if B is believed on the basis of A and gets all of its warrant by virtue of being believed on the basis of A. Then what we have here is a *circular chain* (a chain circular with respect to the *directly warrants* relation): a finite set of propositions A_0 to A_n (ordered by the *directly warrants* relation) such that for any A_i ($i \neq n$), A_i is directly warranted by A_{i+1}, and A_n is directly warranted by A_0. Say further that, for any member A and B of the chain, A *gets all its warrant from B* if and only if A is directly warranted by B or A is directly

---

[16]I therefore erred when in "Coherentism and the Evidentialist Objection to Theistic Belief," p. 121, I wrote, "The foundationalist need not hold, therefore, that if A is believed on the basis of $B_1, \ldots, B_n$, then the warrant of A cannot exceed that of any of the B_i; he holds instead that if A's warrant for S is derived *entirely* from its being believed on the basis of the B_i, then its warrant cannot exceed any of theirs."

warranted by some proposition that gets all its warrant from B. It is clear, first of all, that if a proposition gets all its warrant from *itself*, then it gets no warrant at all; a proposition that gets all its warrant from itself has no warrant.

It is clear, second, that this relation—the gets-all-its-warrant-from relation—is transitive. For suppose C gets all its warrant from B and B gets all its warrant from A. If C is directly warranted by B, then it follows immediately that C gets all its warrant from A; so suppose C is not directly warranted by B. Consider the segment of the chain from B to C (inclusive). Clearly $B + 1$, the proposition that is directly warranted by B, gets all its warrant from A; but then the same will go for $B + 2$, the proposition directly warranted by $B + 1$, and so on all the way to C. Thus C gets all its warrant from A. This relation, therefore, is transitive. But then it follows that, in the circle in question, A_0 will get all its warrant from itself. As we have seen, in that case A_0 has no warrant at all; and the same will go for each of the other members of the circular chain. It is for these reasons, therefore, that the foundationalist rejects circular reasoning. As he sees it, a noetic structure that displays a circle in its basis relation displays a defect—a warrant defect.

II. Coherentism

According to foundationalism, then, a proper noetic structure will not contain a circle in its basis relation; and this is because warrant does not arise just by way of warrant transfer. Current lore has it, however, that the coherentist does not object to circular reasoning at all, provided the circle is large enough. What the coherentist claims (so we are told) is that in a proper noetic structure, every belief is accepted on the evidential basis of other beliefs; since the number of beliefs any of us has is finite, it follows that in such a structure there will be circles in the basis relationship; that, however, is no barrier to their having warrant, if the resulting circles are sufficiently large; and indeed it is in just such circles that warrant arises.

Now this is not at all easy to believe. The intuition relied upon by the foundationalist here—that circular reasoning cannot produce warrant—is very strong.[17] First, it seems wholly obvious that even if a person *could* believe a proposition on the evidential basis of itself, this maneuver would confer no warrant whatever upon that proposition. Suppose I believe that my dog is an alien from outer space, and suppose I could manage, somehow, to start believing this proposition on the basis—the immediate evidential basis—of *itself*. Surely this belief would not thereupon acquire a greater degree of warrant for me than it had before I executed this dubious maneuver. So if the belief in

---

[17]Thus Richard Fumerton: "many philosophers seem not to be quite so squeamish about moving in circles, particularly if the circles are 'big' enough. Still, the idea is difficult to swallow. If someone responds to our request for his justification supporting P by appeal to E, then supports E by appeal to F and F by appeal to P, we feel that he has somehow missed the point of our request for his justification. We feel no more satisfied with his answer than if he had greeted our original request with silence and a knowing wink." *Metaphysical and Epistemological Problems of Perception* (Lincoln: University of Nebraska Press, 1985), p. 43.

question has no warrant for me apart from what accrues to it by virtue of standing in the believed-on-the-basis-of relationship, then in this case it has no warrant at all. Say that a circular chain of the sort under consideration is *of unit circumference* if the set of beliefs involved is a unit set; and say more generally that it is of circumference *n* if the set of beliefs involved is *n*-membered. Then clearly a circle of unit circumference confers no warrant upon its member. But surely the same goes for a circle of circumference 2. If at first I believe both *A* and *B* and then manage to believe each on the basis of the other, I am no better off, epistemically speaking, than I was at first. (If I accept special relativity solely on the basis of the muon decay phenomena and believe in muon decay solely on the basis of special relativity, then neither has any warrant for me at all.) And how could it help to increase the size of the circle? If a circle of circumference *n* does not produce warrant, surely the same will go for a circle of circumference *n* + 1.[18] Warrant cannot magically arise just by virtue of a large evidential circle. (If I go around the circle twice, do I get twice as much warrant?) If the coherentist really holds that circular reasoning is a source of warrant, then his views are unlikely indeed.

A. Coherentism Characterized

But why saddle him with anything so miserably implausible? There is a much more charitable way to construe his characteristic claim. He should not be seen as endorsing circular reasoning or making an implausible remark about the properties of the basis relation; he isn't really claiming that the *basis relation* is a source of warrant. Nor does he hold that the basis relation in a rational noetic structure can sometimes be circular. His suggestion, instead, is that coherence is the sole source of warrant. *He is instead pointing to a condition under which a belief is properly basic*—a condition under which a belief acquires warrant without being accepted on the evidential basis of other beliefs. On his view, a belief *B* is properly basic for a person *S* if and only if *B* appropriately coheres with the rest of *S*'s noetic structure (or with some part of it, or with an appropriately purified version of it, or some part of *that*).[19] If a proposition *B* coheres

[18]In any event, could I not simply interpolate as many items as I need to get a large enough circle? For any proposition *A*, there will be arbitrarily many propositions truth functionally equivalent to *A*; so there will be circular chains of arbitrary length where *A* is a member of the chain and where each *A* + *i* is truth functionally equivalent to *A*. (We can add, if we like, that no member of the chain is *obviously* or trivially equivalent to any other member.) No doubt the coherentist will be able to add a qualification parrying this particular suggestion; but for any such qualification, sufficient ingenuity, one suspects, will produce another similar problem evading it.

[19]Lehrer therefore speaks ("The Coherence Theory of Knowledge") in this connection of my *verific* doxastic system: my doxastic system minus the false beliefs it contains. There are of course many other possibilities. We could take it that what counts here is my *unsullied* noetic structure: the noetic structure I would have if I were a disinterested seeker after truth, undistracted by pride, ambition, hatred, lust, and the like; or my *truth-augmented* structure: the result of removing all false beliefs, substituting their negations, and making other required changes.

It is also worth noting that the account can be generalized: one can be a coherentist with respect to *knowledge,* or *scientific* knowledge, or *certainty,* or the degree of warrant required for *proper basicality* (if that's different from the other three) and so on.

with my noetic structure, then *B* is warranted for me; its warrant does not arise, however, by virtue of my believing it *on the basis of* the rest of my noetic structure, so that those other propositions are my *evidence*—deductive, inductive, or abductive—for *B*. Indeed, if, for any proposition *A* I believe, I accept *A* on the basis of the rest of what I believe, then my noetic structure would contain a host of tight basis circles; for then I would believe *A* on the basis of $B_1, \ldots, B_n$ and each of the B_i on the basis of *A* together with the rest of the B_i. (Of course, if we added a dimension and spoke not of *circular* but of *cylindrical* reasoning, then the cylinders in question could be of considerable *height*, even if only of circumference 2.)

So the coherentist does not really tout circular (or cylindrical) reasoning. What he does instead is suggest an unusual condition for proper basicality, a new source of warrant: he holds that a belief is properly basic for me if and only if it appropriately coheres with the rest of my noetic structure. A *pure* coherentist resolutely rejects warrant transmission altogether; for her, all propositions that enjoy warrant in a noetic structure are basic in that structure. Deduction, induction, and abduction may indeed figure, in one way or another, as elements in the coherence relation, but warrant does not get transmitted by the basis relation from one proposition to another. Of course, a coherentist need not be a *pure* coherentist; she can instead embrace an impure or mixed variety. She could hold, for example, that the *source* of warrant is coherence but add that warrant is sometimes transferred via the basis relation. Thus I may be warranted in my belief that some horses have quirky personalities by virtue of believing that proposition on the basis of my belief that Clyde is a horse and has a quirky personality; and I may be warranted in that latter belief by virtue of its coherence with the rest of my noetic structure. Global coherentism is compatible with local foundationalism; the view that coherence alone is the source of warrant is compatible with the view that warrant is sometimes transmitted. What is really characteristic of coherentism is not a view about the *transmission* of warrant but a view about its *source*. Seen from the present perspective, therefore, the coherentist reveals her true colors as a nonstandard foundationalist with unusual views about what is properly basic.[20]

The pure coherentist holds that all warranted propositions in a noetic structure are basic in that structure; no warrant gets transmitted. The impure

[20]Somewhat similar views about the essential nature of coherentism may be expressed by Ernest Sosa in "The Raft and the Pyramid," in *Midwest Studies in Philosophy*, Vol. V, 1980, ed. Peter French, Theodore E. Uehling, Jr., and Howard Wettstein (Minneapolis: University of Minnesota Press, 1980), p. 18. Coherentism can thus be seen as a special case of axiological Chisholmian internalism, the special case where the value in question is coherence between the belief in question and the doxastic component (or something closely related to it) of the evidential base. Of course, the coherentist may resist this way of characterizing his view—not because it is inaccurate, but because (as at any rate the pure coherentist sees things) the basis relation is epistemologically irrelevant, as is the distinction between those beliefs that are basic and those that are not. A belief has warrant if and only if it appropriately coheres; why add these irrelevancies about the basis relation? One sees her point; still, the view suggested is indeed a (limiting) case of foundationalism: one in which in a proper noetic structure, no beliefs are accepted on the evidential basis of other beliefs, so that all are basic and properly basic.

coherentist holds that some propositions may get their warrant by virtue of being believed on the basis of others; but the ultimate source of the warrant in question is coherence. Both accept the view that coherence is the *only* source of warrant; and this is the central coherentist claim. According to the ancient or medieval foundationalist, perception and self-evidence or reason are sources of warrant. The modern classical foundationalist replaces perception by introspection; Reid restores perception and adds testimony, memory, sympathy, induction, and others. And the coherentist, by contrast, casts her lot with coherence. She holds that coherence alone is a source of warrant.

This is the source of a fateful consequence: on the coherentist view, a belief acquires no warrant by virtue of its relation to experience. The fact that I am indeed being appeared to redly confers no warrant, either on my belief that I am perceiving something red or even my belief that I am being appeared to redly; the fact that the corresponding conditional of *modus ponens* seems to me self-evident confers no warrant, for me, on my belief that that proposition is true; the fact that I find myself powerfully impelled to believe that I had an orange for breakfast, that this memory belief seems *right*—that fact confers no warrant, for me, on that belief. What confers warrant on these beliefs, if indeed they are warranted for me, is no more and no less than their coherence with the appropriate body of beliefs.

B. Coherentism Rejected

Coherentism, therefore, is a special case (a *very* special case) of foundationalism: the variety according to which the only source of warrant is coherence. Hence the characteristic coherentist claim that all beliefs are on an epistemic par; all stand equally before the bar of coherence; and, in case of failure of coherence, all are equally liable to revision. The ordinary foundationalist, of course, balks at this excess of egalitarian fervor (as he sees it); relative to a given set of circumstances, he says, some beliefs are privileged, acquiring warrant just by virtue of being formed or sustained in those circumstances. Thus a perceptual belief—the belief that I see a tree, for example—may have warrant for me, and get it from circumstances having little to do with coherence; it is, we may say, a *starting point* for thought. (It does not follow that it is unrevisable, incorrigible, indefeasible, or certain; what follows is only that it gets at least *some* warrant in some fashion other than by way of coherence.)

Coherentism is clearly mistaken. Note first that coherentist theories are what Pollock calls "doxastic" theories; they hold that the warrant or positive epistemic status of a belief is determined solely by the relations *that* belief bears to *other* beliefs. If you hold precisely the same beliefs in two different circumstances, then any belief you hold in both circumstances will enjoy the same degree of warrant in each circumstance; the nondoxastic circumstances do not matter.[21] The coherentist claims that coherence is *sufficient* for warrant, and

---

[21]Pollock errs, however, when he goes on to add that "no one even considered denying it [the claim that warrant is determined solely by relations to other beliefs] until fairly recently"; see his *Contemporary Theories of Knowledge* (Totowa, N.J.: Rowman and Littlefield, 1986), p. 19. The

necessary for it, in that a proposition has warrant for me if and only if it is coherent with my noetic structure or appropriately (deductively, inductively, or abductively) follows from propositions that are coherent with my noetic structure.

I think we can see that she is mistaken on both counts: coherence is neither necessary nor sufficient for warrant. As to sufficiency: it seems wholly clear that a person's noetic structure might be thoroughly coherent even though some of her beliefs have no warrant at all. Oliver Sacks recounts the case of the Lost Mariner, who suffered from Korsakov's syndrome, a profound and permanent devastation of memory caused by alcoholic destruction of the mammillary bodies of the brain. He completely forgot a thirty-year stretch of his life, believing that he was 19 years old when in fact he was 49; he believed it was 1945 when in fact it was 1975.[22] His beliefs (we may stipulate) were coherent; but many of them, due to this devastating pathology, had little or no warrant.

Or consider someone *S* who, by virtue of some noetic malfunction (due to tumor, Cartesian demon, or Alpha Centaurian) of which he is not aware, believes, whenever he is appeared to redly, that no one else is ever appeared to redly. (Perhaps you think this state of affairs a bit bizarre and unlikely; but what is required is only that it be possible in the broadly logical sense.) Add that *S*'s beliefs, on these occasions, are coherent—coherent in any reasonable sense a coherentist might propose. Nevertheless his noetic structure is grossly defective and his belief lacks warrant. *S* may be *deontologically justified* in this belief; he may be within his rights in accepting it (perhaps it is not even within his power to reject or withhold it): it may be that there are no noetic duties he has flouted. This belief may also be rational in the Foley sense (see chapter 7, p. 132): perhaps the disorder is so deep-seated that even if he reflected long and hard, he would retain his peculiar beliefs, becoming ever more confirmed in them. Nevertheless the belief in question has little or no warrant for him.

Examples can be multiplied. Timothy is a young artist from Firth, Nebraska, with an intense (indeed, pathologically inordinate) admiration of Picasso. Waiting at a supermarket checkout, he idly picks up a copy of the *National Enquirer,* reading therein that Picasso, contrary to what most of us have always thought, was really an alien from outer space. As a result of his overwhelming and diseased veneration of Picasso, Timothy forms the belief that he, too, is really an alien from outer space, having been deserted by his Alpha Centaurian parents on an exploratory field trip to Nebraska. The rest of his beliefs fall into a coherent pattern with this one. His belief that he is an alien from outer space, however, clearly has little or no warrant for him—and even if it happens, by some enormous coincidence, that in fact he *is* an alien, he certainly doesn't know that he is.

---

whole Aristotelian tradition and the whole medieval tradition at least implicitly sees warrant as a function of *experience* as well as belief; the same surely goes for Descartes and Locke (and their epigone) who see the warrant attaching to a self-evident belief, for example, as arising from the phenomenal conditions—that "clarity and distinctness" (Descartes) or "evident luster" and "clarity and brightness" (Locke)—that accompany consideration of it.

[22]In *The Man Who Mistook His Wife for a Hat* (New York: Harper and Row, 1985), pp. 23ff.

Finally, consider the Case of the Epistemically Inflexible Climber. Ric is climbing Guide's Wall, on Storm Point in the Grand Tetons; having just led the difficult next to last pitch, he is seated on a comfortable ledge, bringing his partner up. He believes that Cascade Canyon is down to his left, that the cliffs of Mount Owen are directly in front of him, that there is a hawk gliding in lazy circles 200 feet below him, that he is wearing his new *Fire* rock shoes, and so on. His beliefs, we may stipulate, are coherent. Now add that Ric is struck by a wayward burst of high-energy cosmic radiation. This induces a cognitive malfunction; his beliefs become fixed, no longer responsive to changes in experience. No matter what his experience, his beliefs remain the same. At the cost of considerable effort his partner gets him down and, in a desperate last-ditch attempt at therapy, takes him to the opera in nearby Jackson, where the New York Metropolitan Opera on tour is performing *La Traviata*. Ric is appeared to in the same way as everyone else there; he is inundated by wave after wave of golden sound. Sadly enough, the effort at therapy fails; Ric's beliefs remain fixed and wholly unresponsive to his experience; he still believes that he is on the belay ledge at the top of the next to last pitch of Guide's Wall, that Cascade Canyon is down to his left, that there is a hawk sailing in lazy circles 200 feet below him, that he is wearing his new *Fire* rock shoes, and so on. Furthermore, since he believes the very same things he believed when seated on the ledge, his beliefs are coherent. But surely they have little or no warrant for him. The reason is cognitive malfunction; his beliefs are not appropriately responsive to his experience. Again, he may be deontologically justified in accepting those beliefs; they may also have Foley justification. But they have no warrant for him. Clearly, then, coherence is not sufficient for positive epistemic status.

But neither is it necessary. It is entirely possible that one of my beliefs should have considerable warrant, even if it is neither coherent with the rest of my noetic structure nor appropriately follows from ones that are coherent with it. A necessary falsehood is presumably incoherent with the relevant body of beliefs; but couldn't a necessary falsehood have warrant for me? You are a habitually authoritative mathematician; you tell me T is a theorem, and produce for it a 'proof' so subtle that you yourself cannot see its fallacy; the proof is fallacious, however, and in fact T is a necessary falsehood; but doesn't T have warrant for both of us? (Didn't Frege's axioms for set theory have warrant for him before he received Russell's fateful letter?) Perhaps you are suspicious of this example: you think little should rest on examples resting on necessary falsehood. Very well, there are plenty of examples that do not involve necessary falsehoods. You are an eminent but idiosyncratic Oxford epistemologist; I an unduly impressionable undergraduate. You offer me a battery of complex and subtly powerful arguments for the conclusion that no one is ever appeared to redly. I am unable to withstand the force of your argumentation and am utterly convinced. The next day I am walking along High Street, reflecting on the significance of what you have proved to me, when suddenly a great large double-deck red bus runs up on the sidewalk just behind me. I turn around in terror, see the bus, and am (violently) appeared to redly; since I have been reflecting about these matters, I notice (that is, believe) that I am thus appeared to. Unless my noetic structure undergoes instant metamorphosis (and we can stipulate that it does not), my belief that I am appeared to redly will be incoherent with my noetic structure; nevertheless it will have a considerable degree of warrant.

Another example: I am an arboreal expert giving a lecture on trees; among other things I claim that no oak trees grow in the state of Washington. Naturally I believe that I have never seen an oak tree in any part of that state. I suddenly notice you in the audience. Seeing you jogs my memory; I seem to remember an occasion on which you and I noticed a particularly luxuriant oak flourishing on the campus of Western Washington University in Bellingham. At the moment when it seems to me that I do so remember, the proposition that I have seen an oak tree in Washington has warrant for me, despite the fact that it does not then cohere with my noetic structure. I will find myself believing that I have indeed seen an oak tree in Washington; if for some reason my other beliefs do not alter, the belief in question will not be coherent with my noetic structure. Nevertheless it then has warrant for me, despite the fact that it does not thus cohere. And the change that is called for, of course, is not that of rejecting or trying to reject the memory belief in question; what is called for is revising the rest of my noetic structure in such a way that it is coherent with the belief in question. Coherence, therefore, is neither necessary nor sufficient for warrant.[23]

So coherentism is false; coherence is neither necessary nor sufficient for warrant, and there are sources of warrant in addition to coherence. It does not follow, of course, that coherence is not a source of warrant; what follows is only that it is not the *sole* source of warrant. A foundationalist can accept coherence as *a* source of warrant—one source among others. A perceptual belief that doesn't fit with the rest of what I believe may be quite properly rejected. Climbing Guide's Wall again, Ric seems to see what looks like a cow on a two-foot ledge 200 feet away and 300 feet off the ground. Wise as he is in the ways of cattle, he realizes that there could hardly be a cow there, rejects the testimony of his senses on the grounds of coherence considerations, and concludes that the light or the angle of vision must be deceiving. Here the foundationalist could gracefully concede that the beliefs *there is no cow on that ledge* and *appearances are deceptive* get warrant by virtue of coherence with the appropriate body of Ric's beliefs; and here coherence considerations overcome or outweigh the impulse to the perceptual belief in question. Of course if he climbed over to the ledge and from a distance of 6 feet, say, it *still* appeared to be a cow, he would have to draw a different conclusion—perhaps that the local climbers are unusually playful. Here coherence considerations are outweighed by the powerful impulse toward believing the proposition *there is a cow on that*

---

[23]These examples, I think, are decisive against Laurence BonJour's coherentism (see chapter 5). They are also decisive against the coherentism of Keith Lehrer's *Knowledge* (see my "Coherentism and the Evidentialist Objection to Theistic Belief," pp. 129–37). With minor modifications they pay the same compliment to the view Lehrer suggests in "The Coherence Theory of Knowledge"; we need add only that, in each case, the belief in question is coherent with the subject's *verific* doxastic system, which is his doxastic system minus the false beliefs it contains.

ledge provided by the sort of experience that goes with clearly seeing a large cow from a distance of 6 feet.

Coherence considerations obviously have their own force and sometimes produce warrant: at any rate it is no part of foundationalism as such to deny this suggestion. The foundationalist denies that coherence is the *only* source of warrant, but (at any rate *qua* foundationalist) he has no stake in maintaining that it isn't a source of warrant at all.[24]

III. Classical Foundationalism

Coherentism is therefore to be rejected: coherence is not the only source of warrant. But what are the other sources? According to modern classical foundationalism (an extraordinarily influential picture dominating Western epistemological thought for nearly three centuries), they are *reason* and *experience*— but then both reason and experience narrowly construed. On this view a proposition is properly basic if and only if it is either self-evident or else appropriately about one's own immediate experience—specifying how one is appeared to, for example. Any other propositions that are acceptable for you must be ones that are appropriately supported by propositions of these kinds.[25]

---

[24]There is further discussion of coherentism in chapter 9 of my *Warrant and Proper Function* (New York: Oxford University Press, 1993).

[25]Here and elsewhere I am of course obliged to make sweeping pronouncements that in fact require qualification, nuance, and documentation. What I display as 'the classical foundationalist' is really a sort of type or amalgam that may do less than exact justice to any particular classical foundationalist. Furthermore, many or most of the thinkers mentioned don't clearly speak with a single voice: there are ambiguities, conflicting tendencies, apparent inconsistencies. Thus Locke (for example) speaks of the "certain knowledge" he has of the proposition that his idea "of *Light,* or the *Sun*" is caused in him by some external agency (*An Essay Concerning Human Understanding,* ed. A. C. Fraser (New York: Dover, 1953), IV, 11, 5, p. 329). Say that an 'experiential proposition for *S*' is one that is appropriately about *S*'s experience: then the proposition of which he claims certain knowledge doesn't seem clearly to be self-evident, or experiential for him or an obvious deductive consequence of such propositions. There are a variety of possibilities here; but the fact is, I think, Locke does believe that this knowledge follows immediately from experiential and self-evident propositions. That he *has* this idea of light or the sun is an experiential proposition for him, as is the fact that his having it is in certain conditions outside his voluntary control. He also seems to think it self-evident that if his having this idea is not in those circumstances under his control, then it is caused in him by some external agency: "So there is a manifest difference, between the *Ideas* laid up in my memory; (over which, if they were there only, I should have constantly the same power to dispose of them, and lay them by at my pleasure) and those which force themselves upon me, and I cannot avoid having. And therefore it must needs be some exteriour cause, and the brisk acting of some Objects without me, whose efficacy I cannot resist, that produces those Ideas in my Mind, whether I will, or no" (ibid.). (Alternatively, he may think that the second proposition is, while not self-evident, extremely probable with respect to what is self-evident; he may also think self-evidence comes in degrees, and that the proposition in question, while indeed self-evident, does not display the highest degree of that quality [or quantity].)

It may seem implausible to think the proposition in question is in fact self-evident. The implausibility can perhaps be mitigated by taking the sense of "exteriour" or "Objects without me" to be the same as that of 'external' in the externalism–internalism debate. (I do not mean to

Classical foundationalism has fallen on evil days; and rightly so. As Reid saw and argued, the whole development of modern philosophy from Descartes to Hume shows that classical foundationalism 'taken to its logical conclusion', as they say, yields the consequence that very little, far less than we would ordinarily think, is epistemically acceptable for us. None of the propositions we believe about ordinary material objects, or the past, or other persons—none of these propositions seems to be appropriately supported by propositions that are properly basic according to the classical foundationalist's standards for proper basicality; the latter offer precious little by way of evidence for the former. But these propositions certainly seem to be acceptable for us: why, then, should we accept classical foundationalism? If there were powerful and compelling arguments for it, then perhaps we should have to grit our teeth and accept it; but the powerful arguments are not forthcoming. So classical foundationalism has fallen into disrepute if not desuetude. I don't propose to add my voice to that of the howling mob, except to say that many forms of classical foundationalism look to be self-referentially incoherent. According to these forms, a proposition *A* is acceptable for me if and only if it is either properly basic or believed on the evidential basis of propositions that are (1) properly basic, and (2) support *A*. But this proposition itself is not properly basic by this criterion: it is neither self-evident nor appropriately about someone's immediate experience, and (subject to the indeterminateness of what is to count as support here) it is certainly hard to see that it is appropriately supported by propositions that do meet that condition.[26]

So classical foundationalism fails. This fact has been widely celebrated (sometimes with a sort of foolish extravagance); it has also been widely hailed as requiring rejection of all of epistemology, or even all of traditional philosophy, or even the very idea of *truth* itself. In a moment of anguish, Dostoyevski blurted that if God does not exist, everything is possible. Richard Rorty and his friends go him one (or more) better and without the anguish: if classical foundationalism is wrong, there is no such thing as truth. These intemperate reactions to the demise of classical foundationalism betray agreement with it at a deep level: agreement that the only security or warrant for our beliefs must arise by way of evidential relationship to beliefs that are certain: self-evident or about our own mental states. But why think a thing like that? And why follow these enthusiasts into that grand confusion between metaphysics and epistemology, confusing truth with our access to it, announcing the demise of the latter as a consequence of the failure of classical foundationalism? Here we have confusion twice confounded: first, confusion of truth with our access to it and, second, confusion of knowledge with Cartesian certainty. But as to the first, truth owes nothing to our access to it; and as to the second, Cartesian certainty is indeed a will-o'-the-wisp, but nothing follows for knowledge.

If classical foundationalism is to be rejected, however, if there are sources of

---

suggest, of course, that the terms in question have just *one* sense in that debate.) So taken, what Locke is saying is that if the occurrence of an idea is not under my voluntary control, then it does indeed have a cause, but is not caused by agencies to which I have the sort of epistemic access the internalist requires.

[26]See my "Reason and Belief in God," pp. 60ff.

warrant in addition to reason and experience (construed thus narrowly), if it is
not the case that the only propositions properly basic for me are those that are
either self-evident or about my own immediate experience, then what other
sorts of propositions *are* properly basic? According to Thomas Reid, there is
nothing but an arbitrary partiality in awarding this status only to propositions
of those two sorts; he proposed that certain beliefs acquired by way of perception are also properly basic, as are beliefs acquired by way of memory, or by
way of induction, as well as beliefs about the mental states of others acquired by
way of what he calls "sympathy," and still others. In *Warrant and Proper
Function* I argue that these and other sorts of beliefs are properly basic. There
are still other candidates: perhaps moral or ethical propositions are properly
basic in this way. According to John Calvin, as I understand him, certain beliefs
about God are also properly basic; the *sensus divinitatis* takes its place along
with perception, reason, memory, sympathy, and induction as a source of
warrant.[27]

There is therefore no shortage of candidates. In *Warrant and Proper Function* I shall examine some of the candidates; for now, however, we must continue our scrutiny of coherentism. We therefore turn, in the next chapter, to the
impressive work of Laurence BonJour.

---

[27]Ibid., pp. 65ff. In *Warranted Christian Belief,* I shall explore Calvin's suggestion.

5

BonJourian Coherentism

Coherentism pure and unalloyed shows little promise; but it is important not to leave matters at such an abstract level. Any real, flesh-and-blood coherentist will have her own particular insights; she will make modifications, adaptations, qualifications, and additions; problems, difficulties, and inadequacies of coherentism *überhaupt* might not afflict certain developments of it. Furthermore, a view that was fundamentally coherentist but imported noncoherentist elements—an impure (contaminated?) coherentism, we might say—could be more plausible and enlightening than coherentism pure and unalloyed. Laurence BonJour's *The Structure of Empirical Knowledge*[1] presents just such a chastened coherentism; in this chapter I shall explain and examine it.[2]

I. BonJourian Coherentism Explained

BonJour's book is entitled *The Structure of* Empirical *Knowledge* (my emphasis); in it he aims to work out a satisfying coherentist account of (roughly speaking) perceptual knowledge and the *a posteriori* elements of common sense and scientific knowledge. (As we shall see, he endorses a traditional foundationalist account of *a priori* knowledge.) BonJour sees the traditional justified true belief account of knowledge as "at least approximately correct" (p. 3); he therefore concentrates his attention on the question, *What is justification?* But if the justified true belief account of knowledge is at least approximately correct, then justification (as BonJour explains it) is at least approximately what distinguishes true belief from knowledge; if so, justification is at least very close to warrant or positive epistemic status. I shall therefore take BonJour as offering an account of warrant.[3]

---

[1]Cambridge: Harvard University Press, 1985. (Unless otherwise stipulated, page references in this chapter are to this work.)

[2]In writing this chapter I am indebted to BonJour for comments that were both penetrating and gracious.

[3]This is perhaps less than wholly accurate; there is a question about how he thinks of Gettier problems (see p. 111).

A. *Justification and Warrant*

Suppose we begin by asking what justification *is* as BonJour sees it. What is its basic nature and what sort of animal is it? "The goal of our distinctively cognitive endeavors," he says, "is *truth:* we want our beliefs to correctly and accurately depict the world" (p. 7). (Apparently he thinks it is we ourselves who set this goal for ourselves as cognitive agents.) He continues:

> We cannot, in most cases at least, bring it about directly that our beliefs are true, but we can presumably bring it about directly (though perhaps only in the long run) that they are epistemically justified. And, *if our standards of epistemic justification are appropriately chosen,* bringing it about that our beliefs are epistemically justified will also tend to bring it about, in the perhaps even longer run and with the usual slippage and uncertainty which our finitude mandates, that they are true. If epistemic justification were not conducive to truth in this way, if finding epistemically justified beliefs did not substantially increase the likelihood of finding true ones, then epistemic justification would be irrelevant to our main cognitive goal and of dubious worth. . . . Epistemic justification is therefore in the final analysis only an instrumental value, not an intrinsic one. (p. 8)

So we have the goal of seeking truth, and holding justified beliefs is a means (perhaps the only means available to us) for achieving that goal. BonJour next sounds a Lockean, Chisholmian note: this goal is apparently one we are *obliged* to have and strive to fulfill. At any rate it is irresponsible to neglect it:

> It follows that one's cognitive endeavors are epistemically justified only if and to the extent that they are aimed at this goal, which means very roughly that one accepts all and only those beliefs which one has good reason to think are true. To accept a belief in the absence of such a reason . . . is to neglect the pursuit of truth; such acceptance is, one might say, *epistemically irresponsible.* My contention here is that the idea of avoiding such irresponsibility, of being epistemically responsible in one's believings, is the core of the notion of epistemic justification. (p. 8)

A person is justified in her beliefs, therefore, if and only if she is epistemically responsible in her believings—that is, if and only if she is epistemically responsible in regulating and governing her belief acceptance and maintenance. But she governs her beliefs responsibly only if she accepts all and only those beliefs she has a good reason for thinking true.

Now the task of the epistemologist, says BonJour, is twofold: "The first part is to give an account of the standards of epistemic justification; and the second is to provide what I will call a *metajustification* for the proposed account by showing the proposed standards to be adequately truth conducive." (Here [pp. 11–12] he chides Chisholm for failing to produce such a metajustification; Chisholm gives an account of the standards of epistemic justification, but fails to show or even argue that the proposed standards are truth conducive.) But it isn't only the epistemologist who must come up with a metajustification:

> If a given putative knower is himself to be epistemically responsible in accepting beliefs in virtue of their meeting the standards of a given epistemological

account, then it seems to follow that an appropriate metajustification for those principles must, in principle at least, be available *to him*. For how can the fact that a belief meets those standards give that believer a reason for thinking that it is likely to be true (and thus an epistemically appropriate reason for accepting it) unless he himself knows that beliefs satisfying those standards are likely to be true? (p. 10)

For me to be justified in accepting a belief *A*, therefore, it is not sufficient that there *be* a good reason for believing *A*, or that *someone* have a good reason for it; I must myself (in principle, at any rate) have such a reason, and I must believe *A* on the basis of that good reason. This conception of justification or warrant gives BonJour a perspective from which to criticize what he takes to be the principal alternatives to the coherentist view he favors: traditional foundationalist accounts of warrant (chapter 2), and more recent externalist and reliabilist accounts of it (chapter 3). It is irresponsible and therefore unjustified to accept a belief unless one accepts that belief on the basis of a good reason for thinking it true; hence the foundationalist errs in holding that some beliefs are properly basic and acquire warrant just by virtue (say) of being formed in the right experiential circumstances. Similarly, the reliabilist errs in thinking that a belief can acquire warrant just by virtue of being formed by a reliable belief-producing process or mechanism; if you hold a belief but have no reason for thinking it true, then that belief is not justified and you are irresponsible in accepting it, even if as a matter of fact it is produced by a reliable process.

Of course, BonJour thinks warrant and coherence are intimately connected, but he does not *identify* the former with the latter: "What is at issue here is the connection between coherence and epistemic justification: why, if a system of empirical beliefs is coherent (and more coherent than any rival system), is it thereby justified *in the epistemic sense*, that is, why is it thereby likely to be true?" (p. 93). But if the issue is the connection between coherence and epistemic justification, then it will not be the case that justification (or warrant) just *is* coherence. No: to be justified is to be appropriately *responsible*—to be responsible with respect to the governance of belief formation and maintenance. It is obvious from our discussion of classical and post-classical Chisholmian internalism, I think, that warrant cannot possibly be related in just *that* way to epistemic responsibility (it can't be that, necessarily, a belief has warrant for me if and only if I am epistemically responsible in forming or maintaining it): clearly a person could be as responsible as you please and still (by virtue, perhaps, of cognitive dysfunction) hold beliefs that have little or no warrant for him. But BonJour adds a specific view as to what epistemic responsibility consists in: if a person governs his belief formation and maintenance responsibly, then he accepts a belief only if he has (or thinks he has) good reason to think that belief true. This, in turn, by an alchemy that isn't entirely easy to make out (p. 92), gets transmuted into the claim that what justifies a particular empirical belief is that it is a member of a coherent system of beliefs. Perhaps BonJour's thought here is that the only good reason I *could* have for thinking a particular empirical belief true is that it is a member of a coherent system of beliefs. In any event, "The justification of a particular empirical belief finally depends, not on other particular beliefs as the linear conception of justification would have it, but instead on the overall system and its coherence" (p. 92). As I understand the view, then, (a) a belief is justified for me if and only if I am responsible in forming or maintaining it; (b) I am responsible in forming or maintaining a belief if and only if I have a good reason for thinking that belief true; and (c) the only good reason for thinking an empirical belief true is that it is an element of a coherent system of beliefs.

B. Coherence

What, precisely, *is* coherence, and how does the fact that a belief is an element of a coherent system provide a good reason for thinking it true? "The main points are: first, coherence is not to be equated with mere consistency; second, coherence, as already suggested, has to do with the mutual inferability of the beliefs in the system; third, relations of explanation are one central ingredient in coherence, . . . and, fourth, coherence may be enhanced through conceptual change" (p. 95). BonJour goes on to state five principles governing coherence (pp. 95, 98):

(1)   A system of beliefs is coherent only if it is logically consistent,

(2)   A system of beliefs is coherent in proportion to its degree of probabilistic consistency,

(3)   The coherence of a system of beliefs is increased by the presence of inferential connections between its component beliefs and increased in proportion to the number and strength of such connections,

(4)   The coherence of a system of beliefs is diminished to the extent to which it is divided into subsystems of beliefs which are relatively unconnected to each other by inferential connections,

and

(5)   The coherence of a system of beliefs is decreased in proportion to the presence of unexplained anomalies in the believed content of the system.

These principles have a rough and ready initial clarity except perhaps for the second one: what is probabilistic consistency and inconsistency? The paradigm case: "Suppose that my system of beliefs contains both the belief that P and also the belief that it is extremely improbable that P. . . . it is . . . clear from an intuitive standpoint that a system which contains two such beliefs is significantly less coherent than it would be without them and thus that probabilistic consistency is a . . . factor determining coherence" (p. 95).

Many questions could be raised about these principles. The first principle, for example, seems initially unproblematic; in fact, however, it harbors several deep issues—issues we cannot properly pursue here. I shall mention just one. We may not be able to bring it about directly that our beliefs are true, says

BonJour, but at least we can bring it about directly that our beliefs are coherent (even if only "in the long run"). So (by this first principle) we can bring it about directly that our beliefs are consistent. But then what sort of consistency does the principle speak of? The best candidate, one thinks, would be consistency in the broadly logical sense—truth in some possible world. For, first, it would be wholly arbitrary to claim that consistency in first-order logic, say, is a necessary condition of coherence, while allowing that a coherent noetic structure might harbor mathematical impossibilities and necessary falsehoods of other kinds. Second, insofar as coherence is supposed to be "truth conducive," falsehood in every possible world is just as bad as inconsistency in first-order logic. But it is far from obvious that consistency in that broadly logical sense is any easier for us to attain than truth. Philosophical disputes, for example, are typically about noncontingent propositions—propositions that are necessarily true or necessarily false. In these cases, therefore, broadly logical consistency is exactly as easy to attain as truth; and in these cases truth, as the continuing disputes attest, is an elusive quarry indeed.

And in fact things are not a whole lot better if we stick to logical consistency taken more narrowly—taken as, say, consistency in first-order logic—as many of us (Frege, for example) have discovered to our sorrow. Is there any guarantee that if we try really hard, we will always be able to avoid such inconsistency, or always be able to discover and extirpate it, if we do happen to fall into it? Obviously not; I might try my level best over my entire lifetime, but by virtue of noetic malfunction have a system of beliefs in which first-order inconsistency runs absolutely riot. And even if we disregard noetic malfunction there is of course still no such guarantee. What is really involved in coherence, insofar as it is (broadly speaking) up to us whether we achieve it, is, presumably, not possibility in the broadly logical sense, nor consistency in first-order logic, but something weaker, something like absence of *obvious* impossibility, or perhaps impossibility that *would be* obvious after a certain degree of reflection.

The second principle is equally problematic and in fact thoroughly obscure. What sort of probability is at issue here? Not personal or subjective probability, presumably; so some variety of objective probability. But which variety? Statistical probability—the sort exemplified by *the probability that an American male will be 6 feet tall by the age of 14 is .08*—is what leaps immediately to mind. But there, on the face of it, anyway (and given what appear to be the plausible reference classes), what is improbable is surely the rule rather than the exception. That precisely *that* mosquito should bite you precisely when and where it does, that on your cross-country trip on December 23 at 4:13 P.M. you should be precisely where you are at that time, that there should be precisely the number of blades of grass in your backyard that in fact adorn it (to say nothing about their length, width, thickness, length of life, weight, color, and the like), that there should be just the number of cows that there are, that a given frog's egg should beat the odds and achieve froghood—either these things are all improbable in the relevant sense or else I have no idea what that relevant sense might be. But if improbability is in fact so rampant, why should I (or my noetic structure) suffer demerits for recognizing and recording it?

C. Other Requirements for Warrant

The remaining principles also have their problems. Still, they give us *some* guidance, and in any event perhaps we do not need a really precise and well worked out notion of coherence in order to carry the discussion further. But coherence, according to BonJour, is not the only thing that counts for justification; there are other requirements. First, the idea, of course, is that the belief in question must be a member of some *person's* coherent system of beliefs; the mere fact that one of my beliefs is a member of *some* coherent system of beliefs, whether or not it is *my* system of beliefs, confers no warrant on that belief.

Second, a system of beliefs capable of conferring warrant upon its members must also meet the "Observation Requirement":

> Thus, as a straightforward consequence of the idea that epistemic justification must be truth-conducive, a coherence theory of empirical justification must require that in order for the beliefs of a cognitive system to be even candidates for empirical justification, that system must contain laws attributing a high degree of reliability to a reasonable variety of cognitively spontaneous beliefs (including in particular those kinds of introspective beliefs which are required for the recognition of other cognitively spontaneous beliefs). (p. 141)

A belief is "cognitively spontaneous" when it is not acquired *via* inference but immediately, in the way in which memory beliefs and beliefs formed by sense perception and introspection are typically acquired. And a system whose members are candidates for justification must contain both beliefs that are cognitively spontaneous, and also laws according to which those beliefs are for the most part true (pp. 112–32 and 141–44).

Third, if the members of a system of beliefs are to be candidates for justification, that system must be coherent not only at the time in question, but over "the long run"; furthermore, it must be "stable"; that is to say, it must not undergo undue change from moment to moment; and finally it must "converge" to a stable system in which the only changes are those "allowed or even required by the general picture of the world thus presented" (p. 170).

> The point is that it is only in that latter sort of case—the case in which the belief system converges on and eventually presents a relatively stable long-run picture of the world, thus achieving coherence over time as well as at particular times—that the coherence of the system provides any strong reason for thinking that the component beliefs are thereby likely to be true. (p. 170)

(BonJour adds later on that the system in question must be more coherent than any alternative that also satisfies the Observation Requirement.) How long must this long run be? Presumably we aren't speaking of *the* long run (else a person could know what her name is only if she were immortal, which would yield a powerful epistemic argument for immortality); but (understandably enough) BonJour does not say how long a run is required. And finally, if *S*'s beliefs are to have justification, *S* must have "a reflective grasp" of the fact that his system of beliefs satisfies these conditions, "and this reflective grasp must be, ultimately but perhaps only very implicitly, *the* reason why he continues to accept the belief whose justification is in question" (p. 154).

D. The Metajustification

So S's belief that *p* is justified, has warrant, only if (a) S's noetic structure satisfies the Observation Requirement, displays a high degree of coherence (at the moment and in the long run), and is more coherent than any alternative that also satisfies the Observation Requirement, and (b) S continues to accept *p* because he "reflectively grasps" these facts about his system of beliefs. But even this is not enough to confer warrant upon S's beliefs. What is also required is that there be a *good argument* for the contention that a noetic structure's satisfying those conditions is "truth-conducive," as BonJour puts it. What could that argument be? This question assumes a certain urgency in that, as he sees the matter, *each* of us, if her beliefs are to attain justification, must in principle be able to tell that coherence is truth conducive: "If coherentism is to be even a dialectically interesting alternative, the coherentist justification must, in principle at least, be accessible to the believer himself" (p. 89). Further, each of us must be able to determine this *a priori* (p. 157). (It is no good examining a large number of beliefs from coherent noetic structures, noting that most are true and concluding that membership in a coherent noetic structure is truth conducive.) How is this supposed to work? What kind of coherentist justification is available to each of us? How is such a "justificatory argument" supposed to go?

As follows. Let *B* be one of my beliefs; and suppose *B* meets conditions (a) and (b) noted previously. Then there is an argument of the following sort for the conclusion that *B* is likely to be true:

(P1)   *B* is a member of my set of beliefs; and my set of beliefs is coherent and stable (in the long run) and meets the Observation Requirement ('long-run coherent' for short)

(P2)   Any belief that is a member of someone's long-run coherent set of beliefs is likely (i. e., more likely than not) to be true

So

(3)   *B* is likely to be true.

This argument has two premises; what is my justification for believing *them?*

1. The Second Premise

Consider first BonJour's argument for (P2). Here he argues that:

A system of beliefs which (a) remains coherent (and stable) over the long run and (b) continues to satisfy the Observation Requirement is likely, to a degree which is proportional to the degree of coherence (and stability) and the long-ness of the run, to correspond closely to independent reality. (pp. 170–71)

His crucial premise is:

> The best explanation, the likeliest to be true, for a system of beliefs remaining coherent (and stable) over the long run while continuing to satisfy the Observation Requirement is that (a) the cognitively spontaneous beliefs which are claimed, within the system, to be reliable, are systematically caused by the sorts of situations which are depicted by their content, and (b) the entire system of beliefs corresponds, within a reasonable degree of approximation, to the independent reality which it purports to describe; and the preferability of this explanation increases in proportion to the degree of coherence (and stability) and the longness of the run. (p. 171)

Let S be my system of beliefs; and suppose that S is long-run coherent. Then (a) and (b) together comprise what BonJour calls the "correspondence hypothesis" with respect to S; and "what needs to be shown," he says,

> is that the *correspondence hypothesis* is more likely to be true relative to the conditions indicated than is any alternative explanation. The underlying claim is that a system of beliefs for which the correspondence hypothesis was false would be unlikely to remain coherent (and continue to satisfy the Observation Requirement) unless it were revised in the direction of greater correspondence with reality—thereby destroying the stability of the original system and gradually leading to a new and stable system of beliefs for which the correspondence hypothesis is true. (p. 172)

Well, how *is* this to be shown, and shown *a priori*? What about the suggestions that I could be a brain in a vat, my beliefs being manipulated by an inquisitive Alpha Centaurian superscientist in such a way as to be coherent (and meet those other conditions), but mainly false? What about Descartes' suggestion that he might be a victim of a whimsically malevolent demon, so that although his beliefs form an appropriately coherent system, they are for the most part false? What about all the other possibilities involving cognitive malfunction—possibilities in which my beliefs are coherent but far from the truth? How are these hypotheses to be shown less probable, on the supposition that my system S of beliefs is coherent, than the correspondence hypothesis with respect to S? BonJour argues (pp. 183–84) that these are all less probable, *a priori*, than the correspondence hypothesis with respect to S. That I should be manipulated in this way by a demon or Alpha Centaurian is enormously improbable, where the probability involved is not statistical probability, but *a priori* probability:

> As already suggested, there seems to be only one real possibility at this point: just as the claim was made above that the elaborated chance hypothesis is antecedently extremely unlikely to be true, that its a priori probability or likelihood is extremely low, so also must an analogous claim be made about the elaborated demon hypothesis. (p. 184)

BonJour argues that the correspondence hypothesis, although itself "highly unlikely" (p. 186), is more probable than these various skeptical hypotheses;

that is, its *a priori* probability, though much less than one-half, is nonetheless considerably greater than that of any skeptical hypothesis. This argument is not at all easy to follow but crucially involves the following idea:

> There is available a complicated albeit schematic account in terms of biological evolution and to some extent also cultural and conceptual evolution which explains how cognitive beings whose spontaneous beliefs are connected with the world in the right way come to exist—an explanation which, speaking very intuitively, arises from within the general picture provided by . . . the correspondence hypothesis, rather than being imposed from the outside. (p. 187)

Given that the *a priori* probability of the correspondence hypothesis exceeds that of the skeptical hypotheses, he concludes that the conditional probability of the correspondence hypothesis on the proposition *S is long-run coherent* also exceeds the conditional probability of any skeptical hypothesis on that same proposition. It is not in general true, of course, that for a proposition *C*, if the prior probability of *A* exceeds the prior probability of *B,* then the conditional probability of *A* on *C* exceeds that of *B* on *C;* this does hold, however, where *A* and *B entail C,* and the skeptical and correspondence hypotheses can be stated so as to meet this condition.

2. *The First Premise*

So my justification for the second premise is essentially that I can see *a priori* that the *a priori* probability of the correspondence hypothesis with respect to *S* is greater than that of any skeptical hypothesis; but then the conditional probability of the correspondence hypothesis on the proposition *S is long-run coherent* is greater than that of any of the skeptical hypotheses on that proposition. But how about (P1)? What is my justification for believing that I do indeed believe *B,* that *B* is a member of my system of beliefs? If I need a justificatory reason for each of my empirical beliefs, I shall also need justification for *that.* And of course I must also believe, for some group of propositions $A_1, \ldots A_n$ that they comprise my system of beliefs; again, what is my justification for that? And what is my justification for the belief that $A_1, \ldots A_n$ form a coherent system?

With respect to the third question, the answer, presumably, is that one can determine *a priori* whether a given system of beliefs is coherent.[4] What about the first two questions? Here it is not easy to see precisely what BonJour has in mind. As far as I can see, however, he disclaims any view as to what sort of warrant or justification such beliefs as *I believe A_0* or *I believe each of $A_1, \ldots A_n$* have for me; as a matter of fact he doesn't seem to claim that such beliefs *have* warrant for me. He recognizes that the justificatory argument will be cogent for me only if I do know or justifiably believe such propositions: "But if the fact of coherence is to be accessible to the believer, it follows that he must somehow have an adequate grasp of his total system of beliefs, since it is coherence with this system which is at issue" (p. 102); and "though questions

[4]But see p. 109.

can be raised and answered with regard to particular aspects of my grasp of my system of beliefs, the *approximate* accuracy of my overall grasp of that system must be taken for granted in order for coherentist justification to even begin" (p. 127). To take this for granted is to accept the "Doxastic Presumption"; that is, I accept the Doxastic Presumption if I believe that my beliefs as to what I believe (my 'metabeliefs', we might say) are approximately correct. However, he apparently does not intend to claim that anyone *has* warrant or justification either for the Doxastic Presumption or for his metabeliefs: "no claim is being made that these metabeliefs possess any sort of intrinsic or independent justification or warrant of any kind (nor would such claim be defensible in light of the earlier antifoundationalist arguments)" (p. 147).

So do we or don't we have warrant for *a posteriori* beliefs? In the last analysis, as far as I can tell, BonJour does not commit himself on this issue: "Rather, the approximate correctness of these beliefs is an essential presupposition for coherentist justification, and both such justification itself and any resulting claims of likelihood of truth must be understood as relativised to this presupposition" (p. 147). Apparently, therefore, BonJour takes it that his project is a sort of *conditional* one. The attempt is to show that *if* I make the Doxastic Presumption, *then* I will have available a justificatory argument for my *a posteriori* beliefs:

> Nothing like a justification for the presumption has been offered for the simple reason that if it is properly understood, none is required: there can obviously be no objection to asking what follows about the justification of the rest of my beliefs from the presumption that my representation of my own system of beliefs is approximately correct. (p. 106)

E. The Justification of A Priori Beliefs

The idea, then, is that we are justified in empirical beliefs only if we have good reason to think them true; and that reason must ultimately be *a priori*. I note that I hold a certain belief *B;* I also note that my system of beliefs is comprised by *B* together with $A_1, \ldots A_n$; I note still further that this system of beliefs is coherent (and coherent in a long-enough run); I know or see or believe *a priori* that any such system of beliefs is likely to "correspond to reality"; I conclude that *B* is likely to be true.

Accordingly, the suggestion is that I can argue *a priori,* somehow, that a coherent system of beliefs is likely to correspond to reality; and of course in giving myself this argument I rely upon principles of logic and other *a priori* beliefs. Now those *a priori* beliefs must themselves have warrant or justification; if they lack it, then I won't have a good reason for thinking that my belief *B* is likely to be true. But how shall we think about the justification or warrant of *a priori* beliefs? I said at the beginning of this section that BonJour was an *impure* coherentist. This impurity consists in a certain promiscuity: he embraces a coherentist account of (broadly speaking) empirical warrant and knowledge, but a wholly different account of *a priori* warrant. Here he adopts what he calls a traditional rationalistic account:

The traditional positive view is that of the rationalist: *a priori* justification is ultimately to be understood as intuitive grasp of necessity: a proposition is justified *a priori* when and only when the believer is able, either directly or via some series of individually evident steps, to intuitively 'see' or apprehend that its truth is an invariant feature of all possible worlds, that there is no possible world in which it is false. (p. 192)

So this coherentist account of empirical knowledge rests upon a foundationalist account of *a priori* knowledge. What we know *a priori* gets its warrant not by virtue of being a member of a coherent system, but just by virtue of being self-evident, or such that it follows from what is self-evident by self-evidently valid arguments. More exactly, I am justified in accepting such a self-evident proposition as $2 + 1 = 3$ by virtue of the fact that I can 'see' that it is necessarily true. Hence I do have a reason for accepting such a proposition: my reason is that it is necessarily true. But I do not have (and apparently do not need) a reason for accepting that reason, for accepting the proposition that $2 + 1 = 3$ *is* necessary.

II. BonJourian Coherentism Examined

BonJour raises many points of great interest; there are many fascinating topics here, and much to say about each one. Strictly speaking, for my project of coming to a satisfying view of the nature of warrant I need consider only what BonJour says about warrant. But he offers us much else of real interest; much of what he says invites, nay, cries out for comment; it would be unduly inappreciative to stick churlishly to what is strictly required. Before going on to an explicit consideration of his account of warrant, therefore, I wish to comment on two other interesting facets of his thought: (1) his relationship to classical foundationalism and his partiality to reason, and (2) the success of his argument for a coherentist justification of empirical belief.

A. *Classical Foundationalism and Trusting Reason*

1. Preliminary Questions

Justification, according to BonJour, is a matter of epistemic responsibility. How so? We have the goal of achieving truth; "one's cognitive endeavors are epistemically justified only if and to the extent that they are aimed at this goal, which means very roughly that one accepts all and only those beliefs which one has a good reason to think are true" (p. 8). Questions arise here: first, do we *all* have this goal? Might not some of us have no overarching cognitive goals at all? Might not others have different overarching cognitive goals—comfort, say, or salvation, or fame and fortune, or mental health? Might I not have the primary goal of doing my cognitive duty, *hoping* that this will lead to my holding mostly true beliefs, but not explicitly aiming at the latter? (Just as I might have the more general aim of living aright, living in accord with duty, hoping this will lead to happiness, but not explicitly aiming at it?) And what about avoiding error? According to William James, W. K. Clifford was unduly finicky and squeamish about this matter; he had an inappropriate and ultimately unhealthy horror of believing what is false. But even if James is right, isn't it perfectly proper to try to avoid error as well as believe truth? (If your only aim is to believe truth, then no doubt the thing to do is to believe as many propositions as you possibly can.) And shouldn't the goal of believing the truth be more subtly specified? I am not particularly interested in sheer *quantity* of truth, as if the more truths (no matter how trivial), the merrier. There are some areas of reality such that I have little interest in learning about them (I really don't care how many blades of grass there are on your front lawn). I also value such epistemic excellences as penetrating insight, gaining a deep understanding of such difficult but important phenomena as sets, possible worlds, middle knowledge, and a thousand other things; how are these goals related to the goal of having true beliefs? Second, are we all really *obliged* to have this goal? Suppose we don't: have we gone contrary to a duty of some kind, so that we warrant reproach and blame? That seems a bit strong.

But let us waive these questions, assuming for purposes of discussion that we all have (perhaps as one among others) the overarching cognitive goal of achieving truth. How does it follow that to act responsibly I must believe only on the basis of reasons? Even if I think that believing on the basis of reasons is the best way to achieve truth, how is it that I would be *irresponsible* if I did not try to believe on the basis of reasons? I might be feckless; or I might be heedless or reckless with respect to my own goals, and hence perhaps irrational in some sense of that multifarious term; but would I be irresponsible? And second, couldn't I think that believing on the basis of reasons is not a good way to achieve truth? Perhaps I think (and responsibly think) that truth gives herself, not to those who are crafty and calculating, but to those who believe with a fine impulsiveness, accepting the first idea that pops into their heads. But then it would be hard to see how responsibility requires that I believe only on the basis of reasons.

More important, might I not be perfectly responsible even if I did not always require a reason for belief, but for many beliefs simply trusted my nature, believing what nature inclines me to believe? In my present circumstances I am inclined to believe that I had breakfast this morning; my memory does not, so far as I know, play me tricks. Why isn't it entirely responsible for me, in these circumstances, to believe that I *did* have breakfast this morning, whether or not I can find some reason (that is, some supporting evidence in other beliefs I hold) for the belief that I did?

Indeed, do I have a real alternative to trusting my nature at some point or other? A reading of the first chapter of BonJour's book might suggest that he endorses the quixotic Enlightenment project of refusing to trust or acquiesce in my cognitive nature until I first determine that it is reliable, that it, for the most part, provides me with truth. But of course this is wholly foolish and self-forgetful, worthy only of someone who, like Kierkegaard's Hegel, forgets that she is an existing individual and confuses herself with universal reason in the abstract. For where do I stand when I conclude that since it is possible that my nature should massively deceive me, I should not trust it until I determine that it does not thus massively deceive me? Where shall I stand while making that determination, while investigating whether or not my nature is or is not reliable? Where is this Archimedian πού στῶ?

Obviously I have nothing but my epistemic nature—my natural epistemic faculties—to enable me to see (if that is what it is) that if it is possible that my nature deceive me, then I must determine whether it is reliable before I trust it. And equally obviously I must trust my nature in trying to determine whether it *is* reliable, and thus worthy of my trust. To determine whether it is reliable, I must determine whether for the most part it yields truth. So perhaps I conclude that my cognitive nature yields much error; perhaps I note that I am inclined to believe propositions *P* and *Q* from which by subtle or obvious arguments it follows that both *R* and not-*R*. But, of course, in so noting I rely upon my natural inclinations for the belief that I do indeed believe both *P* and *Q*, that those arguments from *P* and *Q* to *R* and not-*R* are in fact valid, and that if my nature inclines me to believe propositions that by those arguments lead to contradictions, then my nature inclines me to error. To transpose the theme into BonJourian terms, if I need a reason for everything I believe, then I need a reason for believing *that,* as well as a reason for thinking that what I take to be a reason for believing that *is* a reason for believing it, and a reason for that second belief, and a reason for thinking that what I take to be a reason for *it* is in fact a reason for it, and so on. That way, obviously, lies intellectual shipwreck.

As a matter of fact, however, BonJour is not involved in any such absurd and self-defeating stance; for he clearly begins his project with an initial trust in *reason,* the faculty that yields *a priori* and self-evident (or apparently self-evident) beliefs. (Indeed, he sweeps a fair amount of dust under the *a priori* rug.) We have noted that he accepts a traditional rationalist account of *a priori* knowledge, holding that in many cases we can simply *see* that a proposition is true, and in fact necessarily true. In these cases, he says, responsibility does not require that we have a reason for the belief in question (more exactly, for the *necessity* of that belief); and he gives a fine defense of that traditional view against various unpromising recent empiricist attacks. Here BonJour concurs with the classical foundationalist: self-evident propositions are indeed properly basic; they have warrant without receiving it by way of warrant transfer or coherence. (Unlike the classical foundationalist (either ancient or modern) BonJour appears to think that beliefs of the form *Necessarily A* are the only properly basic beliefs; here he differs from the ancient classical foundationalist, who holds that propositions evident to the senses are also properly basic, from the modern classical foundationalist, who holds that certain propositions about one's own mental life are also properly basic, and from both ancient and modern classical foundationalists, since they hold that a self-evident proposition is properly basic, whether or not it is of the form *Necessarily A*.)

Now here we may be inclined to think we detect a sort of incoherence in BonJour's views, or at any rate an arbitrary partiality. If I can responsibly trust my nature with respect to what seems self-evident, why can't I trust it with respect to perception and memory, say, or introspection, the faculty whereby I come to hold metabeliefs about what I believe? To put the matter BonJour's way, if I don't need a reason for believing one of the deliverances of reason, why do I need one for believing one of the deliverances of sense or memory or introspection? Initially, BonJour writes as if we need a reason for *everything* we believe; his objection to internalist and externalist foundationalism is that on these views a person could justifiably accept a belief without having a reason for thinking that belief true. But then, as it turns out later, he *doesn't* think you need a reason for (the necessary truth of) what seems self-evident; one can accept the deliverances of reason in the basic way without irresponsibility. And isn't there an arbitrary partiality there? As Thomas Reid says,

> The sceptic asks me, Why do you believe the existence of the external object which you perceive? This belief, sir, is none of my manufacture; it came from the mint of Nature; it bears her image and superscription; and, if it is not right, the fault is not mine; I ever took it upon trust, and without suspicion. Reason, says the sceptic, is the only judge of truth, and you ought to throw off every opinion and every belief that is not grounded on reason. Why, sir, should I believe the faculty of reason more than that of perception? They came both out of the same shop, and were made by the same artist; and if he puts one piece of false ware into my hands, what should hinder him from putting another?[5]

BonJour neither asks nor answers Reid's question. He writes initially as if responsibility *always* requires believing only if you have a reason, only later beating an unannounced retreat from this position by way of making an exception for self-evident beliefs (more exactly, beliefs of the sort *P is necessary,* where *P* is self-evident). But perhaps there *is* an answer, of sorts, to Reid's question; perhaps Reid is a bit hasty. He often writes as if the skeptic (or the modern classical foundationalist) were just a whimsical, arbitrary fellow who exalts reason and consciousness (Reid's term for the faculty whereby I come to know such things as that I am appeared to redly) over perception and memory for no reason at all—or else an imperceptive fellow, who mistrusts perception and memory because he can't give a noncircular justification of them, foolishly failing to notice that the same thing holds for reason and consciousness. But skeptics need not be as arbitrary and imperceptive as *that.* The skeptic ordinarily begins by pointing to the uncertainty, disagreement, error, and confusion that haunt human life. One of the originating causes of skepticism, says Sextus Empiricus, is that "men of talent . . . were perturbed by the contradictions in things and in doubt as to which of the alternatives they ought to accept." There is often enormous disagreement among human beings, and disagreement about matters of the greatest import, both practical and theoretical. These things—error, confusion and disagreement—show that our noetic faculties are to at least some degree unreliable. If you and I disagree, then either your faculties are misleading you or mine are misleading me. (Of course we rely upon our cognitive nature in making *that* judgment; but if it is mistaken there, then it is deeply mistaken indeed.)

[5] *An Inquiry into the Human Mind,* in *Inquiries and Essays,* ed. Ronald Beanblossom and Keith Lehrer (Indianapolis: Hackett Publishing, 1983), VI, xx.

And the skeptic about perception does not ordinarily mistrust perception merely because he can't give a noncircular justification of it; instead he begins by claiming, plausibly enough, that the senses are sometimes misleading. "I have learned from experience that the senses sometimes mislead me, and it is prudent never to trust wholly those things which have once deceived us," says Descartes; "The same tower appears round from a distance but square from close at hand," says Sextus Empiricus; and he adds that "sufferers from jaundice declare that objects that seem to us white are yellow." (Not all of Sextus's pronouncements on this subject inspire equal confidence; he also holds that those whose eyes are bloodshot see everything as red, and he reports with evident approval Anaxagoras's attack on the common view that snow is white by way of the argument *snow is frozen water; water is black;* therefore *snow is black.*)

So the skeptic about sense perception typically opens his case by pointing out that perceptual appearances are often misleading. And here, of course, he is right. From some angles Mount Teewinot looks higher than the Grand Teton; a flat North Dakota road may look shiny and wet in the distance when in fact it is perfectly dry; parched travelers in the desert may be misled by perceptual appearances into thinking there is an oasis no more than a couple of miles away. On the other hand, we don't know of any such thing in the case of, say, what Reid calls 'consciousness', the faculty responsible for the sort of beliefs we express by saying, 'I am appeared to redly'. We don't know of any cases where it seemed to someone that he was being appeared to redly when in fact he was being appeared to bluely or not at all; we don't know of any case where someone believed he was in severe pain when in fact he was perfectly comfortable, or believed that he was sad when in fact he was euphoric. One reason, then, for following the modern classical foundationalist in trusting reason and consciousness more than sense perception is the fact that the latter sometimes misleads us.

We should pause here to ask *how* we know that sense perception sometimes deceives us. Consider the phantom oasis. At time t it looks to us as if there is an oasis about a mile and a half from the place we stand; we make a thirsty dash to that spot, only to find nothing but sand; we conclude that at t we were mistaken in thinking there was an oasis there. The conclusion that we were thus misled by our senses at t clearly involves several faculties: memory, induction (whereby we come to believe that if there was no oasis there when we arrived, then there was none there at t), and sense perception itself. We might be able to do without induction; perhaps there was an old bedouin at that very spot, enjoying the warm sunshine; he reports that he has been there for at least two hours, and at no time during that time was there an oasis on that spot. Then we rid ourselves of dependence, in this instance, upon induction, but we add a couple of other dependencies; for now we depend upon the faculty or power (Reid calls it *sympathy*) whereby I come to believe, under certain conditions, that someone other than myself believes and is telling us such a thing as that he has been at a certain place for a couple of hours during which time there was no oasis there—as well as *credulity*, the faculty leading me to believe what I take it others tell me. (Alternatively, in this case I don't rely upon credulity, but replace one reliance upon induction by another: I now employ the inductively based belief that when a bedouin seems to say he has been on a certain spot for a couple of hours and there has been no oasis there during that time, then indeed there was no oasis there during that time.)

Of course we also depend, in this instance, upon reason. In some cases of error detection just *one* faculty, in addition to reason, is involved. I seem to remember that *p*, and that on a previous occasion I seemed to remember that not-*p*. In this case it is just reason and memory that are involved in detecting error. Various other combinations of our faculties can lead to the detection of error. It is interesting to note, however, that in every such case *reason* is involved; in every case where we detect error we will be relying upon some inference or self-evident truth. So perhaps we should conclude, by Mill's Method of Agreement, that *reason* is the source of error in all these cases! But of course that is not what we do conclude. "Why, sir," asks Reid, "should I believe the faculty of reason anymore than that of perception?—they both came out of the same shop, and were made by the same artist." But often we *do* believe the faculty of reason more than that of perception, and rightly so. If I put a couple of marbles between my fingers in a certain way, my eyes tell me that there is just one marble there and my sense of touch tells me that there are two. I do not conclude that, contrary to the deliverances of reason, there is just one marble there and furthermore two; I quite properly take it that it is my senses that mislead, not my reason.

So one possible ground for discriminating among our faculties is that some of them seem on some occasion to be misleading, to lead us into error. This is a ground for discrimination against perception and memory in favor of consciousness. Another ground for discrimination is that some but not all faculties can be validated by other faculties. Again, consciousness seems privileged here. I said earlier that we know of no cases where someone thought he was appeared to redly, or thought he was in pain but really was not. It is at least plausible to go further; some of the deliverances of consciousness are such that it is a teaching of reason that we are not deceived with respect to them. Is it not self-evident that a person who carefully considers whether he is being appeared to redly, and *believes* that he is being appeared to redly, *is* being appeared to redly?

Here we must be careful; perhaps I *can* believe *de re, of* the proposition that I am being appeared to redly, that it is true, when as a matter of fact it is false. I may now believe that everything you explicitly believe is true, and know that there is just one proposition you now explicitly believe; I can then believe of *that* proposition that it is true, even if I don't know which proposition it *is* that you now believe, and even if that proposition is (or is equivalent to) the false proposition that I am now being appeared to redly. But I don't see how it could be that I should grasp the proposition that I am being appeared to redly, consider whether it is true, and then believe that I am being appeared to redly when in fact I am not being appeared to that way. If I reflectively believe that I am being appeared to redly, then it is at least approximately true that I am so appeared to. (I say 'approximately true' because perhaps it's not quite *redly* that I am being appeared to, but something closer to pinkly or mauvely.) It is not easy to state the truth here exactly, but there is a truth here, I think, and it is one that distinguishes consciousness from such other faculties as memory and perception.

The skeptic (and the modern classical foundationalist), then, is not being just arbitrary in taking it that consciousness is more worthy of credence than some of our other faculties. But what about reason itself? Is there something about *it* that distinguishes it from other faculties, such that by virtue of that feature it is more worthy of credence than the others? I am inclined to think the answer is *yes,* although I am unable, at present, to see the issues with real clarity. An important difference between reason and my other faculties is the obvious fact that I can't think about the reliability of any of my faculties without in some sense *trusting* reason, taking it for granted or assuming, at least for the time being, that it is reliable. Suppose I reflect on the fact that perception, say, sometimes leads me into error; and suppose I conclude, with the Humes of this world, that perception is not to be trusted—or with Reid that it *is* to be trusted. Either way, of course, I employ the faculty of reason; more than that, either way, if I am serious, and if I accept the conclusions to which I am led and do not also, ironically, half reject them, I am clearly *trusting* reason and its deliverances. But of course the same does not go for perception, or memory; I can think about *their* reliability without employing or trusting them.

This is a *difference,* you say; but is it a *relevant* difference? I think it is, but it is hard indeed to explain exactly why. Perhaps the answer lies in the following slightly different direction: we cannot so much as *raise the question* of the reliability of reason, or any other of our faculties, without taking the reliability of reason for granted. Earlier I said there is a certain laughable foolishness and self-referential folly attaching to the enterprise of refusing to trust one's cognitive faculties before one has certified them as reliable; for of course one has to trust them or some of them in order to try to certify them. This is true *a fortiori* with respect to reason; clearly one cannot sensibly try to determine whether reason is trustworthy, before relying on it, since one has no recourse but to rely on it in trying to make that determination. This foolish futility, however, does not affect the corresponding projects with respect to our other faculties.

So far we have three candidates for the post of being a feature that relevantly distinguishes some faculties from others; two of these favor consciousness and one of them favors reason. But now suppose we think a bit more about the fact that reason displays this feature, a feature that distinguishes it from our other faculties. Does it follow from this fact that one could not sensibly come to the conclusion that reason is unreliable? Not obviously. What would be required for me to conclude, sensibly, that reason is not to be trusted? One suggestion: I may learn or think I learn from divine revelation, say, that some proposition is true, which proposition conflicts with what reason teaches. (Some people think thus—mistakenly, in my view—about the Christian doctrines of the Trinity and Incarnation.) But here there are deep waters. I rely upon reason to conclude that there is a conflict between reason and revelation here; so if I conclude that reason is unreliable, have I not lost my reason for thinking there is a conflict (and hence my reason for thinking reason unreliable)? Further, if I rely upon reason in concluding that there is a conflict, I can of course quite sensibly *continue* to rely upon it and conclude that the alleged divine revelation is not really a divine revelation after all.

What is needed, here, is a case where reason somehow indicts *itself,* and cannot self-servingly point the finger at something else, some other faculty. Suppose there were some propositions that are among the immediate teachings of reason—that is, were apparently self-evident; and suppose they led by argument forms also sanctioned by reason to a conclusion whose denial was an immediate teaching of reason. To put it more simply, suppose I came upon apparently self-evident propositions $P_1, \ldots, P_n$ that led by apparently self-evidently valid arguments to a self-evidently false conclusion Q. If reason is reliable, then $P_1, \ldots P_n$ are true; but if $P_1, \ldots, P_n$ are true, then so is Q, in which case reason is not reliable; so if reason is reliable, it isn't reliable; so it's not reliable. Could I sensibly come to this conclusion and no longer trust reason?

Once I had accepted the argument and stopped trusting reason, then, of course, I could no longer sensibly offer this argument as my reason for mistrusting reason; at first glance the argument seems to defeat itself. At second glance, however, we see that this is not a way out. Consider this remarkable passage from Hume (a passage in which he is echoing Sextus):

> The skeptical reasonings, were it possible for them to exist, and were they not destroy'd by their subtlety, wou'd be successively both strong and weak, according to the successive dispositions of the mind. Reason first appears in possession of the throne, prescribing laws, and imposing maxims, with an absolute sway and authority. Her enemy, therefore, is oblig'd to take shelter under her protection, and by making use of rational arguments to prove the fallaciousness and imbecility of reason, produces in a matter, a patent under her hand and seal. This patent has at first an authority, proportioned to the present and immediate authority of reason, from which it is deriv'd. But as it is suppos'd to be contradictory to reason, it gradually diminishes the force of that governing power, and its own at the same time; till at last they both vanish away into nothing by a regular and just diminution. . . . 'Tis happy, therefore, that nature breaks the force of all skeptical arguments in time, and keeps them from having any considerable influence on the understanding.[6]

Hume's point, or one lurking in the nearby woods, could perhaps be put as follows. I begin in the natural condition of trusting reason; I then encounter these arguments showing by way of reason that reason is not to be trusted; I then stop trusting reason; but once I have done so, I no longer have any reason not to trust reason and my natural tendency to trust reason reasserts itself; but then I once more have reason to stop trusting reason; whereupon I lose my reason for mistrusting reason and fall back into the natural condition of trusting it; whereupon . . . What we have is a nasty dialectic, a movement that proceeds through a distressing loop. And after having gone through the loop a

[6] *A Treatise of Human Nature,* with an analytical index, ed. L. A. Selby-Bigge (Oxford: Clarendon Press, 1888), I, IV, i, p. 18.

couple of times, I may find myself going through it faster and faster, until I am in effect intellectually paralyzed—or until, weary and frustrated, I give up the whole subject and go out to play backgammon with my friends. So couldn't someone in this condition—someone who had encountered a deliverance of reason that by apparently self-evident argument forms led to an apparently self-evidently false conclusion—couldn't someone in this condition sensibly stop trusting reason? I can't see why not.

But, sadly enough, this is precisely the condition in which as a matter of fact we find ourselves. There are apparently self-evident propositions that lead by apparently self-evident arguments to conclusions that are self-evidently false. I am thinking, of course, of some of the Russell paradoxes. It is apparently self-evident that for anything I can correctly say about an object *x,* there is a property *x* displays; it is also apparently self-evident that every property has a complement; and it is apparently self-evident that some properties—*being a property,* for example—exemplify themselves. But then it is an apparently self-evident consequence of apparently self-evident propositions that there is such a property as *non-self-exemplification;* and we all know the rest of the sorry tale. So we are in just the position I said could sensibly lead a person to mistrust reason itself.

Now we need not draw the conclusion that reason is not to be trusted at all; that would be absurdly excessive. But it does follow, I think, that our reason, in our present condition, is not to be trusted wholeheartedly and without reservation; for if it *is* wholly reliable, then it *is not* wholly reliable: in which case it is not wholly reliable.

To return to BonJour, then: there is indeed a sort of partiality involved in his holding that responsibility requires reasons in the case of perceptual and memory beliefs, but not in the case of self-evident beliefs. But perhaps the partiality is not altogether arbitrary: there are differences between the faculties involved, and perhaps these differences partly warrant this sort of differential treatment of them—"partly," because the relevant differences between them are a matter of degree and not nearly as stark as BonJour and the classical foundationalist seem to suppose.

2. BonJour's Justification of Empirical Belief

As we saw earlier, BonJour holds that an empirical belief B has warrant for me if and only if I have a reason for thinking B true; and that reason can only be the conjunction of

(i) B is a member of my system of beliefs $B_1, \ldots B_n$ and that system is coherent

with

(ii)   any belief that is a member of a coherent system of beliefs is probably true.

He then offers an argument (the justificatory argument) for (ii). There are serious problems here: I shall mention four, in order of increasing severity.

(a) Coherence and Likelihood of Truth I

How are we to establish (ii)? "What is needed, in first approximation," says BonJour, "is an argument to show that a system of empirical beliefs that is justified according to the standards of a coherence theory of this sort is thereby also likely to correspond to reality" (p. 169); he then goes on to give an argument for this conclusion. But this conclusion will not quite give us (ii); what it will give us, of course, is that any element of a coherent system of beliefs is an element of a system of beliefs that is *likely* to correspond to reality. And even if a coherent system of beliefs is more likely than not to correspond to reality (and BonJour does not believe that it is), it doesn't follow that each element of such a system is more likely than not to be true. (Maybe a system of beliefs corresponds to reality if, say, nine out of ten of its members are true.) To get (ii) we need an additional premise—something like *if a system of beliefs corresponds to reality then every member of it is true*. Unfortunately this premise is not acceptable to BonJour. It would place an even greater burden on the argument for the claim that a coherent system of beliefs is likely to correspond to reality; that argument would then have to conclude that any coherent system of beliefs is likely to have no false members, whereas what in fact he means to argue for is that a coherent system of beliefs will correspond to reality "within a reasonable degree of approximation" (p. 171).

(b) Coherence and Likelihood of Truth II

This brings us to another and even less tractable problem. Suppose B is a belief of mine; I propose to justify it in BonJourian fashion. How, precisely, does the justification go? I am to note that B is an element of a system S, of beliefs, that has been coherent for some significant period; and I am also to see *a priori* that such a system of beliefs is likely to correspond to reality. But what BonJour actually argues here is not that such a system of beliefs is *more likely than not* to correspond to reality (and hence to contain mostly true beliefs); what he argues is that the correspondence hypothesis with respect to S (CHS) is more likely to be true than any alternative explanation according to which S does *not* correspond to reality. More exactly, he argues that

$$P(CHS/S \text{ is long-run coherent})$$

is greater than

$$P(SKS/S \text{ is long-run coherent})$$

where SKS is any skeptical hypothesis with respect to S. That is, he argues that the conditional probability of the correspondence hypothesis with respect to S, on S's being long-run coherent, is greater than the conditional probability of any of the skeptical hypotheses with respect to S, on that same condition. So the best we can say for CHS, BonJour thinks, is that it is not as unlikely as the skeptical explanations, the explanations according to which S does not correspond to reality.

But then how can I conclude that B is likely to be true? My ground for holding that B is likely is that B is probable with respect to (CHS), an explanation of the coherence of S that is more probable than any skeptical explanation. But if (CHS) is not itself more probable than not, how can the fact that B is probable with respect to it so much as even slyly suggest that B is more probable than not? And even if the CHS were more probable than not, the fact that B is probable with respect to it would not of course show that B is itself more probable than not. It is more probable than not that one of the first 51 tickets of the 100-ticket lottery will win, and probable on *that* that one of the first 26 tickets will win; but the latter is not more probable than not.

(c) Long-run Coherence?

I said above that a justificatory argument for one of my beliefs B involves the premise that

(ii)   any belief that is a member of a coherent system of beliefs is probably true.

But (ii) is not quite accurate; the system of beliefs in question (as we saw on p. 92) must of course be some person's system of beliefs, and it must be coherent *in the long run,* or at any rate in some sufficiently long run. So (ii) is more accurately stated as

(ii′)   If B is a member of S's system of beliefs and S's system of beliefs has been coherent for a sufficiently long run, then B is likely to be true.

The basic idea is this: the most likely explanation of someone's system of beliefs remaining coherent in the long run is that those beliefs are caused in such a way as to be for the most part true. But here another problem rears its ugly head: if I am to use this argument to justify B, then I shall have to know or justifiably believe not only that my system of beliefs *is* coherent, but that it *has been* coherent over the long run, or a long enough run. This is another *a posteriori* belief; and what could be my justification for *it*? There are two possibilities: (i) my beliefs about times other than the present get warrant in some way (via memory, for example) *different* from the way other empirical beliefs get warrant, or (ii) they do not. The first alternative is obviously unsatisfactory for BonJour. But of course so is the second: on BonJour's scheme, I am to be justified in holding a particular empirical or *a posteriori* belief B by noting (among other things) that (1) B is a member of my system of beliefs S and (2) S has been coherent over a sufficient time. But then of course (2) must be justified for me, and justified for me before B is. In the case in question, however, B is (2); hence in the case in question (2) must be justified for me before it is justified for me. It is hard to see a way out.

(d) The Doxastic Presumption

To be justified in believing *B*, I must know that *B* is a member of my system of beliefs and that that system has been coherent for a sufficiently long run; as we have seen, the second conjunct causes real trouble. But so does the first; in fact here there is a problem that threatens the structural integrity of BonJour's whole position. Clearly my justificatory argument for *B* requires that I justifiably believe such propositions as *I believe B* and *I believe each of B₁, . . . Bₙ* (where these are the members of my system of beliefs). And the question is: what sort of warrant or justification do such beliefs have for me? As we have seen (p. 96), BonJour does not give an answer; as a matter of fact he doesn't claim that such beliefs *have* warrant for me. Instead, he represents his project as a *conditional* one, showing that *if* I make the Doxastic Presumption, *then* I will have available a justificatory argument for my *a posteriori* beliefs. But isn't there an error here? The Doxastic Presumption (with respect to myself) is the proposition that my metabeliefs (my beliefs as to what I believe) are approximately correct. BonJour recognizes that a justificatory argument with respect to one of my beliefs requires the Doxastic Presumption:

> Thus when, as in the following discussion, appeal is made to the Doxastic Presumption in setting out a particular line of justification, this should be understood to mean that the justificatory argument depends on the believer's grasp of his overall system of beliefs and is cogent only on the presumption that his grasp is accurate. (p. 128)

BonJour's idea seems to be that a cogent justificatory argument for one of my beliefs requires the truth of the Doxastic Presumption. That is, if the Doxastic Presumption is not true (with respect to me) then my justificatory argument will have a false premise; *I believe B* and *I believe each of B₁, . . . Bₙ* will not be true, or close enough to the truth; and my justificatory argument will be unsound.

But here I think there is confusion. What the cogency of such an argument requires is not just the *truth* of those metabeliefs (*I believe B* and *I believe each of B₁, . . . Bₙ*), but *that I be justified* in holding them. It isn't sufficient that my metabeliefs happen to be true; if I am not justified in those beliefs, then my justificatory argument confers no justification upon *B for me*. And given BonJour's claim that an empirical or *a posteriori* belief (*any* empirical or *a posteriori* belief) is justified for me only if I have a good reason for it, it follows, on his view, that I am not justified in those metabeliefs, and hence not justified in holding any of the *a posteriori* beliefs I do in fact hold. BonJour apparently holds that my justificatory argument is conditional upon the *truth* of the Doxastic Presumption (with respect to me); but in fact it must be conditional upon the *justification*, for me, of that presumption. Other elements of BonJour's position imply, however, that I cannot be justified in this presumption.[7] Hence it looks as if BonJour's position implies that no one has warrant for any empirical or *a posteriori* belief.

Of course BonJour has already made one exception to the general claim that

---

[7] As he himself argues, I cannot have a BonJourian coherentist justification for it; but he also holds that BonJourian coherentist justification is the only kind possible for an *a posteriori* belief.

I am justified in believing *B* only if I have a good reason for thinking *B* true: beliefs of the sort of which *necessarily, 2 + 1 = 3* is an example. Perhaps he could make another: perhaps he could hold that my beliefs about what *I believe* also have warrant immediately and in themselves. Then his position would be an unusual variety of modern classical foundationalism. He would concur with the foundationalist in holding that self-evident beliefs and meta-beliefs have noncoherentist warrant; he would differ from him in two respects: first, in denying that other propositions about one's own immediate experience have such warrant and, second, in holding that warrant transfer to a particular *a posteriori* belief occurs only by way of a justificatory argument.

In concluding this section, I want to point to one more kind of difficulty. This difficulty is presented by BonJour's claim that the *a priori* probability of the sorts of propositions relevant to his argument are knowable *a priori*. The objection is not that there isn't any such thing as *a priori* probability. I see no objection to the claim that there is such a variety of probability, although I think it is better to call it 'logical probability'.[8] But BonJour's argument requires not merely that propositions do have *a priori* probabilities; it also requires the premise that the Correspondence Hypothesis, for a given coherent structure *S* of beliefs, be more probable, *a priori*, than any of the skeptical explanations of the coherence of *S*—that is, any of the explanations according to which it is not the case that *S* corresponds to reality; and of course that too must be knowable *a priori*. This is monumentally dubious. Even if such a hypothesis as (CHS) and these skeptical explanations do have an *a priori* probability, a probability on necessary truths alone, it is surely anyone's guess what that probability might be. Assuming there is such a thing as *a priori* probability, what would be the *a priori* probability of our having been created by a good God who (all else being equal) would not deceive us? What would be the *a priori* probability of our having been created by an evil demon who delights in deception? And which, if either, would have the greater *a priori* probability? Short of being able to argue that God exists necessarily (in which case the first would have a probability of 1), how could we possibly tell?

3. Coherence and Warrant

I now turn finally (and more briefly) to the question central to my concerns here: does BonJour's coherentism give a satisfactory account of warrant? More specifically: suppose a belief is a member of a system of beliefs coherent in BonJour's sense: will this be necessary and sufficient for warrant? Still more specifically, since both coherence in BonJour's sense and warrant come in degrees, is it necessary that the warrant of a belief and the coherence of the system of beliefs to which it belongs vary together?

(a) No Degrees of Warrant
The first thing to see is that BonJour's account seems not to accommodate the obvious fact that warrant comes in *degrees*. I believe both that I live in Indiana

[8]See chapter 9 of my *Warrant and Proper Function* (New York: Oxford University Press, 1993).

and that Aristotle once lived in Stagira; clearly the first has more warrant for me than the second. I believe both that there are oak trees in my backyard and that once there were many cedars in Lebanon; again, the first has more by way of warrant for me than the second. But of course the second member of each pair is as much an element of my system of beliefs as the first (elementhood not coming in degrees); so if what confers warrant on such a proposition for me is my knowing or believing that it is an element of a coherent system of beliefs, then all of my beliefs will have the same degree of warrant. If I know anything, then any true belief of mine constitutes knowledge. Further, high coherence is not *perfect* coherence; BonJour clearly means to hold that a coherent system of beliefs can be sufficient for high warrant, for its members, even if it contains pockets of incoherence. But then suppose a given belief is at the source and center of such a pocket: on BonJour's suggestion that belief would have as much warrant for me as my most secure item of empirical knowledge. Both of these consequences are thoroughly unwholesome.

But perhaps this difficulty can be overcome; a little Chisholming may save the day. Perhaps there are ways of partitioning my system of beliefs into sub-systems, some of which display more coherence (and thus confer more warrant) than others; or perhaps a particularly large and impressive subsystem could be identified as a central core, other beliefs having warrant in proportion to their probability with respect to that central core. There are a number of intriguing possibilities here, most of which look pretty difficult; but perhaps it can be done.

(b) Coherence Not Sufficient for Warrant

Is high coherence sufficient for high warrant? It seems not. It seems clear that a belief could be a member of a highly coherent system of beliefs and still have very little warrant. Return, for example, to the Case of the Epistemically Inflexible Climber (see p. 82), the unfortunate whose beliefs became fixed, no longer responsive to experience, due to an errant burst of high-energy radiation. Stipulate that his system of beliefs is coherent; and to adapt this example to BonJour's specific account of justification, stipulate also that his system of beliefs has both been coherent for some time and that it meets the Observation Requirement.[9] (Many beliefs about the geography of China, say, spontaneously arise in his cognitive system, along with the appropriate introspective beliefs.) His system of beliefs thus meets BonJour's conditions for justification; but then it meets those conditions equally well later on, when he is at the opera and his experience is of a wholly different character. At that later time, however, his beliefs that he is seated on the belay ledge, that there is a hawk floating in lazy circles a couple of hundred feet below his feet, and so on, clearly have little or no warrant for him. If one of these beliefs happens to be true, it will not qualify as an instance of knowledge for him, even though it is a member of a coherent system of beliefs.

Or suppose I am one of Descartes' madmen: I think I am a squash, perhaps a pumpkin. This psychotic delusion is the pivot of my whole system of beliefs

[9]Here I am indebted for a correction to Caroline Simon.

and the rest of my beliefs settle into a coherent pattern around it. (Thus I believe that I was grown in a famous Frisian garden, that I alone among the vegetables have been granted rationality and self-consciousness, that the explanation for my having been thus exalted is to be found in God's middle knowledge about what various possible gourds would freely do in various situations, and so on.) We could also turn to the skeptical hypothesis BonJour mentions. Perhaps I have been captured by Alpha Centaurian cognitive scientists, who make me the subject of a cognitive experiment; their aim is to give me a system of beliefs in which falsehood and coherence are maximized. They succeed in giving me a thoroughly coherent set of beliefs, but in a few cases they slip, giving me a true belief rather than a false one. Or perhaps I am victimized by a Cartesian demon who chooses a set of beliefs at random and then adds enough beliefs so that my noetic system is coherent. (We must add, in each case, that the Observation Requirement is satisfied.) In such cases my beliefs may have a great deal of coherence, but they will have very little warrant. Those that are true, are true just by accident, and surely do not constitute knowledge for me.

BonJour recognizes (p. 150) that in these cases there is not knowledge; he adds that what we have in these cases are or are similar to *Gettier* situations.[10] Now, first, BonJour believes that the traditional justified true belief account of knowledge is "at least approximately correct" (p. 3). Perhaps, then, it would follow that in the present cases, even if the subject doesn't have knowledge, he *almost* does; it would be approximately true, or near the truth to say that he does. But surely not. If my cognitive faculties are subject to malfunction of that degree of seriousness, surely I don't have anything like knowledge; my beliefs have far too little warrant for knowledge. Second, would these really be much like Gettier cases? I shouldn't have thought that a situation in which I was deceived in such wholesale, global fashion was really a Gettier situation. The latter typically involves the subject's cognitive environment's being mildly but not overwhelmingly misleading: someone shows me a lot of evidence for the false proposition that he owns a Ford, or I mistake a wolf in sheep's clothing for a sheep, or am deceived by a lot of barn facades the native Wisconsinites have erected.[11] The sort of case where my cognitive faculties are massively malfunctioning does not seem very similar to these paradigm Gettier situations.

But of course it might be hard to tell what is close to the truth and what not; and equally hard to tell what sorts of situations achieve the distinction of being similar to genuine Gettier situations. What is important here is that high BonJourian coherence is not sufficient for high warrant; indeed, great coherence can go with very little warrant. Furthermore, BonJour gives not so much as a hint as to what further is required for knowledge, or for a degree of warrant high enough for knowledge; he does not discuss Gettier situations at all. So (*pace* the book's title) what we have is not really an account of empirical *knowledge;* it is at best an account of one condition necessary for empirical knowledge. What more might be required? BonJour says nothing at all on this

---

[10]"Of course, for the sort of reason suggested by Gettier examples, his belief would presumably not count as knowledge even if they happened fortuitously to be true."

[11]See *Warrant and Proper Function*, chap. 2, sect. 1, pt. E, for discussion of the Gettier problem.

head. In *Warrant and Proper Function* I suggest that one condition crucially required is the absence of the sort of cognitive malfunction or pathology involved in the above examples.

(c) Coherence Not Necessary for Warrant

But where that condition (plus a couple of others) *is* satisfied, we don't also need high coherence for high warrant; high BonJourian coherence is not sufficient for high warrant, but it isn't necessary either. Couldn't I know what my name is, or that I live in Indiana or that I am not bald even if much of my noetic structure is in disarray and displays little coherence? Concede for purposes of argument that a belief *B* constitutes knowledge for me only if there is a fair degree of coherence *in the near neighborhood of B;* surely it isn't necessary that my noetic structure *overall* displays much coherence. And *a fortiori,* it does not seem necessary, in order for me to know *B,* that *B* be a member of a system of beliefs that is coherent in even a moderately long run. I am captured by Alpha Centaurian cognitive scientists who for a period of a year manipulate my beliefs in such a way that my noetic structure is not coherent to any significant degree; their experiment concluded, they return me back to earth and restore me and my faculties to normal functioning. Couldn't I then know, for example, that I see a sheep, even though I am killed a couple of days later in a car accident, so that the belief in question is not a member of a noetic structure that is coherent for any significant run?

Now of course the resolute BonJourian coherentist might protest that he has an *argument* for holding that in these cases there is little or no justification (and hence no knowledge) and that I am ignoring that argument. The argument, substantially, would be that

(a)   one must have a *reason* to be justified in accepting a belief,

and

(b)   the only possible reason would be that the belief is an element of a system of beliefs coherent in the long run, and such a system probably corresponds to reality.

But as we have already seen, BonJour himself does not accept (a); he makes an exception for some beliefs of the form *Necessarily A.* He must therefore restrict (a) to empirical or *a posteriori* beliefs. But then why distinguish in this way among beliefs; why discriminate, in this fashion, against *a posteriori* beliefs? BonJour doesn't say.

As we saw above, however, perhaps there is a way to make a principled distinction between reason, on the one hand, and perception on the other, trusting the former more fully than the latter. But as we also saw, the differences between the two on the basis of which such discrimination could be justified are both relatively tenuous and a matter of degree. They do not support the claim that I can have maximal warrant for, say, necessarily *2 + 1 = 3,* while a perceptual judgment has warrant for me only if I accept it on the evidential basis of other beliefs. It therefore seems to me that we don't have here the materials for an argument in support of the appropriately qualified version of (a). So why should we accept it; why suppose there is anything even remotely irresponsible in accepting in the basic way the deliverances of memory, say, or introspection, or perception? We all regularly do this; presumably a good argument would be required to show that such behavior is irresponsible; but no such argument seems available.

I conclude, therefore, that BonJour has not provided anything like a satisfactory account of warrant; BonJourian coherence is neither necessary nor sufficient for warrant. In the next chapter I shall turn to still another account of warrant, an account that deserves to be called 'coherentist' even though it is quite thoroughly different from the sorts of views traditionally so-called.

6

Bayesian Coherentism and Warrant

I turn now to a more recent entry into the lists, a contestant that, compared with classical foundationalism, has only lately joined the fray. Some (for example, L. J. Savage) call this new arrival 'personalism'; others call it 'subjectivism'; but most call it 'Bayesianism', on the grounds that its devotees typically recommend change of belief in accordance with a generalization of Bayes' Theorem.[1] Perhaps the best name from our present perspective would be 'probabilistic coherentism', but I shall defer to established custom and concur in 'Bayesianism'. Bayesianism goes back essentially to Frank Plumpton Ramsey's 1926 essay "Truth and Probability."[2] Although there are many varieties of Bayesianism, few explicitly raise the epistemological question of the nature of warrant. Nonetheless many fascinating issues arise here, issues that bear at least obliquely on the main topic of this study.

Now there are certain difficulties in treating Bayesianism as an address to the traditional epistemological problems with which we have been dealing. First, contemporary studies in probability in general and Bayesianism in particular present an extensive and daunting literature, much of it directed to specialized and technical problems of one sort or another. And while many of these problems are of great intrinsic interest,[3] their bearing on the question of

[1]Named after its discoverer, the famous seventeenth-century clergyman Thomas Bayes, who allegedly found it useful in gambling. (It is not recorded whether he found it useful in fulfilling his pastoral duties.) The recommended policy for change of belief is *conditionalization*: see pp. 122–124.

[2]First published in *The Foundations of Mathematics and Other Logical Essays,* ed. R. B. Braithwaite (London: K. Paul, Trench, Trubner, 1931). An important contemporary exponent is Bruno de Finetti; see, for example, his "Foresight: Its Logical Laws, Its Subjective Sources," in *Studies in Subjective Probability,* ed. H. E. Kyburg and H. Smokler (New York: Wiley, 1964; 2d ed., 1980). See also R. Carnap, in particular his *Logical Foundations of Probability* (Chicago: University of Chicago Press, 1950) and "The Aim of Inductive Logic," in *Logic, Methodology and Philosophy of Science,* ed. E. Nagel, P. Suppes, and A. Tarski (Stanford, Calif.: Stanford University Press, 1962).

[3]Just one example: the literature that has grown up around David Lewis's powerful piece, "Probabilities of Conditionals and Conditional Probabilities," *Philosophical Review* 85 (1976); reprinted in *Ifs,* ed. W. Harper, R. Stalnaker, and G. Pearce (Dordrecht: D. Reidel, 1981). Following Ernest Adams, "The Logic of Conditionals," *Inquiry* 8 (1965), we may note that an indicative conditional $A \to C$ is assertable if and only if the (subjective) conditional probability $P(C/A)$ is sufficiently high. (Thus before Reagan's reelection in 1984 it would have been wrong to assert the conditional *if Carter gets elected, we'll have a communist president,* even if one were

the nature of warrant is not always easy to see. Second, Bayesians tend to speak, not of warrant or positive epistemic status, but of *rationality;* for example, they claim that a system of beliefs is rational only if it is *coherent,* conforms to the calculus of probabilities (see pp. 119ff.). But how is rationality related to warrant? The conditions for rationality proposed by Bayesians and their sympathizers (for example, coherence, strict coherence, changing belief by conditionalization or Jeffrey's "Probability Kinematics," van Fraassen's Reflection) do not seem initially plausible as individually necessary or jointly sufficient for warrant. Still, these conditions clearly bear *some* interesting relations to warrant; they are also related to other nearby notions such as justification, the several varieties of rationality,[4] epistemic duty and epistemic integrity, and so on. In this chapter I outline the essentials of Bayesianism and ask whether the latter contributes to a satisfying account of warrant; I conclude that it does not. (Bayesians will find this conclusion neither surprising nor depressing: their interest lies, as I say, not in warrant, but in rationality.) In the next chapter I shall inquire whether the Bayesian conditions are plausibly taken as necessary or sufficient for rationality, in some interesting sense of that elusive and multifarious term. The outcome will be mixed: human beings are not irrational, in any sensible sense, by virtue of failing to conform to Bayesian constraints, but in some areas partial conformity to some of those constraints is something like an ideal to be aimed at.

I. Bayesianism Explained
A. *Statistical versus Normative Probability*

Suppose we begin by contrasting two quite different sorts of probabilities. On the one hand, we have

(a)   The probability that a 19-year-old American male who smokes more than a pack a day will live to be 70 is .87,

(b)   The probability that a radium atom will decompose within the next 1000 years is .5,

(c)   The probability that a female Frisian under the age of 50 attends church more than 4 times a month is .274,

and

(d)   The probability that a 2-year-old Rhode Island Red from southern Wisconsin will contract coccidiosis within the next year is .004;

---

confident of the truth of the conditional [taken truth functionally] by virtue, say, of confidence in the falsehood of its antecedent). The simplest explanation of that fact, says Lewis, would be that $P(A \rightarrow C) = P(C/A)$ (when $P(A)$ is nonzero); for then the assertability conditions for the indicative conditional would not be an exception to the general rule that assertability goes by absolute (subjective) probability. Lewis shows that this simplest explanation can be true only in certain trivial cases.
[4]See chapter 7, pp. 132–37.

on the other there are

(e)   It is likely that Special Relativity is at least approximately true,

(f)   Given what we know, it is likely that there has been life on earth for more than 3 billion years,

(g)   Despite the flat-earthers, it is extremely improbable that the earth is flat,

and

(h)   The Linguistic Theory of the A Priori is at best unlikely.

It is of the first importance to appreciate the difference between these two groups. (a)–(d) are ordinarily established by statistical means, by broadly speaking empirical or scientific investigation. Further, these probabilities are *general;* what is probable is that a thing of one kind (a 19-year-old American male who smokes more than a pack a day) should also be a thing of another kind (a survivor to the age of 70), or that a member of one class (the class of two-year-old Rhode Island Reds from southern Wisconsin) should also be a member of another (the class of chickens that will contract coccidiosis within the next year). These probabilities may change over time (the probability that an American infant will reach the age of 50 is greater now than it was 100 years ago); and they do not depend upon what anyone knows or believes. Turning to the probabilities in the second group, note first that what is probable or improbable here is a *proposition:* Special Relativity, or The Linguistic Theory of the A Priori, or *there has been life on earth for more than 3 billion years.* Note second that these probabilities are explicitly or implicitly relative to some body of information or evidence;[5] it is improbable, with respect to what we now know, that the earth is flat, but not with respect to what was known by a sixth-century Celt. Third, note that scientific or statistical investigation is not ordinarily relevant to the establishment of these probabilities, that is, to the probability of the proposition in question relative to the body of information in question (although of course such investigation is relevant to the establishment of that body of information). And finally, note that these probabilities contain an irreducibly *normative* element. It is epistemically extremely probable (given our circumstances) that the earth is round; hence, there is something wrong, mistaken, substandard in believing (in those circumstances) that it is flat; to believe this in our circumstances you would have to be a fool, or perverse, or dysfunctional, or motivated by an unduly strong desire to shock your friends.

We might call probabilities of the first group *factual* probabilities, and those of the second *normative;* or we might call the first sort *statistical* and the second *epistemic.* According to Ian Hacking these statistical and epistemic probabilities are to be found intermingled in discussions of probability going

---

[5]Of course, there is also a perfectly good sense in which a proposition can also be epistemically probable relative to nonpropositional elements such as experiences of certain kinds; see my *Warrant and Proper Function* (New York: Oxford University Press, 1993), chap 10.

back to the seventeenth century: "It is notable that the probability that emerged so suddenly [in the decade around 1660] is Janus-faced. On the one side it is statistical, concerning itself with stochastic laws of chance processes. On the other side it is epistemological, dedicated to assessing reasonable degrees of belief in propositions quite devoid of statistical background."[6] As a matter of fact, these two faces, like much else, seem to go all the way back to Aristotle. The first thing to see here, however, is that the Bayesian *qua* Bayesian is concerned with *normative* probabilities, not factual probabilities.

B. Degrees of Belief

The second thing to see is that the Bayesian begins his story by observing that belief comes in *degrees;* I believe some propositions much more firmly than others. Thus I believe that the earth has existed for millions and maybe even billions of years, and also that I live in a house (as opposed to a cave or tent); but I believe the second much more firmly, much more fully than the first. I believe that Banff is in Scotland, that there was such a thing as the American Civil War, that I am more than 10 years old, and that $7 + 5 = 12$; and I believe these in ascending order of firmness. Say that a belief of yours is a *partial* belief if you accept it to some degree or other; partial beliefs include those you hold most firmly together with all those which you accept to some degree or other, no matter how small. (Thus the denial of one of your partial beliefs is one of your partial beliefs.) From the perspective of our project, Bayesianism can be seen as essentially suggesting conditions for a *rational* or *reasonable* set of partial beliefs; thus Ramsey himself saw his project as that of setting out a logic for partial belief.

This is a sort of rough-and-ready initial characterization of the idea of degrees of belief; but Bayesians often follow Ramsey in suggesting ways in which degrees of belief can be more precisely measured. Ramsey held that one's degrees of belief are not at all accurately detectable by introspection; he therefore suggested the famous Ramsey Betting Behavior Test for degrees of belief. I claim that the Detroit Lions will win their division and then the Super Bowl; you scoff, inviting me to put my money where my mouth, is and propose a small wager: then the least odds at which I will bet on the Lions represents the degree to which I believe they will win. More exactly, if I will pay seven dollars for a bet that pays ten if the Lions win the Super Bowl and nothing if they do not, then I believe to degree .7 that the Lions will win. More generally, if I will pay n (but no more) for a bet worth m if the Lions win, then my degree of belief that the Lions will win is n/m. Still more generally, for any person S there will be a *credence function* $P_S(A)$ from some appropriate set of propositions (perhaps the propositions S has entertained or encountered) into the unit interval; $P_S(A)$ specifies the degree to which S believes A. ($P_S(A) = 1$ proclaims A's utter and unconditional adherence to A, $P_S(A) = 0$ is true just if he has no inclination at all towards A, while $P_S(A) = 1/2$ tells us that S, like Buridan's ass, is suspended midway between A and $-A$.)

[6]*The Emergence of Probability* (Cambridge: Cambridge University Press, 1975), p. 12.

As Ramsey points out, I may also have *conditional* degrees of belief, corresponding to conditional probabilities; perhaps my degree of belief that Feike can swim, on the condition that he is a Frisian lifeguard, is .98. Such a conditional degree of belief can be defined as:

$P(A/B) = P(A\&B)/P(B)$, provided $P(B)$ does not equal 0.

In the case in question, then, it must be that my confidence that Feike is both a swimmer and a Frisian lifeguard is nearly as great as my confidence that he is a Frisian lifeguard. Although conditional degrees of belief can be so defined, it is worth noting that Ramsey introduces them in a wholly different manner. What he says is that S's conditional belief in A given B is measured by the least odds S would accept for a *conditional bet* on A, given B: "We are also able to define a very useful new idea: 'the degree of belief in p given q'. . . . It roughly expresses the odds at which he would bet on p, the bet only to be valid if q is true."[7] "Such conditional bets," Ramsey observes, "were often made in the eighteenth century." Thus I might be willing to pay you five dollars for a bet that pays ten if the Lions win the Super Bowl, the bet to be in force only if the Lions win their division and the playoffs. This bet, clearly, is one that I win if the Lions get into the Super Bowl and win; I lose it if the Lions get into the Super Bowl and lose; the bet is called off if the Lions don't make it to the Super Bowl. And now the claim is that the least odds at which I will accept a bet on A conditional on B measures my belief in A on the condition that B.

Of course, it is not at all obvious that there really *are* degrees of belief of this sort; perhaps the least odds I will accept for a belief on A measures not the degree to which I believe A (maybe I don't really believe A at all) but the degree to which I (fully) believe that A is probable.[8] And even if there are the right sorts of degrees of belief (both conditional and absolute), it isn't clear that they can really be measured in this way, as Ramsey himself noted. For first, there is the diminishing marginal utility of money; a hundred dollars means a great deal more to me than to a millionaire, and an extra hundred dollars tacked on to a small win (five dollars, say) means much more than the same amount tacked on to a large one (five thousand, say). Furthermore, there are many reasons why someone's betting behavior might not correspond to his degrees of belief. Perhaps you are by nature excessively cautious, so that you won't bet at all unless you get odds at 5 percent better than your degree of belief warrants. Perhaps, on the other hand, you like to live dangerously, often betting at long odds for the sheer excitement of it; or perhaps you bet at odds unwarranted by your degrees of belief because you love to gamble and can't find anyone who will bet at more reasonable odds. Or perhaps the bet can't be settled. You endorse *existentialism* (the view that existence precedes essence in such a way that if Socrates had not existed, then his individual essence would not have existed either); although I recognize some of the attractiveness of this view, I find it on balance implausible and reject it in favor of the view that Socrates' essence exists necessarily. You propose a wager; since it is hard to see how the bet could be settled, I frivolously wager my entire fortune on my position at odds of 999 to 1, even though this does not correspond at all to my relatively modest confidence in it. Or perhaps I am a nineteenth-century Scots Calvinist who believes that betting is wrong, refusing to bet at any odds whatever; and if you forcibly compel me to bet, I will bet completely at random.

Some of these difficulties were familiar to Ramsey (and he proposed a means of dealing with the objection from diminishing utility). In any event, insistence upon the measurability of degrees of belief (or more radically, 'operational' definitions of them) in terms of betting behavior or something similar is not crucial to a Bayesian program;[9] what matters is that indeed there *are* the appropriate degrees of belief, whether or not it is possible to measure them.

C. Conditions of Rationality

1. Coherence

Now the next Bayesian step is to propose a certain normative constraint on partial beliefs: *probabilistic coherence*. The idea is that a system of beliefs that does not conform to this constraint is in some way defective, deformed, not up to snuff, such that it does not measure up to the appropriate standards for proper belief; Bayesians often put this by saying that probabilistic coherence is a constraint on *rational* belief. What *is* probabilistic coherence? According to Laurence BonJour (as we saw in the last chapter) probabilistic coherence is a matter of not believing both A and *it is improbable that* A. According to the present notion, however, a system of partial beliefs is coherent if and only if it conforms to the probability calculus. Here is a handy formulation:

A_1 $0 \le P(A) \le 1$,

A_2 If A and B are necessarily equivalent, then $P(A) = P(B)$,

A_3 If A and B are incompatible (that is, the denial of their conjunction is necessary), then $P(AvB) = P(A) + P(B)$

A_4 If A is necessary, then $P(A) = 1$.[10]

---

[9]On diminishing utility, see his "Truth and Probability," pp. 172ff. Sadly enough, Ramsey himself seems to think we can grasp the notion of degrees of belief only if we *do* have some such means of measuring them:

> It will not be very enlightening to be told that in such circumstances it would be rational to believe a proposition to the extent of 2/3, unless we know what sort of a belief in it that means. We must therefore try to develop a purely psychological method of measuring belief. . . . It is a common view that belief and other psychological variables are not measurable, and if this is true, our inquiry will be vain; and so will the whole theory of probability conceived as a logic of partial belief; for if the phrase 'a belief two-thirds of certainty' is meaningless, a calculus whose sole object is to enjoin such beliefs will be meaningless also. (p. 166)

[10]A_2–A_4 speak of *necessity;* of course we can speak instead, if we like, of truth in propositional logic, or first-order logic, or first-order logic plus mathematics and set theory, or truth that can be discerned *a priori*. (No doubt there are still other plausible candidates.)

If we add the familiar definition of conditional probability in terms of absolute probability

$$P(A/B) = P(A\&B)/P(B) \text{ (provided } P(B) \text{ does not equal 0)},$$

we have as immediate consequence the familiar multiplicative law for conjunction:

$$P(A\&B) = P(A) \times P(B/A).$$

It is easy to see how my beliefs might fail to conform to these axioms. At the beginning of the season, I might inadvertently believe to degree .67 that the Lions will win the Super Bowl but also believe that the Giants have a 50-50 chance of winning (that is, believe to degree .5 that they will win), thus (given A_1) violating A_3. Before I have seen the proof of their equivalence, I might believe the Axiom of Choice more firmly than the proposition that the real numbers can be well ordered, thus violating both A_2 and A_4. Still further, there are plenty of necessary truths I don't believe to the maximal degree. Suppose we ignore necessary truths I have never thought or heard of (and which I therefore don't believe to any degree at all): there are still such necessary truths as, for example, *there are no nonexistent objects,* or Peirce's Law $(((p \rightarrow p) \rightarrow p) \rightarrow p)$ which I believe to a less than maximal degree, thus violating A_4.

Now *why* must my beliefs conform to this coherence condition if I am to be rational? Well, suppose they don't; suppose I believe to degree .67 that the Lions will win the Super Bowl and also believe that the Giants have a 50-50 chance of winning. Noting this fact and having fewer scruples than you ought to have, you propose a couple of bets: for $66.67 you offer to sell me a bet that pays $100 if the Lions win and nothing if they don't; since I believe to degree .67 that the Lions will win, I consider this a fair bet and accept. But you go on to offer me another bet that pays $100 if the Giants win and nothing if they don't; this bet costs $50. Since I also regard this as a fair bet, I accept. And now I am in trouble. I have paid you $116.67 for the two bets, but no matter who wins the Super Bowl, the most I can win is $100. You have made a *Dutch book* against me: a series of bets such that no matter what happens I am bound to lose.[11] So why think my beliefs must be coherent? Here is one possible reason: if they are not, I am vulnerable to a Dutch book.[12]

[11]In contemporary discussions (no doubt under the influence of Bas van Fraassen) it is the *Dutchman* who is clever in a Dutch book situation, so that a Dutch book is a series of bets made against some unfortunate dullard by a clever Dutch bookie. According to the *Oxford English Dictionary,* however, to dutch one's bets is to bollix them up in such a way that no matter what happens, you lose. So it isn't the clever bookie who's Dutch; it's his victim. (In the seventeenth century, English acquired many idioms referring to the Dutch, all of them derogatory: there is, for example, "Dutch bottom," used to refer to vases and people, and meaning a large, ungainly, and awkward-looking bottom.) I shall bow to current custom, however, and continue to refer to clever Dutch bookies.

[12]John Kemeny and Abner Shimony showed that you are vulnerable to a Dutch book if and only if your beliefs do not conform to the probability calculus: see the former's "Fair Bets and

Contemporary discussions often emphasize this answer to the question why rationality demands coherence. Thus Paul Horwich: "if a person is rational, he will distribute his probabilities—his degrees of belief—in accord with these laws. For only if he does this will he be able to avoid a so-called Dutch book being made against him."[13] As I shall argue, however, this is not a good reason for thinking that rationality requires coherence (and as a matter of fact I think rationality requires that we *not* be coherent). And Ramsey himself only mentions in passing that incoherent beliefs imply Dutch book vulnerability; he makes little or nothing of this as a reason for thinking rationality requires coherence. Instead, he points to certain analogies between deductive logic and the probability calculus (taken as the logic of partial belief), proposing that rationality requires coherence among *partial* beliefs, just as it requires consistency among *full* beliefs. The answer to the question, *Why think rationality requires coherence?* he thinks, is the same as the answer to the question, *Why think rationality requires logical consistency?*

So Bayesians propose coherence as a necessary condition of rational belief. But of course this is a very weak condition (although as I shall argue it is also much too strong). For example, I could be coherent but still vulnerable in a less radical way to a Dutch bookie: I might accept a series of bets which is such that, no matter what happens, I can lose but can't possibly gain, a series of bets in which at best I can break even (and at worst do worse). Blinded as I am by misplaced partisan loyalty, I am prepared to wager my entire fortune on the Lions; I am willing to pay you $1,000 for a bet that pays that very amount if the Lions win, but nothing at all if they lose. Then if the Lions win, I break even; if they lose I am ruined. To avoid this unfortunate condition, S must see to it that her beliefs are *strictly* coherent[14]—that is, such that she believes no contingent proposition to the maximum degree; she must satisfy

(SC) $P_S(A) = 1$ only if A is necessarily true.

Strict coherence is of course stronger than coherence; coherence requires that I believe all necessary truths to the maximum but permits similar enthusiasm about contingent truths (indeed, I can be coherent even if I am so misguided as to believe every contingent falsehood to the max). Bayesians and their sympathizers, therefore, sometimes propose strict coherence as a further condition of rationality.[15]

Inductive Probabilities" and the latter's "Coherence and the Axioms of Confirmation," both in *Journal of Symbolic Logic 20* (1955).

[13]*Probability and Evidence* (Cambridge: Cambridge University Press, 1982), p. 20. See also pp. 26–28. (Of course there *are* other ways of avoiding Dutch books—for example, not betting.) See also R. Stalnaker "Probability and Conditionals," in *Ifs*, p. 111: "It is obviously reasonable to require that any function determining odds be coherent. If you are willing to accept bets which you are logically certain to lose, then you are as irrational as if you had beliefs which are logically certain to be false."

[14]Established by Kemeny in "Fair Bets and Inductive Probabilities."

[15]Thus Robert Stalnaker: "This strengthening of coherence seems perfectly reasonable. It is surely irrational to take risk with no hope of gain, even if there is *some* hope of breaking even." "Probability and Conditionals," in *Ifs*, p. 111.

2. Conditionalization and Probability Kinematics

Even if I satisfy strict coherence, however, I am far from out of the woods. In particular, says the Bayesian, my beliefs can *change* in an improper, defective, irrational way. Let $P_{me,t0}$ be my credence function at a time t_0. Suppose I am coherent at t_0 (and every other time); I might still be such that $P_{me,t0}(A/B)$ is high, while at the next instant t_1 I learn that B is true but nonetheless then believe A to a low degree. For example, $P_{me,t0}$ (Feike can swim/Feike is a Frisian lifeguard) is very high—.98, say; at $t + 1$ I learn that Feike is indeed a Frisian lifeguard (and nothing else relevant); but at $t + 1$ my degree of belief in *Feike can swim* falls to .01, the rest of my beliefs settling into a coherent pattern. Then I appear to be irrational, at least at $t + 1$, even though my beliefs are coherent then as well as at t. Here Bayesians propose a further constraint: if I am rational, my beliefs will *change by conditionalization*. This suggestion was already made by Ramsey:

> Since an observation changes (in degree at least) my opinion about the fact observed, some of my degrees of belief after the observation are necessarily inconsistent with those I had before. We have, therefore, to explain exactly how the observation should modify my degrees of belief; obviously if p is the fact observed, my degree of belief in q after the observation should be equal to my degree of belief in q given p before, or by the multiplication law to the quotient of my degree of belief in pq by my degree of belief in p. When my degrees of belief change in this way we can say that they have been changed consistently.[16]

We may put this requirement as follows: suppose C_0 is my credence function at a time t_0; and suppose I then learn (by observation, let's say) that B is true. What should C_1, my credence function at the next instant t_1, be? Since I have learned that B is true, $C_1(B) = 1$, of course, but what about the rest of what I believe? The idea is that I should now believe a proposition A to the degree to which A was probable on B according to my old credence function; I must conform to

(Conditionalization) $C_1(A) = C_0(A/B) = C_0(A\&B)/C_0(B)$ (where $C_0(B)$ is not zero).

We can think of it like this: when I change belief by conditionalization on a proposition B, I retain all my old conditional probabilities on B, but I am now certain of B. Thus in the case where $P_{me,t0}$ (Feike can swim/Feike is a Frisian lifeguard) is .98 and I learn that Feike is indeed a Frisian lifeguard, at $t + 1$ my degree of belief in *Feike can swim* should have been .98. In general, the classical

---

[16]"Truth and Probability," p. 192. Indeed, the idea of changing belief by conditionalization apparently goes back, appropriately enough, to Bayes himself. Although what he writes on the topic is obscure, the third proposition of the first part of Bayes' essay on probability, according to Glenn Shafer, "gives a justification for changing subjective probabilities by conditioning in cases where the possibilities for the step-by-step development of our knowledge are built into our initial subjective probability model." See his "Bayes' Two Arguments for the Rule of Conditioning," *Annals of Statistics* 10, no. 4 (1982), p. 1076.

Bayesian idea is that if I am rational, then as I go through life learning various contingent truths (that is, raising to the maximal degree my belief in those propositions), I will constantly update my other beliefs by conditionalization on what I learn. Given conditionalization, we can see a reason for thinking rationality requires that one's *original* credence function (one's 'Ur-function', we might say) be *strictly* coherent as opposed to coherent *simpliciter:* "it is required as a condition of reasonableness: one who started out with an irregular [that is, not strictly coherent] credence function (and who then learned from experience only by conditionalizing) would stubbornly refuse to believe some propositions no matter what the evidence in their favor."[17]

But why suppose rationality requires changing belief by conditionalization? Why must we do it *that* way? Here as before a Dutch book argument is available: if I don't follow the rule of conditionalization (but do follow some rule or other)[18] in changing belief in response to what I learn, then a *diachronic* Dutch book can be made against me. A cunning bookie who knew my credence function at *t* and my method for changing belief could offer me a series of bets (at odds I consider fair) such that no matter what happens, I am bound to lose. Suppose, for example, that at t_0 my credence function C_0 is such that $C_0(the$ *Lions will get into the Super Bowl)* = .5, and $C_0(the$ *Lions will win the Super Bowl/the Lions get into the Super Bowl)* = .5. (I think it's 50-50 that they will get to the Super Bowl and 50-50 that they will win on the condition that they get into it.) Suppose further that according to my rule or strategy for changing beliefs, my credence function C_1 at a later time t_1 (before it's settled whether they get into the Super Bowl) will be such that $C_1(the$ *Lions will win the Super Bowl)* = 1/6. You gleefully rub your hands and propose the following series of bets. First, at t_0, a bet conditional on the Lion's getting into the Super Bowl: you pay me $30 if the Lions get into the Super Bowl and win it; I pay you $30 if the Lions get into the Super Bowl and don't win it; if the Lions don't manage to get into the Super Bowl, the bet is called off. At t_0 I regard this bet as fair. Second, you propose a small side bet at even money on the Lion's getting into the Super Bowl: you pay me $10 if they do and I pay you $10 if they do not; at t_0 I also regard this bet as fair. So if the Lions don't get into the Super Bowl, I pay you $10. If they do get into the Super Bowl, then at t_1 you propose still another bet; according to this one I pay you $50 if the Lions win and you pay me $10 if they lose; at t_1 I will regard this bet as fair. But now, once more, I am in trouble. If the Lions don't get into the Super Bowl, the first bet is off and I lose $10 on the second. If the Lions get into the Super Bowl and win, then I win $40 on the first two bets but lose $50 on the third for a net loss of $10. Finally, if the Lions get into the Super Bowl and lose, then I win $20 on the second and third bets but lose $30 on the first, again winding up $10 poorer. So no matter what happens, you are into my pockets to the tune of $10.

---

[17]David Lewis, "A Subjectivist's Guide to Objective Chance," in *Ifs*, p. 271.

[18]Or, slightly more modestly, know for each future time *t* and possible course C of my experience up to *t*, what my posterior probabilities at *t* will be if C turns out to be my actual course of experience up to *t*. See Bas van Fraassen's presently unpublished "Rationality Does Not Require Conditionalization," p. 6.

This argument is a specification of an argument due to David Lewis.[19] What Lewis shows is that if my beliefs change by a rule or strategy other than conditionalization, then a shrewd bookie who knew my credence function at t could make a diachronic Dutch book against me (more precisely, he could devise a diachronic Dutch strategy against me). The details of this argument are interesting but too far afield to pursue here. (It is worth noting, however, that the argument holds only on the condition that I change belief according to some rule;[20] if I don't follow a rule, the Dutch bookie is stymied, and he is also stymied if I always follow a rule, but change rules every now and then, having no rules for changing rules.)

Now there is one respect in which conditionalization is not entirely realistic: on many occasions when we learn something—by observation, say—we don't come to have *complete* confidence in what we learn. You see that the scale reads 204; you then see that you weigh 204 pounds; but of course you realize there is some small chance that you are misreading the scale, or that it has gone awry, no longer correctly reporting your weight, or that you are hallucinating. So while you learn by observation that you now weigh 204 pounds, you don't come to believe this with maximal confidence; but it is only the case of maximal confidence that is covered by conditionalization. I might observe something by candlelight, having less than complete confidence in my observation,[21] or hear a phrase in a noisy lecture hall (I am pretty confident he said your thought is deep and rigorous; but just possibly what he said is that it is weak and frivolous). Richard Jeffrey has proposed a natural generalization of conditionalization ("Probability Kinematics," as he calls it) to accommodate such cases. In the simplest case, where my new probabilities arise from a change in my credence in a proposition A, my new credence C_{new} will be given by

$$C_{new}(B) = C_{new}(A) \times C_{old}(B/A) + C_{new}(-A) \times C_{old}(B/-A).$$

The generalization to the generic finite case is just what you would expect.[22]

Bayesians, therefore, propose constraints on rational belief: coherence or perhaps strict coherence, and changing belief by conditionalization or probability kinematics. In his absorbing and instructive "Belief and the Will,"[23] Bas van Fraassen suggests still another constraint:

[19]Reported in P. Teller, "Conditionalization, Observation and Change of Preference," in *Foundations of Probability Theory, Statistical Inference, and Statistical Theories of Science*, ed. W. Harper and C. Hooker (Boston: D. Reidel, 1976), 1:209ff.

[20]See van Fraassen, "Rationality Does Not Require Conditionalization."

[21]Richard Jeffrey, *The Logic of Decision* (Chicago: University of Chicago Press, 1983), p. 166.

[22]Ibid., chap. 11.

[23]Van Fraassen is no classical Bayesian. One way in which he diverges from orthodox Bayesianism is that he rejects conditionalization as a condition of rationality; more generally, he holds that rationality does not require conformance to *any* rule for changing belief. The rational agent, he thinks, will be such that his beliefs, at any time t, will be determined by prior belief plus experience; it doesn't follow, however, that there is some function from full belief and prior opinion to present degree of belief.

(Reflection) $P_t^a(A/P_{t+x}^a(A) = r) = r$

Here P_t^a is the agent a's credence function at time t, x is any non-negative number, and $P_{t+x}^a(A) = r$ is the proposition that at time $t + x$ the agent a will bestow degree r of credence on the proposition A. To satisfy the principle, the agent's present subjective probability for proposition A, on the supposition that his subjective probability for this proposition will equal r at some later time, must equal this same number r.[24]

Suppose I now fully believe that in three weeks I will believe to degree .9, say, that the Lions will get into the Super Bowl; then if I conform to Reflection, my present degree of belief in that proposition must also be .9. More generally, my conditional personal probability for a proposition A, on the condition or supposition that my future credence in that proposition A will be r, will be r. Reflection, as van Fraassen observes, looks (initially, at any rate) unduly exuberant. As he points out, if I conform to it I never believe, with respect to any of what I take to be my future full beliefs, that there is any chance at all that it will be mistaken; more precisely and more strongly, there is no proposition A and future time f such that I put any credence at all in the proposition that I will fully but mistakenly believe A at f. This seems initially a bit too sanguine; given my spotty track record, shouldn't I think I might be wrong again? (In chapter 7 we shall look into this question.)

Further, if I conform to Reflection I place no credence at all in the proposition that at some future time f I will be less than certain of any proposition to which I presently afford full belief. So if I conform to Reflection, then I give zero credence to the suggestion, with respect to any proposition I now know, that at some time in the future I will no longer know it. More generally: let $P(A)$ be my present degree of belief in A, f be any future time, $P_f(A)$ my degree of belief in A at f, and d any degree of belief significantly different from $P(A)$: the greater $P(A)$ (the greater the degree of belief I presently afford A) the more firmly I must believe that $P_f(A)$ is not equal to d.

Still further, if I conform to Reflection, then for any future time f, I am sure that my future degree of belief in some proposition A will be n at f (that is, $P(P_f(A) = n) = 1$, for some degree of belief n), only if that degree of belief equals my present degree of belief in A. In general, for any proposition A and future time f, the more sure I am that $P_f(A) = n$, the closer n will be to my present degree of belief in A. (More exactly, the more sure I am that $P_f(A) = n$, the smaller the interval about n in which $P(A)$ is to be found; the size of that interval is a monotonically decreasing function of $P(P_f(A))$.[25])

[24]*Journal of Philosophy* 81, no. 5 (May 1984) p. 244.
[25]Argument: by Reflection and the definition of conditional probability, we have

$$\frac{P(A\&P_f(A) = n)}{P(P_f(A) = n)} = n \text{ and } \frac{P(-A\&P_f(A) = n)}{P(P_f(A) = n)} = 1 - n$$

As $P(P_f(A) = n)$ increases, so do $P(A\&P_f(A) = n)$ and $P(-A \& P_f(A) = n)$; the former can go as high as n and the latter as high as $1 - n$. Now let $P_1(P_f(A) = n) = m$ and $P_2(P_f(A) = n) = m^*$,

But why think rationality requires conformity to Reflection; why suppose conformity to Reflection a good candidate for a condition of rationality? (And what kind of rationality are we thinking of here?) Well, for one thing, a Dutch argument is once again available: if I do not conform to Reflection then I am vulnerable to a diachronic Dutch book similar in essential respects to the strategy employed by the bookie in the earlier case (p. 123), where I failed to change belief by conditionalization.[26] Van Fraassen himself, however, does not propose this as a reason for thinking that rationality requires conformity to Reflection. In chapter 7 I shall examine *his* reason for thinking rationality requires satisfying Reflection; more generally, I shall outline the main kinds of rationality and ask whether any of them requires satisfaction of any of the Bayesian constraints. For now, however, we turn to the announced subject of this chapter,

II. Bayesianism and Warrant

Coherence, strict coherence, conditionalization, probability kinematics, Reflection—what shall we say about them? It is initially clear, I think, that they show little promise as severally necessary and jointly sufficient conditions for warrant (the condition or quantity, roughly, enough of which is what distinguishes knowledge from mere true belief). First, none of the proposed conditions seems necessary. To satisfy coherence (and *a fortiori*, strict coherence) I must believe each necessary truth—more realistically, perhaps, each necessary truth within my ken—to the same degree: the *maximal* degree. But clearly I can know a great deal without doing that. Either Goldbach's conjecture or its denial is a necessary truth; I don't know which and believe neither to the maximal degree; yet I know that $2 + 1 = 3$ and that I live in Indiana. It is a necessary truth that arithmetic is incomplete; nevertheless I do not believe that truth as firmly as that $2 + 1 = 3$ (it has none of the overwhelming obviousness of the latter). I believe Peirce's Law; it is not trivially easy to see through it, however, and I do not believe it as firmly as the most obvious tautologies. I am therefore incoherent; but that does not prevent me from knowing that I am more than seven years old. Now in these examples, we might say that the locus of the incoherence—the beliefs from which it flows, so to speak—is far distant from the propositions I said I knew. Perhaps we could hope to segregate or localize the incoherence, holding that what is required for a proposition's having warrant is only local coherence, coherence in the appropriate neighborhood of that proposition (perhaps specifying neighborhoods in terms of appropriate sub-

---

$m^* > m$. Then

$P_1(A \ \& \ (P_f(A) = n)) = mn$ and $P_1(-A \ (P_f(A) = n)) = m(1 - n)$.

On P_1, $P(A)$ must be at least mn and $P(-A)$ must be at least $m(1 - n)$; so A must be between mn and $1 - (m(1 - n))$. Similarly, on P_2, $P(A)$ must be at least m^*n and $P(-A)$ must be at least $m^*(1 - n)$; so $P(A)$ must be between m^*n and $1 - (m^*(1 - n))$. But since $m^* > m$, $m^*n > mn$ and $1 - (m^*(1 - n)) < 1 - (m(1 - n))$; hence the lower limit for $P(A)$ at P_2 is greater than the lower limit for $P(A)$ at P_1 and the upper limit for $P(A)$ at P_2 is lower than its upper limit at P_1.

[26]For details, see "Belief and the Will," *Journal of Philosophy* 81, no. 5 (May 1984), pp. 237–38.

algebras of the relevant total set of propositions). But no hope in that direction. I believe both that arithmetic is incomplete and that I feel a mild pain in my left knee; I believe the former slightly less firmly than the latter. But that does not prevent me from knowing either or both of these propositions; hence, in this case the propositions known and the locus of the incoherence coincide. Indeed, I can know much even if my full beliefs are *inconsistent;* no doubt Frege knew where he lived even before Russell showed him that his set theoretical beliefs were inconsistent. There is therefore nothing to be said for the suggestion that strict coherence or coherence *simpliciter* is a necessary condition of knowledge.[27]

Obviously the same goes for changing belief by conditionalization or by probability kinematics: I can know what my name is even if I have just changed belief in some way inconsistent with probability kinematics (and hence inconsistent with conditionalization.) Nearly every philosopher, I suppose, has changed belief in ways inconsistent with probability kinematics. If (like Frege) you have ever changed your degree of belief in a noncontingent proposition, then you have changed belief in a way inconsistent with probability kinematics; but that has little bearing on whether you had knowledge either before or after the change. Again, localization will not help: I might come to see that a proposition—for example, that there is no set of nonselfmembered sets—is necessary, thereby coming to know that very proposition, even though that proposition is also the locus of the allegedly illicit change of belief. Indeed, couldn't it be that I change credence in a proposition that is in fact necessary, and *know* that proposition both before and after the change? Couldn't I know

---

[27]Of course, these constraints can be weakened in one way or another, as in Daniel Garber's "Old Evidence and Logical Omniscience in Bayesian Confirmation Theory," in *Testing Scientific Theories,* ed. John Earman (Minneapolis: University of Minnesota Press, 1983), and Ian Hacking's "Slightly More Realistic Personal Probability," *Philosophy of Science* 34 (1967). Garber's suggestion, however, loses much of the original appeal of the requirement of coherence. More to the point, it still requires that to be coherent I must afford the maximum degree of belief to all the tautologies expressed by sentences in the truth functional closure of some set of sentences (p. 111); but doing that, surely, is nowhere nearly necessary for knowledge. Thus I might know both that I live in Indiana and that China is larger than Fiji, even if I don't fully believe some of the tautologies involving just those two propositions, either because I have never thought of them, or because they are too complicated for me to grasp with any clarity, or because (as with, for example, Peirce's Law) while I can grasp them, I can't see their truth nearly as clearly as that of, say, $2 + 1 = 3$ or $-(p \& -p)$.

Hacking vastly weakens the notion of coherence: he explains the notions of necessity and possibility, as they occur in the probability calculus, in terms of the notion of 'personal impossibility' where a proposition A is personally impossible for me just if I know $-A$. (This results in "slightly more realistic axioms" for the calculus.) "Suppose X knows no more . . . than Y; then if Y's betting rates satisfy the slightly more realistic axioms, X cannot bet with Y in such a way that X knows . . . that he will win from Y" (p. 322). This is a vastly attenuated sense of coherence. Is it necessary for warrant? If it is *necessary,* in the broadly logical sense, that what I know be manifest in my behavior, then presumably it will be impossible that I fail to be coherent in this sense; in that case Hacking coherence is necessary for warrant, but only in the way in which not being a married bachelor is. On the other hand, perhaps it is possible to be Hacking incoherent. If it is, Hacking coherence will not be required for warrant. You propose a complicated series of bets about who will win the Super Bowl, a series that amounts to a Dutch strategy; I don't bother to think the matter through properly, and accept; then (presumably) I am not coherent in Hacking's sense, but I may still know what my name is, that there is such a thing as the Super Bowl, and that the team that scores the most points wins.

some fairly recondite mathematical truth by way of testimony, and then later come to grasp a simple and elegant proof of it, this being accompanied by a small but definite increase in credence?

Similarly, suppose my credence function changes in the following fashion: I come to see (as I think of it) that one of my conditional probabilities $P(A/B)$ is mistaken, so that my conditional probability for A on B changes (and this is the originating change), but there is no change in $P(A)$ or $P(B)$. Then my probabilities have changed in a way inconsistent with probability kinematics.[28] But surely I could come to see that one of my conditional probabilities $P(A/B)$ was inappropriate, make an appropriate change in it without changing my degree of belief in A or in B, and still know what I knew before the change. Being excessively sanguine, I believe that the probability of my getting a Nobel Prize, conditional on my finishing my book by next Christmas, is relatively high (though I think my chances of finishing by then are not very good); you persuade me that this confidence does not fit the facts; I come to a more chastened estimate of this probability, without changing my personal probability for my getting the prize or for my finishing by Christmas. Can't I know much both before and after and during this change?

Changing belief by probability kinematics, therefore, is not necessary for knowledge or warrant. Of course the same goes also for Reflection; clearly I can know something today, even if I also think I may invest full belief in a false proposition tomorrow. Indeed, I can now *know* that there are three pens on my desk, even if my credence in that proposition, on the supposition that 10 years from now my credence in it will be low, is high.

None of the Bayesian conditions, therefore, is necessary for warrant. It is equally obvious, I suppose, that satisfying all of them is not *sufficient* for it. (Of course I don't mean to suggest that Bayesians claim otherwise.) This is obvious because Bayesianism is *incomplete* if taken as a theory of warrant, and incomplete in at least two important ways. First: taken as an account of warrant, Bayesianism (like coherence theories generally) is what John Pollock calls a "doxastic" theory: it holds that the warrant or positive epistemic status of a belief is determined solely by the relation that belief bears to other beliefs, wholly neglecting the relation it bears to experience. Bayesianism says some-

---

[28]Argument: a change in $P(A/B)$ with no change in either $P(A)$ or $P(B)$ is equivalent to a change in $P(A\&B)$ with no change in either $P(A)$ or $P(B)$; so it suffices to show that Jeffrey conditionalization precludes the latter change.

Accordingly, suppose your beliefs do change in the latter way. Let P be your old credence function and P* your new; and let

$P(A) = n$, $P(B) = m$, and $P(A\&B) = x$.

Then

$P^*(A) = n$, $P^*(B) = m$, and $P^*(A\&B) = y$ (y not equal to x).

By Jeffrey, if you come to believe a proposition X to degree n, then for any proposition A, $P^*(A) = n(P(A/X)) + (1 - n)(P(A/-X))$. For the case in question, therefore,

$P^*(-A) = 1 - y(P(-A/-(A\&B))) + y(P(-A/(A\&B)))$
$= 1 - y(P(-A/-(A\&B))) + 0$
$= (1 - y)(1 - n)/1 - x$.

but this last expression can equal $1 - n$ only if $x = y$.

thing about how my credence should be propagated over the rest of my beliefs when I come to hold a new belief in response to experience: that should go by way of conditionalization or Jeffrey conditioning. It says nothing, however, about *how my beliefs should change in response to experience*. If my beliefs *do* change in response to experience, then the Bayesian can tell me how my probabilities should be redistributed over the rest of what I believe; but she has nothing to say about how my beliefs should change (in response to experience) in the first place. Hence my beliefs could change in utterly bizarre ways even if I conform to all the Bayesian principles.

Here we can return to previous examples. By virtue of cognitive malfunction, I might be such that upon being appeared to redly, I form the belief that no one other than I is ever thus appeared to; this is compatible with my credence function's satisfying all the Bayesian constraints. But even if my beliefs do satisfy those constraints, the proposition *Only I am ever appeared to redly* will have little by way of warrant for me. Even if by some wild chance it happens to be true, it will not constitute knowledge. Alternatively, I might be captured by Alpha Centaurian cognitive scientists who run an experiment in which they propose to bring it about that my beliefs satisfy Bayesian constraints, but change with respect to my experience in wholly random ways; then many of my beliefs will have little by way of warrant despite their conformity to Bayesian principles. Again, I might be like the Epistemically Inflexible Climber (chapter 4, p. 82) whose beliefs became fixed, no longer responsive to experience, so that no matter what my experience, I continue to hold the same beliefs. If we suppose that my beliefs satisfy the Bayesian constraints when I am struck by that burst of radiation, they will satisfy them in the Jackson opera; but many of them will have no warrant then. In these cases and a thousand others my beliefs would have little or no warrant for me, even though they meet the Bayesian conditions.

Taken as a theory of warrant, therefore, Bayesianism is incomplete in that it says nothing about the sort of relation between belief and experience required by warrant. But perhaps we could take it as a *partial* theory of warrant, a theory having to do only with what is downstream, so to speak, from the formation of belief on the basis of experience. So taken, it could be thought of as a sort of foundationalism with nothing much to say on the question, Which propositions are properly basic? but as making suggestions as to what warrant requires by way of change in belief in response to change at the basic level. Here too, however, we are doomed to disappointment; for there is a second way in which Bayesianism (taken as a theory of warrant) is incomplete: it provides no account of *evidence* or *evidential support*. It lacks the resources to say what it is for one proposition to offer evidential support for another; hence, it offers no account of the way in which a proposition can acquire warrant by being believed on the evidential basis of another proposition that already has it. The proposition

(1)   99 out of 100 Frisian lifeguards can swim and Feike is a Frisian lifeguard

supports, is evidence for

(2)   Feike can swim.

There is excellent (propositional) evidence that the earth is round; and according to the probabilistic version of the problem of evil, the existence of evil, or of certain particularly horrifying cases of it, is evidence against the existence of God. These evidence relations, furthermore, transfer warrant. If I know the evidence that the earth is round and believe that it is round on the basis of that evidence (and have no defeaters for this belief), that belief will have warrant for me. Clearly these evidence relations hold independently of my degrees of belief; and even if I am certain that (1) is true and (2) false, I still recognize that the first supports the second. But precisely this notion of evidential support is what cannot be explained in Bayesian terms.

We can see this as follows. First, we might try looking to the idea of conditional personal probability or conditional credence for a Bayesian account of the supports relation, claiming that B supports A if $P(A/B)$ is sufficiently high. But first, whose credence function is at issue here? We need a subscript. So suppose we relativize the notion of support to credence functions, so that B supports A *for me* if and only if $P_{me}(A/B)$ is sufficiently high: things still go wildly wrong. For example, on this suggestion it won't be possible for me to know a proposition—that Feike can swim, say—and also know a couple of other propositions, one of which evidentially supports it and the other of which supports its denial; if I know all three propositions, then the conditional probability of any on any will be high. But obviously I might very well know a couple of propositions, one but not the other supporting that proposition: perhaps I know (1) and also know

(3)   99/100 Frisian octogenarians can't swim and Feike is a Frisian octogenarian.

If I know both that (1) is true and (2) is false, then (embarrassingly enough) the conditional probability, for me, of the *denial* of (2) on (1) will be very high, and the probability of (2) on (1) very low, so that (1) supports, for me, the denial of (2). More generally: take any pair of contingent propositions such that the first offers evidential support for the second: even if I satisfy all Bayesian constraints, my personal probability for the second on the first can be as low as you please.

But perhaps this is not how the Bayesian will explain evidential support;[29] perhaps she will say that A supports B in case $P(B/A) > P(B)$—that is, A supports B *for me* in case $P_{me}(B/A) > P_{me}(B)$. But this too can't be right. Due to cognitive malfunction or the machinations of demon or Alpha Centaurian, I might be such that, for example, I know nothing at all about Feike's swimming ability and $P_{me}(2) = .5$, but am also such that $P_{me}((2)/(1)) = .1$ and $P_{me}((2)/(3)) = .9$. Then on the present suggestion, (1) disconfirms (2) 'for me' and (3)

[29]Here I am indebted to Patrick Maher.

confirms it for me! But (if 'evidentially supports for me' [as opposed to 'evidentially supports' *simpliciter*] makes any sense at all) surely they do not.

The real problem, though, is with that subscript; evidential support is not, in this way, relative to individual noetic structures or individual credence functions. (It is not a three-place relation among a pair of propositions and a credence function.) My Alpha Centaurian captors might cause me to reason in such a way that what is in fact the evidence for the roundness of the earth Bayesianly supports, for me, the proposition that the earth is flat. But even if they do, it is not the case then that the evidence for the earth's being round really does support 'for me' the proposition that it is flat—just as it is not the case that the earth is flat 'for me'. If evidence E supports proposition H, then E supports H *simpliciter*, not merely relative to your credence function or mine. (1) is *as such* evidence for (2); the idea of its being evidence for (2) for *you* but not for *me*, if it is to be a sensible idea, can only be taken as something like the idea that you recognize that it is evidence for (2) while I do not, or that when (1) is added to the rest of what you believe, the resulting total evidence supports (2), but when added to the rest of what I believe, the resulting total evidence does not. It is therefore at the least enormously difficult to see how we could explain the supports relation in Bayesian terms.

Bayesianism has little to contribute to a proper theory of warrant. This conclusion, however, is one Bayesians can accept with equanimity; for their interest typically lies not in warrant but in something else, something they call 'rationality'. It is time to turn to that baffling and elusive notion.

7

Bayesian Coherentism and Rationality

Our central focus is on the notion of warrant—that quantity enough of which is sufficient, together with truth, for knowledge. As an account of warrant, Bayesianism clearly won't do the job; for purposes of this book, therefore, no more, strictly speaking, need be said. But Bayesianism is much too interesting to dismiss in such summary fashion. Bayesians typically speak not of warrant, but of *rationality* and they have subtle and fascinating things to say about it. One of the things they say is that conformity to Bayesian constraints is necessary for rationality. But what *is* this rationality of which they speak? In this chapter we shall explore this question: rationality (along with justification) is a crucially significant notion neighboring warrant and is important for coming to a solid understanding of it. We shall explore this multifaceted notion of rationality and ask whether there is any interesting facet of it of which Bayesianism is a good account.

I. The Varieties of Rationality
A. *Means–Ends Rationality and Foley Rationality*

One of the slipperiest terms in the philosophical lexicon, 'rationality' is many things to many people. According to Richard Foley,

> rationality is a function of an individual pursuing his goals in a way that he on reflection would take to be effective. Since epistemic rationality is concerned with the epistemic goal of now believing truths and now not believing falsehoods, the Aristotelian conception suggests that it is epistemically rational for an individual S to believe p just if he on reflection would think that believing p is an effective means to his epistemic goal.[1]

The *generic* notion of rationality of which Foley's is a species is what our Continental cousins, following Max Weber, sometimes call *Zweckrationalität*, the sort of rationality displayed by the actions of someone who strives to attain his goals in a way calculated to achieve them. Clearly there is a whole constellation of notions lurking in the nearby woods: what would *in fact* contribute to your goals, what you *take* it would contribute to your goals, what you *would*

[1]*The Theory of Epistemic Rationality* (Cambridge: Harvard University Press, 1987), p. 66.

132

take it would contribute to your goals if you were sufficiently acute, or knew enough, or were not distracted by lust, greed, pride, ambition, and the like, what you would take it would contribute to your goals if you were not thus distracted and were also to reflect sufficiently, and so on. This notion of rationality has assumed enormous importance in the last 150 years or so. (Among its laurels, for example, is the complete domination of the development of the discipline of economics.) Rationality thus construed is a matter of knowing how to get what you want; it is the cunning of reason. (*Zweckrationalität* might also be called 'Jacobean rationality', after the Old Testament patriarch Jacob, famed for cunning if not integrity.) Foley's specifically *epistemic* rationality is a special case of Jacobean rationality: the case where the goal in question is the epistemic goal of now having true beliefs and now not having false beliefs. Foley rationality is a property one of your beliefs has if, on sufficient reflection, you would think that holding that belief was an effective means to achieving that epistemic goal.

By way of brief digression: Foley rationality is intuitively important; and Foley develops it with depth and subtlety.[2] It is important to see, however, that Foley rationality does not provide the materials for an account of warrant (nor, of course, does Foley claim it does). There may be interesting connections between warrant and Foley rationality; but I can be Foley rational in accepting a belief *B*, even if *B* has no warrant or positive epistemic status for me. Descartes speaks of those "whose cerebella are so troubled or clouded by the violent vapors of black bile, that they constantly assure us that they think they are kings when they are really quite poor, or that they are clothed in purple when they are really without covering, or who imagine that they have an earthenware head, or are nothing but pumpkins or are made out of glass" (Meditation I). So imagine someone doing something that on the face of it looks at best wholly eccentric and at worst insane. Suppose one of your friends takes to wrapping his head with great swaths of cotton batting, cutting tiny holes for his eyes, ears, and nose; then by way of applying a finishing touch, he puts on a necessarily oversize football helmet. He never goes out without this getup, and he makes superhuman efforts to avoid even the most moderate bumps. He does not play football, of course, but he also avoids such apparently unhazardous activity as walking under oak trees when acorns are falling and

---

[2]Perhaps there is a self-referential problem with *reflection* here. According to Foley, a person is epistemically rational in accepting *p* if and only if on reflection he would think accepting *p* an effective means to his epistemic end, that is, if and only if he "has an uncontroversial argument for *p*, an argument that he would regard as likely to be truth preserving were he to be appropriately reflective and an argument whose premises he would uncover no good reason to be suspicious of were he to be appropriately reflective" (ibid., p. 66). But what's so great about reflection? Couldn't I be profoundly convinced that reflection, in particular, reflection on arguments and argument forms, is nearly always misleading? Perhaps I concur with D. H. Lawrence: when an argument gets sicklied o'er with the pale cast of thought, it is impossible to see whether it is a good one. To tell whether an argument is acceptable, you must think with your blood, endorsing your first impulse; reflection only muddies the waters. But if this is one of my most profound convictions, why would epistemic rationality require me to accept a proposition only if it is the conclusion of an argument that *on reflection* I would find acceptable?

apple trees during picking season. This behavior seems egregiously foolish and wholly irrational; but then we discover that (due to black bile or brain lesion) he has come to believe, like Descartes' madmen, that his head is made of glass. (He believes his head is a hollow spheroid, made of thin and fragile crystal.) This belief on his part may be utterly mad; but given that he *has* it, one can see why he acts as he does. From his perspective, which includes that bizarre belief as well as a wholly understandable desire to avoid a shattering experience, this mode of behavior seems perfectly sensible—rational, as we might say.

His behavior displays means–ends rationality; but further, his mad belief may display Foley rationality. For perhaps this belief, due as it is to cerebral malfunction, is deeply ingrained in him and wholly immune to reflection: no matter how much he reflected, he would still hold it—indeed, hold it even more firmly—and still think holding it a good way to achieve his goal of believing truths and not believing falsehoods. But of course the belief would have little or no warrant for him. A high degree of Foley rationality, therefore, isn't anywhere nearly sufficient for warrant; to get a condition sufficient for the latter, we should have to add at the least that the agent's cognitive faculties are not subject to this sort of cognitive disorder.

B. Aristotelian Rationality

According to Aristotle, man is a rational animal. Aristotle was no doubt right in this as in much else: but what did he mean? One of the most venerable uses of the term 'rational' is to denote certain kinds of beings: those with *ratio*, the power of reason. Such creatures are able to hold beliefs; they are capable of thought, reflection, intentionality. Rational beings are those that are able to form concepts, grasp propositions, see relationships between them, think about objects both near and far. This is the sense in which man is a rational animal. Creatures can of course differ with respect to their rational powers, the strength or excellence of their reason or *ratio*. Man is a rational animal, but certain other animals also appear to display some rudimentary powers of reason, and perhaps there are still other creatures (angels, Alpha Centaurians) by comparison with whom, cognitively speaking, we human beings pale into insignificance. So a second sense of the term: a creature is rational if it has the power of reason. (Clearly, being rational in this sense is a necessary condition for having knowledge ; it may also be sufficient for having *some knowledge or other*, but of course it is not sufficient for any particular bit of knowledge.)

C. Rationality as the Deliverances of Reason

Aristotelian rationality is *generic:* it pertains to the power of thinking, believing, and knowing. But there is also a very important more specific sense; this is the sense that goes with reason taken more narrowly, as the source of *a priori* knowledge and belief.[3] Most prominent among the deliverances of reason are *self-evident* beliefs—beliefs so obvious that you can't grasp them without

[3]See my *Warrant and Proper Function* (New York: Oxford University Press, 1993), chap. 6.

seeing that they couldn't be false. Of course, there are other beliefs—*38 × 39 = 1,482,* for example—that are not self-evident, but are a consequence of self-evident beliefs by way of arguments that are self-evidently valid; these too are among the deliverances of reason. So say that the *deliverances of reason* is the set of those propositions that are self-evident for us human beings, closed under self-evident consequence. This yields another traditional kind of rationality: a belief is *rational* if it is among the deliverances of reason and *irrational* if it is contrary to the deliverances of reason. (A belief can therefore be neither rational nor irrational, in this sense.)[4] Rationality in this sense is clearly species (or kind) relative; beings of more impressive intellectual attainments might well find much self-evident that is beyond our cognitive grasp.

There are various analogical extensions of this use of the term 'rational' and its cohorts, and analogical extensions of the concept it expresses. First, we can broaden the category of reason to include memory and experience and whatever else goes into science; this is the sense of the term when reason is contrasted with faith. Second, a person can be said to be irrational if he won't listen to or pay attention to the deliverances of reason. He may be blinded by lust or inflamed by passion, or deceived by pride: he might then act contrary to reason—*act* irrationally, but also *believe* irrationally. Thus Locke:

> Let never so much probability land on one side of a covetous man's reasoning, and money on the other, it is easy to foresee which will outweigh. Tell a man, passionately in love, that he is jilted; bring a score of witnesses of the falsehood of his mistress, 'tis ten to one but three kind words of hers, shall invalidate all their testimonies . . . and though men cannot always openly gain-say, or resist the force of manifest probabilities, that make against them; yet yield they not to the argument.[5]

D. Deontological Rationality

There is another important extension of this sense. Evidentialist objectors to theistic belief say that it is irrational to believe in God without having (propositional) evidence. Here they don't have in mind Foley rationality (they would not be mollified by a demonstration that even after sufficient reflection the theist would continue to think believing in God a good way to achieve his epistemic goals); nor do they mean that believers in God (sadly enough) are not rational creatures; nor do they necessarily mean that belief in God is contrary to the dictates of reason (they need not think that one can deduce the nonexistence of God from propositions that are self-evident to one degree or another). What then *do* they mean? An important clue is the way these critics often assume the moral high ground, sometimes even sounding a bit self-righteous in the process. Thus Michael Scriven:

[4]Here I won't stop to ask whether self-evidence is a matter of degree, whether there are propositions that are self-evident to all of us, whether any proposition self-evident to any of us is self-evident to all of us, what the phenomenology of self-evidence is, and how we are to understand 'in accord with'; for these matters, see ibid., chap. 6.

[5]*An Essay concerning Human Understanding,* ed. A. C. Fraser (New York: Dover, 1953), IV, 20, 12, p. 453.

Now even belief in something for which there is no evidence, i.e., a belief which goes beyond the evidence, although a lesser sin than belief in something which is contrary to well-established laws, is plainly irrational in that it simply amounts to attaching belief where it is not justified. So the proper alternative, when there is no evidence, is not mere suspension of belief, e.g., about Santa Claus; it is disbelief. It most certainly is not faith.[6]

Here Scriven is thinking of *propositional* evidence: the evidence afforded for one of your beliefs by way of an argument from other propositions you believe, for example. Now *why* is it irrational to believe that for which there is no evidence? Return to Descartes and Locke (see pp. 11ff); and suppose you agree with them that there is a *duty* to refrain from believing a proposition (a proposition that is not either self-evident or appropriately about your own mental life) unless there is (propositional) evidence for it. Suppose, more particularly, you agree with them that it is *self-evident,* a deliverance of reason, that there is such a duty. Then to believe a proposition of that sort without evidence is to go contrary to the deliverances of reason: not by believing a proposition that is contrary to reason, but by believing in a way that constitutes flouting a duty, a duty such that it is a deliverance of reason that there *is* such a duty. To flout this duty is to go contrary to the deliverances of reason; it would be natural, therefore, to extend the use of the term and call such beliefs 'irrational'. In that extended sense of the term, belief in God without propositional evidence *is* irrational, if indeed it is self-evident that there is the sort of duty Locke and Descartes say there is. (Of course, the fact is that is *not* self-evident.)

Rationality in this sense, clearly, is very close to the classical notion of *justification,* as in chapter 1. Indeed, this claim that proper belief in God requires propositional evidence is often put in terms of justification; in these contexts, 'justification' and 'rationality' are often used interchangeably (a fact we understand when we see that this variety of rationality, like classical justification, is essentially deontological). Note that here, as with 'justification', there are many analogical extensions and additions to the use of the term, and many cases where it is used in forgetfulness of the original basis of its application. It is in this way that the term 'irrational' can come to be used as simply a *name* for a certain kind of behavior, a kind of behavior that, by many earlier users of the term, was thought to have the property (say, that of going contrary to duty) it expressed on the earlier use of the term. In this way someone can come to think that it is irrational to believe without propositional evidence even if she no longer believes that there are those epistemic duties Locke and Descartes say there are—although then it is no longer clear just what she is saying about such believings when she says that they are irrational, or why their being irrational should be thought a mark against them.

E. Rationality as Sanity and Proper Function

One who suffers from pathological confusion, or flight of ideas, or Korsakov's syndrome, or certain kinds of agnosia, or manic depressive psychosis will often

6*Primary Philosophy* (New York: McGraw-Hill, 1966), p. 103.

be said to be irrational; after the episode passes, he may be said to have regained rationality. Here 'rationality' means absence of dysfunction, disorder, impairment, pathology with respect to rational faculties. So this variety of rationality is analogically related to Aristotelian rationality; a person is rational in this sense when no malfunction obstructs her use of the faculties by virtue of the possession of which she is rational in the Aristotelian sense. Rationality as sanity does not require possession of particularly exalted rational faculties; it requires only normality (in the nonstatistical sense) or health, or proper function. This use of the term, naturally enough, is prominent in psychiatric discussions—Oliver Sack's man who mistook his wife for a hat,[7] for example, was thus irrational. In this sense of the term, an irrational impulse may be rational: an irrational impulse is really one that goes contrary to the deliverances of reason; but undergoing such impulses need not be in any way dysfunctional or a result of the impairment of cognitive faculties. To go back to some of William James's examples, that I will survive my serious illness might be unlikely, given the statistics I know and my evidence generally; perhaps we are so constructed, however, that when our faculties function properly in extreme situations, we are more optimistic than the evidence warrants. This belief, then, is irrational in the sense that it goes contrary to the deliverances of reason; it is rational in the sense that it does not involve dysfunction. (To use the terminology of my *Warrant and Proper Function*, the module of the design plan involved in the production of this belief is aimed, not at truth, but at survival).

II. Bayesian Constraints and Rationality

Now which, if any, of these concepts of rationality does the Bayesian have in mind when she declares that rationality requires satisfying coherence, conditionalization or probability kinematics, and perhaps Reflection? Note that these Bayesian constraints are thought of in two quite different spirits. First, the *Kantian* way: the conditions in question are proposed as norms for our epistemic behavior—epistemic rules or maxims, perhaps—which, like norms generally, are none the worse for being seldom met:

> Bayesian decision theory provides a set of norms for human decision making; but it is far from being a true description of our behavior. Similarly, deductive logic provides a set of norms for human deductive reasoning, but cannot be usefully reinterpreted as a description of human reasoning.[8]

To the extent that we fail to obey these rules or conform to these norms (on this way of thinking of the matter) we are allegedly irrational or, at any rate, less than wholly rational.

But second, there is the *Platonic* way: the Bayesian constraints may be thought of as descriptive of the intellectual life of ideal cognizers, as charac-

---

[7]*The Man Who Mistook His Wife for a Hat* (New York: Harper and Row, 1987).
[8]Richard Jeffrey, *The Logic of Decision* (Chicago: University of Chicago Press, 1983), p. 167.

teristic of ideally rational persons, knowers with maximal *ratio*. Thus Paul Horwich:

> More specifically, the Bayesian approach rests upon the fundamental principle: (B) That the degrees of belief of an ideally rational person conform to the mathematical principles of probability theory.[9]

So here we are idealizing, perhaps in the way in which we do physics by thinking about frictionless planes and point masses. Human beings are not in fact coherent, but then automobiles are not point masses and roads are not frictionless plains; still, we can learn a lot about the way automobiles move on roads by treating them as if they were point masses and frictionless plains. Perhaps the Bayesian means to be talking about how human beings *would* function if there were not the intruding analogues of friction. Or perhaps we are idealizing in a different way: we are describing the intellectual characteristics of an ideal knower, a being of maximum reason, maximum *ratio*, whether or not an idealized *human* knower. In either case, the thought is that the Bayesian constraints form a pattern for us, a sort of Platonic *eidos* that constitutes an ideal for us and our intellectual life. And of course there is an intimate connection between these two: if the Bayesian conditions describe the intellectual life of an ideally rational person, then insofar as we do not conform to them taken as maxims or rules, we fall short of that ideal.

A. Coherence

But now we must ask a question that has been clamoring for attention: *Why* must we conform to the Bayesian constraints, if we are not to be irrational? Why, for example, must we be *coherent* to be rational? Here there are substantially three answers: first, what for want of a better name, I shall call "the argument from means–ends rationality," initially in the form of a Dutch book argument and then in a deeper form; second, the argument from ideality; and third, the analogical argument.

1. The Dutch Book Argument

The *conclusion* of the Dutch book argument is that I am irrational if not coherent.[10] Why so? And how are we to think of this irrationality that allegedly

---

[9]*Probability and Evidence* (Cambridge: Cambridge University Press, 1982), p. 12.

[10]There are some initial problems with the coherence requirement. For example, my credence function is *gappy*; there are many propositions on which I have no opinion at all (perhaps for the very good reason that I have never heard of them). Perhaps my opinions are also vague, in the sense that there is no precise numerical answer to the question 'How firmly do you believe *A*?' Further, we need not suppose that just any two beliefs of mine are comparable; perhaps there are pairs of propositions *A* and *B* I believe, such that it isn't true that I believe *A* more firmly than *B* but also isn't true that I believe *B* at least as firmly as *A*. (The *believes at least as firmly as* relation might not be connected in my noetic structure.) But then, of course, it follows immediately that my credence function is not coherent. Bas van Fraassen therefore proposes a less demanding sense of 'coherence'. Say that a probability function *P* (a function that conforms to the calculus of

fastens, like a rapacious lamprey, to one who does not conform to Bayesian constraints: what sort of irrationality is this? Which (if any) of the previously noted forms of rationality is at stake? Clearly not Aristotelian rationality or rationality as sanity; one can be a sane and properly functioning rational animal without being coherent. Nor is it among the deliverances of reason that there is a duty to be coherent. So perhaps it is means–ends rationality that is at stake. Perhaps the thought is that if I am not coherent, I am vulnerable to a Dutch bookie, and that does not fit well with my aims (which include among other things hanging on to my fortune, meager though it is).

But just how is the argument supposed to run? No doubt in general it would be means–ends irrational (*ceteris paribus*) to accept knowingly a series of bets such that no matter what happens, I lose. (It would also be irrational to accept such a series of bets even if I *didn't* know it was of that distressing character; this would be irrational in a broader means–end sense in which taking any action guaranteed to frustrate my ends is [*ceteris paribus*] irrational, whether or not I know it is guaranteed to frustrate my ends.) But suppose I *do* bet on *A;* why must I also be prepared to bet on not-*A?* Indeed, who says I have to bet at all? Dutch book arguments picture us as wildly enthusiastic and totally committed bookies, posting odds (perhaps on a giant board on the front lawn) on every proposition we come across, ready to take on all comers and cover any bets that are fair according to those odds. (I'll give you 100 to 1 that Caesar crossed the Rubicon, 10^{10} to 1 that arithmetic is incomplete, 1 to 3 that there are two John Paul Jones's in the phone book on Fiji, 4 to 1 on Existentialism, . . .) If I *were* to do this, then no doubt a logically omniscient bettor could drain my pockets; for, of course, I am not logically omniscient and, as I will argue in sec. 4 (p. 145), not even consistent with respect to my full beliefs (for the paradox of the preface, see p. 145). But *are* there any such bettors—more relevantly, am I likely to encounter one? And if I do encounter one, can't I just refuse to bet? Are these logically omniscient bettors a problem worth worrying about?

What means–ends rationality requires is not that I be coherent or post coherent odds. What it requires is that if I am not coherent, I avoid betting with logically omniscient bookies, just as I avoid betting on historical facts with historians or on points of law with lawyers. But in fact means–ends rationality requires something vastly stronger: it requires that I stay out of that whole miserable betting situation. I don't have the time to get involved with all that odds posting, all those efforts to figure out what I believe about this and that (whether, for example, I believe that the theory of evolution is more likely than, say, supralapsarianism); I don't have the time or money to put up that big

---

probabilities) *satisfies my credence function* if P(A) > P(B) when I believe A more firmly than B, P(A) ≥ P(B) when I believe A at least as firmly as B, and so on. Then (given that my beliefs are gappy and not connected) if there are any probability functions that satisfy my credence function, there are many. And now say that I am coherent only if there is at least one probability function that satisfies my credence function. See his "Belief and the Will," *Journal of Philosophy* 81, no. 5 (May 1984), p. 251, and "Empiricism in the Philosophy of Science," in *Images of Science*, ed. P. Churchland and C. Hooker (Chicago: University of Chicago Press, 1985), pp. 247–48.

board. Why should I waste time doing things as silly as all that? There are other ways in which I would much rather spend my allotted three score and ten—other ways that will contribute much better to my goals. The Dutch book argument, therefore, clearly goes nowhere, as an argument for the conclusion that it is irrational not to be coherent. No doubt it would be irrational for me to engage in wagers with logically omniscient bookies if I am incoherent or know that I am, but it doesn't follow that I am means–ends irrational if not coherent.

We can say something stronger: *it would be means–ends irrational for me to try to become coherent.* This is evident as follows. A principal source of my incoherence is my lack of what is sometimes called 'logical omniscience'. But this is not quite the right term. I am less than logically omniscient, all right, just by virtue of the fact that there are many necessary truths I have never heard of. But the problem for my being coherent is not just that there are necessary truths I have never heard of; the problem is that many of the necessary truths I *have* heard of are such that it would be irrational for me to believe them to the maximal degree. Consider Goldbach's Conjecture, for example, or the claim that each object has a qualitative individual essence, or the view that objects have haecceities and that Socrates' haecceity could not have existed if Socrates himself had not. I have little idea which if any of these are true; I therefore give some credence to each of them, but also some credence to each of their denials. But, of course, each is noncontingent, necessarily true if true at all; I am therefore incoherent. Many other noncontingent propositions are such that while I *think* I can see that they are true, I can't see their truth as clearly as that of elementary truths of logic or arithmetic: for example, the propositions that no propositions are sets,[11] that (*pace* Meinong and Castañeda) there are no objects that do not exist, and (*contra* existentialism) that even if Socrates had not existed, the possible worlds in which he exists would still have existed, and so on. Hence I believe them to some degree less than the maximal degree. But isn't this just what rationality requires? Would it be rational in the means–ends sense, given my limitations, for me to try to achieve coherence, thus trying to believe every noncontingent proposition I think of to the maximal or minimal degree? Of course not. According to John Locke, the wise man proportions his belief to the evidence: but this holds for noncontingent truths as well as contingent truths. One of my goals is to try to achieve a wise and judicious frame of mind in which I proportion my degree of belief, with respect to noncontingent truths, to their degree of obviousness, or their obviousness with respect to what is obvious, or the enthusiasm with which they are endorsed by those who know. But then means–ends rationality does not require that I be coherent;[12] it

[11]See my "Modal Realism and Modal Reductionism," in *Philosophical Perspectives, 1, Metaphysics, 1987*, ed. James Tomberlin (Atascadero, Calif.: Ridgeview, 1987), pp. 206ff.

[12]We might note here again what we noted in the preceding chapter: the Bayesian could claim that what coherence requires is not that you never believe a necessary truth to a less than maximal degree, but that you never believe a *truth functional tautology* to a less than maximal degree. But first, this seems utterly arbitrary. On this showing, you are irrational if you assign some complicated tautology less than maximal credence, but not if you believe, for example, that $2 + 3 = 7$. And second, it is clearly not true that rationality requires believing, say, $((p \rightarrow p) \rightarrow p) \rightarrow p$ ("Peirce's Law") as firmly as, say, $-(p \& -p)$. The rational condition here, for a human being, is to

requires, instead, that I recognize my limitations and believe a noncontingent proposition with maximal firmness only if it is maximally evident for me.[13]

2. The Deeper Means–Ends Argument

But perhaps we could think of Dutch book arguments as dramatizing and pointing to a deeper sort of problem: if I am not coherent, then my views will be such as to necessarily diminish my chances of being right; and since I have a stake in being right, isn't that means–ends irrational? Isn't it also Foley irrational in that it interferes with my goal of now believing truth and not now believing falsehood? Thus van Fraassen:

> Let me clarify this by means of the distinction between reasonableness and vindication in the evaluation of right action, right decision, and right opinion. Whether or not you were vindicated in a decision or action depends on the outcome it led to in the actual circumstances that obtained—much of which you could not have known or reasonably expected. Whether or not your present opinion about tomorrow's weather will be vindicated depends on tomorrow's actual weather. Lack of vindication can be a reproach, as Machiavelli pointed out, but it cannot impugn the rationality of the action or opinion. Whether or not that was reasonable depends on factors settled at the time and, in some sense, accessible. The paradigm of irrationality is to form or organize your actions, decisions, or opinions so as to hinder needlessly your chance of vindication. If your opinion is self-contradictory, you have sabotaged yourself in the worst possible way—you have guaranteed that your opinion will not turn out correct—but milder forms of self-sabotage are easily envisaged.[14]

believe the latter to the max but the former just a bit more tentatively, even if you are convinced (you have just made a truth table analysis) that it is indeed a tautology. The reason, of course, is that the latter is utterly obvious, but the former is not.

[13]I have dwelt here on noncontingent propositions; but a similar problem arises for their contingent colleagues. Consider a countably infinite collection $C = \{A_0, A_1, \ldots, A_n \ldots\}$ of mutually exclusive (in pairs) and jointly exhaustive propositions such that I don't know of any that it is false and such that I have no more reason to accept one than another: for example, *there are no angels, there is exactly 1 angel, there are exactly 2 angels, . . . , there are exactly n angels*. We can easily see that I am vulnerable to a Dutch book unless my credence function is countably additive, that is, such that the sum of the probabilities afforded the members of C equals my probability that at least one member of C is true. But any such distribution of credence over the members of C seems wrong. A probability function that assigns them all the same probability, will assign them all zero credence; but then their sum will also have zero credence, unlike my credence for the proposition that at least one member of C is true. Any function that assigns some zero and others a nonzero credence also seems wrong: if I have no more reason to think the one true rather than the other, how can I afford the one more credence than the other? But any function that assigns them all a nonzero credence must approach zero as a limit and hence must assign some member A vastly smaller credence than some member B; how can this be proper when I have no less reason to think A true than B? Nor will it help to follow David Lewis and assign them *infinitesimal* credence. First, it is not even remotely clear that there could *be* infinitesimal degrees of credence; and second, even if there could, it will still turn out that for any kind of object (witches, demons, Siberian Cheesehounds) such that for any positive integer n it is possible that there be just n objects of that kind, my credence, for any positive integer m, that there are more than m such objects would be infinitesimally close to 1. But that too seems wrong.

[14]"Empiricism in the Philosophy of Science," p. 248.

Among those milder forms of self-sabotage, we might think, is incoherence: if we are incoherent, we cannot be completely vindicated, and "A decision is unreasonable if vindication is *a priori* precluded."[15] What is the force of 'unreasonable' here? Perhaps van Fraassen is thinking of means–ends rationality: among my goals is vindication, or rather a style of epistemic life in which vindication is not *a priori* excluded. Incoherence, however, is incompatible with achieving that style of life; so incoherence is means–ends irrational. Here we have an argument from means–ends rationality that is independent of Dutch book considerations and is both deeper and more plausible than Dutch book arguments. Still, I think the reply is essentially the same. After all, we have already ruined the possibility of (complete) vindication by accepting any non-contingent truth to a degree different from 0 or 1. Here there is at best a conflict among my goals. Perhaps it would be good (if possible) not to preclude *a priori* the possibility of complete vindication; but it is also good to respond appropriately to the difference in warrant, for me, between different noncontingent propositions. I want to believe noncontingent propositions to the degree to which they are obvious to me, or clearly supported by propositions that are obvious to me, or attested to by those in the know. And the fact is I want this a good deal more than I want to avoid precluding *a priori* the possibility of complete vindication. I could achieve that latter condition only by believing all necessary propositions (or all those that come within my ken) to the maximal degree and all impossible propositions to the minimal degree. This seems to me to require a degree of opinionation inappropriate for beings such as we, who know of our own limitations.

3. The Argument from Ideality

But isn't it true that an *ideal* intellect would satisfy these conditions? Surely an ideally rational person, a person possessed of perfect *ratio* or reason, a perfect knower, would satisfy them, just by virtue of being thus ideally rational. And if an ideal intellect would be coherent, then isn't coherence an ideal for any intellect? According to J. Howard Sobel, "*Logical omniscience,* being certain of every necessary truth, and *high opinionation,* having quite definite degrees of confidence in all propositions, are further aspects of an ideal for intellects." He adds that "A person has a stake in intellectual perfection, a deeply personal stake, and compromises made here are always degrading in a sense.")[16] Are we not therefore irrational or at any rate less than wholly rational to the extent that we fail to achieve coherence? We could see the argument of the preceding section as related to this one. Part of my reason for rejecting coherence as required by means–ends rationality is just that some necessary truths seem

[15]Van Fraassen, "Calibration: A Frequency Justification for Personal Probability," in *Physics, Philosophy and Psychoanalysis,* ed. R. S. Cohen and L. Laudan (Dordrecht: D. Reidel, 1983) p. 297. (Of course, as Michael DePaul points out, it could be that even if your goal is to get as close as possible to perfect vindication, the rational thing to do is to accept a policy that will guarantee that you miss perfect vindication.)

[16]"Self-Doubts and Dutch Strategies," *Australasian Journal of Philosophy* (March 1987), pp. 68, 75.

much more obvious to me than others; but of course an ideal intellect would not labor under that handicap; so for such an ideal intellect, means–ends rationality as well as ideality would require coherence.

Now an ideal intellect, an ideal knower, would indeed conform to most of these conditions. God, for example, is omniscient; further, we may suppose he believes every true proposition to the maximal degree and every false proposition to the minimum, so that his beliefs are coherent. True, they probably are not *strictly* coherent (for him many[17] true contingent propositions probably have a subjective probability of 1), but that is only because he is not subject to the sorts of limitations that make it inappropriate (if it is) for us to believe contingent propositions to the max. Since he knows that he never makes a mistake, absence of strict coherence is not *hubris* for him. Furthermore, since his opinions do not change (or rather, do not change in the relevant fashion),[18] he trivially satisfies conditionalization and probability kinematics. Of course he also satisfies Reflection: since he is essentially omniscient, at any time t he believes all truths to the max, including the truth, with respect to any later time t^* and any truth B, that at t^* he will believe B to the max. There are or may be intellects less exalted than God but more exalted than we who also conform to the Bayesian conditions—intellects characterized by logical omniscience, say, even if they are not perfect (or even very good) with respect to contingent truth. (There may also be intellects more ideal than we who do not display logical omniscience, but approach more closely to it than we; and there may also be intellects more ideal than we who are further from coherence than we, but superior in other respects.) A wholly ideal intellect would certainly meet these Bayesian conditions; indeed, a *completely* ideal intellect, an ideal cognizer, a knower than which none greater can be conceived, would be *essentially* coherent—such that it is not possible that it fail to be coherent; for such a person would be essentially omniscient (omniscient in every possible world in which it exists). Perhaps we should go still further (following Anselm) and argue that a *really* ideal intellect would be *necessarily* coherent, coherent in every possible world; for such an ideal person, we might argue, would be necessarily omniscient—essentially omniscient and necessarily existent. (So if it is *possible* that there be a completely ideal intellect, it is *necessary* that there is one.)

But even if this last is too extravagant, the premise that an ideal intellect would indeed be coherent seems correct. What follows, however, for *us?* Not much, so far as I can see. Of course, it does not follow that we should try hard or even at all to achieve coherence. In an ideal world, the Red Cross does not exist; despite our knowledge of that fact, the Red Cross has nothing to fear from us. In an ideal world there are no lawyers, police, cancer research, or

---

[17]But perhaps not all: some would exempt certain future contingent propositions and others might exempt counterfactuals of freedom.

[18]I don't propose to enter, here, the question whether some propositions are temporally contingent, varying in truth value over time, so that an omniscient being would change his mind constantly about, for example, what time it is, and frequently about whether, say, Socrates is sitting.

dishwashers; we know better than to try in consequence to eliminate lawyers, cancer research, dishwashers, and the police force. The same goes for intellectual ideality. Trying hard to achieve coherence would deprive us of other goods, indeed, of other *epistemic* goods. An ideal intellect would be maximally opinionated, and that in a dual sense: it would have opinions on everything and would hold all its opinions to the max. But should I try to do that? Of course not. I can't sensibly try to achieve coherence with respect to noncontingent truths; but even for contingent truths it might be foolish to invest much effort in it. If I spend too much time trying to detect incoherence in my credence function, I may have little time left to learn new truths or appropriately reflect upon those I have already learned.

Accordingly, I am not irrational in any of the senses distinguished previously by virtue of failing to conform to these conditions. I am not means–ends irrational for so failing; nor am I insane; nor do I then fail to be a rational animal; nor do I then act or believe contrary to the deliverances of reason; nor is there a duty (for me) to be coherent. I am not intellectually defective or worse than I ought to be simply because I am nowhere near being an ideal intellect, that is, simply because there are or could be intellects vastly superior to mine. An ideal intellect would know everything—certainly everything in the past, maybe everything in the future as well. It does not follow that I am irrational in any sense or in any way intellectually defective because I know nothing about the language spoken by pre-Celtic Scots. Am I locomotionally deficient by virtue of the fact that I can't run as fast as a cheetah or fly like a falcon (to say nothing of a *really* ideal locomotor)? Am I deficient with respect to power simply because I am not omnipotent?

True, I am not an *ideally* rational intellect; but it does not follow that I am (in any sensible sense) *ir*rational. *Ideal rationality* and *irrationality* are not complementary properties, even within the class of intellectual beings. *Being less than ideally rational* is a state one achieves simply by being the sort of intellect for which there are or could be superiors; only God manages to avoid this condition. It does not follow that the rest of us are all irrational, defective in some way. I am irrational if I fail to function properly from a cognitive point of view; but I can function perfectly properly even if I am nowhere near ideality. A Model T Ford can be in perfect running order, even if it can't keep up with a new Thunderbird.

As we have already seen, the states and conditions of an ideal intellect are not by that very fact appropriate ideals or standards for me; and, indeed, my so taking them might be arrogant (as when I condescendingly insist on speaking German with German speakers whose English is much better than my German), or means–ends irrational, or merely ludicrous (as when I persist in vainly trying fancy dunks, because that's how Michael Jordan and Dominique Wilkins do it). I display nothing but *hubris* in taking for myself goals not suited to my powers, or measuring myself by standards inappropriate for the kind of being I am, even if there are beings—beings superior to me—who do meet these ideals and standards. The argument from ideality therefore fails.

4. The Analogical Argument

According to Ramsey, the probability calculus is no more than an extension to partial beliefs of formal logic. But then coherence is analogous to consistency in full belief: I should strive for the former just as I should for the latter, and failure to be coherent is irrational just as is failure to be consistent. Jeffrey[19] and others endorse this idea.

It is by no means obvious, of course, either that I should strive for consistency in every context or that failure to achieve it is irrational. After all, there is the Paradox of the Preface: I write a book named *I Believe!* reporting therein only what I now fully believe. Being decently modest, I confess in the preface that I also believe that at least one proposition in *I Believe!* is false (although I have no idea which one[s]). Then my beliefs are inconsistent, in the sense that there is no possible world in which they are all true; but might they not nevertheless be perfectly rational? Given my sorry track record, is it not perfectly sensible and rational for me to suppose that at least one proposition in the book is false? True: I can't rationally entertain any proposition in the book and believe that it is true and furthermore false; but I can rationally believe of each that it is true, while also believing that their conjunction is false. I believe every proposition in the book; I do not believe their conjunction and in fact think it is false;[20] and isn't this precisely what rationality, following the evidence, requires?

Still, in *some* way—a way difficult to specify, given the enormous diversity and articulation of the human cognitive design plan—one obviously ought to strive for consistency. In the same way, then, shouldn't we also strive for coherence? Initially, however, there looks to be an absolutely crucial disanalogy between coherence and consistency: for while I can *withhold* full belief, it looks initially, at any rate, as if I can't withhold partial belief. I have an option with respect to consistency; if I see that A and B are inconsistent, I can withhold full belief with respect to one or the other, thus running no risk of inconsistency. Not so (it initially seems) for incoherence; I can't withhold partial belief; for no matter what I do, I will be apportioning credence between the proposition in question and its denial. To avoid inconsistency, I simply become less opinionated; this won't help with respect to incoherence, and indeed *guarantees* it in the case of noncontingent propositions.

But perhaps this initial appearance is deceiving: am I really obliged to assign some degree of credence or other to just any proposition I encounter? Can't I withhold credence altogether—even when I entertain the proposition in question? Isn't there a difference between withholding credence with respect to some belief A, on the one hand, and, on the other, affording the same degree of credence to A and its denial? You ask me how likely it seems to me that A is true; all I can say is that it seems at least as likely as $2 + 1 = 4$ and no more

[19]*The Logic of Decision* (Chicago: University of Chicago Press, 1983), p. 167.

[20]I don't *entertain* the conjunction of all the propositions I believe; it's too complicated for me to hold before my mind. But I do believe of it that it is false; I pick it out by way of a description ('the conjunction of all the propositions I believe') and believe that the proposition thus specified is false.

likely than $2 + 1 = 3$; and the same goes for B. It would then be true that they seem about equally likely to me, but also true, perhaps, that I don't assign either any nontrivial credence. If I *can* in this way withhold credence, then the objection to the analogy does not hold. If I can withhold belief altogether, believing neither A nor its denial to any degree at all, then I have the same option with respect to coherence as I have with respect to consistency: if I see that my beliefs are incoherent, I can locate the problem and withhold credence from the offending beliefs.

But there is still a crucial disanalogy. I can see that my beliefs are incoherent just by noting that there are noncontingent propositions to which I do not assign either the maximum or minimum degrees of belief; if I am obliged to withhold credence in all these cases, I will have an opinion on a noncontingent proposition only if I have absolute certainty with respect to it—that is, believe it or its denial to the max. But surely this is not required by rationality. I believe that arithmetic is complete, but I am not absolutely certain of it; does rationality really require that I either assign no credence at all to this proposition, or else believe it to the max? I don't think so. The most we can say, I think, is that there is a certain state of affairs I recognize as valuable (and as an epistemic value at that) such that absence of coherence guarantees (*a priori*) that the state of affairs in question is not actual. It does not follow, however, that there is a sensible sense in which I am irrational if I am not coherent. It would also be good to have blinding speed—to be able to run as fast as a greyhound, say; but it doesn't follow that I am locomotorily deficient if I have some property that precludes blinding speed. It would be very good to be able to play the piano better than any human being can in fact play; those who can't are not necessarily musically deficient. A coherent philosopher would be a strange and unlovely creature. Philosophical propositions are for the most part noncontingent; so for nearly any philosophical proposition you pick, either she would have no views at all on it—assign it no credence at all—or else she would be absolutely certain of it or of its denial. Hardly an ideal philosophical interlocutor.

I conclude that none of the forms of rationality we distinguished requires coherence, and some of them require incoherence.

B. Conditionalization and Probability Kinematics

If coherence is not a sensible ideal for us, neither is changing belief by conditionalization or probability kinematics; furthermore, neither is required for rationality. Before arguing the point, however, I want first to defend Bayesians against a certain complaint. Consider my *first* credence function—my Urfunction, we might say: according to Bayesians it is privileged in that any deviation from its pristine conditional probabilities is irrational. But why should *that* credence function be thus exalted? (As the forty-five-year-old dentist said, Why should some sixteen-year-old have the right to decide that I must spend the rest of my life being a dentist?) What is so special about that original Ur-function? According to Bayesians themselves, it is no more rational *an sich* than any of indefinitely many others.

Now here the following complaint is sometimes lodged against Bayesians.[21] Suppose *U* is the conjunction of propositions to which I afforded full belief in my Ur-function; and let *e* be the conjunction of propositions on which I have since come to bestow full belief: then there are many coherent states *S* of belief such that there are coherent credence functions C^* coinciding with my Ur-function on *U*, and such that C^* conditionalized on *e* yields *S*. So suppose I change from my present belief state to a new coherent belief state S^* and do not do so by conditionalization: according to the Bayesian, this is irrational. But, says the complainant, why so? There are any number of coherent credence functions (coinciding with my Ur-function on *U*) from which S^* comes by conditionalization on *e*; any of those functions is as rational as my Ur-function; any could have been my Ur-function, if one of them *had*, then I would have been rational to reach S^*; so what is irrational about my now changing to some other function in that family? But of course the Bayesian has a reply: what is irrational about that is just that it is changing belief in some way other than by conditionalization or probability kinematics. Although the objection is indeed suggestive, its precise bearing is not quite clear. It seems to beg the question against the Bayesian, refusing to take seriously his suggestion that changing belief in some other way is irrational. Perhaps it is less an argument than a cry of incredulity.

So this isn't a serious objection. But the real question, as it seems to me, is this: why can't I sensibly come to *see* that my credence function, though coherent, needs to be changed? The simplest cases would again involve non-contingent propositions. Perhaps I believe to the max that even if Socrates had not existed his haecceity would have; I believe this just as firmly as *2 + 1 = 3*. You get me to see that even if I am right, it isn't genuinely *obvious*, not nearly as obvious, anyway, as *2 + 1 = 3*. I then pull in my horns and believe it more moderately (not changing belief in any other proposition); have I not in fact done the rational thing? Yet I have changed belief in a way inconsistent with probability kinematics. Furthermore, my original maximal belief (supposing it true) was consistent with my being coherent; my later, less than maximal belief was not; and yet the change from one to the other seems perfectly rational, perfectly sensible, and perhaps even required by rationality. Wouldn't I be irrational if I persist in my opinionation?

But of course the same can go for credence in contingent propositions. Couldn't a change in my credence function originate from my coming to see that one of my conditional credences P(*A*/*B*) is improper—even if I continue to invest the same degree of credence in *A* and in *B*? I think more about this proposition *B* I thought provided excellent if nonconclusive evidence for *A*; I come to see that its evidential value is not as significant as I believed, although my degree of credence in *A* and in *B* does not change. Thus a change in my credence function originates from this change in P(*A*/*B*) with no change in P(*A*) or P(*B*). And then my credence function changes, but not by way of probability kinematics. Couldn't this nonetheless be a perfectly rational change?

[21]See Henry Kyburg, Jr., *The Logical Foundations of Statistical Inference* (Dordrecht: D. Reidel, 1974), p. 119.

C. Reflection

1. Explanation

Van Fraassen's Reflection (see chapter 6, p. 125)[22] is of great interest in itself, and van Fraassen has subtle and fascinating things to say about it; to do justice to it or them would require more space (and insight) than I can command. (I shall try not to make a sow's ear out of a silk purse.)

In "Belief and the Will" he put the principle as follows:

$$P_t^a(A/P_{t+x}^a(A) = r) = r$$

where P_t^a is the agent a's credence function at time t, P_{t+x}^a is the agent's credence function at a later time $t + x$, and $P_{t+x}^a(A) = r$ is the proposition that at $t + x$, a believes A to degree r.[23]

I now fully believe that in three weeks I will believe to degree .8, say, that the Athenians won the Peloponnesian War; a little calculation shows that if I conform to Reflection, my present degree of belief in that proposition will also be .8.[24] I am now convinced that truth is not merely what my peers will let me get away with saying; to conform to Reflection, I must now also believe that there is no chance at all that by a year from now I will have changed my mind. I now believe to about .9 that nominalism is false; if I conform to reflection, then I do not now accord .2 credence to the supposition that a year from now I will believe the denial of nominalism to that degree (see n. 35). More generally, an agent satisfies reflection at t just if her degree of belief in A at t, on the condition or supposition that her belief at the same or later time $t + x$ in A will be r, is r. She violates it if, for example, she does not completely reject the proposition that at some future time she will come to believe a false proposition fully.[25]

Reflection so stated applies only to 'sharp' subjective probabilities; it does not accommodate the case where, for example, you think it at least twice as likely as not that it will rain tomorrow afternoon (you're on a summer hiking trip in the Colorado Rockies), but no more than six times as likely as not, and

---

[22]I call it *van Fraassen's* reflection; but according to van Fraassen's unpublished "Belief and the Problem of Ulysses and the Sirens" (hereafter, "Ulysses") "When I was writing 'Belief and the Will' . . . , I did not realize that the statistician Michael Goldstein formulated essentially the same argument for an equivalent principle of iterated expectation ("The Prevision of a Prevision," *Journal of the American Statistical Association* 78 [1983] 817–819)."

[23]"Belief and the Will," p. 244.

[24]Let A be the proposition *The Athenians will win*; let P be my present credence function and P_t my credence function at time t, three weeks from now. Then if I conform to Reflection, $P(A/P_t(A) = .8) = .8$, that is,

$$\frac{P(A\&P_t(A) = .8)}{P(P_t(A) = .8)} = .8$$

Since I now fully believe that in three weeks time my credence for A will be .8, the denominator is 1; therefore $P(A\&P_t(A)=.8) = .8$; since my probability for the right conjunct is 1, my probability for A must be .8.

[25]"Belief and the Will," pp. 236–37.

your opinion is no more definite than that. Then your credence in that proposition is *vague*. We could represent your credence by an *interval* of real numbers (rather than a specific number): [.67, .86]. You might think it at least as likely as not that Paul will be more than ten minutes late, but have no more definite opinion; we could then represent your degree of credence for this proposition as the interval [.5, 1]. Many or most of our credences, I suppose, are vague. Partly to accommodate vague belief, van Fraassen recently proposed a more general version of reflection:

> *Opinion Reflection Principle.* My current opinion about event E must lie in the range spanned by the possible opinions I may come to have about E at later time t, as far as my present opinion is concerned.[26]

You are about to throw a fair coin; at the moment you think it as likely to come up heads as tails; you also believe that in a few seconds you will believe the proposition *it came up heads* either to the maximal degree or to the minimal degree; you satisfy *Opinion Reflection Principle* (call it 'New Reflection') because your present credence in that proposition lies within the range spanned by the possible opinions you now think you will have in a few seconds. You are beginning a course in philosophy; you are presently rather undecided about nominalism, thinking it no more likely than its denial. The instructor, however, is known to be both a nominalist and a persuasive teacher; you think it quite likely that by the end of the course you will afford a higher degree of credence to it than you do now; in fact, you think that at the end of the course you will believe nominalism at least twice as likely as its denial. Then your current degree of belief in nominalism does not lie within the range of opinion you now think you will have at the end of the course and you violate New Reflection. To conform to it you must *now* think nominalism is at least twice as likely as its denial (your current degree of credence for nominalism must lie in the interval [.67, 1]).

Now it looks initially as if van Fraassen means to propose Reflection (both old and new) in the familiar way: as a *condition of rationality;* you are rational only if you (or your credence function) conform to Reflection.[27] So taken, it looks vulnerable to certain kinds of criticism, (and indeed has not lacked for critics).[28] It is tempting to suggest examples of the following sort: suppose you foresee that you will soon be suffering from some condition interfering with the proper function of your intellectual faculties. You learn that the glass of Kool-Aid you have just drunk was laced with the psychedelic drug LSQ, which you know causes those who drink it to believe very firmly that they can fly;[29] or you believe that you will soon begin a drinking spree and will firmly believe, after

[26]"Ulysses," p. 15.

[27]"The Principle we are thereby led to postulate as a new requirement of rationality, in addition to the usual laws of probability calculation is . . . [reflection]"; see "Belief and the Will," p. 244.

[28]See especially David Christenson "Clever Bookies and Coherent Beliefs," *Philosophical Review* C, no. 2 (April 1991), pp. 229–46; Patrick Maher "Diachronic Rationality," *Philosophy of Science,* forthcoming; and W. Talbott, "Reflections on Two Principles of Bayesian Epistemology," presented at the American Philosophical Association, Eastern Division, 1987.

[29]Christenson, "Clever Bookies," p. 234.

ten drinks, that you can drive home perfectly safely.[30] (As you presently see things, your future credence in the offending propositions lies in a very narrow interval bounded above by 1). But then conformity to Reflection (both old and new) requires that you endorse those foreseen future opinions: to conform to it you must *now* believe that you can fly, or that you will be able to drive home perfectly safely after those ten drinks—and *that* seems ridiculous.

Van Fraassen has a rejoinder—a rejoinder that is initially puzzling. A proposed counterexample, he says, must squeeze between the Scylla of my refusing to recognize that future opinion as genuinely *mine*, and the Charybdis of my acting in a way inconsistent with my integrity as an epistemic agent. (*Integrity* seems to seize center stage here, supplanting rationality.) On the one hand, in some of these cases I would not really see those future credences as really mine:

> The question is not only what foreseen transitions—ways of changing my mind—I, the subject, classify as pathological or reasonable. The question is also what I am willing to classify as future opinions of mine. When I imagine myself at some future time talking in my sleep, or repeating (with every sign of personal conviction) what the torturer dictates or the hypnotist has planted as post-hypnotic suggestion, am I seeing this as myself expressing my opinion as they are then? I think not.[31]

This is the death or disability defense.

On the other hand, integrity as an epistemic agent requires that I now commit myself to following epistemic policies that I now stand behind, that I now endorse as rational or right. Suppose a scientist learns that materialism is caused by a certain dietary deficiency, and that for the last year his diet has been deficient in just that way. How should he respond? Not by saying: "I know that materialism is false, of course, but it looks (sadly enough) as if I shall soon believe it is true." No; what epistemic integrity requires, van Fraassen thinks, is that such a person now say (to himself if not to others) "Forewarned as I am, and as no one before us could be, I shall take good care to change my mind about materialism only for good reasons, and not in an irrational fashion."[32] Perhaps, though, he recognizes that the deficiency will be too much for him; it will obstruct proper function, making it impossible for him to regulate my opinion in a rational way: "In that case," says van Fraassen,

> he will no longer be able to formulate a considered opinion, but be at the mercy of strong impulses which he himself classifies as irrational. He will not be in control. From his present point of view, his future behavior will then be a sad parody of epistemic activity. The death or disability defense comes into play.[33]

Now how, precisely, shall we understand this defense? The basic claim is that in a proposed counterexample, a proposed alleged rational violation of Reflection, either the agent is not clearly recognizing the future opinion as really

[30]Maher, "Diachronic Rationality."
[31]"Ulysses," p. 21.
[32]Ibid., p. 23.
[33]Ibid., p. 24.

hers, or else she is not making the commitment (required by integrity as epistemic agent) to allow her beliefs to change only in ways she now sees as right. (Perhaps this is less a *claim* than a *challenge.*)

But the defense is initially baffling. There are two problems: first, can I sensibly claim that those foreseen opinions won't really be mine? Second, how is the commitment that epistemic integrity allegedly requires—how is that commitment relevant to alleged counterexamples to the claim that a rational person conforms to Reflection? Take the first, and consider the materialism case. I bleakly foresee that I won't be able to resist the onslaught any better than anyone else; it is clear to me that I won't be able to make sure that I change my opinion in reasonable ways: can I really claim, with any show of propriety, that the future opinion I sadly foresee really won't be *mine?* It is hard not to sympathize with Patrick Maher: "A defender of Reflection might try responding to such counterexamples by claiming that the person you would be when drunk is not the same person who is now sober. . . . But this is a desperate move. Nobody I know gives any real credence to the claim that having 10 drinks, and as a result thinking they can drive safely, would destroy their personal identity."[34] True: we might say "When she gets drunk, she's a wholly different person." But this is only a manner of speaking. Can I really claim, with any show at all of plausibility, that this materialist I foresee will not be me? It hardly seems so.

And now take the second question about van Fraassen's response. A proposed counterexample that manages to avoid the Scylla presented by the previous considerations is likely to founder in the Charybdis created by the requirement that I must now resolve to change opinion rationally. But how is that commitment so much as relevant? What counterexample candidates does it defeat? How is it part of a defense of Reflection?

So how shall we understand van Fraassen here? Perhaps as follows. His critics,[35] I think, have paid insufficient attention to a distinction he clearly thinks crucially important: the distinction between, on the one hand, making an autobiographical statement about your credence function and, on the other, *expressing* or *avowing* your opinion. Consider promises, he says. Today I say sincerely, "I promise you a horse"; I am not making an autobiographical statement about what I am presently doing, not reporting on my current activities. (Could a bystander sensibly respond, "You are in error; you aren't really promising him anything at all"?) I am not reporting or commenting on my behavior, but promising you a horse, thus instituting and accepting an obligation to you I didn't have before. Now epistemic judgments (judgments of the sort *A seems to me more likely than not,* or *my personal probability for C is high*) resemble promises in that they are not, says van Fraassen, statements of autobiographical fact. I say, "It seems likely to me that he did her wrong"; what I do in making this judgment is less like saying that I was born in

---

[34]"Diachronic Rationality."

[35]Including myself. In the 1986 summer Institute in Philosophy of Religion in Bellingham, Washington, I made some criticisms of Reflection some of which depended, as I now see it, upon failing to appreciate the distinction in question.

Michigan than like promising you a horse. Epistemic judgments are even more like expressions of commitment or intention:

> It seems then, that of the alternatives examined, epistemic judgments are most like expressions of intention. . . . If I express this intention to an audience, then, just as in the case of a promise, I invite them to rely on my integrity and to feel assured that they now have knowledge of a major consideration in all my subsequent deliberation and courses of action.[36]

Van Fraassen's critics have had little to say about this suggestion; but surely *something* like it is both true and important. Creeds—the Apostles' Creed, for example—are also sometimes called 'confessions' (The Augsburg Confession, The Belgic Confession); but to confess your faith is not (or not merely) to make an autobiographical statement about the condition of your psyche. (Nor is it to admit, shamefacedly, that unfortunately you do hold the opinions in question.) Creeds typically begin with 'Credo' or 'I believe': "I believe in God the Father Almighty, maker of heaven and earth." But if I use this creed to express what I believe, I am not merely reporting the result of self-examination, as I might be if I told you that every now and then I am subject to doubts about one or another element of the creed. I am doing something quite different: something that involves making or renewing a commitment. I am calling to mind an epistemic stance I have taken; I am renewing, restating, retaking that stance. Seriously using a creed, furthermore, is only a special case of a more general phenomenon: stating or expressing one's considered opinion.

According to van Fraassen, therefore, there is an important distinction between autobiographical statement of fact and expression of opinion, epistemic judgment. I say to you: "You tell me that you believe that democracy is a good thing, but given that you believe it's a good thing, what do you think are the chances that it really *is* a good thing?" Here the right *first* response, van Fraassen thinks, would not be a factual, autobiographical remark based, perhaps, on the available statistics about the frequency with which you've been wrong in the past, or the frequency with which other people are wrong in similar beliefs, or anything of that sort. The right first response must be either to reject the question as an impertinence or to say something like "Are you serious? They're very good, of course." This is a synchronic case; but something similar holds in the diachronic case. You ask me, "What is your opinion of the likelihood that democracy is a good thing, given the supposition that tomorrow you'll believe that it is?" Again, the right first response, he thinks, the response required by integrity, is: "That it is very likely, of course." But this response is not to be thought of as an autobiographical report; it is an epistemic judgment, an expression of opinion, more like a promise or commitment than a factual report.

Suppose we try to get a closer look. To satisfy New Reflection, my current opinion about an event E must lie in the range spanned by the possible opinions I now think I may come to have about E at future time t. But *what is it,* exactly, to satisfy this condition? The 'factualist' says something like this: there

[36]"Belief and the Will," p. 254.

are beliefs or opinions, which are mental states of some sort, and they come in degrees. For Paul to satisfy Reflection (in this instance) is for the third-person statement (as made, perhaps, by Eleanor)

> Paul's opinion about *E* lies in the range spanned by the possible opinions he presently thinks he may come to have about *E* at future time *t*

to be true. That is a factual statement about Paul. (It "is a proposition.")[37] And according to the factualist, Paul satisfies Reflection if and only if this proposition is true.

So says the factualist; van Fraassen, however, is no factualist but a voluntarist:

> I have argued that it [Reflection] is in fact indefensible if we regard the epistemic judgment . . . as a statement of autobiographical fact. The principle (Reflection) can be defended, namely as a form of commitment to stand behind one's own commitments, if we give a different, voluntarist interpretation of epistemic judgment. I call it 'voluntarist,' because it makes judgment in general, and subjective probability in particular, a matter of cognitive commitment, intention, *engagement*.[38]

What is it, then, to satisfy Reflection on a voluntarist reading? I'm not sure, but perhaps the following can bring us to the right neighborhood. When Eleanor uses such sentences as,

> Paul's current opinion about *E* is .6, and he now thinks that at *t* his opinion about *E* might lie in the interval <.5, .7>,

or

> Paul's personal probability for *A*, on the condition that a week from now his probability for it will be .9, is .9,

she makes a factual, biographical, general or specific remark about Paul and his credence function. However when *Paul* uses the first person analogue of these sentences

> My current opinion about *E* is .6, and I now think that at *t* my opinion about *E* might lie in the interval <.5, .7>,

or

> My personal probability for *A*, on the condition that a week from now my probability for it will be .9, is .9,

---

[37]"I think there is something to the view that the statement that my opinion is such and such 'is not a proposition'" ("Belief and the Will," p. 243).
[38]"Belief and the Will," p. 256.

then on the voluntarist view he is not asserting what Eleanor asserts; he is instead expressing his opinion, making an epistemic judgment; this is something like making a promise or avowal or commitment. When he expresses (avows) his opinion, he is committing himself to something or other—perhaps to continuing to hold this opinion unless some reason for no longer holding it shows up, perhaps to changing opinion only in an acceptable, rational, proper way—acceptable and proper, of course, by *his* lights, and by his *present* lights. In making epistemic judgments, on the voluntarist view, I commit myself to managing my opinion properly, to changing opinion only in ways consistent with my integrity as a responsible maker of judgments, a rational agent, a player in the judgment and assertion game (which is no game, but a deeply important feature of human life). Whatever precisely it is to satisfy Reflection, on a voluntarist reading, it is at least to be *committed* in a certain way, to make or be prepared to make commitments of some kind. (Someone who is more sympathetic to dispositions than van Fraassen might think of it as something like being disposed to make, being willing to make, setting oneself to make Reflectionlike expressions of opinion.) It is to be in the state of mind, epistemic and otherwise, that can properly be expressed by epistemic judgments. Thus "Belief and the Will,"

> I conclude that my integrity, qua judging agent, requires that, if I am presently asked to express my opinion about whether A will come true, on the supposition that I will think it likely tomorrow morning, I must stand by my own cognitive *engagement* as much as I must stand by my own expressions of commitment of any sort.[39]

"If I am presently asked . . . I must stand by . . ."; that suggests satisfying Reflection is a matter of being disposed to make Reflectionlike judgments or expressions of opinion (commitments) on the appropriate occasions.

Now return to the two problems with van Fraassen's defense of Reflection (that I can hardly claim that materialist won't be me and that it is hard to see how voluntarism figures in); how does this voluntarism help? Well, in the materialist case I foresee that I won't be able to withstand the onslaughts of disease or dietary deficiency. Those future opinions won't be arrived at by free and rational activity on my part. Of course, I recognize that the future may bring intellectual dysfunction, disability. If it does, I will no longer be able to regulate my opinion properly; it will be out of my control and out of my hands. And to the extent that I foresee that my future opinion will in fact be out of my control, I can't properly make Reflection-like judgments about it; I can't sensibly make commitments about it, anymore than I can make a commitment not to be subject to the ills our flesh is heir to. I don't take responsibility for *those* opinions; and perhaps in that sense we can say that they aren't really mine.

> Integrity requires me to express my commitment to proceed in what I now classify as a rational manner, to stand behind the ways in which I shall revise my values and opinions. It is on this basis that I rely with confidence on my

[39]Ibid., p. 255.

future opinion, to the modest extent of satisfying the Reflection principle. But integrity pertains to how I shall manage what is in my power. My behavior, verbal or otherwise, is no clue to opinions and values when it does not bespeak free, intentional mental activity.[40]

Reflection is to apply to free, intentional epistemic activity—epistemic activity insofar as it is within my control.

2. Does Rationality Require Reflection?

As I understand it, then, van Fraassen's view is that integrity requires making Reflection-like commitments; apparent counterexamples will either be cases where the agent is not making such commitments, or cases where she foresees that her future epistemic activity will not be within her control. What shall we say about this view? First, I shall set aside the important question of the degree to which my beliefs *are* in fact within my power, the degree to which it is within my power to regulate them. This is a difficult and thorny issue;[41] but clearly we have *some* degree of control (even if it is only indirect), and that provides Reflection, construed voluntaristically, with an area of application. We should note next that we have drifted a considerable distance from the typical Bayesian project of proposing conditions or criteria for rationality. What is at issue here is less rationality (at any rate in the senses distinguished at the beginning of this chapter) than *integrity*—integrity as a rational, judging agent. There is such a thing as integrity as a parent, teacher, judge, expert; there is also integrity as a rational agent, a player in the belief and assertion game. So suppose we think about Reflection and integrity in those terms, and suppose we think about the former voluntaristically. Does rational integrity demand that I conform to Reflection in the sense of being committed to Reflectionlike expressions of opinion (or being in the state properly expressed by such judgments) in the appropriate circumstances? (Of course, it isn't all that easy to see precisely what integrity as a rational agent amounts to, but for the moment we can perhaps make do with the sort of rough-and-ready grasp of it we initially have.)

I think not; but perhaps the way in which it does not need not disturb van Fraassen much. According to van Fraassen, Old Reflection, the version proposed in "Belief and the Will" (see my p. 125) is entailed by New Reflection, the more general version proposed in Ulysses.[42] Old Reflection seems to run

---

[40]"Ulysses," p. 25.

[41]See p. 23; and also see William P. Alston's "The Deontological Conception of Epistemic Justification," in *Philosophical Perspectives, 2, Epistemology, 1988* ed. James Tomberlin (Atascadero, Calif.: Ridgeview, 1988), pp. 260ff. This essay is reprinted in Alston's *Epistemic Justification: Essays in the Theory of Knowledge* (Ithaca: Cornell University Press, 1989).

[42]It is not initially obvious that this is so, however; it seems possible to violate the former without violating the latter. For consider Bertrand Russell. He believes N (nominalism) to .9, but, knowing as he does that he frequently changes his mind, also assigns .2 credence to the proposition that at future time f (five years from now) he will believe N to .1. If he satisfies Old Reflection,

$$P(N/pf(N) = .1) = .1,$$

into trouble, particularly with respect to extreme cases of belief to degrees 1 and 0. Thus (on the assumption that full belief is to be represented by a personal probability of 1), if I conform to this principle, I can't now invest any credence at all in the proposition that at some future time t I will fully believe a false proposition: for example, I can't accord any credence at all to the proposition that the theory of evolution is false, but a year from now I shall fully believe it.[43] Similarly, if I now fully believe some proposition, I can accord no credence at all to the proposition that at future time t I shall have less than full belief in that proposition.

Now perhaps we should ignore these extreme cases on the grounds that the peculiar results we get there are just artifacts of the model; or perhaps we should say that Reflection is not designed to apply to them. A more interesting response would be as follows: these unhappy consequences arise only if we take Reflection in a factualist, autobiographical fashion; they disappear if we take Reflection voluntaristically. But *how,* exactly, does taking it voluntaristically help? This is not clear to me, and I don't think van Fraassen gives us much help here.

But suppose there is a good answer along these lines. Even so, there remains a problem with Reflection, both Old and New. For consider forgetting. At present I firmly believe (to about .99, say) that I spoke with my friend Fred at about 2:00 P.M. on October 15, 1991. (That was this afternoon, and I remember it clearly.) A little calculation shows that if I conform to Reflection, my

hence

$$P(-N/pf(N) = .1) = .9;$$

hence

$$\frac{P(-N \& pf(N) = .1)}{P(pf(N) = .1)} = .9.$$

If he satisfies Old Reflection, therefore, the quotient $P(-N \& pf(N) = .1)$ divided by $P(pf(N) = .1)$, equals .9. But clearly it doesn't. $P(-N) = .1$; hence the numerator can't be more than .1, but the denominator is .2; hence the quotient is at most .5. (I am assuming that Russell has sharp probabilities and that he is sure he will have sharp probabilities at f.) But can't he have these credences and also invest some credence in the proposition that he will, at f, believe N to degree .9 (just as as he does now)? Then his present degree of belief in N lies within the range spanned by what he foresees as the opinions he may have at f; if so, he is in conformity with the general Reflection principle.

Van Fraassen's reply (personal communication), as I understand it, is that the correct way to express opinion is by way of *expectation*, the expected value of a random variable such as $v(A) =$ the degree to which I believe or will believe A. This variable can of course assume different values at different times; and for a given future time f I may presently have different probabilities for the different values I think v may assume at f. My expectation for $v_f(A) = \Sigma(P_i v_i(A))$ where the v_i's are the values I think $v_f(A)$ may assume and P_i is my present probability for its assuming v_i. Van Fraassen's idea is that New Reflection must apply to expectation as well as to opinion *simpliciter;* and a little calculation serves to show that in the present example Russell's expectation for his present degree of belief in A ($v_p(A)$) does not equal his expectation for $v_f(A)$.

The suggestion that Reflection is to apply to expectation values raises fascinating new issues; it would take us too far afield to enter them here, however, so I shall regretfully ignore them.

[43]"Belief and the Will," pp. 236ff.

present degree of belief in the proposition that at some future time f I will believe this proposition to .1—that is, $P(P_f(A) = .1)$—can be no greater than .0012. But isn't this disconcerting? The fact is I believe $P_f(A) = .1$ (f a year from now, say) quite strongly. My present degree of belief in the proposition that a year ago today I was speaking with Fred at 2:00 P.M. would be in the neighborhood of .1 (it seems to me that I speak to him at about that time maybe one out of ten days); and I expect that (assuming I survive the year) my degree of belief in the corresponding proposition a year hence will be about the same.[44] Nor would matters be improved by thinking in terms of New Reflection: my present high credence for this proposition is not within the range of opinions I now suppose I may have a year from now. Examples of this kind are legion. I have just looked up your telephone number; I believe it is n; by the day after tomorrow I shall have forgotten what it is and shall bestow on the proposition that it is n a relatively low degree of belief.

And here is the point: my integrity as a player in the belief-and-assertion game does not require that I do or try to do anything different here. It does not require that I do my best to bring it about that I continue to believe these things to the same degree that I now believe them; that would be at best foolish. I now believe that there are three books on my desk and believe this very firmly; I now firmly believe that there are two squirrels chasing each other in my backyard; I don't expect to believe either of these things at all firmly a couple of weeks from now. (Call the present time 't'; I don't now expect that then I will firmly believe that at t there were two books on my desk.) But there is nothing here threatening my integrity. I *can't* remember all these trivial things, of course; but I am not required by integrity to *try* to remember each particular one or as many as I can. Doing so, indeed, might clutter my mind in such a way as to inhibit other cognitive functioning that is more important.

A good bit of what van Fraassen says, however, suggests that he doesn't mean to say that Reflection *should* apply to cases like forgetting. He speaks of 'considered opinion'; his examples are drawn from cases like that of a weatherman, whose job it is to have reliable views and make reliable pronouncements on the weather, or a scientist who discovers that materialism is due to dietary deficiency. It is in cases like this, cases of what we might call *considered opinion,* that Reflection (voluntaristically construed) is most plausible. That is, it is in cases of this sort where it is plausible to suppose that integrity as a player in the belief-and-assertion game requires me to make Reflectionlike epistemic judgments. I am now a serious nominalist; if I take part with integrity in the belief-and-assertion practice, I must resolve or be prepared to resolve to see that this opinion changes, so far as in me lies, only for good reason. But the same does not go for forgetting the thousands of trivial things I now rather passively believe. Here my beliefs change, but not because I have acquired a reason for

---

[44]W. J. Talbott proposed counterexamples of this kind (counterexamples involving forgetting) in "Reflections on Two Principles of Bayesian Epistemology," presented at the American Philosophical Association, Eastern Division, 1987, in a colloquium on Logic, Probability, and Methodology. There is a discussion of Talbott's examples in F. Bacchus, H. E. Kyburg, Jr., and M. Thalos, "Against Conditionalization," *Synthese* 85 (1990).

giving them up (not by acquiring new evidence, say); and this is of course in no way a violation of integrity.

Accordingly, suppose we restrict attention to the areas where van Fraassen intends Reflection to apply. Let's suppose further (as seems right to me) that truth lies somewhere in van Fraassen's neighborhood: there is indeed an element of commitment or expression of intention involved in epistemic judgments, and integrity as a participant in the activity of belief and assertion requires that one be prepared to make such Reflectionlike avowals (whatever precisely they are). It's worth noting first, that this does not, of course, preclude making autobiographical judgments as well. Consider promising again. Although (as van Fraassen points out) 'I promise you a horse' does not ordinarily function as a statement of autobiographical fact, I can certainly note that I *am* promising you a horse even as I do so (to his amazed chagrin, he heard himself promising her a *horse*!). So why can't *I* believe, as *you* clearly can, that I am promising you a horse? And why can't I believe, as you clearly can, the factual proposition that my credence in a given proposition is high? I make whatever commitment integrity requires; I resolve to change belief only in rational ways and for good reason; but can't I also and quite sensibly have a personal probability for the proposition that I will do what I commit myself to doing? I promise to be faithful to you; if you ask me how likely it is that I *will* be faithful, I can't properly respond by citing statistics about the frequency with which promises of this sort are indeed followed by faithfulness. But can't I nevertheless *have an opinion* (a subjective probability) on the question how likely it is that I will keep the promise? I resolve to lose 15 pounds in two months; can't I also ask myself how likely it is that I will really stick to the diet this time? And perhaps conclude that it isn't very likely?

Of course, these two (making the resolve or commitment or promise, and also opining that there is a good chance that I will not maintain the resolve or keep the promise) seem to interfere with each other. It isn't simply that the proprieties governing promising require that when asked how likely it is that I will keep the promise I just made, I respond by reaffirming it. That is indeed so; but there is also the fact that my believing it unlikely that I will stay on the diet this time (my having a low subjective probability for this proposition) saps my resolve to do so. My knowledge that I sometimes lie and the consequent belief that I am likely to do so again interferes, in a way, with my resolving henceforth to tell the truth. In the same way, my thinking it likely that I will not change opinion only in ways that I now endorse, saps my resolve to change opinion only in those ways.

Still, won't the mature cast of mind contain both elements? Perhaps not both in the same thought, so to speak; perhaps I can't commit myself to really staying on the diet *this* time, and also, simultaneously, and with full awareness, judge on the basis of past performance that it is unlikely that I will do so. Perhaps I can't resolve to keep my promise to be faithful this time, and in the same breath (the same thought) assign a rather low subjective probability to the proposition that I will indeed do so. In order to do both—in order to commit myself fully but also recognize that there is a good chance I won't do what I commit myself to doing—I must maintain a sort of *distance* between the two. I do indeed thus commit myself; at the next moment I recall how things have gone in the past and how they are likely to go again, assigning a fairly high probability to the proposition that I will fail again; and I can rapidly switch between these two frames of mind. No doubt, this attitude requires a certain flexibility or subtlety of mind (some might even call it doublemindedness); but isn't this just what integrity and self-knowledge, in the human condition, require? Integrity requires that we resolve and commit ourselves wholeheartedly, unreservedly, to keeping our promises, staying on the diet, fighting our tendencies to self-aggrandizement and to pursuing our own goals and seeking our own welfare even at the expense of others; but self-knowledge requires the reluctant and rueful realization that the chances of failure here are very good indeed. No doubt this doublemindedness is to be regretted from some perspectives; in a perfect world there would be no such thing. But the world is not perfect: given what the world *is,* such an attitude seems the appropriate one.

As with promises and resolves generally, so with the epistemic resolves and commitments connected with Reflection. Let's agree that van Fraassen is right; integrity requires that I resolve to form and change opinion only in ways I now fully endorse (insofar as this is within my power); and suppose we also agree that the way in which this resolve is to be expressed is by way of making first-person Reflectionlike judgments. As van Fraassen suggests, this is the first thing to do in many situations, as when you are asked what your personal probability for nominalism (or the existence of God, or that there are individual essences) is on the condition that a year from now you will firmly believe it. The *first* thing to do is to make a Reflectionlike commitment. But there is also a *second* thing to do. There is that *proposition* about me, which others can believe or disbelieve; and if they can, why can't I? *You* can reflect on the question how likely it is that I will keep the promise I have just made; your personal probability for my keeping it (given my track record) may be considerably short of maximal. I too can reflect on that question, almost (but not quite) as I make the promise; and I too may have to conclude, sadly, that the chances of my keeping it are considerably less than maximal; and if I conclude this, then my personal probability for my keeping it (like yours) will be less than maximal. In the same way, perhaps, in making the Reflectionlike judgment, I express a certain state of mind, perhaps the state of being committed to forming and changing opinion only in ways I now endorse; but in almost the same thought I can undergo the chastened realization that things may very well not go this way. Chances are good that I will continue to form too high an opinion of my own powers and accomplishments; I may continue to be sometimes careless and biased in the ways in which I form judgments about others; I may continue to let fatigue, desire for ease and enjoyment, reluctance to put forth the necessary effort, lack of patience, desire for immediate reward and gratification—I may continue to let these prevent me from managing my opinion as well as I should and from coming to learn or see what I would if I *did* manage it properly.

Van Fraassen is right: integrity as knowing agent, as player in the belief-and-assertion game, requires that I make the sorts of commitment he calls us to. But rationality and self-knowledge may nonetheless require me to violate Reflection, taken factually, taken in the third-person mode, as a proposition about myself. In fact it does so require, and that even when it is free, rational, and considered opinion (not epistemic malfunction, nor the vagaries of inconsequential fact I now know but will have forgotten by tomorrow) that is at issue. If I satisfy Old Reflection, I don't afford any probability at all to the proposition that at future time *t* I will fully believe what is false; that must be as unlikely, as far as I am concerned, as that I will become a married bachelor. But of course it isn't. You may think the problem here is just the extreme value of full belief; but not so. I now firmly (to about .98, say) believe Serious Actualism: the view that objects have no properties in worlds in which they do not exist (not even nonexistence). A little calculation shows that if I conform to Reflection, my present degree of belief in the proposition that at future time *f* (a year from now, say) I will believe the denial of this proposition to degree .9—$P(P_f(\text{-SA}) = .9)$—can be no greater than .002 (see n. 42). But that seems to me unrealistically low; I have changed my mind about this before, and obviously it can happen again.

I believe to a much higher degree that it is wrong to try to advance one's career by lying about others. But, like others, I am liable to corruption. I must sadly realize that there is some likelihood that I will be corrupted in this matter, coming to see my own interests as of such overwhelming importance that I endorse any means at all of serving them. The probability, as I see it (based on what I know of myself and others), of my coming to believe that there is nothing wrong with so doing is low, but not nearly as low as Reflection requires. I believe more strongly yet that some things are right and others wrong; but again, must I not realize that there is a nonnegligible probability that 5 years from now I will have become a moral nihilist? I have never seriously considered the thought that the moral distinctions we all think we see are really illusory; what would happen if I were to look into this possibility, seriously studying the works of moral nihilists and antirealists? There is the possibility that I would change my mind, be corrupted; can I claim that the probability of this possibility is vanishingly small? I'm afraid not.

Again, distance is important. When I consider, entertain the proposition that some actions are genuinely wrong, the idea that I should reject this belief, becoming a moral antirealist or nihilist, seems wholly ridiculous. But when I reflect on the inconstancy we humans display, when I think about what I know about myself and others, I must regretfully admit that the idea, sadly enough, is very far from ridiculous. What rationality and integrity require of me, therefore, is indeed the sort of commitment van Fraassen suggests; but they also require a concomitant and chastened personal probability for the proposition that I will indeed carry out my commitment—a probability that in many cases will violate Reflection.

By way of conclusion: perhaps the most interesting aspect of van Fraassen's defense of Reflection is his voluntarism, and his suggestion that an epistemic judgment really involves a sort of commitment or resolve to regulate opinion, form and change belief, in ways that you now see as right and proper. This suggestion is fascinating (if a bit obscure); I believe there is something true and important about it. But there are also those propositions about me and my credence function; there are also those propositions to which the factualist draws our attention. Here a mature self-awareness requires that I have opinions; and these opinions, even if I am rational, or rather in particular if I am rational, need not conform to Reflection.[45]

[45]Responses to some of these critical points are perhaps to be found in a very recent and unpublished paper by van Fraassen "Fine-Grained Opinion and Full Belief, Without Infinitesimals," which came into my hands too late for me to take account of it.

8

Pollockian Quasi-Internalism

For classical internalism, the characteristically internalist nisus comes from deontology: warrant is conceived as epistemic duty fulfillment, and this, in the presence of plausible assumptions, leads directly to internalism. The Chisholm of *Theory of Knowledge* and *Foundations of Knowing* concurs; for the post-classical Chisholm, however, internalism persists but has lost its raison d'etre. Coherentism and Bayesian coherentism are also forms of internalism, and are properly thought of as forms of post-classical Chisholmian internalism. Still further, however, there is also the interesting theory of John Pollock's "Epistemic Norms"[1] and *Contemporary Theories of Knowledge,*[2] a theory Pollock says is internalist. In this chapter I shall examine Pollock's conception of warrant. I propose to argue that Pollock is an internalist in name only; I shall also argue that his official view of warrant is deeply flawed; and I shall conclude that there are hints, in his thought, of a wholly different and much more promising conception.

I. Pollockian Epistemic Norms

Our question is, What is warrant or positive epistemic status? John Pollock offers a systematic and highly articulated answer—if not to that very question, then to one lurking in the nearby neighborhood. Suppose we begin by considering his account of justification and norms.

A. *Justification*

The important epistemological questions, says Pollock, bear on *justification* rather than knowledge:

> Epistemology is 'the theory of knowledge' and would seem most naturally to have knowledge as its principle focus. But that is not entirely accurate. The theory of knowledge is an attempt to answer the question 'How do you know?', but this is a question about *how* one knows, and not about knowing *per se*. In asking how a person knows something we are typically asking for his

---

[1]*Synthese* 71 (April 1987), pp. 61–95.
[2]Totowa, N.J.: Rowman and Littlefield, 1986. (Page references in this chapter are to this work.)

grounds for believing it. We want to know what justifies him in holding his belief. Thus epistemology has traditionally focused on epistemic justification more than on knowledge. (p. 7)

So the central questions in epistemology, says Pollock, have to do with justification rather than knowledge; still, he does offer an analysis or account of the latter, and hence an account of warrant or positive epistemic status. To examine it, however, we must first consider his explanation of justification.

Neither the term 'justification' nor the notion of justification, of course, is unproblematic. To turn to the term, one might use it for whatever it is (enough of which) distinguishes knowledge from mere true belief. Pollock does not adopt this strategy, and (as I argued in chapter 1) there are excellent reasons for not doing so. First, it may be that what distinguishes mere true belief from knowledge is complex, something like the vector sum or product of two or more simpler qualities or quantities. Second, the term 'justification' has a deontological ring; it is redolent of rights and duties, permission and prohibition, blame and exoneration. As we saw in chapter 1, there is a long and impressive tradition—one going back at least to Descartes and Locke— according to which what distinguishes knowledge from true belief just *is* justification taken thus deontologically. But of course that is just one tradition among others; simply to *baptize* what distinguishes knowledge from true belief 'justification' is to give that tradition a confusing and undeserved advantage over its rivals.

So 'justification', as Pollock uses it, does not simply name whatever it is that epistemizes true belief: but then how does he use it? First, justification, he says, is essentially normative: "A justified belief is one that it is 'epistemically permissible' to hold. Epistemic justification is a normative notion. It pertains to what you *should* or *should not* believe" (p. 7). What is it that governs what it is permissible or impermissible to believe? Here we meet *epistemic norms*, the central characters in Pollock's epistemological drama:

> Rules describing the circumstances under which it is epistemically permissible to hold beliefs are called 'epistemic norms'. (p. 8)

Thus we can give an entirely adequate analysis of epistemic justification as follows:

> A person's belief is justified if and only if he holds it in conformance to his epistemic norms. (p. 168)

B. Norms

So my beliefs are justified if and only if they are permitted by my epistemic norms. But what sort of flora or fauna are they: how do they arise and how do they work? What is the source of their normativity? Am I *obliged* to follow them? (The previous quotation suggests that if I don't, then I do what I should not do, what is in some way impermissible.) Suppose I don't appropriately conform to one of these norms: what sort of criticism is then appropriate to my condition?

1. The Nature of Norms

First, norms govern what Pollock calls 'reasoning': any change in belief, whether resulting from reasoning in the more narrow sense or not.[3] (Perceptual and memory beliefs, therefore, will be acquired by reasoning.) Any belief can be evaluated epistemically; and any belief I hold will either be justified—epistemically correct or permissible—or else epistemically impermissible. (Not so for digestion: a given peristaltic contraction is neither permitted nor impermissible, not being subject to permission or prohibition at all.) His favorite example of an epistemic norm: "If something looks red to you and you have no reason for thinking it is not red, then you are permitted to believe it is red" (p. 169). He most often compares epistemic norms to what he thinks of as *internalized* norms for such activities as riding a bicycle, hitting a tennis ball, and typing—such norms as (for bicycle riding), " 'If you feel yourself losing momentum then push harder on the pedals', and 'If you think you are falling to the right then turn the handlebars to the right' " (p. 168). A crucial difference, as he sees it, between norms for activities of that sort and epistemic norms is that the former speak of what to do or what you *ought* to do, but the latter speak only of what you are *permitted* to do. A norm for bicycle riding tells you that you ought to do A under condition B; an epistemic norm tells you only that you may believe P under condition C.

So epistemic norms govern reasoning (broadly conceived) and are relevantly like internalized norms for bicycle riding and hitting a tennis ball. But *how* do they govern reasoning? Norms for some activities guide our behavior by way of our consciously holding them before the mind and explicitly conforming our actions to them. You follow a recipe for Mulligan Stew, or, more poignantly, a step-by-step set of directions for assembling a cardboard toy refrigerator for your daughter—the kind where the advertisement says "Takes no more than 20 minutes of your valuable time to assemble!" but in fact takes every evening for a week. This, says Pollock, isn't at all how things go with epistemic norms: we aren't typically aware of them or conscious of them; we don't bring them before our minds and consciously set out to form beliefs in accordance with them. We don't typically think: "now I am being appeared to redly; when one is appeared to redly (and all else is equal) it is permissible to believe that there is something red lurking in the neighborhood; so I'll believe that."

But then how *do* epistemic norms guide our behavior? We already have the answer: they do so in the way in which internalized norms for bicycle riding or hitting a golf ball guide behavior. In such cases, when we first learn how to perform the activity in question, we begin by consciously following norms we explicitly think of or entertain. My cycling teacher says: "Remember: when falling to the right, turn the handlebars slightly to the right"; my driving instructor says "When you shift from first to second, let up on the accelerator pedal a split second before you depress the clutch; wait just an instant for the engine to slow down before you slip (not force) the gear lever into second." I

---

[3] "Reasoning is not, strictly speaking, an action, but it is something we do, and we do it by doing other simpler things. We reason by adopting new beliefs and rejecting old beliefs under a variety of circumstances" ("Epistemic Norms," p. 75).

heed her words and at first consciously hold these directives before my mind. But soon such norms get *internalized* (however exactly that is to be understood); after some practice I can shift without thinking of the norms at all; after more practice the whole procedure becomes automatic. The same (says Pollock) goes for epistemic norms, except that typically we don't have to internalize them; they are, so to speak, internalized from the start. "The point here," he says, "is that *norms can govern your behavior without your having to think about them.* The intellectualist model of the way norms guide behavior is almost always wrong. . . . Reasoning is more like riding a bicycle than it is like being in the navy [where they do things by the book]" (p. 129; Pollock's emphasis).

2. *The Normativity of Epistemic Norms*

But what makes just *these* norms—the ones that actually govern our belief acquisition and change, or the ones that *should* govern them—the *right* norms for reasoning? (Perhaps we should put it like this: of all the candidates for normhood, what is it that confers normhood on those candidates that are actually successful?) Pollock's characteristically bold answer: these norms are the *right* norms for reasoning because *the norms we use are constitutive of the concepts we have.* If, in doing a bit of reasoning, I had employed norms *different* from those I *did* employ, then I would not have done *that* bit of reasoning. More specifically, if, in forming a given belief *B*, I had employed norms different from the ones I did employ, then it would not have been *B* that I would have formed.

Let's see if we can come to a better understanding of this initially dark saying. Pollock begins by rejecting what he calls "the logical theory of concepts." In essence, he says, this theory holds that what *individuates* a given concept, what *makes it the concept it is,* is its logical relations to other concepts (pp. 143–44). This idea generates the "picture of a 'logical space' of concepts, the identity of a concept being determined by its position in the space, and the latter being determined by its entailment relations to other concepts"[4] (p. 143). So what *constitutes* a concept, what makes it the concept it is, on this theory, are its logical relations to other concepts. The concept *being red*, for example, entails the concept *being colored* (that is, it is not possible [in the broadly logical sense] that something exemplify the former but fail to exemplify the latter); it precludes the concept *being a prime number* (that is, it is not possible that there be an object that exemplifies both concepts); and it neither includes nor precludes the concept *being square*. Further, given any standard understanding of necessity, it is *necessary* that *being red* is related to these other

[4]A preliminary question: how are we to think of concepts—that is, what sorts of objects (if indeed they are objects) are they? The above quotation would sound just as plausible if 'concept' were replaced throughout by 'property': how do concepts differ from properties? Or would the term 'concept' function not simply to denote a property, but in a more complicated, semicategorematic fashion, so that to speak of John's concept *horse* is to speak of John's grasp of the property *being a horse,* and to say that John has the concept *horse* is to say that John has a grasp of that property?

concepts in those ways; it is necessary that it includes *being colored,* precludes *being a prime number,* and neither includes nor precludes *being square.* But of course a concept C precludes a concept C^* if and only if it includes the complement $-C^*$ of C^*; it suffices, therefore, to think about the concepts C includes. So consider the *conceptual train* of *being red*—that is, consider the concepts it includes: it is not possible, on the logical theory, that *being red* should have failed to have that conceptual train. But it is also impossible, on the logical theory, that some concept distinct from *being red* should have had that very conceptual train. Having that conceptual train, therefore, is, on the logical theory, the (or an) *individual essence* of the concept *being red.*[5] Indeed, it is something even stronger, since on this theory having that conceptual train is what *makes being red* the concept it is.

Now Pollock rejects this view—quite rightly, since it seems clearly false.[6] In its place he proposes "the epistemological theory of concepts" (p. 147) according to which

> concepts are individuated by their roles in reasoning. What makes a concept the concept that it is is the way we can use it in reasoning, and that is described by saying how it enters into various kinds of reasons, both conclusive and prima facie. Let us take the *conceptual role* of a concept to consist of (1) the reasons (conclusive or prima facie) for thinking that something exemplifies it or exemplifies its negation, and (2) the conclusions we can justifiably draw (conclusively or prima facie) from the fact that something exemplifies the concept or exemplifies the negation of the concept. My proposal is that concepts are individuated by their conceptual roles. The essence of a concept is to have the conceptual role that it does. (p. 147)

On Pollock's view, therefore, the essence of a concept is its conceptual role rather than, as on the classical view, its conceptual train. Of course, conceptual role and conceptual train significantly differ: one belief can be a *prima facie* reason for another even if it does not entail it; and one belief can entail another even if it is not a *prima facie* reason for it.[7]

But precisely how is this relevant in the present context? Our question was, What makes a given norm or norm candidate—for example, *when appeared to redly, you may form the belief that you see something red if you have no reason to the contrary*—a *correct* norm or a *real* norm? The answer: *being appeared to redly* is *necessarily* a reason (a *prima facie* reason) for judging that you are

[5]See my *The Nature of Necessity* (Oxford: Oxford University Press, 1974), chap 5.

[6]If it were true, there would be no concepts that were distinct but equivalent in the broadly logical sense; there would be no distinct concepts C and C^* that included each other, for if C and C^* entailed each other, they would have the same conceptual train and hence (by the logical theory) would be the same concept. But clearly there are distinct but equivalent concepts. *Being the sum of 2 and 4* entails and is entailed by *being the square root of 36* and *being the second smallest composite natural number* (and of course many much more recondite items). Surely these are not the *same* concept: a person could grasp the first, for example, without grasping either of the others. The concept *being a married bachelor* is equivalent to the concept *being a prime number divisible by 4;* yet these are clearly different concepts.

[7]*There are no married bachelors* entails that arithmetic is incomplete but is not a *prima facie* reason for the latter.

perceiving something red. This norm is constitutive of one or more of the concepts involved in my judgment that I see something red; and *that* means at the least that it is necessary, in the broadly logical sense, that it is a correct norm for that judgment. So the answer to the question, *What makes this norm correct?* is much like the answer to the question, *What makes modus ponens valid?* About all one can say is that it couldn't have been otherwise.

There is one further and fateful consequence Pollock draws from his epistemological theory of concepts:

> Because concepts are individuated by their conceptual roles, it becomes impossible for people's epistemic norms to differ in a way that makes them conflict with one another. The epistemic norms a person employs in reasoning determine what concepts he is employing because they describe the conceptual roles of his concepts. If two people reason in accordance with different sets of epistemic norms, all that follows is that they are employing different concepts. Thus it is impossible for two people to employ different epistemic norms in connection with the same concepts. (p. 148)

II. Justification and Objective Justification

Pollock's official account of epistemic justification goes as follows:

> Epistemic justification consists of holding beliefs in conformance to correct epistemic norms. But as we have seen, our epistemic norms are constitutive of the concepts we have and hence it is a necessary truth that our actual epistemic norms are correct. Thus we can give an entirely adequate analysis of epistemic justification as follows:
>   A person's belief is justified if and only if he holds it in conformance to his epistemic norms. (p. 168).

Now clearly a person could be justified, in this sense, with respect to a true belief even if that belief does not constitute knowledge for him; justification, so construed, is not an apt candidate for warrant. For example, I might look at a red ball that is in fact but unbeknownst to me illuminated by red light, so that it would look red even if it were white. Then, says Pollock, I might be *justified* in believing the ball red but would not *know* that it was. Or consider such self-evident and nearly self-evident beliefs as *2 + 1 = 3, 7 + 5 = 12* and *4 is not prime.* What would the norms governing such beliefs be like? The best candidates, I suppose, would refer to the phenomenology that goes with such belief. Two kinds of phenomenology accompany beliefs of this sort. First, there is something like a sort of broadly speaking sensuous phenomenology, a sort of phenomenal imagery (possibly variable from person to person). But second and more important, there is also a strongly felt inclination to believe the proposition in question; it is as if the belief in question has a sort of powerful perceived attractiveness. More accurately, there is a strongly felt inclination to believe that the proposition in question *must* be so, couldn't be false.[8] Presumably norms

[8]See my *Warrant and Proper Function* (New York: Oxford University Press, 1993), chap. 6, sec. 1.

for these beliefs would take the form of permitting such beliefs when they are accompanied by phenomenology of that kind.

Clearly, a belief could conform to *that* sort of norm when it had little or no warrant. Return to an example from chapter 3 (p. 59): I am captured by a group of Alpha Centaurian superscientists intent upon a cognitive experiment; in the course of conducting their experiment, they so modify my cognitive faculties that I believe every third proposition of the form *n is prime* (where *n* is a natural number between 23 and 200), disbelieving the rest. (Thus I believe that 23 and 24 are not prime, that 25 is prime, that 26 and 27 are not, and so on.) They further modify my faculties so that whenever I consider one of those propositions I believe—*25 is prime, 28 is prime, . . . , 67 is prime, . . . , 199 is prime*—I undergo the very sort of phenomenology that for me goes with simply seeing that, say, 5 is prime: I can apparently see that it is true in just the way I can see that *4 + 3 = 7* is true. Then in believing that proposition I am conforming to my norms for such belief; for they permit me to believe any proposition of this sort if it is accompanied by the right sort of phenomenology. So such propositions are justified for me, but they have little warrant for me.

For warrant, says Pollock, we must turn to *objective* justification, which together with truth (and a codicil to accommodate "socially sensitive truths") *is* sufficient for knowledge. The basic idea of objective justification is something like this. Suppose I am justified in believing *P;* I am also *objectively* justified in so doing, if, no matter what true propositions I came to believe, I would *still* be justified in believing *P,* and for the same reason that I *am* justified. We can put it a bit more formally as follows:

> *S* is objectively justified in believing *P* if and only if: (1) *S* is subjectively justified in believing *P* and (2) There is a set *X* of truths such that, given any more inclusive set *Y* of truths, necessarily, if the truths in *Y* were added to *S*'s beliefs (and their negations removed in those cases in which *S* disbelieves them)[9] and *S* believed *P* for the same reason then he would still be (subjectively) justified in believing *P*. (p. 185)

This account, Pollock thinks, is insufficiently explicit; he therefore proposes a more complicated 'official' account of objective justification. The official account is of considerable interest (see Appendix); but the less explicit account will adequately serve our present purposes. Now "Objective epistemic justification," says Pollock, "is very close to being the same thing as knowledge" (p. 185); all that remains to be added is a smallish qualification having to do with what (following Gilbert Harman) he sees as a social dimension of knowledge. "We are 'socially expected' to be aware of various things": what is in our mail, what is announced on television, what any sixth grader has learned in

[9]This won't quite do the job: we must also appropriately delete items that entail denials of members of *Y*, items that together with members of *Y* entail the denials of members of *Y*, and so on. I won't try to state the condition exactly. There is another (and nastier) problem here. Pollock thinks this account guarantees that all objectively justified beliefs are true (p. 185). He believes this, presumably, because if *S* believes *P* and *P* is false, then there will be a set *Y* of truths—a set containing ~*P*—that doesn't meet the condition laid down by the second clause. Strictly speaking, however, every such set *Y* trivially meets the condition in question, since (as a little reflection makes clear) that condition, specified to a set containing ~*P*, has an inconsistent antecedent.

school, and the like. A proposition is "'*socially sensitive for* S' if and only if it is of a sort S is expected to believe when true" (p. 192). Warrant, therefore, is given by objective justification plus a small qualification to take account of socially sensitive propositions.[10]

III. Problems

Pollock displays a certain degree of diffidence with respect to his account of knowledge: "At this stage in history it would be rash to be very confident of any analysis of knowledge" (p. 193). This diffidence, I think, is not entirely misplaced. I propose to argue that Pollock's account of warrant or positive epistemic status is seriously flawed, foundering on the possibilities of cognitive malfunction; I shall go on to argue that this account really represents a sort of transitional stage, an uncomfortable halfway house on the way to a more satisfactory view.[11]

A. Degrees of Warrant

First, a small problem I shall simply note without comment. Obviously warrant or positive epistemic status comes in degrees; obviously some of my beliefs have more by way of warrant than others. Pollock concurs (p. 5); yet his official account of objective justification makes no provision for degrees of justification, either objective or subjective. Pollockian norms are permissive (and possibly also prohibitive); and a person is justified in a belief "if and only if he holds it in conformance to his epistemic norms" (p. 168), that is, if and only if his holding that belief is permitted by those norms. But of course there aren't degrees of permission. You are permitted (or not) *simpliciter:* you can't be permitted to degree .3, say, or be more permitted to do one thing rather than another. (This points to a difficulty for any wholly deontological conception of positive epistemic status.) Similarly for objective justification. You are objectively justified in believing P, to put it crudely, if and only if (a) you are justified in believing P and (b) each truth is such that if you believed it, you would still be justified (for the same reason) in believing P; clearly then, there is no room for degrees of objective justification. It isn't at all easy to see how to handle this problem, but there are some possibilities,[12] and sufficient ingenuity might do the trick.

B. Incorrect Norms and Identity of Concepts

I turn now to the deepest and most important difficulty with Pollock's account of warrant. It isn't easy to see precisely what the Pollockian norms are; but couldn't someone reason in accordance with *mistaken* or *incorrect* norms, so

---

[10]For the final definition of knowledge, see the Appendix.
[11]A view, as I see it, to be found in my *Warrant and Proper Function*.
[12]Personal communication from Pollock.

that even though her reasoning conforms to *her* norms, and even though she is objectively justified (again, according to *her* norms) nonetheless she fails to know what she believes? Return to Paul's plight in chapter 2 (p. 42). As the story went, Paul suffers from a brain lesion induced by radioactive fallout from a Soviet missile test. He now reasons differently from the rest of us; when appeared to in the church-bell fashion, he forms the belief that something is appearing to him in that fashion, and that it is orange. His noetic system is altered by the lesion in such a way that he now reasons according to the norm *when you are appeared to in the church-bell fashion (and have no reason to think that what is appearing to you is not orange), it is permissible to believe that you are being appeared to by an object that is orange;* he is appeared to in the familiar church-bell fashion and, in accordance with his norms, forms the belief that he is being appeared to by something that is orange. It isn't entirely easy to say when someone is objectively justified, but couldn't it be, in this case, that no matter what other relevant truths he had known, his norms would still have permitted him to form that belief in that fashion? Add that his belief— that he is being appeared to by something that is orange—is by happy coincidence in fact true: due to that cognitive malfunction he still wouldn't know; in fact he would be nowhere near knowing.

Or consider an epistemic agent *S* whose cognitive nature has been so altered—due to demon or black bile or perhaps to the "warmed or overween- ing brain" to which Locke attributed the enthusiasm of religious enthusiasts— that whenever he is appeared to redly, he finds himself with the belief that no one other than himself is ever appeared to redly. Objective justification, in Pollock's sense, is not an easy notion to work with; it can be difficult to determine what could be objectively justified and what not; but couldn't such a person be objectively justified in such beliefs? Add that his belief to this effect on a given occasion is true: perhaps there has been a nuclear holocaust; *S*'s cognitive faculties are affected in the way suggested; the rest of us are so modified that we are no longer appeared to redly; due to trauma-induced amnesia, *S* is not aware of any of this. So when he forms his pathologically induced belief that no one else is appeared to redly, the belief he forms is true. Still, one wants to say, neither *S* nor Paul knows the relevant proposition; it is just by happy accident, here, that belief matches fact. And don't we have here an argument for the conclusion that the proposed necessary and sufficient condition for knowledge or warrant is not in fact sufficient?

Pollock's response, so far as I understand it, is that these examples, contrary to appearances, are not really possible. They are not possible, because different people cannot, contrary to appearances, employ appropriately different norms in reasoning:

> Because concepts are individuated by their conceptual roles, it becomes impos- sible for people's epistemic norms to differ in a way that makes them conflict with one another. The epistemic norms a person employs in reasoning deter- mine what concepts he is employing because they describe the conceptual roles of his concepts. If two people reason in accordance with different sets of epistemic norms, all that follows is that they are employing different concepts.

Thus it is impossible for two people to employ different epistemic norms in connection with the same concepts. (p. 148)

In the above example, Paul has and uses a nonstandard norm for the concept *x is appeared to by something that is orange*—a norm that is not employed by the rest of us. This norm differs from ours in such a way that the reasoning it sanctions is not sanctioned by our norms. But then, says Pollock, it follows that Paul has not employed the same concepts as we. In particular he has not employed the concept *x is appeared to by something that is orange;* therefore he has not formed the belief *I am being appeared to (in that church-bell fashion) by something that is orange.* But then we don't have a case of someone's employing an incorrect norm and thereby failing to have knowledge: what we do have is someone's employing a *correct* norm for a concept distinct from *x is appeared to by something that is orange*—perhaps a concept the rest of us don't have at all.

Here we must be careful. Pollock does not hold that it is impossible to reason in a way out of accord with the correct norms for a concept; you can make a *mistake*, fail to reason in accord with your norms. You can *fail* to reason in accord with the *correct* norms for a concept; what you can't do is reason in accord with *incorrect* norms for a concept. What is not possible is that you *have* a norm for a concept that is not in fact a *correct* norm for that concept. Pollock's claim is that one can't reason in accord with incorrect norms.

But why not? What leads Pollock to this startling conclusion? How does the argument go? Recall that "the *conceptual role* of a concept" is "(1) the reasons (conclusive or prima facie) for thinking that something exemplifies it or exemplifies its negation, and (2) the conclusions we can justifiably draw (conclusively or prima facie) from the fact that something exemplifies the concept or exemplifies the negation of the concept"; Pollock's proposal is that "the essence of a concept is to have the conceptual role that it does" (p. 147); and what this means is that for any concept C and norm N, N is a norm for C if and only if it is necessary that N is a norm for C.

Suppose we concede for present purposes that this is correct.[13] Let's agree first that there are norms for concepts; second, that these norms are typically *permissive*, as he says, so that they take such forms as *In circumstances C you may believe that concept C* is exemplified;* and third that if a given norm N is a norm for a concept C* then it is necessary that N is a norm for C*. How does the conclusion follow; that is, how does it follow that if I form the belief that C* is exemplified but do not form it on the basis of a correct norm for C*, then I haven't really formed the belief that C* is exemplified (so that it is not in fact possible to form that belief on the basis of an incorrect norm)?

It doesn't. Clearly there are incorrect norms for a concept (for example, Paul's and S's norms of a couple of paragraphs back) as well as correct norms. More exactly, it is possible to form beliefs involving a concept, employing the norms that are not correct norms for that concept. Clearly a person could form beliefs involving a concept on the basis of what are not in fact correct norms for

---

[13]I shall argue below that it is not.

that concept. Such a person would not, of course, be forming beliefs on the basis of the norms for the concept, that is, on the basis of the *correct* norms for the concept; but it does not follow that he wouldn't be forming beliefs involving that concept. If *having such and such norms* is an essence of a concept, then any statement falsely specifying that N is a norm for concept C will be necessarily false; but it does not follow that I can't reason in accordance with an incorrect norm—that is, a norm that is not in fact a norm for the concept in question. It is part of the essence (let's suppose) of the concept *orange* to have just the norms it does; but it does not follow that it is part of the essence of the belief *this thing exemplifies orange* to be formed only by someone whose norms for *orange* are *those* norms.[14] Suppose one of Paul's norms for *orange* conflicts with the correct norms for that concept, so that he forms the belief *orange is exemplified here* on the basis of an incorrect norm for *orange;* it does not follow that this belief is not the belief, with respect to some object, that it exemplifies that concept. What follows is only that Paul's norms for *orange* are not the correct norms for it. If he does form that belief that way, then his reasoning is incorrect; but it does not follow that he can't form the belief that way. Here Pollock apparently fails to distinguish the claim that a given concept has essentially the norms it has (which follows from his theory of concepts) from the claim that a given belief has essentially the property of being such that it is formed by someone whose norms for the concepts it involves are correct norms (which does not follow from his theory).

Consider an ethical analogy. No doubt it is part of the essence of some (or all) actions to be permitted and enjoined in just the circumstances in which they *are* permitted and enjoined; there are correct norms for their performance. Suppose then that A is some such action and N_{1-n} the correct norms for it; it will then be part of the essence of A that N_{1-n} are its correct norms. But it does not follow that *being performed by someone who has N_{1-n} for A* is part of the essence of A, so that A cannot be performed by anyone who does not have N_{1-n} as her norms for A. Perhaps it is part of the essence of such an action as *causing someone severe pain* that it is always wrong to do it just for the fun of it; it does not follow that I can't myself have norms for that action that permit doing it just for the fun of it. I would be acting wrongly; but I would still be performing the action *causing someone else severe pain.* In the same way, if Paul has incorrect norms for orange, it does not follow that he can't form beliefs of the sort *that thing is orange;* all that follows is that he is reasoning incorrectly.

So the argument begins from a dubious premise and is in any event inconclusive. What the argument really requires is a premise entailing that it is part of the essence of a concept, not just to have the norms N it does have, but to be such that no one can have other norms for it. The argument is unsound, therefore; and isn't the conclusion of the argument—that two people can't have or employ conflicting norms with respect to the same concept—wholly implausible? Consider the Pyrrhonian skeptic. Sextus Empiricus recommends that

[14]More exactly if more pedantically, it doesn't follow that it is part of the essence of the proposition *this thing exemplifies orange* that it can be believed only by someone who reasons in accord with the correct norms for *orange.*

"in the hope of attaining quietude," we withhold ordinary perceptual beliefs (among others), not acceding to our natural tendencies to form such beliefs when appeared to in the familiar ways.[15] Thus "we are brought firstly to a state of mental suspense and next to a state of 'unperturbness' or quietude" (chapter 4). Sextus urges us to adopt different norms: his recommendation is that we replace such norms as

> *when you are appeared to redly and consider whether you perceive something red and have no reason to think that you do not, you may form the belief* I am appeared to by something red

by such norms as

> *when you are appeared to redly and consider whether you perceive something red and have no reason to think that you do not, you may* withhold *the belief* I am appeared to by something red

or, more radically, by the norm

> *when you are appeared to redly, you should* not *form the belief* I am appeared to by something red.[16]

As Reid and Hume point out, it is at the least very difficult to withhold ordinary perceptual beliefs under the conditions in which, in the course of ordinary life, we form them. Still, given sufficient effort and training, perhaps a talented person could do it; perhaps Sextus himself managed to govern his belief in the way he recommended. At any rate it clearly seems *possible* (in the broadly logical sense) that he do so. Of course, if he did manage this feat, *his* formation of such beliefs as *I see something red* would be governed by norms different from the one that governs *our* formation of such beliefs—different, and conflicting in the relevant way. A belief in accord with his norms would not be in accord with ours. But then on Pollock's view, Sextus wouldn't so much as have the concept *x sees something red;* hence he could not form the belief in question. So (on Pollock's view) it is not just unwise or ill-advised to follow Sextus's recommendation; it is logically impossible. Indeed, if Sextus managed to follow his own advice, he would no longer be able to conceive that advice. For if he followed it, he would no longer be able to form the belief *I see something red* and *a fortiori* could form no belief of the sort *when appeared to redly, it would be good to withhold the belief* I see something red. But surely this is much too strong. It may be difficult to follow the instructions in question; it may be foolish to do so; but it is not logically impossible. Surely there could be or could have been beings who formed beliefs in accordance with the norms Sextus suggests.

[15] *Outlines of Pyrrhonism*, chap. 4.
[16] Or perhaps his suggestion is just that we reject the norm *when you are appeared to redly, you may form the belief* I am appeared to by something red.

For another example, consider John Locke, who deplored the ways in which the generality of mankind forms belief. There is one "wrong measure of probability," he says, that "keeps in ignorance, or errour, more people than all the others together"; this is "the giving up our assent to the common received opinions, either of our friends, or party, neighbourhood, or country"[17] His idea is that the unreflective run of mankind form their beliefs in accord with what Reid calls "The Principle of Credulity"; when one of our peers tells us something, we tend to believe it, at least in the absence of countervailing reasons. (Reid plausibly thinks this belief-forming principle is native to us.)[18] So the generality of mankind reasons in accord with such norms as *if practically everyone I know believes p, then I may (or ought to) believe p;* Locke recommends that we eschew norms of that sort and try to form our beliefs on the basis of such quite different (and conflicting) norms as *I may (or ought to) believe p only if that proposition is sufficiently probable with respect to my evidence.* But then on Pollock's view Locke's advice has nothing whatever to be said for it. For if in fact some of us *do* form the belief in question in accordance with the first norm but not the second, then it is not even possible that someone should form beliefs of that sort in accord with the second but not the first. So the advice is either logically impossible to follow or else such that everyone already follows it.

Once more, this is surely incorrect. Locke's recommendation is not defective in *that* way, even if it is unrealistic (perhaps even Quixotic and foolish). Clearly there could be people who formed beliefs in accord with the first norm but not the second, and people who formed beliefs in accord with the second but not the first. On the face of it, people can form beliefs in accordance with all sorts of conflicting norms. The paranoid forms the belief that Fred is out to get him and seems to do so in accord with norms the rest of us do not employ ("that subtle, slightly squinty-eyed look gives him away"): but isn't it the belief *Fred is out to get him* that he forms? If not, why think he is paranoid? And isn't it possible (even if improper) to form one's beliefs according to the norm *if believing p is in your best interests (or would afford you pleasure or comfort) then you may believe p?*

Second, recall that there must be norms, not only of the form *when in circumstances C you may believe P* but also *when in circumstances C you may believe P to degree d.* Or rather, recall that norms will *typically* be of the latter sort, not the former; what one does, when one forms a belief, is to form a belief of a certain strength, and obviously not just any degree of strength is appropriate. (You are driving through Chicago; you catch a quick glimpse of what appears to be a hippopotamus in the median strip; if you form the belief *that's a hippopotamus* and hold it as firmly as you believe that Chicago is in Illinois, then your degree of belief is inappropriate.) Now even if it is psychologically impossible to withhold ordinary perceptual beliefs, it certainly seems possible to hold these beliefs with a somewhat different degree of firmness than is

[17]*An Essay Concerning Human Understanding,* ed. A. C. Fraser (New York: Dover, 1953), IV, xx, 17.
[18]See *Warrant and Proper Function,* chap. 4, pt. 2.

customary. Couldn't Sextus adopt and come to exemplify norms licensing degrees of belief somewhat different from those of the rest of us? Perhaps he holds pretty much the same perceptual beliefs as the rest of us, but holds them more tentatively. But again, on Pollock's suggestion, even this would be impossible; for, on his suggestion, if the skeptic's norms are different from ours—if (under given circumstances) they license forming a belief with a degree of strength different from what our norms license—then the skeptic wouldn't so much as have the relevant concepts.

Still further, our norms are modified or shaped by what we learn. We learn to trust some people under some conditions, but distrust others under others. We learn to exercise a certain skepticism about what we are told by politicians; we learn to take more seriously what someone tells us when what she says does not redound to her own credit (unless she is the sort of person whose apparent self-deprecation is a subtle form of self-aggrandizement); we learn not to form beliefs about marital discord without speaking to both parties; and so on. But then our norms are also thus shaped and altered by what we learn. It would be monumentally implausible to suppose that whenever my norms alter under the pressure of experience, I lose a concept I previously had, replacing it with a new one.[19]

The same goes for a wide variety of cases. You and I both have the concept *red;* we therefore exemplify norms for the formation of beliefs of the sort *I see something red* or *that thing is red.* For a given set of circumstances, there will be an interval $d–d^*$ such that my norms license the formation of a belief of that sort to any degree within that interval. But surely there is no reason to think it is necessary, in order for us both to have the concept *red,* that our norms coincide on these intervals; why couldn't they diverge, even if only slightly? Hume points out (and this may have been known even before Hume) that we reason inductively; we form beliefs reflecting a sort of expectation that the future will be like the past in relevant but hard to specify respects. So there are norms licensing my belief that the sun will rise tomorrow (given my past experience); these norms, no doubt, will involve intervals of degrees of belief. Perhaps your norms specify slightly different intervals from mine: must we conclude that we do not have the same concepts? Similar remarks obviously hold for memory, and for *a priori* beliefs. You and I both believe, say, that there neither are nor could be nonexistent objects; but I believe it more firmly than you. Couldn't this reflect a difference in the norms governing our belief here? For a given phenomenology of apparent obviousness, say, couldn't my norms specify a slightly different interval from yours? It is surely hard to see why not, and hard *in excelsis* to see that this is logically impossible.

Still further: clearly there could have been creatures capable of the same beliefs as we, but with different cognitive powers; and we ourselves could have

---

[19]Of course we could simply redefine the term 'concept', using it, say, to denote something like an ordered pair of a concept in the old sense with a set of norms or a conceptual role. Then, naturally enough, we would get the above result. But then it would no longer follow that persons using different concepts could not form the same beliefs; hence it would not follow that we could not form the same beliefs while exemplifying or employing conflicting norms.

been differently constituted. Take the concept *orange,* for example; and suppose the world had been different in such a way that there is always something orange near anything that is blue. Surely God could have so created us that among our norms would have been such items as *when you are appeared to bluely, you may form the belief that there is something orange nearby*—even though that norm is not in fact a correct norm for *orange.* Or (to take an example that involves what Pollock calls an attribute rather than a concept) we could have been like pigeons, having a built-in way of telling directions. Then we could be taken blindfolded through a complicated maze, spun around repeatedly, and still been able to tell which way is south. If we had been so constructed, we could have had norms for *south* that are different from the ones we do have—norms involving a sort of phenomenology that none of us has ever experienced. But we should still have been able to form such beliefs as *Mexico City is south of Minneapolis.* And here we don't just have variation, within the relevant norms, with respect to degree of belief sanctioned, but with respect to the formation of the belief itself.

Once it is clear that we can share a concept even though we differ in the above fashions with respect to the norms we adopt, it is hard to see why we can't differ even more radically. To return to the examples with which I began: doesn't it seem possible that (due to pathology) Paul should begin to form his beliefs quite differently, exemplifying norms different from those he exemplified before, exemplifying such norms as *when you are appeared to in the church-bell fashion, you may form the belief* I am appeared to by something that is orange? Doesn't it seem possible that (due to psychic disorder) *S* could come to exemplify such a norm as *when you are appeared to redly, you may form the belief* no one else is appeared to redly?

Pollock claims that what are in fact the correct norms for a given concept are *constitutive* of that concept, where this means at any rate that it is necessary that those norms are correct for that concept: from this he infers that it is not possible that different people form the same belief while employing or exemplifying conflicting norms. What we have seen, however, is that the argument is invalid, and the conclusion implausible. But then Pollock's view as to what it is that distinguishes mere true belief from knowledge—that is, being objectively justified—is incorrect; an unfortunate of the sort just described could be objectively justified in his belief despite its having little or no warrant or positive epistemic status for him.

IV. New Directions

I believe that Pollock's position is an uncomfortable way station on the journey from the traditional and explicitly deontological conception of warrant in his first book *Knowledge and Justification* to a wholly different sort of view. Suppose we begin by noting a certain problem with his account of norms. He suggests that on the "intellectualist model" the picture as to how norms direct our reasoning is *too* intellectualistic; but doesn't the same hold for his own official view? He compares the process of belief formation, retention, and change to such activities as bicycle riding, typing, hitting a golf ball, and so on (p. 171), and argues that epistemic norms govern belief in the way norms for those activities govern them. There are analogies here: each is something one comes or can come to learn to do; each requires a certain maturing process; each can be done without paying much conscious attention to the process, and so on. But there are also significant differences. In the first place, *every* well-formed human being learns to reason, in Pollock's broad sense (and learns to do so by an early age); not so, of course, for typing and cycling. In this respect, reasoning is more like walking and running. But it differs significantly even from them: it is not typically under direct and conscious control. If I want something from the refrigerator, it is up to me whether or not to walk to it (as opposed to crawling or running to it, or asking you to go to it for me). I can refrain from walking and running; I can give them up for Lent if I choose. But I can't give up reasoning for Lent—not, at least, without giving up a great deal more.

Furthermore, I can *undertake* to walk or run; and I can decide, if I choose, how long to make each stride, and which direction to walk in. I can also decide to walk backward, or in some weird, ridiculous way.[20] Pollock sometimes seems to suggest that the same goes for reasoning. He sometimes speaks as if he thinks we typically *undertake* to form beliefs: "The sense in which the norms guide our behavior in doing X is that the norms describe the way in which, once we have learned how to do X, our behavior is automatically channeled in undertaking to do X" (p. 131); and he sometimes speaks as if he thinks we typically deliberate about what to believe, the epistemic norms guiding us in coming to a decision as to what to believe: "I have taken the fundamental problem of epistemology to be that of deciding what to believe. . . . Considerations of epistemic justification guide us in determining what to believe" (p. 10).

But the fact is in typical cases I neither undertake to believe (anymore than I undertake to breathe) nor make any decisions as to what to believe. I have too little direct control over my beliefs for that. I consider the corresponding conditional of *modus ponens:* I find myself with an ineluctable inclination to believe that this proposition is true and indeed necessarily so. You ask me what I had for breakfast: I find myself believing that what I had for breakfast was a grapefruit. I am appeared to redly; I find myself with the belief that I am perceiving something red. I consider the question what Caesar had for breakfast the morning he crossed the Rubicon: I find myself with no belief on that topic. In each of these cases (as in general), I have little or no direct or conscious control. I can't just *decide* to accept, say, Affirming the Consequent (or Ignoring the Antecedent) instead of *modus ponens;* I can't just decide not to believe that I had a grapefruit for breakfast; and I can't just decide to form a belief as to what Caesar had for breakfast that fateful morning (although I can decide to go to the library and look it up). Or rather, whether or not I can *decide* to do

---

[20]As in Monty Python's "Ministry of Silly Walks."

these things, I can't in fact *do* them. As Thomas Reid says, "My belief is carried along by perception, as irresistibly as my body by the Earth. And the greatest sceptic will find himself to be in the same condition. He may struggle hard to disbelieve the informations of his senses, as a man does to swim against the torrent; but ah: it is in vain."

This is not to say, of course, that I have no control *at all* over my beliefs. I can arrange that I will have beliefs on certain topics by putting myself in the right conditions; I may also resolve to be less credulous (or less skeptical), pay more attention to the evidence, not insist on evidence when it is not appropriate, fight my tendency to form beliefs by wishful thinking, and the like. Nor am I saying that a person couldn't learn to inhibit her natural belief-forming tendencies. Perhaps I could follow Sextus's advice and (by dint of long and arduous training) attain a state in which I do not believe that I see something red when I am appeared to redly. (Perhaps I could even train myself to believe that I am appeared to by something green under those conditions.) But the point is that if these things are humanly possible at all, they are very difficult: for the most part we have little direct control over what we believe, and neither undertake nor decide to form specific beliefs.

Pollock compares epistemic norms most explicitly to norms we first consciously grasp and follow in a step-by-step explicit fashion and then internalize: "[Epistemic norms] describe an internalized pattern of behavior that we automatically follow in reasoning, in the same way we automatically follow a pattern in bicycle riding. This is what epistemic norms are. They are the internalized norms that govern our reasoning" (p. 131). But for the most fundamental kinds of beliefs, there is typically nothing like *internalizing* our epistemic norms. Under the right conditions, I believe that I am appeared to redly, or that there is a tree outside, or that $7 + 5 = 12$, or that you are coming for dinner. Perhaps, in a semi-Pickwickian way, it is correct to say that I know how to believe these things and have learned how to do it; but it isn't as if there is anything like internalizing a set of directions for forming such beliefs. We don't first learn how to believe such things by thinking about maxims or norms for beliefs, explicitly following them by noting that we are in the condition in which, according to the norm, it is permissible to form the belief in question, and then forming that belief. Norms for bicycling or driving get internalized and become second nature; most epistemic norms, by contrast, are first nature. They don't have to *become* internalized; they regulate our doxastic carryings on long before we so much as notice them. Epistemic norms are more like the 'norms' that govern perspiration, or adrenaline flow, or blood pressure, or rate of respiration. To think about them on the pattern of internalized rules or directions is to think about them in too intellectualistic a way.

In a remarkable section of *Contemporary Theories of Knowledge,* Pollock himself suggests a wholly different way of thinking about norms. He remarks that "a fuller understanding of the nature of epistemic norms can be obtained by seeing how they are integrated into the broader picture of man as a cognitive machine" (p. 149); he suggests that "considerable light can be thrown on human epistemology by reflecting on the working of cognitive machines in general"; he considers how we might try to build an information processing machine ('Oscar') that simulates our cognitive behavior. In such a machine, he says,

> Sensory input results in behavioral output, and an important part of the connection is provided by thought. The thought processes constitute reasoning and are governed by rules for reasoning. . . . The rules for pure reasoning constitute epistemic norms. *In effect, epistemic norms comprise a "program" for the manipulation of sentences in the language of thought in response to sensory input.* (p. 161; emphasis added)

Since Pollock sees a *belief* as something like a sentence in the language of thought (a sentence treated in a certain special way), his view is that epistemic norms relevantly resemble a program for an information-processing machine. Such a program describes how the machine will behave under various conditions (if it is functioning properly). Figuratively speaking, it instructs the machine to take certain lines of action in response to a certain state of affairs (when you are in state S and condition C obtains, move to state S^*); among other things it specifies the conditions under which the machine in question will 'believe' certain propositions. To turn to human beings and remove the quotation marks, epistemic norms will be very much like descriptions of the doxastic behavior of a properly functioning human being. When appeared to in a certain characteristic way, I will form a certain characteristic belief (if there are no defeaters); when I consider an instance of *modus ponens*, it seems obviously valid and I form the belief that indeed it is; when you tell me that your name is 'Alexander Hamilton', I believe you. Epistemic norms will be like generalizations of these descriptions.

But note how very different this conception of norms is from the one to be found in Chisholm or, indeed, the entire Lockean–Cartesian tradition—the tradition in which the notion of justification has its natural home. When Oscar fails to function in accord with her specifications, we may rightly think she is defective, or isn't working properly; but we can hardly claim that she isn't *justified* in functioning that way. (She should be ashamed of herself?) The notions of duty, obligation, permission, exoneration, blameworthiness, justification—that whole deontological stable—these seem irrelevant to Oscar and her functioning. Here we have a conception of epistemic norm that differs *toto caelo* from the deontological conception. Norms thought of this new way are more like specifications for a piece of machinery. Thus the specifications for a 1985 GMC van say something like (I'm just guessing) "After a cold start, the engine idles at 1,500 RPM until the coolant temperature reaches 180°F; then it slows to 750 RPM." Such specifications describe how a machine of a certain sort functions when it is working properly.

So epistemic norms in this new conception are like specifications for a mechanism, or descriptions of how a certain kind of device functions when it is working properly. Perhaps you think it is stretching things to call specifications or descriptions 'norms'. But the fact is that term is correct (if analogical); and there is a sense of 'ought' to go with it. Referring to the engine, we may correctly say "It ought to slow to 750 RPM when it heats up"; referring to the engine's thermostat we may say "It ought to open when the coolant temperature hits 180°F"; referring to your newly purchased but recalcitrant word-processing program you may say "When you strike the option and Q keys, it ought to align the right margin." (This use of 'ought' is not predictive; we can say the same sort of thing even if we are constructing a new machine that has not worked properly so far and probably won't for the next month.) So such descriptions or specifications can rightly (if analogically) be called 'norms'; they specify the behavior of a normal, properly functioning human person, that is, one whose functioning conforms to the relevant norms. In *Warrant and Proper Function* I argue that a crucial element of what confers warrant upon a belief for me is its being produced in me by my faculties functioning properly in a congenial epistemic environment. Equivalently, I argue that a belief has warrant for me when it is produced by my cognitive faculties functioning in accord with my design plan in an appropriate epistemic environment (where the element of the design plan governing its production is successfully aimed at truth). Pollock's deep view of the nature of epistemic norms is very much in accord with that suggestion; his norms, so thought of, begin to look very much like elements of the design plan.

There is another way to see that the conception of norm here adumbrated is wholly different from that to be found in the deontological tradition (the tradition of Pollock's earlier epistemological work and the tradition where the notions of justification and permission are at home). Consider the sense in which Pollock's new view is *internalist:*

> It is easy to see that they [that is, epistemic norms] must be internalist norms. This is because when we learn how to do something we acquire a set of norms for doing it and these norms are internalized in a way enabling our central nervous system to follow them in an automatic way. . . . In general, the circumstance-types to which our norms appeal in telling us to do something in circumstances of those types must be directly accessible to our automatic processing systems. The sense in which they must be directly accessible is that our automatic processing system must be able to access them without our first having to make a *judgment* about whether we are in circumstances of that type. We must have non-epistemic access. (p. 133)

In what way, then, is Pollock's theory internalist? A person is justified in a belief if and only if the belief is formed in accord with her norms; such a norm must specify conditions under which it is permissible to form a certain belief; and the norm is internalist in the sense those conditions must be "directly accessible to our automatic processing systems"—that is, accessible to those systems without our having to make any judgments. So those conditions must be accessible to our central processors, whatever those are, in approximately the way in which the ambient temperature is accessible to a thermostat. The thermostat embodies such norms as *when it gets below 70°F., close the switch.* But then of course the ambient temperature (or something appropriately connected with it) must be 'accessible' to the thermostat.

So Pollock's theory is internalist in that on his theory there are norms that are internalist in the sense just outlined. But *that* sense is at best attenuated (not to say eviscerated and emasculated). It does not require, of course, that S is or even could become *aware*, either of the norms or of those conditions; the conditions have to be accessible to S's *automatic processors*, but of course they don't have to be accessible to S. The ph level of my blood is too low; my body makes the appropriate response; so the ph level of my blood must be accessible to my "automatic processors." Does my believing this justify me in claiming to hold an internalist theory of acidulous behavior? You might concede that under certain conditions accessible to your "automatic processors," your gallbladder will pump bile into your stomach. Would it follow that you endorse an internalist theory of bilious behavior?

And couldn't even the most blatant externalist be an internalist in this sense? You are an externalist; you think that what confers warrant upon a belief is its being produced by a reliable belief-producing mechanism. But you could consistently add that there are Pollockian norms governing the formation and sustenance of belief, and that conditions specified in the norms are accessible to the relevant "automatic processing system." That wouldn't make you much of an internalist. Again, note how far this alleged sort of internalism is from that implied by the classical deontological conceptions of warrant. There the idea was that we ourselves can consciously regulate our beliefs, and are obliged to do so in a certain way. According to Locke, for example, I am blameworthy if I accept a belief B when it does not (after reflection) seem to be probable with respect to what is certain for me. But then of course I must be aware of or know or be able to know whether I accept B, and what is certain for me, and whether (after reflection) B seems more probable than not with respect to what is certain for me. Nothing at all like this is involved in Pollock's alleged internalism.

There is a strain, a tension, a schism in Pollock's thinking about norms. He thinks about them partly in ways appropriate to a deontological conception of warrant, as if they specified conditional duties or obligations: he speaks of permission, justification, being within one's rights, and the rest of the deontological panoply. But he also thinks of them as if they were more like directions embodied by a piece of machinery, or specifications of how an organism works when it is functioning properly—part of the *design plan* that is featured in the account of warrant I give in *Warrant and Proper Function*; and this is to think of them (and of warrant) very differently indeed. This latter way of thinking of warrant seems to me to have great promise. In *Warrant and Proper Function* I shall try to develop it in detail.

9

Reliabilism

The views so far considered have all been examples of internalism—some very close to the deontological heart and soul (and origin) of the internalist tradition, and others at some analogical distance. None of these views, as we saw, offers the resources for a proper understanding of warrant or positive epistemic status. Chisholm's dutiful but malfunctioning epistemic agents, Pollock's agent who reasons in accordance with incorrect norms, the coherent but inflexible climber—all have come to epistemic grief. None of the suggestions so far considered is anywhere nearly sufficient for warrant. And the reason is not far to seek. Internalism is a congeries of analogically related ideas centering about *access*—special access, of some kind, on the part of the epistemic agent to justification and its ground.[1] What holds these ideas together, what is the source of the motivation for internalism, is *deontology:* the notion that epistemic permission, or satisfaction of epistemic duty, or conforming to epistemic obligation, is necessary and sufficient (perhaps with a codicil to propitiate Gettier) for warrant. Deontology generates internalism. Upon reflection, however, it is wholly clear that satisfaction of epistemic duty is nowhere nearly sufficient for warrant. I may be ever so dutiful; I may be performing works of magnificent epistemic supererogation, and nonetheless, by virtue of cognitive malfunction, be such that my beliefs have next to no warrant at all. Warrant is indeed a profoundly normative notion; it contains a deep and essential normative component; but that normative component is not or is not merely deontological.

It is equally clear, however, that internalism cut loose from deontology won't do the trick. Think of the conditions or states to which I can plausibly be thought to have the requisite sort of privileged access: *doing my epistemic duty* and *trying my best,* of course, but also *being appeared to in such and such a way, having a coherent noetic structure* (perhaps), *following the epistemic policies that I think are appropriate,* or the policies that upon sufficient reflection I would think are appropriate,[2] and so on. For many (perhaps most) of these

[1]See chapter 1.

[2]This is of course Foley rationality. See my pp. 132ff. The sort of privileged access I have in this case is attenuated: I don't *now* have much by way of special access to what I would think after sufficient reflection. Further, if what is at issue is my present deepest standards, wouldn't we have to add that what is involved is what I would think after sufficient reflection, given that those

states it is far from easy to spell out a plausible notion of privileged access such that we do indeed have that sort of privileged access to them. These are monumental difficulties. Even if we ignore them, however, what we have seen is this: things can go as well as you please with respect to the states in question and some particular belief of mine; but that belief may still (by virtue of cognitive malfunction of one sort or another) be without warrant.

Internalism, therefore, is quite insufficient; for an account of warrant we must look elsewhere. But if internalism seems not to do the job, what more natural than to try externalism? I shall think of externalism as the complement of internalism; the externalist holds that it is *not* the case that in order for one of my beliefs to have warrant for me, I must have some sort of special or privileged access to the fact that I have warrant, or to its ground. Clearly externalism thus conceived is something of a catchall. Recently, however, there has been a great flurry of quite appropriate interest in a certain specific kind of externalism: the original and exciting reliabilist and quasi-reliabilist views of David Armstrong,[3] Fred Dretske,[4] and Alvin Goldman,[5] and of those who take inspiration from them, such as William Alston,[6] Marshall Swain,[7] Robert Nozick,[8] and many others. Reliabilism is the new boy on the block; it is innovative and original in the contemporary epistemological context. As a matter of fact, however, it isn't quite as original as it initially seems; Frank Ramsey proposed the germ of a reliabilist account of warrant in his 1926 essay "Truth and Probability."[9] According to Ramsey (roughly) the "reasonable" degree of belief is the proportion of cases in which the "habit" producing the belief produces true beliefs.[10] Reliabilism, therefore, goes back at least to Ramsey; but externalism (taken broadly) goes back much further, back to Aquinas, back, in fact, all the way to Aristotle.[11] Indeed (apart from some of

deepest standards don't change? And do I have any sort of privileged access to answer to the question whether my deepest standards have changed? And finally, how much reflection is enough, and do I have privileged access to the answer to the question whether I have reflected enough?

[3] *Belief, Truth and Knowledge* (London: Cambridge University Press, 1973).

[4] *Knowledge and the Flow of Information* (Cambridge: MIT Press, 1981).

[5] See, for example, "What Is Justified Belief?" in *Justification and Knowledge: New Studies in Epistemology,* ed. George Pappas (Dordrecht: D. Reidel, 1979), and *Epistemology and Cognition* (Cambridge: Harvard University Press, 1986).

[6] This work is to be found in, for example, his "Concepts of Epistemic Justification" and "An Internalist Externalism" (see nn. 12 and 13) and in several of the articles collected in *Epistemic Justification* (Ithaca: Cornell University Press, 1989).

[7] *Reasons and Knowledge* (Ithaca: Cornell University Press, 1981).

[8] *Philosophical Explanation* (Cambridge: Harvard University Press, 1981). For animadversions on the views presented there, see my "Positive Epistemic Status and Proper Function," in *Philosophical Perspectives, 2, Epistemology, 1988,* ed. James Tomberlin (Atascadero, Calif.: Ridgeview, 1988) pp. 15ff.

[9] First published in The *Foundations of Mathematics and Other Logical Essays,* ed. R. B. Braithwaite (London: K. Paul, Trench, Trubner, 1931), pp. 195–96.

[10] Ramsey recognizes that we can't consider only the *actual* proportion of truths among beliefs produced by the habit in question: the crucial notion of reliability is in some way crucially counterfactual. He also notes that we must consider not only the habit that produces the belief in question, but also the habit-producing habit that produces that habit.

[11] See Aristotle's *De Anima* and *Posterior Analytics,* II, where there is a sort of anticipation of

the skeptics of the later Platonic Academy), it isn't easy to find internalists in epistemology prior to Descartes. On the long view it is really externalism, in one form or another, that has been dominant in our tradition. Armstrong, Dretske, Goldman, and their *confreres* are not so much proposing a startling new view as recalling us to the main lines of our tradition. (Before you take this as a point against them, remember that, as Hobbes observed, he who says what has never been said before says what will probably never be said again.)

Externalism, taken broadly, is right about warrant. But externalism as such is simply the denial of internalism: and what is needed is not simply the denial of deontology and internalism. What is needed is a positive (and, we hope, *correct*) account of warrant. In this chapter I propose to examine three externalist and reliabilist accounts of warrant: those offered or suggested by Alston, Goldman, and Dretske—offered or *suggested,* I say, because Alston and Goldman speak explicitly of *justification* rather than warrant. I shall argue that these accounts look in the right direction; but each also overlooks an element absolutely essential to our conception of warrant. Then in *Warrant and Proper Function* I shall spell out what I take to be the sober epistemological truth of the matter.

I shall argue, however, that no brief and simple, semialgorithmic account of warrant carries much by way of illumination. Our epistemic establishment of noetic faculties or powers is complex and highly articulated; it is detailed and many-sided. There is knowledge of (or, to beg no questions, belief about) an astonishingly wide variety of topics—our everyday external environment, the thoughts and feelings of others, our own internal life (an internal soliloquy can occupy an entire novel), the past, logic and mathematics, beauty, science, morality, modality, God, and a host of other topics. These faculties work with exquisite subtlety and discrimination, producing beliefs on these and other topics that vary all the way from the merest suspicion to absolute dead certainty. And once we see the enormous extent of this articulation and subtlety, we can also see that warrant has different requirements in different divisions or components or compartments or modules (the right word is hard to find) of that establishment; perhaps in some of these areas internalist constraints are indeed necessary for warrant.

I. Alstonian Justification

A. The Concept

I begin with William P. Alston's account of justification as presented in "Concepts of Epistemic Justification"[12] and "An Internalist Externalism"[13] (cited hereafter as CEJ and IE). As the the second title indicates, Alston's thought here is a sort of bridge between internalism and externalism, a sort of halfway house

---

reliabilism (more accurately, a statement of what reliabilism is a return to), and see Aquinas's *Summa Theologiae,* I, q. 84, 85.

[12] *Monist* (January 1985).

[13] *Synthese* 74, no. 3 (March 1988).

between the two; beginning our transition to externalism with it may therefore reduce the shock. The account is *externalist* and even *reliabilist* in that, as we shall see, he holds that a person is justified in believing a proposition only if she believes it on the basis of a reliable indicator. Of course Alston's account is of *justification,* not warrant. Warrant is that (whatever it is) such that enough of it together with truth (and perhaps a codicil aimed at Gettier) is necessary and sufficient for knowledge; as we shall see, Alston does not claim that justification (as he conceives it) fills that bill. Still, I think we may be able to make progress toward a deeper understanding of warrant by considering his account of justification.

Anglo-American epistemologists of this century have concentrated on the notion of *epistemic justification;* but exactly what, asks Alston, *is* justification? Much more energy has gone into the question under what conditions beliefs *have* justification than into investigation of the *nature* of justification, into analyzing and making explicit our concept (or concepts) of justification. Setting out to redress the balance, Alston initially points out that justification has at least the following four features: it is a concept of something that applies to beliefs or believings; it is evaluative, and *positively* evaluative, so that rating a belief as justified is to attribute a desirable or favorable character to it; more specifically, it is *epistemically* evaluative, having to do with a favorable position with respect to truth (or the aim of acquiring true beliefs); and finally, it comes in degrees (CEJ, pp. 58–59). (We may therefore prefer to think of it as a *quantity* [rather than a property], a quantity that perhaps varies as a function of other quantities or properties.) Of course this gives us only a distant view of the concept. Trying for a closer look, Alston asks the following question: what *is* this favorable status which, according to the central core of the idea of justification, accrues to a justified belief? Here he notes an important watershed:

> As I see it, the major divide in this terrain has to do with whether believing and refraining from believing are subject to obligation, duty, and the like. If they are, we can think of the favorable evaluative status of a certain belief as consisting in the fact that in holding that belief one has fulfilled one's obligations, or refrained from violating one's obligations to achieve the fundamental aim in question [that is, "the aim of maximizing truth and minimizing falsity in a large body of beliefs"]. If they are not so subject, the favorable status will have to be thought of in some other way. (CEJ, p. 59)

There is a hint here that the notion of justification as a matter of permission, of freedom from blameworthiness, of fulfillment of epistemic duty and obligation—in a word, the *deontological* notion of justification—is more natural, or at any rate more familiar than alternatives. This is surely plausible; as we saw in chapter 1, deontological notions of justification have been overwhelmingly dominant in twentieth-century Anglo-American epistemology. Exploring this family of ideas with care and insight, Alston pays particular attention to the ways in which doxastic phenomena can be within our voluntary control. His verdict is that none of the deontological notions will do the job: even the most promising of the bunch, he says, "does not give us what we expect of epistemic justification. The most serious defect is that it does not hook up in the right way with an adequate, truth-conducive ground. I may have done what could reasonably be expected of me in the management and cultivation of my doxastic life, and still hold a belief on outrageously inadequate grounds" (CEJ, p. 67).

So the deontological answer to the question 'What sort of evaluation is involved in justification?' can't be right. "Perhaps it was misguided all along," he says, "to think of epistemic justification as freedom from blameworthiness. Is there any alternative, given the non-negotiable point that we are looking for a concept of epistemic evaluation?" (CEJ, p. 69) The answer, of course, is that there are *many* alternatives. After another careful exploration of the field, he chooses his candidate:

> S is J_{eg} ['$_e$' for 'evaluative' and '$_g$' for 'grounds'] justified in believing that p iff S's believing that p, as S did, was a good thing from the epistemic point of view, in that S's belief that p was based on adequate grounds and S lacked sufficient overriding reasons to the contrary. (CEJ, p. 77)

Here "grounds" would include other beliefs, but also experience (as in the case of perceptual beliefs); I refer the reader to the text for the qualification "as S did" (CEJ, p. 70) and for discussion of the nature of the basing relation (CEJ, pp. 71–72; IE, pp. 265–77). But why this emphasis upon *grounds?* Because, says Alston, in asking whether S's belief that p is *justified* (in the evaluative but nondeontological sense) "we are asking whether the truth of p is indicated by what S has to go on; whether given what S had to go on, it is at least quite likely that p is true. We want to know whether S had *adequate* grounds for believing that p, where adequate grounds are those sufficiently indicative of the truth of p" (CEJ, p. 71). Alston explains the idea of grounds being indicative of the truth of p in terms of conditional probability: "In other terms, the ground must be such that the *probability* of the belief's being true, given that ground, is very high" (IE, p. 269).[14]

A belief is epistemically justified, therefore, only if it is accepted on the basis of adequate grounds. But there is a further condition: these grounds must be *accessible* to the believer:

> I find widely shared and strong intuitions in favor of some kind of accessibility requirement for justification. We expect that if there is something that justifies my belief that p, I will be able to determine what it is. We find something incongruous, or conceptually impossible, in the notion of my being justified in believing that p while totally lacking any capacity to determine what is responsible for that justification. (IE, p. 272)

The specific form of the internalist requirement Alston offers is determined by what he takes to be the origin of the intuitions supporting the accessibility requirement:

> I suggest that the concept [that of epistemic justification] was developed, and got its hold on us, because of the practice of critical reflection on our beliefs, of challenging their credentials and responding to such challenges, in short the

---

[14]This probability, of course, is to be *objective* (IE, p. 269).

practice of attempting to justify beliefs. Suppose there were no such practice; suppose that no one ever challenged the credentials of anyone's beliefs; suppose that no one ever critically reflected on the grounds or basis of one's own beliefs. In that case would we be interested in determining whether one or another belief *is* justified? I think not. (IE, p. 273)

(Alston argues that what must be accessible to the agent is only the *ground* of the belief;[15] the relationship between ground and belief by virtue of which the ground supports or is a reliable indicator of the belief need not be accessible.) And finally, how accessible must the ground be to the agent? Here (naturally enough) there is no very precise answer: "What is needed here is a concept of something like 'fairly direct accessibility'. In order that justifiers be generally available for presentation as what legitimates the belief, they must be fairly readily available to the subject, available through some mode of access much quicker than that of lengthy research, observation, or experiment" (IE, p. 275).

B. *Questions about Alstonian Justification*

1. *Where Does It Come From?*

Alston begins by arguing that the deontological family of concepts of justification won't do, despite their naturalness and familiarity. What we need, he says, is an *evaluative* conception that is not *deontological;* he settles on one of a wide variety of possibilities. But what guides the search here? How do we determine which of all the many epistemic nondeontological values is the right one? There are hosts of epistemically valuable but nondeontological states of affairs: *usually* believing the truth; *now* believing the truth; having a belief formed by a reliable belief-producing mechanism; *knowing* that one's beliefs are formed by a reliable belief-producing mechanism; being Foley rational with respect to one's beliefs; having true beliefs on topics important for survival, or a good life, or deep understanding, or spiritual excellence; being such that one's cognitive faculties are nondefective, being such that one's beliefs are proportioned to the evidence; being suited to one's epistemic environment; being able to forget what would otherwise clutter one's memory; believing on the basis of a reliable indicator; believing on the basis of an *accessible* reliable indicator; believing on the basis of an accessible reliable indicator you *know* or *justifiably believe* is reliable; and many more. The rejectees as well as the lucky winner are all epistemically desirable; each is an epistemically valuable state of affairs. How does Alston decide among them, and what guides him in selecting one of them as the one that goes with epistemic justification?

To answer this question we must return to the brief historical excursus of chapter 1. First, the dominant tradition in Anglo-American epistemology has certainly been heavily deontological. The "justified true belief" account of knowledge is of course the one we learned at our mother's knee;[16] a belief

[15]More exactly, the ground must be "the sort of thing that in general, or when nothing interferes, is available for citation by the subject" (IE, p. 275).

[16]But bear in mind the caveat of chapter 1, p. 6: there are few explicit statements of a justified true belief theory of knowledge prior to Gettier.

constitutes knowledge only if it is a *justified* belief. Justification is necessary for knowledge, and (along with truth) nearly sufficient for it; perhaps a fillip or epicycle ("the fourth condition") is needed to appease Gettier, but the basic contours of the notion of knowledge are given by justification and truth.

And the fundamental notions of justification in this tradition—the 'received tradition', as we may call it to mark its dominance—have been deontological notions, or notions analogically but intimately related to deontological notions. Think, for example, of the classical Chisholm (see chapter 2): positive epistemic status, for him, is aptness for epistemic duty fulfillment. No doubt Chisholm is the dominant figure among contemporary deontologists, but he is only one deontologist among many.[17] Indeed, the very term 'justification' is redolent of deontology. To be justified is to be blameless, to have done what is required, to be, like Caesar's wife Calpurnia, above reproach. It is to be such as not to be properly subject to censure, blame, reproach, reproof. Alston therefore objects to the use of the term 'justification' for any concept that is *not* deontological:

> I must confess that I do not find 'justified' an apt term for a favorable or desirable state or condition, when what makes it desirable is cut loose from considerations of obligation and blame. Nevertheless, since the term is firmly ensconced in the literature as the term to use for any concept that satisfies the four conditions set out in section II, I will stifle my linguistic scruples and employ it for a non-deontological concept. (CEJ, p. 86 n. 21)

But of course 'justification' occupies the field; it is the term typically used to denote warrant, that which (Gettier to one side for the moment) stands between mere true belief and knowledge.

So the first thing to see is that in the received tradition, justification is necessary and nearly sufficient for warrant; and the second is that justification, in the received tradition, is thought of deontologically. But the next thing to see is that the received tradition follows John Locke in being inclined to see the central epistemic duty here as that of believing only on the basis of *evidence,* of proportioning belief to evidence. This tradition goes back to Locke; it has boasted clouds of witnesses ever since. (Among them, as we saw in chapter 1, are W. K. Clifford, Sigmund Freud, Brand Blanshard, H. H. Price, Bertrand Russell, Michael Scriven, and, more recently, Richard Feldman and Earl Conee.[18]) Perhaps this duty arises, as Alston and Chisholm suggest, out of a more basic Ur-duty to try to achieve the right relation to the truth; or perhaps (as Locke seems to suggest) the duty in question is *sui generis,* one attaching to

---

[17]For a short but diversified list, consider, for example, Laurence BonJour's deontologism (see pp. 88ff); Brand Blanshard in *Reason and Belief* (London: Allen & Unwin, 1974), pp. 406ff; perhaps Bas van Fraassen in "Belief and the Problem of Ulysses and the Sirens" (at present not published); Carl Ginet in *Knowledge, Perception and Memory* (Dordrecht: D. Reidel, 1975), p. 28; John Pollock in *Knowledge and Justification* (Princeton: Princeton University Press, 1974); and A. J. Ayer with his suggestion that your belief constitutes knowledge if it is a true belief for which you have "the right to be sure," in *The Problem of Knowledge* (London: Macmillan, 1956), p. 28ff. See my discussion (pp. 199ff) for the conception of justification—a conception analogically related to the deontological conception—in Alvin Goldman, *Epistemology and Cognition.*

[18]"Evidentialism," *Philosophical Studies* 48 (1985), pp. 15–34.

a person whether or not conforming to it leads for the most part to truth; but in any event a fundamental duty is that of believing only on the basis of evidence. And when this thought is combined with the deontological conception of justification, the result is a powerful emphasis upon *evidence,* a strong tendency to see justification as in most cases a function of quality and quantity of evidence. "In most cases"; for of course insofar as modern classical foundationalism is an important part of the received tradition, beliefs that are either self-evident or appropriately about one's own introspectable states will have warrant without being accepted on the basis of evidence.

The shape of the concept of justification in the received tradition is clear: it involves a marriage of the idea that deontological justification is central to warrant (and hence to knowledge) with the notion that—at any rate over vast areas of the epistemic terrain—a fundamental intellectual duty is that of believing only on the basis of evidence.

Now return to the question: what guides Alston's search for the right or appropriate conception of justification? Why, of all the epistemically valuable states of affairs to link with justification, does he settle on the one he picks? What exactly is his project here? Perhaps the answer is to be found along the following lines: he aims to make explicit the various notions of justification lurking in the contemporary neighborhood, and aims to select the candidate that best fits the conditions laid down by the received tradition. As we have seen, there are three essential elements to that tradition: (a) justification is conceived deontologically, (b) justification heavily involves evidence or grounds, and (c) justification is necessary and nearly sufficient for warrant. We can understand Alston's choice among all those epistemically valuable states of affairs as a matter of trying to select the candidate that best fits these three conditions. Of course he quite correctly sees that *no* concept fits really well; no deontological concept is anywhere nearly sufficient for warrant; hence the received position (as I argued in chapter 1) is incoherent. He therefore looks for another epistemically valuable state of affairs—one that is perforce nondeontological—that will fill or nearly fill the bill.

An initial problem looms, however. In the tradition in question, justification is thought to be necessary for warrant and nearly sufficient for it (in the sense that in addition to justification all that is needed for warrant is a proviso to appease Gettier). Alstonian justification, however, is not in (Alston's view) necessary for knowledge (and hence not necessary for warrant): "Beliefs that, so far as the subject can tell, just pop into his head out of nowhere would not be counted as justified on this position" (IE, p. 281)—because there would not be an accessible ground for the belief. Such beliefs, however, might nonetheless constitute knowledge: "I do hold that mere reliable belief production, suitably construed, is sufficient for knowledge" (IE, p. 281). So Alstonian justification, unlike justification on the received conception, is not necessary for warrant.

But perhaps this problem is less real than apparent. Alston expresses skepticism as to whether there *is* knowledge that isn't based on grounds, even though he thinks perhaps there could be; he doubts that it ever happens that an item of knowledge consists in a belief that is reliably produced but simply pops into the subject's head.[19] There *could be* knowledge of that sort, and if there *were*, it would be knowledge unaccompanied by justification; but perhaps the idea is that justification is a necessary condition for knowledge in the case of any belief that *does not* just pop into the agent's head. (And if, as Alston thinks likely, *no* cases of knowledge are in fact of that sort, every case of knowledge would be a case of justified belief, even if not *necessarily* so.)

If we understand him thus, it is easy to see why Alston's notion of justification takes the shape it does. First, it is no wonder, given the heavy emphasis upon evidence in the received tradition, that Alston gives pride of place to *grounds.* Second, it is equally easy to see the source of the requirement that these grounds be *accessible* to the agent. Alston finds "widely shared and strong intuitions in favor of some kind of accessibility requirement for justification" (p. 186). These intuitions, I suggest, are to be accounted for in terms of the widely shared deontological conception of justification; deontology, as I argued in chapter 1, requires accessibility. Alston recognizes that deontology cannot play the role it is assigned in the received tradition: nonetheless a *prima facie desideratum* for a reconstruction of the received notion of justification, he thinks, is that it recognize and accommodate those widely shared intuitions in favor of an accessibility requirement for justification. But what, finally, about the specifically *externalist* component of Alstonian justification, the suggestion that the grounds on which I believe *p* must in fact be an indicator of its truth, if I am to be justified? How does this fit in? Perhaps in a double way. In the first place (as I argued), the received tradition prominently features the notion that a chief epistemic duty is that of believing only on the basis of *evidence;* that tradition also features the deontological conception of justification; and these two together yield the thought that being justified in believing *p* requires having evidence for *p.* Further, where *q* is indeed evidence for *p, q* presumably will indeed be an indicator of the truth of *p.* We can therefore see Alston's suggestion—that being justified in believing *p* requires that one believe *p* on the basis of a ground that is an indicator of the truth of *p*—as a generalization or broadening of the received tradition's emphasis upon evidence.

2. Alstonian Justification Nowhere Nearly Sufficient for Warrant

I think we can see that Alstonian justification is itself by no means either necessary or nearly sufficient for warrant. Of course Alston does not claim that it *is* necessary; as we have seen, he suggests that a belief that just popped into my head could possibly be knowledge, but would not be justified because it was not grounded. But neither is it sufficient, or even sufficient up to Gettier problems. *S*'s belief that *p* is Alston-justified if it is based on a ground that is both accessible to *S* and is a reliable indicator of the truth of *p.* Clearly, however,

---

[19]But isn't this really the way it goes with memory? Do we form memory beliefs on the basis of an accessible ground? I don't think so (see *Warrant and Proper Function,* chap. 3). And what about *a priori* beliefs such as that 2 + 1 = 3? Here too, I think, there is nothing relevantly like grounds (see ibid., chap. 6). (For Alston's contrary view, see CEJ, pp. 77–78.) I am therefore inclined to think that memory and *a priori* beliefs don't typically have Alstonian justification; but doesn't that cast something of a pall over the notion?

a belief could meet that condition even if it had little or no warrant. There are different kinds of examples here. Note that Alstonian justification does not require that *S know* or *justifiably believe* that the ground of her belief is in fact reliably connected with the truth of that belief (although it may preclude your believing that the ground in question is *not* a reliable indicator: that belief would be a defeating and possibly overriding condition). Accordingly: suppose I often believe that someone I meet is a fine fellow on the basis of a certain kind of facial appearance, a sort of scrunched-up look around the eyes. I now form beliefs in this way only because once years ago I very much admired a comic book character who looked like that. Even if it turns out that the look in question really is a reliable indicator of being a fine fellow, my belief still has little or no warrant for me. Even if it is a powerful indicator and I believe the proposition very firmly, I still wouldn't know it.

A second kind of case: suppose that some standard set of axioms for real analysis has the consequence that there are 4 successive 7s in the decimal expansion of π; suppose further that I believe those axioms, and believe that there are 4 successive 7s there on the basis of them. This is not, however, because I can see or show that they do have that consequence, or because I believe that someone else has shown that. Instead, it is due to a nasty little glitch in my belief-forming apparatus: on the basis of those axioms I believe for *any* number n I've thought of that there are n successive 7s in the decimal expansion of n. Under these conditions, I may be justified in accepting these beliefs, but none of them has any warrant for me, not even the ones entailed by the axioms in question.

A third kind of case: suppose (contrary to what most of us believe) the *National Enquirer* is in fact extremely reliable in its accounts of extraterrestrial events. One day it carries screaming headlines: STATUE OF ELVIS FOUND ON MARS!! Due to cognitive malfunction (inducing the "epistemic incontinence" Alston speaks of elsewhere), I am extremely gullible, in particular with respect to the *National Enquirer,* always trusting it implicitly on the topic of extraterrestrials. (And, due to the same malfunction, I don't believe anything that would override the belief in question.) Then my belief that a statue of Elvis was found on Mars is in fact based on a reliable indicator which is appropriately accessible to me; and I don't know or believe anything overriding this belief. But surely the belief has little by way of warrant.

A fourth example. Where the ground of a belief is in fact a reliable indicator, this will be, naturally enough, because of the nature of the indictor and the relation between it and the proposition in question. More generally, it will be because of the character of the cognitive environment in which the subject finds himself. Imagine, therefore, that I suffer from a rare sort of malady. A certain tune is such that whenever I hear it, I form the belief that there is a large purple animal nearby. Now in my cognitive environment, this is not in fact an indicator of the truth of this belief; so the belief has no Alstonian justification. But imagine that I am suddenly transported without my knowledge to some foreign environment—Australia, say; and imagine further that there, when that tune is heard, there is almost always a large purple animal nearby. (The tune in question, as it turns out, is the love call of the double-wattled purple cassowary.) In my new cognitive environment, the tune is indeed a reliable indicator of the truth of the belief; but of course the belief in question would (initially, at least) have no warrant—it would have no more warrant for me in Australia than it did in my original cognitive environment.

It is easy to see a recipe for constructing examples here. All we need are cases where some phenomenon is in fact a reliable indicator of the truth of a proposition, but my believing the proposition in question on the basis of that phenomenon arises from cognitive malfunction. A last example, then: suppose I suffer from two maladies. First, I visit a neural clinic for orthopedic surgery. Due to an appalling mix-up, I emerge from the operation with a serious disorder: whenever I have a pain in my right shoulder I form the belief, on the basis of that pain, that there is something wrong with my left knee. Next, I fall victim to a brain tumor that involves a specific and highly characteristic symptom: every so often it causes a vascular disorder—a constriction in a certain vein—in my left knee, and at the same time a sharp pain in my right shoulder. (I am entirely unaware of mix-up and tumor.) As things now stand, then, the pain in my shoulder, which is the ground of my belief that there is something wrong with my knee, is a reliable indicator of a disorder there. (We may add that this belief is not overridden by anything else I know or believe; perhaps the tumor also suppresses any beliefs that would otherwise defeat the belief in question.) I therefore meet the conditions for Alstonian justification; but surely that belief has little or no warrant for me. What is important to see in this case is that an indicator may in fact be a reliable indicator, but only *accidentally* reliable—reliable in a way that from an epistemic or cognitive point of view is merely accidental. This presages a problem that arises much more generally for reliabilism. A ground, or indicator, or a belief-forming mechanism, can be reliable just by accident—due, for example, to a freakish malfunction; and in those cases there will be no warrant even though there is reliability.

Once more, the important thing to see here, I think, is the central role, for warrant, of the idea of proper function, of absence of cognitive dysfunction.

II. Dretskian Reliabilism

A. *The Basic Idea*

Reliabilists come in at least two styles. The first sees warrant in terms of origin and provenance: a belief has warrant for me if it is produced and sustained by a reliable belief-producing mechanism. The second sees warrant as a matter of *probability;* a person is said to know a (true) proposition *A* if he believes it, and if the right probability relations hold between *A* and its significant others. On the first style, probability may figure in the account of what it is for a belief-producing mechanism to be reliable, but nothing need be said about the probability, conditional or otherwise, of the particular belief in question. On the second what matters is the probability of the belief in question; pedigree counts only as it figures into probability. Alvin Goldman's account of warrant is of the first sort, and I shall turn to it in the next section. The most powerfully developed account of the second sort, however, is to be found in Fred Dretske's *Knowledge and the Flow of Information* (hereafter cited as *KFI*), to which I now turn.

According to Dretske,

(D₁) *K* knows that *s* is *F* = *K*'s belief that *s* is *F* is caused (or causally sustained) by the information that *s* is *F*. (*KFI*, p. 86)

Two preliminary comments: Dretske is primarily concerned with *perceptual* knowledge; in particular his account is not designed to apply to *a priori* knowledge, such as *K*'s knowledge that, say, 7 + 5 = 12. Secondly, the account is restricted to what he calls "de re content" (*KFI*, p. 66); it is restricted, he says, to the kind of case where what *K* knows is a piece of information of or about *s*.

Now what sort of animal is this "information that *s* is *F*"? And what is it for a thing of that sort—presumably an abstract object or ensemble of abstract objects—to *cause* or causally sustain a belief? So far as I can see, Dretske gives little by way of answer to the first question. What he does give are many examples of the sort *the information that s is F*. There is, for example, the information that Sam is happy, that the peanut is under shell number 3, that Susan is jogging. One might say that these are *bits* of information, except that the term 'bit' has been preempted for a *measure* of information. We are to think of information as being generated by or associated with states of affairs; and the amount of information generated by a given state of affairs depends upon the number and probability of the possibilities that state of affairs excludes. Suppose I throw a fair-64-sided die. The information that the die came up on a side numbered from 1 to 32 reduces the possibilities by a half and carries 1 bit of information; the knowledge that the die came up on a side numbered from 1 to 16 reduces the possibilities by another half and accordingly carries 2 bits; the information that the die came up (say) 3 reduces the original 64 possibilities to one and carries 6 bits of information. As you can guess from the example, if a piece of news reduces *n* (equally probable) possibilities to 1, then the amount of information that piece of news boasts is given by log (to base 2) *n*. In the general case, where the possibilities involved need not be equiprobable (and where P(*A*) is the probability that a given possibility *A* is realized) the amount of information generated by *A* is given by

(D₂) $I(A) = \log (1/P(A))$, that is, $-\log P(A)$.

There are deep perplexities here. What are the relevant alternative possibilities for, for example, *Susan is jogging?* (D₂) is applicable only where the possibilities involved are finite in cardinality; is that so for such an uncontrived real life possibility as *Susan is jogging?* What would be the probability of something like *Susan is jogging?* These are pressing questions for an account of this kind, and I don't know of any even reasonably satisfactory answers to them. They are also less urgent than they look, however, because the notion of the *amount* of information does not crucially enter into Dretske's account of knowledge. Nor need we know, for Dretskian purposes, just what information *is;* all we really need to know is what it is for a piece of information to *cause* or *causally sustain* a belief. Here the answer is disarmingly straightforward:

> Suppose a signal *r* carries the information that *s* is *F* and carries this information in virtue of having the property *F*. That is, it is *r's being F* (not, say, its being *G*) that is responsible for *r's* carrying this specific piece of information. Not just any knock on the door tells the spy that the courier has arrived. The signal is three quick knocks followed by a pause and another three quick knocks. . . . It is the temporal pattern of knocks that constitutes the information-carrying feature (*F'*) of the signal. The same is obviously true in telegraphic communication.
>
> When, therefore, a signal carries the information that *s* is *F in virtue* of having property *F'*, when it is the signal's *being F* that carries the information, then (and only then) will we say that the information that *F causes* whatever the signal's being *F'* causes. (*KFI*, p. 87)

Given (D_1), then, what we have is that a person *K* knows that *s* is *F* if and only if (1) *K* believes that *s* is *F*, (2) there is a signal *r* such that *r* has some property *F'* in virtue of which it carries the information that *s* is *F*, and (3) *r's* having *F'* causes *K* to believe that *s* is *F*. Since we can safely drop the reference to the property *F'* of the signal by virtue of which it carries the information that *S* is *F*, what the analysis boils down to is the idea that *K* knows that *s* is *F* if and only if *K* believes that *s* is *F* and this belief is caused by a signal that carries the information that *s* is *F*. So what we still need to know is what it is for a signal to carry the information that *s* is *F*. This is given by

(D_3) A signal *r* carries the information that *s* is *F* = the conditional probability of *s's* being *F*, given *r* (and *k*) is 1 (but, given *k* alone, less than 1). (*KFI*, p. 65)

Now, *k*, as Dretske explains, is the *background knowledge* of the receiver. (D_3) must therefore be *relativized* to be accurate; a signal may carry the information that *s* is *F* relative to you but not to me. You already know that *s* is *F;* so the probability of *s's* being *F* relative to your background knowledge is 1; no signal carries the information that *s* is *F* relative to you. I don't know that *s* is *F;* so any signal *r* which is such that the probability of *s's* being *F* on *r&k* equals 1 (where *k* is my background knowledge) carries the information that *s* is *F* with respect to me. If you know that *s* is *F*, then no signal carries the information that *s* is *F* with respect to you; if you don't know that *s* is *F*, then that information is carried with respect to you by any state of affairs whose conjunction with what you do know entails that *s* is *F*. We can therefore rewrite (D_3) as

(D_4) *r* carries the information that *s* is *F* relative to *K* iff $P((s \text{ is } F)/(r\&k)) = 1$ and $P((s \text{ is } F)/k) < 1$.

And now we can say that

(D$_5$) K knows that s is F if and only if K believes that s is F and there is a state of affairs r's *being* G such that (1) r's *being* G causes K to believe that s *is* F and (2) P((s *is* F)/(r's *being* G & k)) = 1 and P((s *is* F)/k) < 1.

We saw that the disturbing notion of the *amount* of information associated with a specific event or state of affairs can safely be ignored, since that notion plays no role in Dretske's final account of knowledge. But now we see that the same goes for the other specifically information theoretic concepts; this analysis of knowledge, when spelled out, involves only the notions of probability, belief, and causation, and doesn't involve them in the problematic ways in which they show up in information theory.[20]

B. Problems

As we have already seen, deontological internalism, coherentism, Bayesianism—all come to grief when we reflect on the ways in which our noetic faculties can malfunction. But the same sorts of problems plague Dretske's account. Consider D$_5$. To see that it won't do the trick, consider The Case of the Epistemically Serendipitous Lesion. Suppose K suffers from a serious abnormality—a brain lesion, let's say. This lesion wreaks havoc with K's noetic structure, causing him to believe a variety of propositions, most of which are wildly false. It also causes him to believe, however, that he is suffering from a brain lesion. K has no evidence at all that he is abnormal in this way, thinking of his unusual beliefs as resulting from an engagingly original turn of mind. Now according to D$_5$, it follows that K knows that he is suffering from a brain lesion. His having this lesion causes him to believe that he is thus afflicted; the probability of his suffering from a brain lesion on his background knowledge k is less than 1; but of course its probability on k & *K is suffering from a brain lesion* is 1. But surely K does *not* know that he is suffering from a brain lesion. He has no evidence of any kind—sensory, memory, introspective, whatever— that he has such a lesion; his holding this belief is, from a cognitive point of view, no more than a lucky (or unlucky) accident.

Indeed, we can add, if we like, that K has powerful evidence for the conclusion that he is *not* thus suffering; he has just been examined by a trio of world famous experts from the Mayo Clinic who (mistakenly) assure him that his brain is entirely normal. In this case, then, K's belief that he has a brain lesion not only is such that he has no evidence for it; he has first-rate evidence *against* it. In such a situation K clearly does not know that he has a brain lesion, despite the fact that this belief meets Dretske's conditions for knowledge.

Examples of this kind can be multiplied; so let's multiply a couple. You have wronged me; you have stolen my Frisian flag. By way of exacting revenge I sneak into your house at night and implant in your dog a source of extremely

[20]See Richard Foley, "Dretske's 'Information Theoretic' Account of Knowledge," *Synthese* 70 (Fall 1987), pp. 159–84.

high frequency electromagnetic radiation. This radiation has no effect on you or your dog, except to cause you to form the belief that aliens from outer space have invaded your house and replaced your dog with a nonterrestrial look-alike that emits ultraviolet radiation. You christen this creature (who is in fact your dog) 'Spot'. Your belief that Spot emits ultraviolet radiation then satisfies Dretske's conditions for knowledge: Spot's emitting ultraviolet radiation causes you to believe that he does; relative to what you know this is not probable, but relative to the conjunction of what you know with *Spot emits ultraviolet radiation,* its probability is, of course, 1. Surely you do not know that Spot emits such radiation. Indeed, as in the previous case we can add that you have powerful (though misleading) evidence *against* this proposition. You have had Spot examined by a highly competent group of physicists based at the Stanford linear accelerator; I have corrupted them, bribing them to tell you that Spot is wholly normal; but you are nevertheless unable to divest yourself of the belief in question. Surely you don't know.

A third example. You and I each hold a ticket for a valuable lottery; first prize is an all-expenses-paid week in Philadelphia. (Second prize, of course, is *two* weeks in Philadelphia.) I approach the person designated to make the official draw and offer him a bribe to fix the lottery: I am to coat my ticket with a substance S^* and he is to coat his hand with a substance S in virtue of which my ticket will stick to his hand. After I leave, you appear and offer him twice as much; he accepts. He then coats his hand with a substance S^{**}; this causes *your* ticket to stick to his hand, thus causing you to win. It also causes me, by virtue of an otherwise undetectable abnormality on my part, to *believe* that you will win. You and I witness the drawing; I suddenly and unaccountably find myself with the belief that you will win. On Dretske's account, I know that you will win, despite my knowledge that I have fixed the lottery. For (where T_5 is your ticket) T_5's *being coated with* S^{**} causes me to believe that you will win; that you will win (we may suppose) has a probability of 1 on the conjunction of my background knowledge with T_5 *has been coated with* S^{**} but a lower probability on my background knowledge alone. But surely I *don't* know, under these conditions, that you will win.

Someone might object[21] that these examples have conformed to the letter but not the spirit of (D_5). On that definition, K knows that s is F if there is a signal r having some property G such that r's *being* G causes K to believe that s is F, and the probability of the latter on the former (plus k) is equal to 1 and greater than that of the latter on k alone; but in my examples, r's *being* G is *identical* with s's *being* F. That is quite true; in these examples I did indeed collapse r's *being* G with s's *being* F. I did so, however, only in order to avoid avoidable problems as to whether P(s's *being* F / r's *being* G) really equals 1. (After all, if the same state of affairs is both r's *being* G and s's *being* F, then it will be beyond dispute that the probability of s's *being* F on r's *being* G (and k) is 1.) The identity of r's *being* G with s's *being* F, however, is an inessential feature of these examples; we can easily amend them in such a way as to mollify the objector. In The Case of the Missing Frisian Flag, let r's *being* G be as before

---

[21]As Dretske did, in correspondence.

and let *s's being F* be *Spot is emitting radiation,* or *Spot would cause a Geiger counter to go crazy,* or *Spot is composed of atoms many of which are unstable.* For the sake of concreteness, revise the example as follows. I implant a source of high-energy radiation in your dog Spot; it is a lawlike truth that any dog in which a source of high-energy radiation has been implanted will lose its hair within seven days; Spot's emitting this high-energy radiation causes a brain lesion in you which in turn causes you to form a large number of wildly false beliefs about Spot (that he is in fact a mermaid, that he can speak fluent French but refuses to out of sheer obstinacy, and so on), but also causes you to form the true belief that Spot will lose his hair within the next two weeks. You have no evidence of any sort for your belief and much evidence against it. (You have just had Spot examined by a team of veterinarians who assure you that he is entirely normal along tonsorial lines.) Here *r's being G* is not collapsed into *s's being F;* you satisfy the conditions laid down by D_5 for knowledge; but surely you don't know. (The Philadelphia lottery example can be amended similarly.)

Clearly, there are as many examples of this sort as you please. One recipe for constructing them is just to consider some event *e* that causes *K* to believe that *e* occurs (or to believe some proposition entailed by *e's* occurrence, or some proposition whose probability with respect to *e's* occurrence is 1) where *e* causes *K* to form the belief in question by virtue of some cognitive abnormality, and in such a way that it is just an accident, from a cognitive point of view, that the belief is true. The problem for Dretske's account is clear. If we restrict ourselves to the sort of knowledge he is thinking of, then indeed if I know that *s* is *F* there must be a signal *r's being G* related to *s's being F* in something like the way he suggests. But the problem is that this isn't sufficient for knowledge; knowledge can be absent even if *r's being G* and *s's being F* are related in the way Dretske suggests; for they can be related in that way when it is merely a cognitive accident that *s is F* is true. As I argue in *Warrant and Proper Function,* they can be related in this way but fail to be related in the way required by the design plan of our noetic structure; but then my belief that *s* is *F* does not constitute knowledge. What these examples show is that something further must be added to Dretske's account; we must add, somehow, that *K's* noetic faculties, or those involved in the production of the belief in question, are functioning properly, are in good working order.

Dretske's account, then, like the others, suffers because it fails to pay explicit attention to the notion of the proper function of our cognitive equipment.[22]

III. Goldmanian Reliabilism
A. *The Old Goldman*

Alvin Goldman's first version of reliabilism is reliabilist indeed: "The justificational status of a belief," he says, "is a function of the reliability of the process

[22]I must retract a criticism of Dretske I made in "Positive Epistemic Status and Proper Function," pp. 21–22, where I argued that there is no currently available conception of objective probability that will serve Dretske's purposes in his analysis of warrant. I now believe there is such a conception; see *Warrant and Proper Function,* chap. 8.

or processes that cause it, where (as a first approximation) reliability consists in the tendency of a process to produce beliefs that are true rather than false." After some interesting preliminary skirmishes, he gives his official account in a sort of recursive form:

(a) If *S*'s belief in *p* results from a reliable cognitive process, and there is no reliable or conditionally reliable process available to *S* which, had it been used by *S* in addition to the process actually used, would have resulted in *S*'s not believing *p* at *t*, then *S*'s belief in *p* at *t* is justified.

(b) If *S*'s belief in *p* at *t* results ("immediately") from a belief-dependent process that is (at least) conditionally reliable, and if the beliefs (if any) on which this process operates in producing *S*'s belief in *p* at *t* are themselves justified, then *S*'s belief in *p* at *t* is justified.[23]

He then adds an appropriate closure clause. Here Goldman speaks of *justification* rather than warrant. As I argued in chapter 1, however, Goldman does not use the term 'justification' as a name for justification (properly so-called); he uses it instead as a near synonym for warrant. (Only a *near* synonym, because what he calls justification is not quite sufficient for warrant; he adds a fourth condition, 'local reliability', to justification to get warrant.)

This is reliabilism pure and unalloyed: call it *paradigm reliabilism*. Although its initial appeal is undeniable, it faces many difficult problems— problems I have explored elsewhere.[24] In particular, it is clear that the conditions laid down by paradigm reliabilism as necessary and sufficient for warrant are nowhere nearly sufficient. Perhaps we can summarize this point as follows. Note first that (on Goldman's showing) what determines the justification of a belief is a process *type* (not token).[25] Now clearly any given concrete cognitive process will be a token of many different cognitive process types—types with varying degrees of reliability. So consider a given belief—Paul's belief that he is watching "Dynasty," for example—and the concrete process that yields it. There are many types of which that process is a token: which is the *relevant* type—that is, which of these types is the one such that *its* degree of reliability determines the degree of justification Paul's belief enjoys? Here we encounter the *problem of generality,* noted by Goldman and developed by Richard Feldman:[26] if we take the relevant type to be relatively narrow, then we face one set of unhappy consequences; if we take it to be broad, we face other unhappy consequences.

Let me put this problem my own way. What determines the *degree* of justification, according to Goldman, is the degree of reliability of the relevant process type. But then the relevant process type, the one that determines the degree of warrant of the belief in question, must be a very narrow type: it must

23"What is Justified Belief?" pp. 10, 13, 20.
24"Positive Epistemic Status and Proper Function," pp. 24ff.
25"On this interpretation, a process is a *type* as opposed to a *token*. This is fully appropriate, since it is only types that have such statistical properties as producing truth 80 percent of the time; and it is precisely such statistical properties that determine the reliability of a process." "What Is Justified Belief?" p. 11.
26Goldman, "What Is Justified Belief," p. 12; and Feldman, "Reliability and Justification," *Monist* (1986).

be such that all the beliefs in its output have the same degree of warrant. (It couldn't be a broad type like *vision,* say, because the outputs of processes exemplifying this type will have many different degrees of warrant: perceptual beliefs resulting from examining a middle-sized object from ten feet in bright and sunny conditions, obviously, will have more warrant than beliefs arising from distant vision on a dark and foggy night.) So suppose we take relevant types narrowly enough so that all the beliefs in the output of a relevant type have the *same* degree of justification or warrant: then first, it will be extremely difficult to *specify* any relevant type. Indeed, if, as Goldman suggests, the relevant type must be specified in psychological or physiological terms, we won't be able to specify any such types at all; our knowledge is much too limited for that. But second and more important, there will be many processes (thus narrowly construed) that are reliable, but not such that the output beliefs have much by way of warrant.

There are many kinds of examples here; I shall mention just one. Adapt The Case of the Epistemically Serendipitous Lesion. There is a rare but specific sort of brain lesion (we may suppose) that is always associated with a number of cognitive processes of the relevant degree of specificity, most of which cause its victim to hold absurdly false beliefs. One of the associated processes, however, causes the victim to believe that he has a brain lesion. Suppose, then, that S suffers from this sort of disorder and accordingly believes that he suffers from a brain lesion. Add that he has no evidence at all for this belief: no symptoms of which he is aware, no testimony on the part of physicians or other expert witnesses, nothing. (Add, if you like, that he has much evidence *against* it; but then add also that the malfunction induced by the lesion makes it impossible for him to take appropriate account of this evidence.) Then the relevant type (while it may be hard to specify in detail) will certainly be highly reliable; but the resulting belief—that he has a brain lesion—will have little by way of warrant for S.[27]

B. The New Goldman

Goldman's paradigm reliabilism has deep and debilitating problems. This isn't the only brand of reliabilism he offers, however, and I turn now to the significantly different account of warrant to be found in his book *Epistemology and Cognition* (hereafter cited as *EC*).[28] He quite properly begins by pointing out (p. 3) that there is an important *normative* element in such crucial epistemic notions as warrant, justification, evidence, and the like. No doubt epistemological deontologism is false; no doubt warrant cannot be explained in terms of satisfaction of duty; nonetheless the central notions of epistemology are profoundly normative. Goldman sees this normativity as essentially a matter of permission and obligation, of conformity to *standards* or *rules*. His notion of warrant, therefore, while it is not deontological, is *analogically related* (related by the analogy of rule governance) to deontological notions of warrant. And

[27]For a more complete exposition of the point, see "Positive Epistemic Status and Proper Function," pp. 28ff.

[28]Cambridge: Harvard University Press, 1986.

what is perhaps of greatest interest here is his combining this idea with the notion that what he calls 'justification' (call it 'Goldmanian justification') and warrant crucially involve reliability. Suppose we begin with Goldmanian justification. A belief is *justified* for a person, says Goldman, if it is permitted by a right rule of justification; a justification rule is *right* if it is an element of a right system of justification rules; and a *system* of rules is right if it is appropriately reliable—that is, has a high enough "truth ratio." But the actual spelling out of Goldman's view isn't quite so simple. Suppose we follow him in approaching his conception of justification (Goldmanian justification) by stages. At the first stage, we have

(P$_1$) S's believing P at time t is justified if and only if (a) S's believing p at t is permitted by a right system of justificational rules (J-rules), and (b) this permission is not undermined by S's cognitive state at t. (*EC*, p. 63)[29]

"Systems of J-rules," says Goldman, "are assumed to permit or prohibit beliefs, directly or indirectly, as a function of some states, relations, or processes of the cognizer. . . . Thus someone being 'appeared to' in a certain way at t might be permitted to believe p at t" (*EC*, pp. 60–61).

Why does Goldman speak here of rule *systems* rather than rules *simpliciter*? Perhaps for the following sort of reason. The justification of a belief B at a time t may very well depend upon the justificational status of one or more other beliefs $B_1 - B_n$ at earlier times $t_1 - t_n$—or, indeed, on the justificational status of a belief B^* at a later time t^* (*EC*, p. 78). For it could be that some processes are fairly reliable (have a fairly high associated truth ratio) themselves but are such that their combination with certain other processes are unreliable. For example, some processes take *beliefs* (among other things) as input and yield other beliefs as output. Thus what leads to my present assessment of your intentions toward me is (in part) my opinion of how you are ordinarily disposed toward me together with my grasp of your present behavior. And even if this process—this way of coming to beliefs about someone's intentions toward me—is ordinarily reliable, its *combination* with some unreliable process for forming the input beliefs may be quite unreliable. I am pathologically paranoid; I believe you (and everyone else) have been biding your time, waiting for a propitious opportunity to do me in; I also believe that in your opinion the time is now ripe. You (a world-class karate expert) approach me, your hand upraised in friendly greeting; I form the belief that you are about to deal me a deadly blow and run off in terror. My belief that you are about to strike has little by way of Goldmanian justification or warrant, even though the process yielding this belief is in general highly reliable. So a J-rule that certified just any belief produced by just any reliable process would certify beliefs that have little

[29]Some of the conditions in which justification is undermined: (1) the sort of case in which you (mistakenly) believe that p is not permitted by such a system of J-rules, (2) the sort of case in which you are *justified* in believing that p is not permitted, even if you do not in fact believe it, (3) the sort of case in which you believe that the source of belief in question is unreliable, and (4) the sort of case in which you believe that some condition holds, which is such that if in fact it *did* hold, then the belief in question would not be permitted by any right set of J-rules.

by way of justification. Whether a given belief in the output of a process like this one has justification will depend in part upon the epistemic status of the beliefs forming its input. In cases of this sort, therefore, we shall have to think of a given belief as the result of a *series* of processes, where the beliefs produced at earlier stages must themselves have been formed according to right rules; accordingly, what is at issue (as Goldman sees it) is systems of rules—or, if single rules, then rules of great complexity. Further, the rule systems in question must have a certain *completeness*—a completeness I shall forebear to explore, remarking only that the relevant rules or rule sets will have to take account of a good deal of an agent's epistemic history.

Now Goldman argues that J-rules should be stated, not in terms of cognitive state transitions (*EC*, p. 77) but in terms of what he calls 'cognitive processes' "where by 'process' we mean a determinate kind of causal chain" (p. 85)—that is (I take it), a set of events $e_1, \ldots, e_n$ so related that the earlier e_i stand in the relevant causal relation to the later e_j. So the "framework principle":

(P$_1$*) A cognizer's belief in p at time t is justified if and only if it is the final member of a finite sequence of doxastic states of the cognizer such that some (single) right J-rule system licenses the transition of each member of the sequence from some earlier state(s). (*EC*, p. 83)

But now for the crucial question: under what conditions is a system of J-rules a *right* system? Here Goldman specifies a criterion, a set of necessary and sufficient conditions for a set of J-rules' being right (and it is here that we see what, according to him, warrant *is*):

(ARI) A J-rule system R is right if and only if R permits certain (basic) psychological processes, and the instantiation of these processes would result in a truth ratio of belief that meets some specified high threshold (greater than .5). (*EC*, p. 106)

How shall we understand this? Here we encounter some real problems. First: these rules, says Goldman, take the form of *process permissions;* a rule permits or authorizes certain processes, processes typically involving a belief or a kind of belief. The processes in question, furthermore, are to be thought of as process *types:* "no criterion will be plausible unless the rules it authorizes are permission rules for specific (types of) cognitive *processes*" (*EC*, p. 85; Goldman's emphasis). The reason, he says (mistakenly, as I shall argue), is that it is only cognitive process *types*, not tokens, that can properly be said to be reliable or unreliable. So the J-rules are rules that apply to specific process *types*. Of course not just *any* cognitive process type will be the sort in terms of which the rules are to be stated. Any given concrete process (obviously enough) will be a token of many different types—types of widely differing degrees of reliability. Suppose Paul is in general fairly reliable, but unfortunately forms the false belief that he is Napoleon. Then his belief is a token both of the type *process terminating in the belief that Paul is Napoleon,* and of the type *cognitive process taking place in Paul;* the latter but not the former is reliable. Of course the belief in question has little warrant. The latter type, then, despite its reliability, is not such that every token of it will have warrant, and a J-rule set that licensed processes of that sort will not be a right J-rule set, even if it only licenses processes that are reliable. This means that the J-rules do not concern just *any* type: only certain kinds of types will be the ones to which J-rules are addressed, the ones that J-rules permit or prohibit. These relevant types—the types to which the J-rules are addressed—will be of great specificity. They will not be such types as *the visual process,* or even *the visual process in a 40-year-old Australian male* but much more specific types—"the critical type," says Goldman, "is the narrowest type causally operative in producing the belief token in question" (*EC,* p. 50). So J-rules permit or prohibit types, and the types they permit or prohibit will be very narrow or specific.

But (and here is the first problem) what would such a narrow type be like? Goldman gives us no guidance at all. When he argues for the plausibility of reliabilism, he mentions such types as memory, perception, deductive reasoning, and the like. As he points out, we think of these as reliable and as for the most part issuing in beliefs that have warrant; we contrast them with, for example, wishful thinking and paranoia, which we think unreliable, and such that the beliefs *they* issue in have little or no warrant. But of course perception, memory, deductive inference, and their kin are not at all the sort of types for which the J-rules must be stated; they are much too broad. Goldman does not give any examples of relevant types—no doubt for the very good reason that we don't know of any. Take your belief that Aberdeen, Scotland, is some thousand miles north of Aberdeen, South Dakota: we have no ideas at all as to what might be the narrowest type causally operative in producing this belief (if there is one: perhaps a pair of types tie for narrowest). Indeed, we have no ideas as to what the *candidates* for this post might be. Goldman says that "by 'process' we mean a determinate kind of causal chain" (*EC,* p. 85)—a causal chain, presumably, consisting of events taking place in someone's cognitive system, the last item of which is a belief. But what are these events like? What sort of events are they? Neural events, presumably, and ones we aren't at present so much as able to describe or think about. Perhaps all we can say is that the relevant types will be ones of this sort: *event of kind e_1, followed by event of kind e_2, . . . , followed by event of kind e_n* (where the class of eligible e's is to be specified in psychological or physiological terms [and will thus have to be left to future science], and where that class is to be restricted in some way so as to eliminate captious and not so captious counterexamples.)

Further: these process types, naturally enough, have or can have *instantiations.* If a process is a type, then an instantiation of a process will be a token of that type, a sequence of concrete specific events the last item of which is a belief; and the events in the sequence will be so related that the earlier events are causes (or part causes) of the later events. So the J-rules will be or contain such items as *process A is permitted,* where process A will be a type $k_1, . . . k_n$ of sequences of cognitive events, k_n being, for example, *the belief that p* for some proposition p. (If we say that the types must be stateable in terms of psychological or physiological terminology, k_n will presumably have to be the cortical or (more broadly) physiological correlate of the belief that p (if indeed there is any such thing). An instantiation or token of A will be a sequence of cognitive events; the last item in the sequence will be a belief that p, and will be appropriately caused by earlier members of the sequence.

And now we come to a really thorny problem. The criterion for rightness of systems of rules is *counterfactual:* a J-rule system R is right if and only if R permits certain psychological processes, and the instantiation of these processes *would* result in a high truth ratio of belief. Would, if *what?* What is the antecedent of the relevant counterfactual and what is its modality? Goldman does not say. Perhaps, however, we can make progress as follows. A system of J-rules, he says, has a *truth ratio* associated with it in a given possible world W (*EC*, p. 107). How can we understand that? Again, Goldman does not say. Perhaps, however, we are to think of it as follows. First, a system S of J-rules, says Goldman, will permit or certify certain patterns of processes; process P is permissible, provided that it has been preceded by any of processes $P^*_1 - P^*_n$; a process taking a belief B as input is permissible provided B is the output of some permissible process. So consider the process patterns that are permitted by S. These, of course, will be patterns of types of cognitive processes. We can combine these permitted patterns of such types into a megatype T: for example, *displaying processes $P_1 - P_n$ (in that order), or $P^*_1 - P^*_n$, or $P^{**}_1 - P^{**}_n$, or* . . . Now some (but of course not all) of these megatypes will be instantiated: a megatype T is *instantiated* if there is a person who displays the ordered sets of processes it permits in the order it permits them. And to determine the truth ratio of a set of rules (that is, the *actual* truth ratio, its truth ratio in the actual world), we compute the ratio of true beliefs to total beliefs in the instantiations of the megatypes it permits. (There are problems here, but I shall resolutely ignore them.)

Once we see what the truth ratio of a set of J-rules is, then of course it is easy to see what the truth ratio of a set of rules in a possible world is: the truth ratio of S in W is simply the truth ratio S would have had, had W been actual; to put it differently, the truth ratio of S in W is the ratio of true beliefs to beliefs *simpliciter* taken over all the instantiations, in W, of all the megatypes licensed by S. (So of course a system of rules will have different truth ratios in different possible worlds.) And Goldman's idea is that the relevant truth ratio for a given system S of J-rules in a possible world W is not simply its truth ratio in the *actual* world; what counts, he says, is the truth ratio of a system of rules in possible worlds *close* to W:[30]

[30]In *EC* Goldman proposed that a system of J-rules is right if and only if it has a sufficiently high truth ratio in 'normal' worlds—worlds consistent with our general beliefs as to what the actual world is like. As he came to see, this is an error. For suppose God had created both us and the world quite differently, so that some nonnormal world would have been actual, and suppose he had created us with cognitive faculties quite different from the ones we do in fact display. (He could have created us with faculties of the sort enjoyed, for example, by pigeons, who are said to be able to detect the strength and gradient of a magnetic field by means of a process involving an electromagnet; or pit vipers, who have a heat detection organ quite different from anything we have; or bats, who navigate with incredible rapidity and delicacy by means of a sort of sonar.) So suppose God (or evolution, if you prefer) had created us in a quite different cognitive environment with quite different faculties that were highly reliable, because well-suited to that cognitive

(ARI*)   A J-rule system S is right in a possible world W if and only if S has a sufficiently high truth ratio in the worlds close to W.[31]

Technical and quasi-technical problems still lurk;[32] but the main and crucial problem is that the suggested necessary and sufficient condition of warrant is vastly too weak to be anywhere nearly sufficient. *Justification,* for Goldman,

environment. And now suppose no set of J-rules with a high truth ratio in *normal* worlds—that is, worlds that are *in fact* normal—licensed our cognitive processes. Then (according to the Goldman of *EC*) it would follow that our beliefs would not have been justified. But that is surely mistaken. Under the conditions in question our beliefs clearly could have had both warrant and justification; indeed, under the conditions in question we could surely have had knowledge.

Put the point in terms of possible worlds. Consider a nonnormal possible world W in which God has created creatures with cognitive faculties quite different from ours. Suppose the cognitive faculties he has given these creatures are highly reliable; suppose still further that there is no set of J-rules with a high truth ratio in *normal worlds* (that is, worlds like what we think the actual world is like) that permit these processes, although of course there are sets of J-rules with a high truth ratio in worlds *like* W that permit them. Then according to *EC* their beliefs would not have warrant. But again, surely that is mistaken. What counts for warrant is whether the relevant cognitive faculties work well in the situation they are designed for; it isn't necessary that they also work well in the sorts of circumstances to be found in worlds similar to what we think is to be found in α, the actual world. Accordingly, in "Strong and Weak Justification" (presented at Brown University in November, 1986, at a conference celebrating Roderick Chisholm's seventieth birthday and published in *Philosophical Perspectives, 2, Epistemology 1988*) Goldman moved to (ARI*).

[31]"It seems advisable to assess its [that is, a rule system's] performance in a set of worlds very close to W" ("Strong and Weak Justification," p. 17). Goldman suggests that his approach can be generalized; we could see a system of J-rules as licensing not beliefs *simpliciter*, but *partial* beliefs: subjective probabilities, beliefs to some degree or other. You are in the Everglades; you catch a quick glimpse of an alligator at fifty yards. Under those conditions the permissible processes would have outputs involving your believing the proposition *there's another alligator* more tentatively, with less firmness than, say is displayed by your belief in *modus ponens*. So the processes permitted by J-rules would be processes whose last members were types of the sort *believing P to degree r*. Goldman notes that a cognizer might have the following interesting property: it might be that about half of the beliefs she holds to degree .5 would be true, three-quarters of the beliefs she holds to degree .75 would be true, and the like; more generally for any degree of belief r, the proportion of truths among beliefs she holds to degree r is r. (We shall have to assume that this cognizer's degrees of belief are rational (he doesn't believe any proposition to, say, $1/\pi$); we shall also have to assume that none of his degrees of belief are very close to but distinct from 1; otherwise he would have to hold an enormous number of beliefs to that degree.) Such a cognizer is *well calibrated*.

But it isn't only cognizers that can be well calibrated; a rule system S, we might say, is well calibrated if and only if for any r in the unit interval, the output (that is, the final member) of a megatype M permitted by S is a partial belief to degree r if and only if the truth ratio of M is r in normal worlds. And now the criterion of rightness is

(ARI**)   "a J-Rules system is right if and only if it is well calibrated" (*EC*, p. 114).

Being thus well calibrated, however, is clearly nowhere nearly sufficient for a system of rules being right. A system S of rules might be well calibrated and nonetheless permit me to believe a large number n of obvious falsehoods (falsehoods of elementary arithmetic, say) to degree .7 provided I also believed $7n/3$ obvious truths of elementary arithmetic to degree .7. If I did this my beliefs would be permitted by a well calibrated set of J-rules, but obviously my belief that (say) 7 + 5 = 11 would have little by way of epistemic justification or positive epistemic status for me. Calibration introduces problems all its own; since there are already plenty of fundamental problems here, I shall ignore it.

[32]First, what is the similarity relation under which the relevant worlds are to be close to W? Can it be specified in a noncircular manner? And second (for plausible similarity relations) there won't be a *single* truth ratio that a given system S of J-rules has in *all* worlds close to W; it will have

isn't quite warrant; it is not the case that a sufficient degree of justification is (together with truth) necessary and sufficient for knowledge. What must be added for the latter is "local reliability," a codicil designed to handle Gettier problems: "a true belief fails to be knowledge if there are any *relevant alternative situations* in which the proposition p would be false, but the process used would cause S to believe p anyway. If there are such relevant alternatives, then the utilized process cannot *discriminate* the truth of p from them; so S does not know" (*EC*, p. 46). So on the complete account a belief has warrant if and only if it is justified (sanctioned by a right set of J-rules) and displays local reliability.

It is easy to see, however, that this alleged necessary and sufficient condition isn't anywhere nearly sufficient. There are many kinds of cases here. To see the first, let *S* be any system of J-rules that is right in the sense of (ARI*). Now in the typical case, we can adjoin to *S* further rules of equal or greater truth ratio without reducing *S*'s truth ratio;[33] let *S**, therefore, be the result of adding

R₁   Any process is permitted whose output is a tautology

to *S*. Obviously the truth ratio of *S** will be at least as high in the worlds close to the actual world as that of *S*; hence *S** will be right in the sense of (ARI*). But then any belief whose content is a tautology will be in the output of a process sanctioned by a set of J-rules right in the sense of (ARI*); clearly the belief meets the above condition for local reliability, since there aren't any alternative situations in which it is false; hence any such belief will have warrant on Goldman's account. Yet not just any belief of a tautology has warrant (as Goldman himself observes); it could be that I believe a complicated tautology *T* not because I see that it is true (perhaps it is too complicated for that) but because you have asserted the denial of *T* and I, due to excessive contrariness, have a powerful tendency to believe the denial of anything you assert—or because I have a pathological tendency to believe whatever looks complicated and is found in a logic book.

Now here it might be objected[34] that the J-rules ought to be stated in psychological or physiological terms; they shouldn't involve terms like 'tautology', which guarantee the truth of the permitted beliefs. Fair enough. (Of course we don't know how to state the relevant J-rules that way, since we don't know anything about the sorts of narrow psychological processes that the J-rules are to permit or prohibit.) But clearly the rules must be such that they do license certain beliefs or classes of beliefs: otherwise the whole project fails. And clearly there will be processes in Goldman's sense whose last items are

---

different truth ratios in different normal worlds. When Goldman says that a set of rules that is right in *W* has a high truth ratio in worlds close to *W*, I take it he does not mean that such a set has a high truth ratio in *every* such world; presumably we shall need some analogue of the notions of averaging or integrating.

[33] "In the typical case" I say; in some cases *S* may be such that the addition of a rule *R* will cause problems. Suppose *R* permits a given belief *B* (and suppose *R* has at least as high a truth ratio as *S*); perhaps *S* contains the conditional rule *if you believe B, you may believe anything*. Then clearly adjoining *R* to *S* may result in a rule system *S** with a lower truth ratio than *S*. So in this example, choose *S* in such a way that this problem does not arise.

[34] As it was by Goldman, in correspondence.

beliefs whose contents are tautologies. So choose some large class *C* of processes whose last items are tautological beliefs (some of them being fairly
complicated); there will be a (possibly complex) psychological or physiological
property *P* had by all and only the members of *C*. Then let *S* be any suitable
right rule system and adjoin

R_1^* Any process having *P* is permitted

to form rule system *S**. On Goldman's showing, any belief permitted by *S** will
have a high degree of warrant, at least if it meets the condition of local reliability (as all the beliefs permitted by R_1^* do). But of course many such beliefs
will in fact have no appreciable degree of warrant at all. Paul is in awe of
logicians: if he runs across a complicated logical sounding proposition replete
with *p*'s and *q*'s, he invariably believes it. He sees such a proposition in a logic
book (in a "Prove or give a counterexample" exercise); it is in fact a tautology,
but he can't see that it is and has no other reason for believing it; this belief,
then, has little by way of justification for him, despite its being certified by the
above rule.

Of course it isn't just processes whose outputs are tautologies that cause a
problem: we get the same problem by adjoining to a right system *S* a rule
sanctioning any process whose output is a proposition true in all the worlds
sufficiently similar to the actual world. Goldman doesn't say much about what
these worlds would be like, but presumably the basic laws of physics that
characterize the actual world would also characterize them. So start from a
right system *S* of J-rules and add

R_2 Any process is permitted whose output is the belief that the velocity
of light is constant[35]

(or that it is about 186,000 miles per second, or that planets travel in elliptical
orbits, or whatever) and you will have a right system of J-rules. But then my
belief that the velocity of light is a constant will be justified, on Goldman's
view, no matter how it is formed—even if I believe it only because it turned up
in a letter to the editor in the *National Enquirer* and I believe everything I read
there. Similarly for any philosophical truth: that there are at least uncountably
many possible worlds, for example. If we add

R_3 Any process is permitted whose output is the belief that there are at
least uncountably many possible worlds[36]

[35]If it is suggested that a J-rule can't permit just a single belief, amend R_2 to

R_2^* Any process is permitted whose output is a truth of physics.

Here we may accommodate the requirement that the rules be stated in psychological or
physiological terms in the way we did with R_1.

[36]Let 'α' name the actual world; Del Ratzsch points out that

R_4 Any process is permitted whose output is the belief that α is not actual

if adjoined to a right system, will yield a right system; for presumably there will be infinitely many to a right set of J-rules, the resulting set will be right; but then any belief that there are at least uncountably many possible worlds will be justified, no matter how bizarre the process that produces it. (Even if it is formed, for example, on the Oscar Wilde Principle of Belief Formation: *Always believe what will cause maximum consternation and dismay among your colleagues.*)

A second kind of example: return to The Case of the Epistemically Seren-dipitous Lesion. As a result of this lesion (and we can stipulate, if we like, that it develops prenatally), most of my beliefs are absurdly false. It also causes me to believe, however, that I am suffering from a brain lesion. This belief of mine, pathologically caused as it is, is clearly one that has little or no warrant. But there will be a cognitive process, in Goldman's sense, whose output is this belief; and we may suppose that this process—call it 'P_1'—occurs only in conjunction with a lesion of the sort in question. So the result of adding

R$_4$ P_1 is permitted

to a right system of J-rules will itself be a right system. Hence Goldman's account yields the conclusion that this belief is justified and, indeed, that under these conditions I *know* that I am suffering from a lesion.[37]

Indeed, perhaps we can argue that on Goldman's account nearly *all* human beliefs are justified. First, a plausibility argument. No doubt the vast majority of human beliefs are true; most of the myriads or millions of our quotidian beliefs, after all, are such relatively unrisky items as *it looks like another rainy day, there's that pain in my left knee again, she looks bored this morning, that cereal tastes no better than the last time I tried it,* and *the miserable lawn needs to be mowed again.* If so, however, the rule

R$_5$ Any cognitive process on the part of a human being is permitted

will have a high truth ratio in the actual world. But then presumably the same will go for the worlds sufficiently similar to the actual world; if the vast majority of human beliefs are in fact true, then any world in which most human beliefs are false will be very different. There is therefore reason to think that R$_5$ has a relatively high truth ratio—a truth ratio higher than $1/2$—in all the relevant worlds. (More to the point [since it is all that is needed for my argument] there is reason to make the weaker claim that an appropriate infinitary analogue of an *average* truth ratio of R$_5$, taken over all the relevant worlds, is appropriately high.) Of course, if R$_5$ does have a high truth ratio in those worlds, then (depending upon how high a truth ratio is required for epistemic justification) on Goldman's showing all human beliefs—at any rate, those produced by processes that are locally reliable—will be justified and have warrant.

But perhaps you are inclined to doubt that most human beliefs are in fact true; perhaps you doubt that R$_5$ has a high truth ratio in the relevant worlds.

worlds appropriately near to α, and of course none of them is actual. So a process producing the belief in question will have a very high truth ratio indeed.

[37]This example is similar to one Goldman uses against Armstrong's account of knowledge.

Very well; then consider

R_6 Any triple of processes are permitted, provided two of them have as output theorems of elementary arithmetic.[38]

Clearly R_6 will have a high truth ratio in all worlds, and hence in all relevant worlds (and if you do not think a truth ratio of $2/3$ is high enough, adjust the example to suit). It does not follow, of course, that all of my beliefs will be justified, on Goldman's account; but it does follow that they will all be justified, provided I believe two theorems of elementary arithmetic for each nonarithmetical proposition I believe—even if my nonarithmetical beliefs are absolute paradigms of lack of epistemic justification.

The main point, I think, is this: contrary to Goldman's suggestion, what determines whether the output of a process has warrant is not simply the truth ratios of the J-rule sets permitting it. To confer warrant or positive epistemic status, the process in question must meet another condition. It must be non-pathological; we might say that the process in question must be one that can be found in cognizers whose cognitive equipment is working properly; it must be the sort of process that can occur in someone whose faculties are functioning aright.

IV. Concluding Peroration

Goldman's *EC* account is complex—complex enough to obscure the main lines of the accounts and introduce extraneous difficulties. In some ways, the earlier paradigm reliabilism is more attractive, if only because of its simplicity. Let me conclude, therefore, by a brief but more general consideration of paradigm reliabilism. The basic idea is that a belief has warrant if it is produced by a reliable belief-producing mechanism or power or faculty. Now initially, I think, the natural way to understand this suggestion would be in terms of actual concrete belief-producing faculties such as Paul's memory, or Paul's visual system. Then the idea would be that one of Paul's beliefs has a good deal of warrant if it is produced by his memory or vision, say, but not if it is produced by way of wishful thinking. Here what counts is the reliability of the concrete system, or organ, or faculty, or source of the belief, however exactly that is to be construed.

The early Goldman, however, demurs: he proposes that it is not concrete systems or faculties, but abstract *types* that are relevant. A belief has warrant for me if it is produced by some concrete process (a series of events of some kind) which process is an example of the relevant type—the *relevant* type because, of course, every process will be an instance of very many different types. Which types *are* the relevant types? This question precipitates the generality problem (see pp. 198–99) and is exceedingly hard to answer. Suppose we had a way to answer it, however: then a belief has warrant for me just in case

[38]To state this rule precisely, we should have to guarantee that no belief is counted as a member of more than one of the triples associated with a cognizer.

the relevant type *T* of the process that produces it is *reliable*. (And perhaps we can understand this as the claim that *T* is such that most of the beliefs produced by processes falling under *T* [in the appropriate nearby possible worlds as well as in the actual world] are true.) Now why does Goldman turn away from concrete faculties or powers and toward these types? The answer: "On this interpretation, a process is a *type* as opposed to a *token*. This is fully appropriate, since it is only types that have such statistical properties as producing truth 80% of the time; and it is precisely such statistical properties that determine the reliability of a process."[39] But as it stands this seems quite mistaken. An actual concrete barometer (as opposed to the type *barometer*) can perfectly well be reliable, and can have the statistical property of correctly registering the atmospheric pressure 80 percent of the time. My eight-dollar digital watch is much more accurate than any of those expensive spring-driven seventeen-jewel Bulovas that seemed so elegant 30 years ago. Here it isn't *types* that are compared for accuracy: what I say is that my digital watch, that very concrete mechanism, is more accurate than any spring-driven Bulova. So this isn't a good reason for developing paradigm reliabilism in terms of types rather than tokens.

But I think there *is* a good reason, from the Goldmanian perspective, and it emerges when we try to accommodate *degrees* of warrant. Goldman says that the degree of warrant enjoyed by a particular belief is a function of the degree of reliability of the relevant process type. Now suppose we try to develop the theory, not in terms of types, but of such concreta as Paul's vision. First, we should have to invoke the notion of proper function: the visual beliefs Paul forms when drunk or when his vision is otherwise impaired won't have much by way of warrant for him, even though his vision is overall pretty reliable. But then the theory would not be a reliabilist theory anymore; it would be a theory more like the one to be presented in *Warrant and Proper Function*. Second and just as important, the problem will be that some of Paul's vision-induced beliefs will have a good deal more warrant than others; his beliefs about what he sees up close in a good light will have more warrant than what he sees in a dim light at some distance; and then it can't be that what determines the degree of warrant of one of Paul's vision-induced beliefs will be just the overall reliability of his vision. So if we try to explain degree of warrant in terms of concrete faculties or powers such as vision, we run into a dead end.

Of course, there are subfaculties as well as faculties: and just as vision is a subfaculty of perception, so there may be subfaculties of vision. Perhaps there are subfaculties narrow enough so that all of their outputs have the same degree of warrant, so that the reliabilist could say that the degree of warrant enjoyed by the outputs of these subfaculties are a function of the reliability of that subfaculty (although she would still have to stipulate that the subfaculties in question were functioning properly). Perhaps there are subfaculties as narrow as all that—but then again perhaps there *are not*. We can't just *make up* subfaculties and organs; there presumably isn't any organ that is the sum of my heart and my left knee, for example, and there isn't any subfaculty whose output consists, say, in visual beliefs produced on Saturdays together with the

---

[39]"What Is Justification?" p. 11.

belief that 4 + 1 = 5. We can't gerrymander concrete processes or mechanisms just any way we want. There is the faculty or power of speech; but there isn't any such thing as a faculty or organ whose output is, say, exactly half the words I speak. There is no organ whose output is half of what my larynx outputs, together with half of what your heart does. The questions what subfaculties there are and whether there are subfaculties of the right degree of generality are empirical questions to which we do not at the moment have even the beginnings of decent answers.

So we can't be at all sure that there are concrete faculties or subfaculties of the right narrowness; and just here is where types are handy. We can make up types *ad libitum* (more realistically, any type we might find useful is already there). So, for example, there is the type *is either a heart or a stomach* and there is also the type *visual belief about tiger lilies in Martha's backyard;* there is even the type *belief on the part of Paul that is either produced on Saturday or is the belief that 4 + 1 = 5.* More to the present point, there are types of the sort mentioned above: *(cognitive) event of kind e_1, followed by event of kind e_2, . . . , followed by event of kind e_n,* where the last item is a belief. These types can clearly be of the relevant degree of specificity, since they can be of any degree of specificity you please.

Sadly enough, however, if we develop the theory in terms of types of that sort, then we have the problems I just mentioned: for example, the type *process whose last item is belief in a tautology* (or the appropriate cortical correlate thereof) is highly reliable, but not nearly all the outputs of that type have warrant. And of course we also have that problem of generality. Let me give one final example to illustrate that problem. Suppose I am struck by a burst of cosmic rays, resulting in the following unfortunate malfunction. Whenever I hear the word 'prime' in any context, I form a belief, with respect to a randomly chosen natural number less than 100,000, that it is not prime. So you say "Pacific Palisades is prime residential area" or "Prime ribs is my favorite" or "First you must prime the pump" or "(17') entails (14')" or "The prime rate is dropping again" or anything else in which the word occurs; in each case I form a belief, with respect to a randomly selected natural number between 1 and 100,000, that it is not prime. The process or mechanism in question is indeed reliable (given the vast preponderance of nonprimes in the first 100,000 natural numbers) but my belief—that, say, 41 is not prime—has little or no warrant. The problem is not simply that the belief is false; the same goes for my (true) belief that 631 is not prime, if it is formed in this fashion. So reliable belief formation is not sufficient for warrant. The belief-producing process or mechanism is indeed reliable; but it is only *accidentally* reliable; it just happens, by virtue of a piece of cognitive serendipity, epistemic good fortune, to produce mostly true beliefs; and that is not sufficient for warrant. In *Warrant and Proper Function* I shall try to explain what it is for a process to be only accidentally reliable; once we see that, we shall also be able to see what is required for warrant.[40]

[40]I am grateful to Tom Senor for help in writing this chapter.

10

Prospect and Retrospect

It is time to take stock. We noted in chapter I that twentieth-century British and American epistemology has been dominated by internalist notions, the most important of which is *justification*. We also noted that contemporary epistemology presents a vast, confused, and confusing welter of views, and that in two crucial respects. First, there is a great deal of confusion as to what the connection is between justification, on the one hand, and knowledge, evidence, and internalist constraints on the other. Second, there is the same confused and confusing welter of opinion as to what justification itself is. Among some of the more popular candidates: justification is taken as a matter of epistemic responsibility or aptness for epistemic duty fulfillment, as an "evaluation" of how well you have fulfilled your epistemic goals, as being believed or accepted on the basis of an adequate truth-conducive ground, as being produced by a reliable belief-producing mechanism, as being supported by or fitting the evidence, and as a matter of everything's going right, for the knowing subject, with respect to cognitive processes 'downstream from experience'.

We saw that order can be introduced into this chaos by tracing the notion of justification back to its source in the classical deontologism of Descartes and (perhaps more important) Locke. Descartes and Locke speak of epistemic *duty* and *obligation*. Descartes seems to say that one is obliged not to believe anything that is not clear and distinct; Locke sees our main epistemic duty as that of proportioning belief to the evidence afforded by what is certain: my duty is to believe a proposition that is not certain for me to the degree to which it is probable with respect to what *is* certain for me. Now some of our contemporaries (BonJour, the classical Chisholm) explicitly explain justification in terms of responsibility or aptness for epistemic duty fulfillment, thus following the deontological lead of Descartes and Locke; others (Alston, Conee and Feldman, many others) explain justification as believing on the basis of evidence, that is, in terms of the *content* of what Locke sees as the principal epistemic duty. Still other views (Lehrer, Cohen) can be understood as related to that original deontological notion by way of analogical extensions of one sort or another. And in still other cases (Goldman), there is no real conceptual connection with that deontological notion, but a verbal connection instead: justification is used as a *name* for that quality or quantity, whatever it is, enough of which is sufficient to turn true belief into knowledge (and in Goldman's view that quality or quantity is not justification properly so-called). Finally, we saw that the internalist concerns characteristic of contemporary epistemology are also to be understood in terms of that original deontology; for internalism flows from deontology and is unmotivated without it.

We then turned to an examination of contemporary internalist accounts of *warrant*. What is characteristic of internalist accounts is that they see warrant as essentially a matter of justification: that quality or quantity that turns true belief into knowledge just is, according to internalists, justification, or perhaps justification together with a fillip to mollify Gettier. We began with the impressive work of Roderick Chisholm. There is a great deal to be learned from Chisholm; but what we saw was that justification, fulfillment of epistemic duty, is neither necessary nor anywhere nearly sufficient for warrant. As we also saw, both the classical and the post-classical Chisholmian accounts founder on the rock of epistemic malfunction. We noted that considerations of proper function also demonstrate the inadequacy of coherentism, whether taken neat or in the perceptive, sophisticated form put on offer by Laurence BonJour. Turning to Bayesianism, a specifically twentieth-century form of coherentism, we observed first that it has little to contribute to an account of warrant, being focused instead on that baffling, elusive, and pluriform notion of rationality; and a consideration of Bayesianism offered an opportunity to explore that notion. What the Bayesian offers us is a picture of one aspect of an ideally rational creature—or rather a picture of rationality (in the traditional sense of capability of thought, reflection, and inference) extended and idealized in one particular direction.

Failing to find a satisfying account of warrant among the unequivocal internalists, we turned next to the equivocal internalism of John Pollock, whose work occupies an interesting but uneasy halfway house between internalism and externalism. Fundamentally, according to Pollock, you are justified in believing a proposition *A* if you have arrived at it in conformity to your epistemic norms. The chief problem was that it seems to be perfectly possible to proceed in terms of *incorrect* norms, in such a way that one's beliefs would be Pollock-justified but still have no warrant. We then moved to the explicitly externalist and reliabilist accounts of Alston, Goldman and Dretske. Reliabilism is a substantial step in the right direction; perhaps we could see reliabilism as a zeroeth approximation to the truth of the matter. Still, it suffers from deeply debilitating problems—problems that need not be recounted here (since, after all, they appear only one chapter back) but which center, again, on the notion of proper function.

The idea of proper function figures prominently in the difficulties with the main current views of warrant; that suggests that this notion is much more deeply involved in our idea of warrant than is currently recognized. That suggestion, I think, is no more (or less) than the unvarnished truth. In *Warrant and Proper Function* I develop this idea in detail; here I shall briefly note its major features. What I propose to explain and explore is our notion of warrant, a notion nearly all of us have and employ in our everyday pursuits. This notion is not best explained, I think, just by producing a set of severally necessary and jointly sufficient conditions. Such a procedure is at home in logic and mathematics; it works somewhat less well or less directly in, say, the metaphysics of modality, and it works still less well (or still less directly) in epistemology. What we really have are *paradigms:* central, clear, and unequivocal cases of knowledge and warrant. But there is also a sort of penumbral zone of possible cases surrounding the central cases; these cases don't conform exactly to the conditions characterizing the central cases, but are instead related by way of analogical extension and similarity. And there is an even more shadowy belt of possible cases beyond that one, an area that is constituted by borderline cases, cases where it is not really clear whether what we have is knowledge (warrant) or not. More exactly, there are borderline cases between the central paradigmatic cases and those comprising the analogical zone, and borderline cases between the latter and cases that are not cases of warrant at all.

Accordingly, a good way to characterize our concept of warrant (more precisely: our system of analogically related concepts of warrant) is to specify the conditions governing the central paradigmatic core (here necessary and sufficient conditions are appropriate) together with some of the analogical extensions and an explanation of the analogical basis of the extension. This procedure is less elegant and regrettably more complex than the straightforward analysis we learned in our youth; it is certainly less stylish than setting out, in an austerely elegant clause or two, the necessary and sufficient conditions governing the concept. Following the procedure I advocate also makes the task of evaluating a proposed account much more difficult: is the putative counterexample a genuine counterexample to the conditions put forward as necessary and sufficient for the central and paradigmatic core concept? Or does it instead fall into one of those penumbral areas? All I can say by way of self-exculpation is first, we must heed Aristotle's dictum not to expect more clarity than the subject permits, and second, this procedure, if less elegant, is also more realistic and can take us closer to the truth.

The notion of proper function, I say, is crucial to the central paradigms of knowledge and warrant. But that notion is inextricably involved with another: that of the *design plan* of the organ or organism or system in question—the way the thing in question is supposed to work, the way it works when it works properly, when it is subject to no dysfunction. *Design plan* and *proper function* are interdefinable notions: a thing (organism, organ, system, artifact) is functioning properly when it functions in accord with its design plan, and the design plan of a thing is a specification of the way in which a thing functions when it is functioning properly. So we might say, as I did, that the central notion with respect to warrant is proper function; but we might as well say that the central notion is that of the design plan. In any event, the first condition for a belief's having warrant, as I see it, is that it be produced by faculties functioning properly. But this is by no means nearly sufficient. A second condition is that the cognitive environment in which the belief is produced must be the one or like the one for which it is designed. Your epistemic faculties may be functioning with perfect propriety; you may have passed your yearly cognitive examination at MIT with flying colors; but if you have been suddenly transported to a wholly different and alien cognitive environment, your beliefs may have little or no warrant. The basic picture, here, is that we have cognitive faculties that are adapted (by God or evolution or both) to our surroundings, our cognitive environment; and when a belief is produced by these faculties functioning properly, then we have warrant.

But we do have to add another condition or two. First, not nearly every case of cognitive proper function is aimed at the truth, at the production of true beliefs. Suffering from a usually fatal disease, you may form unrealistic beliefs about the probability of your recovery; you may think that probability much greater than the statistics at your command would warrant. This need not be a case of epistemic malfunction; perhaps we are so designed that under such conditions we form beliefs more optimistic than the statistics warrant, because such optimism itself increases the chances of survival. (Compare William James's case of the climber whose confidence that he can leap the crevasse is too high from one point of view [he has never before leapt a crevasse of that size], but is also required if he is to have any chance at all of leaping it.) More generally, many beliefs are formed partly as a result of (for example) wishful thinking; and it is not at all clear that what we have there is epistemic malfunction. Wishful thinking has its purposes, even if forming beliefs with maximal verisimilitude is not among them. Beliefs of this sort, then, are produced by properly functioning cognitive faculties in the environment for which those faculties were designed; nevertheless they lack warrant. So a further condition must be added; to have warrant, a belief must also be such that the purpose of the module of the epistemic faculties producing the belief is to produce true beliefs. Another way to put it: the belief has warrant only if the segment of the design plan governing its production is aimed at truth, at the production of true beliefs.

Being produced by properly functioning faculties aimed at truth in the environment for which those faculties are designed—these are central aspects of our concept of warrant. There is one more central aspect of it, however: and that is that the design plan of the faculties in question must be a *good* one. An angel might design my faculties, aiming at producing a rational creature whose beliefs were for the most part true. If this angel is one of Hume's lazy or incompetent or immature angels, however, then the fact that my beliefs are produced by faculties functioning properly (that is, just as they were designed to) in the environment for which they were designed, and according to a design plan aimed at the truth—that fact will not be sufficient for warrant. It is also necessary that the design in question be a *good* design: that is, that there be a substantial objective probability that a belief of that sort produced under those conditions is true. We might call this *the presupposition of reliability;* it is the condition of warrant the reliabilist seizes upon. Although it is not the whole truth, it is indeed a part of the truth, and it is for this reason we may see reliabilism as an approximation (if only a zeroeth approximation) to the truth.

After outlining the central idea, I shall turn to a number of qualifications having to do with the design plan. There is functional multiplicity: the fact that a given bit of the design plan may be aimed at the fulfillment of more than one purpose; there is the distinction between the design plan and the max plan, between purpose and design, between intended results and unintended by-products, between responses that fulfill the main purpose of a system and those that are there as a result of trade-offs and compromises, and so on. (This last distinction gives us a way of handling an analogue of the dreaded Gettier problem.) Then in the next few chapters I shall explore some of the main areas of our epistemic establishment, turning successively to memory, knowledge of one's self, knowledge of other persons, perception, *a priori* knowledge and belief, induction, and probability. I next explore certain *general* features of the epistemic design plan: its foundationalist structure, the defeater and overrider system, and the place of evidence. In the final two chapters, I shall argue, first, that it is extremely difficult to see how to give anything like a *naturalistic* account or analysis of the notions of proper function, design plan, and their colleagues in that circle of interdefinable notions. I shall then conclude by arguing that while the view that I am proposing indisputably falls under the rubric of naturalistic epistemology, the latter flourishes much better in the garden of supernatural theism than in that of metaphysical or theological naturalism.

Appendix

In this appendix I wish to outline and briefly comment upon John Pollock's official definition of objective epistemic justification, which goes as follows:

> S is objectively justified in believing P if and only if S instantiates some argument A supporting P which is ultimately undefeated relative to the set of all truths.[1] (p. 189)

(We can recast the account of *subjective* justification to conform: S is subjectively justified in believing P if and only if S instantiates an ultimately undefeated argument supporting P [p. 188].)

This does not wear its meaning upon its sleeve; it is worth trying to understand it both for its own sake, and because in so trying we encounter Pollock's account of defeasibility—perhaps the fullest and most satisfactory account extant of that crucial but puzzling notion. To understand the definition, we must know five things: what an *argument* is, what it is for someone to *instantiate* an argument, what it is for an argument to be *defeated,* what it is for an argument to be *ultimately undefeated,* and what it is for an argument to be *ultimately undefeated with respect to a set of truths.* I shall try to convey the essential idea in each case, referring the reader to the text for details.

1. *Arguments.* The basic idea here is familiar from elementary logic, where an argument is a series of items (typically sentences), each member of which is either a premise or a consequence (by way of an argument form) of preceding items, which may be thought of as *reasons* for the item in question. Adapting this familiar idea, Pollock thinks of an argument as a finite series of *epistemic states* (not sentences). These states will include beliefs, being perceptually appeared to, seeming to remember something, and the like:

> We must take arguments to proceed from internal states (both doxastic and nondoxastic states) to doxastic states [that is, beliefs], the links between steps being provided by reasons . . . reasons are internal states. . . .
>
> Our epistemic norms permit us to begin reasoning from certain internal states without those states being supported by further reasoning. Such states can be called *basic states.* Paramount among these are perceptual and memory

---

[1](For the moment please refrain from raising such embarrassing questions as whether there is or could be any such thing as the set of all truths.) Page references in this appendix are to Pollock's *Contemporary Theories of Knowledge* (Totowa, N.J.: Rowman and Littlefield, 1986).

states. Arguments must always begin with basic states and proceed from them to nonbasic doxastic states. . . . [They] proceed from basic steps to their ultimate conclusions through a sequence of steps each consisting of a belief for which the earlier steps provide reasons. (p. 187)

So an argument is a series of epistemic states beginning from basic states and terminating in a belief; and for each belief in the sequence there will be a reason, which may be either another belief or a nondoxastic state (for example, being appeared to thus and so).

2. *Instantiation.* To *instantiate* an argument is to be in the basic states from which the argument begins and to believe the conclusion of the argument on the basis of that argument.

3. *Defeat.* What is noteworthy about Pollock's account of defeasibility is his recognition that it cannot be properly explained merely in terms of the relation between a single belief and a defeating belief or condition: "To handle defeasibility in a general way, we must recognize that arguments can defeat one another and that a defeated argument can be reinstated if the arguments defeating it are defeated in turn" (p. 48). Although he does not give an account of what it is for one *argument* to defeat another, he does say what it is for one *proposition* or belief to defeat another:

If P is a reason for S to believe Q, R is a defeater for this reason if and only if R is logically consistent with P and P&R is not a reason for S to believe Q. (p. 38)

(So let's say provisionally, if not wholly accurately, that a defeater argument for an argument *A* with conclusion *C* is an argument that supports a defeater of *C*.) Thus I meet someone at a party: he tells me his name is 'Alexander Hamilton', thus giving me a reason *P* (*he says his name is 'Alexander Hamilton'*) for believing that that is his name; you take me aside and tell me that he is a notorious practical joker who is really named 'Melvin Hamilton' but invariably introduces himself as 'Alexander'; you thus provide me with a defeater *R* (*he is really named 'Melvin'*) for that reason *P*.

Now a (propositional) defeater *R* for a reason *P* to believe a proposition *Q* is a defeater for *me* only if I *believe R*. This reveals a certain incompleteness in the definition of defeater: for of course (as Pollock recognizes)[2] I can believe a proposition to different degrees. I believe *R* with great fervor; I also believe *P*, but much less firmly; then (if no other beliefs are relevant) I do not have a reason for believing *Q*. It is consistent with this, however, that if I believed *P* fervently and *R* much less firmly, then I would still have a reason for believing *Q*. I believe that the moon is sometimes visible from the floor of Deepwater Canyon on the basis of the rather dim and infirm belief that I once saw it from there; I learn (beyond the shadow of a doubt) that you (the world's premier expert on deep canyons) believe that the former is never visible from the latter; then I no longer have a reason for believing that it is. But suppose I believe very

[2] "If we reflect on our beliefs, we will find that we are more confident of some than of others. It is reasonable to place more reliance on those beliefs in which we have greater confidence, and when beliefs come in conflict we decide which to reject by considering which we are least certain of" (p. 5).

strongly that I *saw* the moon from the canyon (I was there just last night and distinctly remember seeing it); even if I come to believe that you think it is not visible from there, I may still have a reason for thinking that it is. As things stand, therefore, *P&R* will on some occasions be a reason for *S* to believe *Q* and on other occasions not; we must add a qualification to the definition of defeater, specifying that whether a potential defeater *R* of *P* *actually defeats P* will depend (among other things) upon the relative strengths of belief in *P* and *R*. Whether a given strength of belief in *P&R* constitutes a reason for believing *Q* will presumably depend upon the relevant norms; so some of them will have to take the form *if you believe P to degree d_1 and R to d_2, then you may believe Q (to d_3); but if you believe P to d_3 and R to d_4, then you may not believe Q to d_3.*[3]

Further, Pollock points out that it is not only propositions or beliefs for which there can be defeaters. It may seem to me that the sheet of paper on the table is red; taking 'reason' in a broad sense, says Pollock, being in this state gives me a reason for believing that the sheet of paper is red. But if you point out that the sheet of paper is being illuminated by red light, then you provide me with a defeater for that reason. He therefore broadens his definition of 'defeater':

> If M is a reason for S to believe Q, a state M* is a defeater for this reason if and only if it is logically possible for S to be in this combined state consisting of being in both the state M and the state M* at the same time, and this combined state is not a reason for S to believe Q. (p. 176)[4]

4. Being Ultimately Undefeated. Here we must quote Pollock's account in full:

> Every argument proceeding from basic states that S is actually in will be undefeated at level 0 for S. . . . Some arguments will support defeaters for other arguments, so we define an argument to be undefeated at level 1 if and only if it is not defeated by any other argument undefeated at level 0. Among the arguments defeated at level 1[5] may be some that supported defeaters for others, so if we take arguments undefeated at level 2 to be arguments undefeated at level 0 that are not defeated by any arguments undefeated at level 1, there may be arguments undefeated at level 2 that were arguments defeated at level 1. In general, we define an argument to be undefeated at level n + 1 if and

[3]Alternatively, if norms are only permissive, never prohibitive, then there will be a norm permitting belief of *P* to d_3 under the first set of conditions but none permitting it to that degree under the second.

[4]Here, as with respect to the previous case, we need some notion of the *strength* of a reason. I look out of my office window and seem to see Paul playing frisbee golf with his similarly frivolous friends; this gives me a reason for believing *Paul is playing frisbee golf*. At the same time, however, I am on the phone with Paul's wife who says he is upstairs in his study still vainly trying to prove the Fundamental Theorem of the calculus; this is a reason, for me, for the denial of that proposition (and hence a rebutting defeater for it). In this case perhaps the defeater is the stronger; I will then be justified in believing that Paul is at home and that the frisbee player, despite appearances, is not Paul but perhaps a ringer, made up to look like Paul and brought in to teach his calculus class, in which the Fundamental Theorem is now up for discussion. Here the (potential) defeater is the stronger; but in other cases the (potential) defeater might not actually suffice to defeat.

[5]The text here says 'level 0', which must be a typographical error.

only if it is undefeated at level 0 and is not defeated by any arguments undefeated at level n. An argument is ultimately undefeated if and only if there is
some point beyond which it remains permanently undefeated; that is, for some
N, the argument remains undefeated for every n > N. (p. 189)

Restricting attention to arguments S instantiates, perhaps we can simplify
this as follows. An argument A is defeated at level 1 if (I suppress the 'only if's')
some argument defeats it; A is *undefeated at level 1* in case no argument defeats
it; hence if A is undefeated at level 1, it is undefeated at every subsequent level
and is ultimately undefeated. A is *defeated at level 2* in case some argument
undefeated at level 1 defeats it; if A is defeated at level 2, therefore, it is defeated
at every subsequent level (since it is defeated by an argument undefeated at
every subsequent level). A is *undefeated at level 2* if it is not defeated by an
argument undefeated at level 1—if, in other words, any argument that defeats
it is defeated at level 1 (that is, defeated by some argument or other). In general,
A is *defeated at level n + 1* if it is defeated by some argument undefeated at
level n; A is *undefeated at level n + 1* if it is not defeated by any argument
undefeated at level n. A little reflection shows that an argument is ultimately
undefeated if it is undefeated at every even-numbered level and is also undefeated at some odd-numbered level. Some arguments not defeated at any even
level are nonetheless not ultimately undefeated; such arguments are defeated at
every odd level and undefeated at every even (for an example, see p. 220).

5. *Conditionality.* We need just one more idea to complete the account of
objective epistemic justification. Say that an argument A is *conditional on Y for*
S (where Y is a set of propositions) if A proceeds from basic states S is in
together with doxastic states consisting of believing members of Y (p. 189).
Then,

> Roughly, a belief is objectively justified if and only if it is held on the basis of
> some ultimately undefeated argument A, and either A is not defeated by any
> argument conditional on true propositions not believed by S, or if it is, then
> there are further true propositions such that the initial defeating arguments
> will be defeated by arguments conditional on the enlarged set of true proposi-
> tions. (p. 189)

More explicitly,

> We then say that an argument instantiated by S . . . is undefeated at level n + 1
> relative to Y if and only if it is undefeated by any argument undefeated at level
> n relative to Y. An argument is ultimately undefeated relative to Y if and only if
> there is an N such that it is undefeated at every level n relative to Y for every
> n > N. (p. 189)

A person S, therefore, is "objectively justified in believing P if and only if S
instantiates some argument supporting P which is ultimately undefeated relative to the set of all truths" (p. 189).[6] As we saw above, objective justification,

---

[6]Foley points out a problem here. Suppose I believe p upon no reflection or investigation; if I
were to think about p at all, I would immediately encounter a defeater q for it. However, if I were
to think about p and q at great length, I would encounter a defeater r for q, and in fact p is
undefeated relative to the set of all truths. According to Pollock's account, I would be objectively
justified in believing p, and if the social requirement were also satisfied, I would know p according

Pollock believes, is very close to knowledge; we need add only a small qualification to accommodate what Pollock, following Harman, sees as "the social side of knowledge."

"We are 'socially expected' to be aware of various things: what is in our mail, what is repeatedly announced on television, what any sixth grader has learned in school, and the like. A proposition is '*socially sensitive for S*' if and only if it is of a sort *S* is expected to believe when true" (p. 192). The final definition of knowledge, therefore, goes as follows:

> *S* knows *P* if and only if *S* instantiates some argument *A* supporting *P* which is (1) ultimately undefeated relative to the set of all truths and (2) ultimately undefeated relative to the set of all truths socially sensitive for *S*.[7]

I mention a small problem—one that probably requires no more than a little more Chisholming. Suppose *P* is a proposition that happens (unbeknownst to me) to be true: can I know (on this account) that I do not believe *P*? Suppose that

> *P*   Caesar had scrambled eggs for breakfast the morning he crossed the Rubicon

is in fact true, but suppose I don't believe it, having no views at all on the subject (as in fact I don't) and believing that I don't believe *P*. For me to be objectively justified in this belief, according to the official definition, I must instantiate some argument that (a) supports the proposition

> *Q*   I do not believe that Caesar had scrambled eggs for breakfast the morning he crossed the Rubicon

and (b) is ultimately undefeated relative to the set of all truths (p. 189). Recall that an argument is conditional on the set of all truths for me if it proceeds (in accordance with my norms) from basic states I am in together with doxastic states consisting of believing members of the set of truths. Now presumably the same norms are to be used both in an argument proceeding from the doxastic states I am in and an argument proceeding from members of the set of truths. But among my norms is the following: *if you are considering a proposition A but do not believe it, then you may believe that you do not believe A.* Among

---

to Pollock's account. Yet that seems anomalous at best: if I miss an obvious and nearby defeater *q*, then I don't really know *p*, even if *q* is in turn defeated by some defeater I would encounter, if at all, only after enormously protracted reflection and investigation. What is needed here is some notion of the *degree of obviousness* of a defeater, or of its *distance*.

[7]This may appear initially a bit puzzling: unless *S*'s society is unusually well informed (or unusually demanding), the set of truths socially sensitive for *S* will be a very small subset of the set of all truths (again, supposing, perhaps counterfactually, that in fact there is such a set). But could an argument be ultimately undefeated relative to the set of truths but not ultimately undefeated relative to some subset of that set? Certainly: an argument *A* might be defeated by argument *B*, which in turn is defeated by an argument *C* proceeding from some proposition included in the set of truths but not in the set of socially sensitive truths: then it could be ultimately undefeated with respect to the set of all truths but not with respect to the set of socially sensitive truths.

the truths, of course, is P itself; so relative to the set of truths there will be for me an argument (call it 'A') from the doxastic state of believing P to the denial of Q (call it '-Q'); this argument will proceed by the above norm.

Can this argument for -Q be ultimately defeated, as it would have to be for me to have an ultimately undefeated argument for Q? I don't see how. An argument (relative to the set of all truths) for Q (hence an argument that defeats the argument for -Q) would be, for example, Q, *therefore* Q (perhaps another such argument would be one from the basic state of not-believing P to Q). Call this argument 'B'. Arguments A and B are so related, as a little reflection shows, that (if there are no other arguments defeating either) each is defeated (by the other) at all the odd-numbered levels; hence neither is undefeated at any odd-numbered level and hence neither is ultimately undefeated. The same will go, so far as I can see, for any other argument for Q. No such argument will be ultimately undefeated; any argument defeating A will itself be defeated at all the odd-numbered levels by A. But then Q won't be objectively justified for me, so that a necessary condition of my knowing it, according to Pollock's account, cannot be fulfilled. Yet surely I do know that I don't believe that Caesar had scrambled eggs for breakfast the morning he crossed the Rubicon.

No doubt this problem requires no more than a bit of tinkering; perhaps, for example, we must say that the norm just mentioned is to be applied only to doxastic states I am in, not to members of the set of truths. More exactly, what is needed is some generalization of that suggestion, since the problem will reappear if the norm in question may be applied to steps of an argument that are *dependent* upon basic steps that are not doxastic states I am in. Reflexive propositions about what one believes (or does not believe) clearly require special treatment when taken in the context of the account of an argument conditional on the set of all truths.

Index

224	*Index*

Coherentism, 77–84. *See also*
Foundationalism
Bayesian. *See* Bayesian coherentism
BonJourian. *See* BonJourian
coherentism
and circular reasoning, 77–78
and coherence as only source of
warrant, 78–80
impure, 79, 87, 96
and properly basic belief, 78–79
pure, 79
special case of post–classical
Chisholmian internalism, 51, 55,
65, 66–67, 79 n. *See also* Post–
classical Chisholmian internalism
and warrant transfer, 79
Concepts
and conceptual role, 165
and conceptual train, 166
distinct but broadly logically
equivalent, 166 n.
epistemological theory of, 166, 167
inclusion and preclusion among,
165–66
logical theory of, 165–66
v. properties, 165 n.
Conditionalization, 122–24, 129, 143,
146–47. *See also* Probability
kinematics
diachronic Dutch book argument for,
123–24
and rationality, 146–47
and Ur-function, 146–47. *See also*
Credence function
and warrant, 127
Conee, Earl, 8, 10, 25–26, 28, 188, 211
Consciousness (Reid), 100, 101–03
Credence function, 117, 123, 146–47
and Ur-function, 123, 146–47

David, Marian, ix
Defeasibility, 217–19
de Finetti, Bruno, 114 n.
DePaul, Michael, 142 n.
Descartes, René, v, vii, 4, 11, 12–13, 14,
19–24, 26, 30, 31, 38, 47, 58, 67,
68, 71, 81 n., 85, 94, 101, 110,
133, 136, 163, 184, 211. *See also*
Classical deontologism
Donagan, Alan, 17 n.
Dostoyevsky, F., 85
Doxastic Presumption. *See*
Metajustification
Dretske, Fred, vii, 183, 184, 193–95,
196, 197, 211

Dretskian reliabilism, 193–97
and causation, 194
and *de re* perceptual knowledge, 193
and information theory, 193–95
Dutch book. *See* Conditionalization;
Probabilistic coherence; Reflection
Duties/obligations
epistemic, 12–14, 19–21, 53–54
ethical, 15–19
objective, 16–17, 18–21, 53
subjective, 16–17, 18–20, 53

Edidin, Aron, 42 n.
Epistemic norms, 163–65, 166–81, 218,
220–21. *See also* Justification
correct, 165, 166–67, 171–76
and degrees of belief, 174–75
determine concepts employed in
reasoning, 165, 166–67, 171–73,
175–76
as generalized descriptions of doxastic
behavior of properly functioning
human beings, 179–81
govern reasoning, 164–65
internalized, 164–65, 178
and learning, 175
permissive (*v.* obligatory), 163, 164,
171, 218 n.
as programs for properly functioning
cognitive machines, 178–79
and special epistemic access, 180–81
Epistemic pairs. *See* Purely psychological
properties
Epistemic principles, 30, 31–32, 36–43,
47–48. *See also* Classical
Chisholmian internalism
as noncontingent, 30, 36, 45 n.
P1, 36–40
P5a, 40–43
and properly functioning cognitive
faculties, 45 n., 65
quasi-epistemic, 48
and self-presenting conditions, 37–40,
47–48. *See also* Internalism, special
epistemic access
Evidence base. *See* Purely psychological
properties
Evidentialism, 25–26, 28–29
and classical deontologism, 26
and internalism, 28–29
special case of post–classical
Chisholmian internalism, 51, 55.
See also Post–classical Chisholmian
internalism
Externalism, 6, 183–84

Kant, Immanuel, 41
Karmo, Toomas, 56 n.
Kemeny, John, 120–21 n.
Knowledge. *See also* Gettier problem;
 Justification
 a priori, 96–97
 v. Cartesian certainty, 85
 and deontology. *See* Classical
 deontologism
 and evidence, 26. *See also*
 Evidentialism
 justified true belief account of, 4, 6–7,
 14, 26, 87, 187–88
Kornblith, Hilary, 8, 10, 25
Kyburg, Henry, Jr., 147 n., 157 n.

Lawrence, D. H., 133 n.
Lehrer, Keith, 9, 10, 11, 25, 27, 28, 29,
 66, 78 n., 83 n., 211
Leibniz., G. W., 68
Lewis, C. I., 7
Lewis, David, 114–15 n., 123 n., 124,
 141 n.
Locke, John, vii, 4, 11, 12, 13, 14, 15,
 19–24, 26, 28, 30, 31, 38, 45, 47,
 51 n., 58, 67, 68, 71, 81 n., 84–85
 n., 135, 136, 140, 163, 174, 181,
 188, 211. *See also* Classical
 deontologism

Maher, Patrick, 130 n., 149 n., 150, 151
Malebranche, Nicolas, 68
Mavrodes, George, ix
Metajustification, 88–89, 93–96,
 105–13. *See also* BonJourian
 coherentism
 and correspondence hypothesis,
 94–95, 106–7, 109
 and Doxastic Presumption, 95–96,
 108–9
 as good argument for claim that an
 empirical belief is likely to be true,
 89, 93
Mill, J. S., 102

Noetic structure, 69, 72. *See also*
 Foundationalism
 design plan of, 197, 213. *See also*
 Warrant, and design plan
 proper, 73–74
Nozick, Robert, 183

Paradigm reliabilism, 27, 198–99,
 208–10
 and cognitive process types *v.* tokens,
 198, 208–10

and degrees of reliability, 198, 209
and problem of generality, 198–99,
 208, 210
Paradox of the Preface, 145. *See also*
 Probabilistic coherence, analogical
 argument for
Partial belief, 117–19 *See also* Bayesian
 coherentism
 and Betting Behavior Test, 117, 118
 conditional, 118–19
 and credence function, 117
 vague, 138 n., 149
Partridge, Michael, ix
Paul, St., 16
Peirce, C. S., 72
Plato, vi, 11 n.
Pollock, John, vii, 28 n., 80, 128,
 162–71, 173, 174, 175, 176–81,
 182, 188 n., 212, 216–21
Pollockian quasi-internalism
 and defeasibility, 217–19
 and degrees of belief, 217–18
 and degrees of warrant, 169
 v. deontological justification, 163,
 176–81. *See also* Classical
 deontologism
 and doxastic voluntarism, 177–78
 and epistemic norms, 163–65,
 166–81, 218, 220–21. *See also*
 Epistemic norms
 and objective justification, 168–70,
 176, 216–21
 and socially sensitive propositions,
 168–69, 220
 and subjective justification, 163,
 167–78
Positive epistemic status. *See* Warrant
Post–classical Chisholmian internalism
 as axiological *v.* deontological, 48–53.
 See also Classical deontologism
 and internalism, 51, 53–54
 and reasonability, 51
 and reduction of epistemic concepts to
 theory of intrinsic value, 50, 55–56
 special case of broad justification, 64.
 See also Justification, broad
 and special epistemic access, 50, 51,
 54
 and warrant as relation between
 beliefs and purely psychological
 properties, 49–51, 52–53, 54–65.
 See also Purely psychological
 properties
Price, H. H., 26, 188
Prichard, H. A., 12 n.